E. T. A. Hoffmann

TALES

The German Library: Volume 26

Volkmar Sander, General Editor

E. T. A. Hoffmann

TALES

Edited by Victor Lange

CONTINUUM · NEW YORK

1982

The Continuum Publishing Company
575 Lexington Avenue, New York, NY 10022

Copyright © 1982 by The Continuum Publishing Company

Introduction © 1982 by Victor Lange

Printed in the United States of America

Library of Congress Cataloging in Publication Data

Hoffmann, E. T. A. (Ernst Theodor Amadeus), 1776–1822.
Tales.
(The German library; v. 26)
Contents: Introduction/Victor Lange—The golden
pot—Councillor Kespel—[etc.]
I. Lange, Victor, 1908–   . II. Series.
PT2361.E4A14 1982   833′ .6   82-7316
ISBN 0-8264-0254-2   AACR2
ISBN 0-8264-0264-X pbk.

For acknowledgments of previously published material, please see
page 309, which constitutes an extension of the copyright page.

Contents

v

Introduction

If we have come to recognize in the "romantic" imagination not only gently lyrical, picturesque, and touching features, but elements of the fantastic, the eccentric, even the pathological, this is in large measure due to the extraordinary work of E. T. A. Hoffmann, one of the key figures in German early nineteenth-century literature, as startling in his personality as in his work. Hoffmann was born in 1776 in Königsberg, that remote but important city in East Prussia. He was orphaned early and brought up by decent but severe relatives. Throughout his life he craved the warmth and immediacy of close human relationships; yet he was inclined to withdraw, to mask his identity, to assume roles, to lead a life divided between strict conformity to a society he distrusted and despised, and a stubborn faith in the liberating energies of the imagination. As a civil servant of the strictest observance, he used his baptismal name, Ernst Theodor Wilhelm; as an artist, in fervent admiration of Mozart, he called himself Ernst Theodor Amadeus.

He read voraciously, developed his talents as a painter and caricaturist, and, after completing his legal training, held a number of administrative and judicial positions, the most important of these during the last eight years of his life as a member of the Prussian Supreme Court in Berlin. But while he discharged these official obligations with meticulous care, his constant preoccupation was with music and literature. When in 1808 he lost his first position as civil servant, he was appointed Kapellmeister at Bamberg. Here, and later in Dresden, he became a music critic of rare perception, an effective man of the theater and a prolific composer: he wrote no fewer than ten operas, two masses, cantatas, chamber music, and two symphonies. The most successful of his operas, *Undine,* performed in Berlin in 1816, was praised by C. M. von Weber as one of the finest and most original works of the age. As Kapellmeister he performed Bach, Handel, Haydn, Beethoven, and the great masters of Italian church music, and interpreted them in his critical essays.

It was in Bamberg and Dresden that he began to write that series of powerful, baffling and bizarre stories that reflect in unforgettable figures his deepening awareness of the gulf, nearly unbridgeable, between the world of obtuse normalcy and the hidden but incessantly challenging presence of elemental spirits, of powers glorious and terrifying, that he was determined to invoke and to articulate. Much of Hoffmann's fiction, published occasionally in almanacs and journals, is ephemeral and little more than the means of supporting his often extravagant life. But the half-dozen volumes of his collected tales have remained singularly fascinating contributions to the rich history of German storytelling in the early nineteenth century.

The very title of his first work suggests a mood of Hoffmann's art that was to remain the unmistakeable signature of all his writing: *Fantastic Pieces in the Manner of Callot* [*Phantasiestücke in Callots Manier*]. The reference to the meticulously executed figures and scenes of the French engraver Callot (1592–1638) was to indicate something of the style of these stories. He had originally thought of "Pictures after Hogarth," but he accepted the publisher's suggestion that Callot was an artist not unlike Hoffmann himself. "Even the commonest subjects of everyday life," he wrote of Callot in an introductory essay, "—his peasant dance, for which musicians, seated like birds in the trees, are playing— appear in the shimmer of a certain romantic originality, to the wondrous delight of anyone whose spirit is inclined to be fanciful." These four small volumes, published anonymously in 1814 and 1815, contain not only the quasi-biographical sketches *"Ritter Gluck"* and *"Don Juan,"* but the first six of the *Kreisleriana,* fictitious portraits of the exuberant and eccentric Kapellmeister Johannes Kreisler, that were to be the oblique but most revealing inventions of his genius as musician and writer. This figure was in subsequent works an ever more complex and telling medium for

Hoffmann's own thoughts and feelings. He reappears in one of Hoffmann's last (and provocatively entitled) works, *The Life and Opinions of Murr the Tomcat, Together with a Fragmentary Biography of the Kapellmeister Kreisler, Written on Scrap-Paper* [*Lebens-Ansichten des Katers Murr . . . in zufälligen Makulaturblättern*] (1820–22). The astonishing incidents and encounters Kreisler here and later reports are made credible by the very ambivalence of his judgment, half susceptible to the narrated incidents of often dubious logic, half detached and incredulous.

The most accomplished of these early tales and, in Hoffmann's own opinion as well as that of his readers, his best, is "The Golden Pot," a "modern fairy tale" in which the student Anselmus is drawn from his accustomed Dresden world into a configuration of magic and supernatural relationships to discover himself transformed from a divided and fragmented mind into a perceptive poet.

This simple summary becomes entirely inadequate when we attempt to interpret the intricate texture of ambivalence and illusion that is here spread lavishly before the reader: Anselmus has fallen in love with two pairs of eyes—those of the pretty but unexciting Veronica and those of the green-golden snake Serpentina, the daughter of the archivist Lindhorst, for whom Anselmus works as copyist of Arabic and Coptic manuscripts. He becomes more and more deeply involved in a magic world in which his judgment and sensibilities are tested. He learns that Lindhorst is in fact an elemental spirit, a salamander, who must, in the trivial drudgery of an archivist, do penance for an offense committed in ages long past. He owns that radiantly polished golden pot, the token of happiness and fulfillment that is to be Serpentina's dowry. It mirrors an abundance of real and imagined figures, permits an insight into the contradictions and agonies of love—for only the love of a "childlike and poetic" young man for each of Lindhorst's daughters will release the archivist from his bondage. Anselmus chooses Serpentina and finds himself imprisoned in a glass bottle on a shelf in Lindhorst's house; against all the machinations of evil spirits, he keeps faith with Serpentina, is freed and in the end united with her in the dreamworld of Atlantis, where the lily that blossoms in the golden pot protects their happiness and reveals to them the deepest secret of nature, the mysterious unity of all living creatures.

However curious and puzzling the plot, however surprising the disguises and transformations in the supernatural world, "The Golden Pot" is yet a narrative of brilliantly rendered states of mind, shifting constantly from the sober Biedermeier life of the Dresden citizens to the blinding magic of Lindhorst's dwelling. The real and the imagined are deliberately interlocked, a "heavenly ladder" leads us imperceptibly into a sphere where we come to recognize the truly significant and radiant elements of life.

Many of the motifs of this strange myth Hoffmann owed to contemporary philosophy, especially to G. H. Schubert, whose *Ansichten von der Nachtseite der Naturwissenschaft* (1808) gave currency to a preoccupation with the dark, "nocturnal," and irrational elements of experience. Yet it will not do to label Hoffmann, in this early story or later, a romantic: he does not juxtapose the real and the fantastic in order to devalue the one and extol the other; for him the fantastic is the real, bared and stripped of its incrustations of dullness and insensitivity. He needs no recourse to any philosophical sort of idealism, nor does he employ that "romantic irony" by which the Schlegel brothers asserted the absolute freedom of the creative spirit. It is obvious that Hoffmann shares the romantic contempt for every form of philistine behavior, but his art considers the platitudinous and trivial, however hollow and blind it may seem, as the stuff that must be drawn into the magic circle of the imagination. In "The Golden Pot" art and love are the impulses that spring from a life that appears empty of color and fragrance, of beauty and enthusiasm. Here and elsewhere in Hoffmann's work it is madmen, lovers, and artists who become, for an instant of bliss, the witnesses of that liberating and transcending power that life conceals under its comforting everyday surface.

Something like redemptive grace Hoffmann attributes, as well, to death—death as fact and concept, as the premise of our most profound acts of creativity, the very "gateway to life." To this conviction, never merely sentimental, he returns often enough. In *The Devil's Elixir* (1815–16) he formulates it in a sentence that was to remain the creed of poets and musicians from Wagner and Baudelaire to Thomas Mann: "Love's highest ecstasy, the fulfillment of the mystery, is manifest in death."

The "elixir" in this "Gothic novel" is the mysterious liquid that is kept as a sacred relic in a monastery; Brother Medardus, in a fit of hubris, drinks from it and is seized by a demonic passion for a girl of "heavenly charm." His adventures in pursuit of this love are astounding; puzzling encounters between figures of frightening identity elaborate Hoffmann's favorite device, the double. Murder, lust, adultery, and incest are, of course, the ingredients of a kind of horror fiction familiar from M. G. Lewis's *The Monk* or Maturin's *Melmoth*. Yet Hoffmann's often wildly erratic inventions of gripping episodes and characters do not vitiate his central purpose of illuminating the dissolution of a mind. The two protagonists, the monk Medardus and the Count Victorin, are so thoroughly interchangeable that neither can be certain of his own identity. The disjointed or multiple personality is a motif to which Hoffmann returned again and again, whether it involved the dissociation of a single consciousness or the synthesis, or sympathetic identification, of two separate individuals. In *The Devil's Elixir* the suspension and confusion of identity and the loss of self in madness are the inescapable consequences of evil in its most radical and existential sense.

Hoffmann's next collection, with the characteristic title *Night Pieces* [*Nachtstücke*] (1817), contains a story of exceptional dramatic and psychological force, "The Sandman," where the clash between reality and the deeply troubling magic that emanates from terrifying figures and actions produces in the reader that sense of the uncanny which Freud has analyzed in one of his most searching literary essays. Two images—the Sandman, who recurs in different impersonation to threaten the power of vision, and the mechanical doll Olympia, who appears to represent perfection—derive their unsettling force from states of mad ecstasy in the student-artist Nathanael. A sequence of almost hysterical events illustrates Hoffmann's conviction that on its most problematical level reality defies unambiguous representation; the line that divides actuality and its hallucinatory reflection must remain undefined, and denies even the storyteller the advantage of a detached and rational narrative perspective. "The Sandman" is a masterpiece of modern European fiction if only because, without the help of a mediating narrator with a fixed point of view, it puts the burden of belief or doubt, of understanding and interpretation, upon the reader's capacity to become a participant in the truth of fiction.

The technique of shifting narrative perspectives is Hoffmann's means of blurring or echoing disparate modes of experience, of alternating paralyzing supernatural appearances and cheerful gatherings. The joining of romantic love and the committing of crime as though under the compulsion of an elusive and destructive demon provides the key to "The Deed of Entail," once more a concatenation of mysterious but plausibly documented actions and events. What is here practiced with unsuspecting abandon, whether music or love, implies a terrifying negativity.

Only a few years later, 1818–21, Hoffmann published his last richly orchestrated cycle of tales—the first, incidentally, to appear under his own name. In these four volumes are the stories told by the Serapion Brotherhood [*Die Serapionsbrüder*], a group of friends who meet occasionally to read from their own works and to discuss them critically or with playful irony. By the "serapiontic principle," stories that may seem incompatible in theme, mood, or genre follow one another: detective fiction alternates with fairy tales, historical memoirs with accounts of the tortures and glories involved in artistic creation. The theme that holds these diverse tales together is, again, the relationship, forever threatened, between actuality and fantasy, body and mind, the offered evidence and the doubts in its reliability, all of these brought into play by the emergence of mythical memories and their capacity to unravel the threads of insight.

The precarious balance of these elements and its failure provide the topics of most of these tales. What makes the bizarre figure of Councillor Krespel and the tragic affirmation of the power of music in the death of his daughter Antonia so moving is Hoffmann's demonstration (which anticipates one of the central assumptions of Dostoevsky or Thomas Mann) of eccentricity and disease as the mainspring of art, of the power of baffling objects and of startling gestures to reveal the threat of destruction and the promise of beauty beneath the surface of the banal or the absurd.

Krespel and Antonia are among Hoffmann's unforgettable incarnations of the terror of the imagination; they offer us constellations of psychological coherence no less compelling than the demonic obsession in "Mademoiselle de Scudéri" of the goldsmith Cardillac, who murders the buyers of his most treasured masterpiece in order to recover it again and again as his own unsurpassed creation. In a setting of carefully drawn historical accuracy, and in a plot of several levels of intrigue and bewildering mystery, Hoffmann explores the mind of an artist whose criminal deeds remain unsuspected until this ugly and grotesque figure, protected by the mask of honorable normalcy, is exposed. He is possessed by satanic voices that are silenced only when he is no longer separated from the work to which he has devoted his supreme artistry.

Here and in the other "unheard-of" accounts—to use Goethe's definition of the form of the novella—that make up the entertainment of the Serapion Brotherhood, in "The Fermata" as well as in "The Mines of Falun," familiar topics are developed in a variety of keys. "The Fermata," for instance, invokes the power of music in its sublime and civilizing as well as its deeply disturbing character; the musician, that paradigm of Hoffmann's artistry, matures as he detaches himself from what at one time may have seemed an ideal, passionately but uncritically embraced. The anecdote on which "The Mines of Falun" is based Hoffmann found in Schubert's *Ansichten von der Nachtseite der Naturwissenschaft;* he expanded it into the magic biography of a young man who is persuaded to go to the mines of Falun that he might enter the magic world of the Queen of the Mountains. Torn between his love for Ulla, the daughter of the director of the mine, and the enchantment of a timeless existence within the mountain, he resolves to choose life with Ulla; but as on the morning of his wedding he sets out to find the glittering stone Almandin as his gift to Ulla, he is held captive by the Queen of the Mountains. Fifty years later his body is found, and Ulla dies next to him in fulfillment of a constant love that seems to transcend and heal the isolation and alienation into which her lover's fascination with the visions and compulsions of inwardness had driven him.

The often varied but never substantially modified theme of Hoffmann's tales is the conflict between a dull and conventional everyday existence and the insistent claims of the spirit; it is the constant topic, richly and colorfully embroidered, of his prolific life. But what distinguishes his treatment of this often invoked conflict is the refusal, wholly uncharacteristic of the idealistic and romantic disposition of his age, to bridge the gulf between a social and political reality depleted of poetic creativity and his own passionate belief in the power of the imagination, of the spirit, of beauty.

These two realms, the pragmatic and the ideal, remain in Hoffmann's tales radically separate. They are not harmonized in optimistic or utopian schemes; their inexorable confrontation, to the point of improbable exaggeration, is the pervasive tenor of his writing. Figures of incredible intensity of purpose and of a stubborn faith in their role as representatives of convictions beyond the commonplace are the carriers of this existential dilemma. The musician Kreisler seems mad in a bourgeois world to which he cannot or will not accommodate himself—he is the genius in an indifferent society. Eccentricity and insanity are, therefore, for Hoffmann those modes of behavior that contain in their shocking or puzzling outward appearance the essence of inspiration and idealism.

If magnetism, somnambulism, hypnotism, and other such states beyond rational consciousness are among Hoffmann's favorite metaphors, they represent not so much the improbable machinery of Gothic fiction as a record, poetically illuminated, of experiences in which Hoffmann himself seems to have shared. His strength as a writer was not any excellence in the style of his prose but his ability to render elusive figures in action, platitudinous characters suddenly made transparent by the perception of intensely felt and unsettling forces. These figures seem abruptly to move from one state of mind to another, from familiar behavior to outrageous actions, from idyll to savage satire. It is at just such moments of shifting gestures and performances, such changes in levels of involvement, that the irrepressible force of the most powerful human impulses—hope and desire, love and hatred, beauty and horror—can be given presence and shape.

Hoffmann died in June 1822, his legs and hands paralyzed, but to the end dictating the last part of his novel *Master Flea* [*Meister Floh*] and a story entitled "The Recovery" [*"Die Genesung"*]. In his own time Hoffmann's reputation was fairly limited. Goethe thought of him as a pathological human being whose invented figures struck him as unnatural, impossible, even insufferable. French, English, and Russian readers, on the other hand, seemed fascinated by Hoffmann's work. Sir Walter Scott suggested that he had the imagination of an opium eater; Gerard de Nerval spoke of Germany as "the land of Hoffmann"; for Balzac he was "notre grand Hoffmann"; Pushkin and Gogol are unthinkable without Hoffmann; Poe and Hawthorne, Baudelaire, Dostoevsky, and Andersen read him with a strong sense of affinity.

In several major musical compositions, Hoffmann's genius has touched countless listeners. In 1838 Robert Schumann composed his "Kreisleriana" with Hoffmann's Johannes Kreisler, "that eccentric, wild, gifted conductor," in mind. Offenbach's delightful opera weaves together three of the tales of Hoffmann—"The Sandman," the Venetian episode of "A New Year's Adventure," and the story of the singer Antonia from "Councillor Krespel"— all told by the poet himself in the wine cellar of Lutter and Wegner in Berlin, where Hoffmann was a constant guest. Mahler composed a funeral march "in Callot's manner" for his first symphony.

A mercurial, gnomelike person, the very model of a judicious official but far from conventional in his private life, Hoffmann transcribed much of his own nervous, agitated sensibility, his sense of the incongruous and paradoxical, his recognition of the unresolvable tensions between freedom and contingency, into his many-faceted work, his stories, his music, his letters. He struck his friends as a figure of almost hypnotic power, shifting quickly from carefully maintained seriousness to the histrionic manner of a mind torn between bitter irony and a tenacious faith in his creative power, from the role of light-hearted storyteller and musician to that of a profoundly melancholy introvert. His attention was ceaselessly upon the discrepancies and contradictions in the lives of the figures who, like himself, recognize the improbable, the absurd, the ominous as the agonizing realities of the mind. His own life seemed often enough driven by forces beyond the control of reason and decorum. We must believe him and the testimony of his *Notebooks* when he confesses to being seized by a demon of creativity, driven by an irresistible power, immersed in a flood of inspiration and held in the grip of overwhelming visions, visions as concrete and precise in their detail as any scene of Breughel or Füssli.

In the recording of these onslaughts of the imagination, in the stubborn pursuit of his art, he seems to have found the means of articulating his obsessive groping for the telling images of magic and the greatness of spirit; but these served also as a mask or shield to protect him from the very powers that threatened to derange his own life. His letters and the testimony of his acquaintances give us evidence enough of a mind forever alternating between depression and elation, generosity and hatred, frustration and exuberant productivity. As the musician in him turned into the novelist, the listener to sublime melodies into a teller of intricately composed fictions, he must have hoped to banish the demons that threatened to destroy him. His remarkable dedication to a career of bureaucratic efficiency was a self-imposed uniform of order and discipline, an indication of his resolution to submit to the conventions of a society in which at times he participated in disarming conviviality, but whose fundamental insensitiveness and modish superficiality he caricatured as depraved and deformed, as malevolent, lifeless, and mechanical.

Hoffmann's work gives expression and shape to that historical experience of diminishing philosophical and institutional certainties, of a growing discrepancy between accepted social and imaginative forms of life and their inadequacy in the eyes of a perceptive observer. What lends unity to Hoffmann's inexhaustible universe of experience and invention is the relentless scrutiny with which he illuminates the ambivalent nature of the world. What may seem to us an intoxicating display of romantic chimera was for him a faithful recording of his search for the true character of reality. Reality—of this he would leave no doubt in the minds of his readers—was that substance of feeling and reflection, that core of the imaginative energy, which is contained and imprisoned and concealed under the thin veneer of commonplace behavior and trivialized judgment.

Hoffmann never ceases to reach out for those signs of imaginative integrity, those spiritually galvanizing myths and symbols that an age of pedestrian, bourgeois normalcy seemed to have forgotten or chosen to ignore. To uncover this hidden truth in its ennobling as well as debasing force, in its divine as well as diabolical attraction; to rescue the essence of courage and intelligence, of beauty and love that appears so fatally disfigured in our everyday existence—this is the purpose of Hoffmann's art. Yet he is not content to pit his vision of truth against sham; he explores the act of that confrontation with a deep suspicion of sentimentality and easy rhetoric. He is one of the first of the modern novelists to develop forms of self-conscious storytelling by which the unwary reader is by subtle degree drawn into states of mind far beyond normal comprehension, addressed by an intelligent narrator who provides every possible historical or scientific proof to make his account credible. His art looks beyond romantic illusion toward the analytical fiction of the later nineteenth century. Like this later work, Hoffmann's also testifies to the agony of the soul and also to a will to fathom its capacities of insight and vision.

V.L.

The Golden Pot

A Modern Fairy Tale

FIRST VIGIL

The Misfortunes of the Student Anselmus,
Assistant Dean Paulmann's Medicinal Tobacco,
and the Gold-green Snakes.

About three in the afternoon on Ascension Day, a young man in Dresden came running out through the Black Gate, directly into a basket of apples and cakes that a hideous old woman was offering for sale, so that everything fortunate enough to survive the tremendous crush was scattered to the winds, and urchins in the street joyously divided the booty that was thrown their way by this precipitous gentleman. At the shriek of "Murder!" unleashed by the hag, her cronies deserted their cake-and-brandy tables, encircled the young man, and cursed him with such vulgarity that, speechless from chagrin and shame, he merely offered his small and by-no-means especially full purse, which the hag clutched greedily and quickly pocketed. Now the tightly closed circle around him opened, but as the young man dashed out, the hag shouted after him: "Yes, run! Run, you spawn of the Devil! Run into the crystal which will soon be your downfall—run into the crystal!" There was something frightful about the shrill, creaking voice of the woman that caused strollers to freeze in amazement; and the laughter, which had at first been general, suddenly was silenced.

Despite the fact that he did not begin to understand these ex-

1

traordinary phrases, the student Anselmus—and the young man was none other—nevertheless felt himself gripped by a certain involuntary dread, and he quickened his pace even more in an attempt to escape the curious looks the multitude cast upon him from all sides. As he worked his way through the crowd of well-dressed people, he heard them murmuring on all sides: "The poor young man! Oh, the damned old hag!" Peculiarly enough, the hag's cryptic words had cast over this amusing adventure an aura of the tragic, so that the youth now provoked a certain sympathy, even though he had before remained unnoticed. Because he was a splendid figure of a man and had a face whose handsomeness and expressiveness were enhanced by the anger that glowed within him, the ladies forgave him not only his clumsiness but even the clothing he wore, though it was completely out of fashion. His pike-gray coat was cut as if the tailor had only known of contemporary styles from hearsay, and his worn and shiny black satin trousers gave him a certain schoolmasterish air that was at odds with the gait and bearing of the wearer.

When the student had almost reached the end of the alley which leads out to the Linke Baths, he was almost out of breath and he began to walk instead of run; but he heardly dared to raise his eyes from the ground because he still saw apples and cakes dancing on all sides of him, and every sympathetic look bestowed upon him by this or that pretty girl seemed to be only a reflex reaction to the laughter that had mocked him at the Black Gate. It was in this frame of mind that he ultimately arrived at the entrance to the baths, which were usually thronged by one group of festive visitors after another. The music of a brass band resounded from within, and the din of merrymaking grew increasingly louder. Tears were about to flow from the poor student because he too had expected to take part in the festivities in the Linkean paradise. Ascension Day had invariably been a family celebration for him; indeed, he had even intended to go so far as to indulge in half a pot of coffee laced with rum and to have a bottle of strong beer. To assure proper dissipation, he had even put more money into his purse than was either altogether convenient or advisable. And now, because of his unfortunate step into the apple basket, all that he had carried with him had simply vanished. Of coffee, of beer, of music, of looking at beautifully dressed girls—in short, of all of his anticipated pleasures—there was nothing more to be thought. He slipped slowly past the baths and finally turned down the road along the Elbe River, which happened to be deserted at the time. Beneath an elder tree that had sprouted through a wall, he found an inviting, grassy resting place. He sat down here and filled his pipe from the canister containing the medicinal tobacco that had recently been given to him by his friend, Dean Paulmann. Immediately before him the golden waves of the beautiful Elbe rolled and tossed; behind this, lordly Dresden rose, boldly and proudly stretching its luminous towers into the fragrant sky, which, in the distance, dipped down toward flowery fields and fresh spring woods, while a range of jagged mountain peaks revealed Bohemia in the dim distance. But the student Anselmus, unmindful of all of this, stared ahead gloomily and puffed smoky clouds into the air until, finally, he articulated his misery, saying, "In truth, I was born unlucky. Even as a schoolboy I could never win a prize; I always guessed wrong at odds and evens; my bread and butter always fell butter side down—I will not say anything about all these miseries. But isn't it a frightening fate that assures that even now when I have become a student in spite of everything, I remain a clumsy fool? Do I ever wear a coat without immediately staining it with tallow or catching it on some poorly fastened nail or other and tearing an accursed hole in it? Do I even greet any councillor or any lady without hurling my hat away, or even slipping on the smooth pavement and stumbling disgracefully? Didn't I, while in Halle, regularly have to pay a total of three of four groschen for broken pottery every shopping day, because the devil instilled in my head the need to walk straight ahead, like a lemming? Have I ever managed to get to class—or to any other place where an appointment had been arranged—on time? What good did it do me to start out a half hour early and stand at the door, for just as I was about to knock—swish!—some devil emptied a washbasin on me—or made me bump against some fellow coming out and got me involved in endless quarrels, and so I was late for everything? Ah! Where have you flown, you blissful dreams of future fortune, when I so proudly thought I might even rise to the height of Privy Secretary! Has not my evil star estranged me from my best patrons? I know that the Councillor to whom I have a letter finds cropped hair intolerable; with enormous effort the barber attaches a small plait to the back of my head, but at the first bow the unhappy knot surrenders and a little pug dog that has been blithely sniffing all around me frolics to the Privy Councillor with the plait in his mouth. Horrified, I dart after it, only to stumble against the table where he has been working while breakfasting, so that cups and plates and inkwell all tumble to the floor with a clatter, even as a flood of chocolate and ink flows over the important public document he has just been writing. "Sir, has the Devil got into you?" the incensed Privy Councillor bellows and shoves me out of the room.

"What good does it do me that Dean Paulmann has made me hopeful about a secretaryship? Will the malicious fate that hounds me everywhere allow it to happen? Just today—think about it! It was my intention to celebrate a happy Ascension Day with appropriate cheer; for once I was prepared to stretch a point and would, like any other guest, have gone into the Linke Baths and proudly have called out, 'Waiter, a bottle of beer, the best in the house please!' I might have sat there till late in the evening, moreover, quite close to this or that splendid group of beautifully dressed girls. I know it! Courage would have come; I would have been an entirely different man. I would certainly have pulled it off so well that when one or another of the young ladies asked, 'What time is it?' or 'What is it they are playing?' I would have gracefully sprung to my feet—without overturning my glass or stumbling over the bench—and, bowing, moving forward one and a half steps, I would have responded, 'By your leave, Mademoiselle, it is the *Donauweibchen* overture,' or 'It is just about to strike six.' Could anyone in the world have thought badly of me for this? I say, no!—for the girls would have glanced in my direction and smiled that mischievous smile they always show when I muster the courage to let them know that I too am acquainted with the light tone of society and with the manner in which ladies should be amused. But Satan himself directed me right into the damned apple basket, and now I sit here in solitude, with only my tobacco—"

Suddenly the soliloquy of the student was interrupted by a singular rustling and crackling that began near him in the grass, but which soon glided up into the leaves and branches of the elder tree spreading over his head. First it seemed as if an evening breeze were shaking the leaves, then as if little birds were twittering on the branches, their small wings mischievously fluttering to and fro. Then a whispering and a lisping began, and it seemed as if the sound of little crystal bells was coming from the blossoms. Anselmus listened and listened. Then—he himself knew not how—the whispering and the lisping and the tinkling turned into half-heard words:

"Betwixt, between, betwixt the branches, between the blossoms, shooting, twisting, twirling we come! Sister, sister, swing in the shimmer—quickly, quickly, in and out. Rays of sunset, whispering wind of evening, sounds of dew, singing blossoms—we sing with the branches and the blossoms; stars soon to sparkle—we must descend; betwixt, between, twisting, turning, twirling, sisters we!"

And thus did the confusing, hypnotic sounds continue. Anselmus thought, "It is only the evening wind that tonight whispers distinct words." But at that instant there was a sound over his head—like a triad of pure crystal bells. He glanced up and saw three little snakes, glistening in green and gold, which had twisted around the branches and stretched forth their heads toward the evening sun. Again there came the whispering and the twittering in the same words as before, and the little snakes went sliding and slithering up and down and through the leaves and the branches; and because their movements were so quick, it was as though the elder tree was scattering a thousand sparkling emeralds through the dark leaves.

"It is the rays of the evening sun playing in the elder tree," Anselmus thought; but the bells once more sounded, and Anselmus saw that one snake was stretching its little head out toward him. A shock like electricity raced through his every limb; he quivered all over, stared upwards, saw a pair of marvelous blue eyes looking down at him with unspeakable desire, so that an unknown feeling of both supreme bliss and deepest sorrow seemed to tear his heart apart. And as he continued to stare, imbued with intense longing, into those charming eyes, the crystal bells sounded harmoniously and the playing, sparkling emeralds fell, encircling him in a thousand glittering flames like golden threads. There was movement in the elder tree, and the tree spoke: "You were lying in my shadow; my perfume surrounded you, but you did not understand me. Fragrance is my speech when it is kindled by love."

The evening wind drifted by, saying, "I played round your temples, but you did not understand me. The breeze is my speech when it is kindled by love."

The sunbeams broke through the clouds, their rays burning with words, as if to say, "I drenched you with glowing gold, but you did not understand me. That glow is my speech when it is kindled by love."

More and more deeply absorbed in gazing into those glorious eyes, his longing grew stronger, his desire more passionate, and everything rose and moved around him as if all were awakening to joyous life. Flowers and blossoms released their odors about him—the fragrance was like the heavenly singing of a thousand flutelike voices; and what they sang was, like an echo, carried on the evening clouds of gold which sailed away with them into remote lands. But as the last ray of sun suddenly sank behind the hills and the twilight's veil covered the scene, a voice that was hoarse and deep seemed to reach Anselmus from a great distance:

"Hey there! What kind of gossiping and whispering is going on up there? Hey there! Who is seeking my ray behind the hills! Sufficiently sunned, sufficiently sung. Hey there! Through bush and grass, through grass and mist. Hey there! Come dow-w-wn, dow-w-wn!"

Thus the voice faded away, as if in the murmur of distant thunder, but the crystal bells shattered in sharp discord. All became mute; and Anselmus saw how the three snakes, shimmering and sparkling, slipped through the grass toward the river. Gliding, sliding, they rushed into the Elbe; and a green flame crackled over the waves where they had vanished, a green flame which, glowing obliquely ahead, vaporized in the direction of the city.

SECOND VIGIL

How the Student Anselmus Was Taken
for a Drunk and a Madman.
The Crossing of the Elbe. Kapellmeister Graun's Bravura.
Conradi's Medicinal Cordial, and the Bronze Apple Woman.

"The gentleman is mad!" said a respectable citizen's wife, who had paused as she was returning from a walk with her family, and now, with her arms crossed, was observing the mad antics of Anselmus. He had clasped the trunk of the elder tree and was continuously calling up to the branches and leaves, "Oh, gleam and glow one more time, you dear golden snakes. Let me once more hear your little bell voices! Oh, you lovely blue eyes, look once more upon me, once more or I must die in agony and longing!" And, along with this, the most pitiful sighing and sobbing escaped from the deepest recesses of Anselmus's soul while, eager and impatient, he shook the elder tree back and forth. But the tree, rather than replying, merely rustled its leaves somberly and inscrutably and seemed as if it were mocking Anselmus and his sorrows.

"The gentleman is mad!" the citizen's wife repeated. And Anselmus felt as if he had been shaken from a deep dream, or as if someone had poured icy water on him to rouse him suddenly from sleep. Only then did he clearly perceive where he was, and only then did he remember what a strange apparition had assaulted his senses so that he had been forced to begin talking loudly to himself. He gazed at the woman in amazement. At last, snatching up his hat, which had fallen off him to the ground, he was about to dash off. Meanwhile, the citizen himself had approached; after placing on the grass the child he had been carrying in his arms, he rested on his staff, listening and staring at the student in astonishment. Now he picked up the pipe and the tobacco that Anselmus had dropped, and extending them to the student, he said, "My worthy sir, do not behave so abominably or take to alarming people in the dark when in fact there is really nothing the matter with you except that you have had a drop too much. Go home and sleep it off like a good lad."

Anselmus was deeply ashamed, and only a very pitiful "Ah!" escaped from him.

"There, there," the citizen continued, "don't take it so to heart. Such a thing can happen to the best of us. On good old Ascension Day it is easy for a man to forget himself in his happiness and to guzzle one drink too many. It can happen even to a clergyman. I take it, my worthy sir, that you are a *candidatus*. But, with your permission, sir, I will fill my pipe with your tobacco. I used all of mine a short while ago."

The citizen uttered this last sentence as Anselmus was about to put his pipe and tobacco away; and now the good citizen cleaned his pipe slowly and deliberately, and just as slowly began to fill it. Several girls from the neighborhood had approached, and they were talking confidentially with the citizen's wife and each other, giggling as they glanced at Anselmus. For the student it was like standing on prickly thorns and glowing hot needles. Just as soon as his pipe and tobacco were returned to him, he rushed off as quickly as he could.

All of the incredible things that he had seen were completely wiped from his memory; he could only remember having babbled all kinds of foolishness beneath the elder tree, and this he found especially horrifying because he had long had an aversion to all soliloquists. His Dean had once said that it is the Devil himself who chatters out of these people, and Anselmus had sincerely believed him. But to be regarded as a *candidatus theologiae* and as being drunk on Ascension Day!—the thought was intolerable. He was about to turn into Poplar Lane near Kosel Garden when a voice behind him called out: "Anselmus! Anselmus! In heaven's name, where are you running so quickly?" The student stopped as if rooted to the spot, because he was certain that some new misfortune was now about to descend upon him. The voice was heard again: "Anselmus, come back, we are waiting for you by the water!" And now Anselmus realized that the voice he heard belonged to his friend Dean Paulmann. He returned to the Elbe and found the Dean and both of his daughters and Registrar Heerbrand about to embark in a boat. Paulmann extended an invitation to Anselmus to join them in crossing the Elbe and to spend the evening at his house in the suburb of Pirna. Anselmus very happily accepted this invitation, thinking that it was a good way to escape from the evil destiny that had all day pursued him.

By chance, a display of fireworks was taking place on the far bank, in Anton Garden, just as they were crossing the river. Sputtering and hissing, the rockets soared on high, scattering blazing stars through the air, a thousand crackling sparks and flashes bursting all about. Anselmus was sitting near the helmsman, lost in thought; but when he saw the reflection of the darting and crackling sparks and flames in the water, it seemed to him as if the little golden snakes were playing in the waves. All the marvels he had seen under the elder tree now once more came alive in his heart and his thoughts, and he was again seized by that ineffable desire, that glowing passion which had shaken him before.

"Ah, my little golden snakes, is it you again? Just sing, sing! Let those lovely, dear dark blue eyes once more come to me through your song. Ah, ah! Are you then beneath the waves!"

Thus cried Anselmus, while at the same instant moving violently, as if he were about to plunge into the river from the boat.

"Is the gentleman mad?" the helmsman shouted and grabbed him by his coattails. The girls, who were close to him, screamed in fear and escaped to the other side of the boat. The Registrar said something in Dean Paulmann's ear, to which the latter lengthily responded, but of which Anselmus could only understand the words: "Attacks like this—haven't you noticed them?" Immediately following this, the Dean rose and then sat down beside Anselmus, with a certain earnestness, seriousness, and official air, taking his hand and saying to him, "How are you feeling, Anselmus?" The student was almost fainting because deep within himself there had risen an insane conflict that he desired in vain to reconcile. He clearly saw now that what he had assumed to be the gleam of golden snakes was really nothing more than the reflection of the fireworks being fired in Anton Garden. But a feeling he had never before known, one he could not identify as either rapturous or painful, convulsed his heart; and when the helm sliced through the water so that the waves, curling as if in anger, splattered and foamed, Anselmus heard a soft whispering in their sound: "Anselmus! Anselmus! Do you not see how we glide ahead of you? Little sister is looking at you again. Believe, believe, believe in us!" And he thought that he could see three streaks of glowing green in the reflected light; but when he gazed somberly into the water to see whether the lovely eyes would not once more look up at him, he saw only too well that the gleam was merely a reflection emanating from the windows of neighboring houses. He sat there, silent, engaged in a struggle with himself. And now Dean Paulmann repeated more sharply, "How are you feeling, Anselmus?"

Utterly despondent, the student answered, "Ah, my dear sir, if only you knew what I, while completely awake and with my eyes wide open, have just dreamed under an elder tree close to the garden of Linke Baths, you would not blame me for being a little absent-minded."

"Well, well, now, dear Anselmus!" the Dean interrupted, "I have always believed you to be a steady young man, but to dream—to dream while your eyes are wide open—and then to suddenly want to leap into the water, this, if you will allow me to say so, is only possible for lunatics or fools!"

Anselmus was extremely distressed by his friend's harsh talk; then Veronica, Paulmann's eldest daughter, a truly lovely, blooming girl of sixteen, said, "But my dear father, surely something extraordinary must have happened to Herr Anselmus. Perhaps he only thinks he was awake when, in truth, he may really have been asleep—and therefore all kinds of foolishness entered his head and still remain in his thoughts."

"And, dearest Mademoiselle, worthy Dean!" Registrar Heerbrand added, "is it not possible for one to sink sometimes into a kind of dreamy state even while awake? I have myself had such an experience; for instance, one afternoon while at coffee, in the kind of mood produced by that special time of salutary physical and spiritual digestion, I suddenly remembered—as if by inspiration—where a misplaced manuscript lay—and only last night a magnificent large Latin paper came dancing before my open eyes in the very same way."

"Ah, most revered Registrar," the Dean responded, "you have always been inclined to the *poetica,* and one thus lapses into fantasies and romantic flights." But Anselmus felt better that anyone should side with him in this very perplexing situation while he was in peril of being considered either drunk or crazy. Despite its already being quite dark, for the first time he noticed that Veronica truly had very lovely dark blue eyes—and he noticed this without recalling the marvelous eyes he had seen in the elder tree. On the whole, the adventure that had taken place under the elder tree had again completely disappeared from his thoughts. He felt at ease and happy; indeed, he became so high spirited that he offered a helping hand to Veronica, his lovely advocate, as she was stepping from the boat, and when she put her arm in his, he readily escorted her home with such skill and good fortune that he only slipped once—this being the only wet spot in the entire road—

Veronica's white gown merely being slightly spattered by the accident.

Dean Paulmann observed this happy change in Anselmus. His fondness for him returned immediately, and he begged to be forgiven for the harsh words that had earlier escaped him. "Yes," he admitted, "there are many examples we possess that indicate that certain fantasies may appear to a man and then prey upon and truly plague him. But this is a physical disease, and leeches are beneficial for it—if they are applied to one's bottom, as proved by a certain learned physician who is now deceased."

Anselmus did not know whether he had been drunk or crazy or sick—in any event, the leeches seemed absolutely superfluous because these alleged fantasies had completely disappeared. The more Anselmus found himself successful in bestowing a variety of delicate attentions on the pretty Veronica, the happier he became.

As usual, there was music after the modest meal. Anselmus had to sit at the piano, and Veronica, her voice pure and clear, sang. "Dear Mademoiselle," Registrar Heerbrand said, "you have a voice like a crystal bell!"

"Indeed not!" Anselmus exclaimed, for a reason unknown to himself; and they all looked at him in astonishment and perplexity. "Crystal bells in elder trees make a wondrous sound—wondrous!" Anselmus continued, half murmuring to himself.

Veronica laid her hand on his shoulder and asked, "What is it you are saying now, Anselmus?"

The student immediately became wide awake again and started to play. Dean Paulmann looked at him morosely, but Registrar Heerbrand placed a sheet of music on the stand and enchantingly sang one of the bravura airs by Kapellmeister Graun. Anselmus played the accompaniment, as he did for many other songs that followed; and a fugue duet played by him and Veronica, which had been composed by Dean Paulmann himself, once more restored everyone to very good spirits.

It had grown rather late; Registrar Heerbrand was reaching for his hat and cane when the Dean secretively drew near him and said, "Hm, do you not wish, honored Registrar, to mention to Anselmus himself—hm!—that about which we spoke before?"

"With enormous pleasure," Registrar Heerbrand replied, and

after they had sat down in a circle, he began as follows without further ado:

"There is in this locality an old, strange, noteworthy man. They say that he engages in all manner of occult sciences, but since no such sciences exist, I take him for an antiquarian, and also for an experimental chemist. I mean none other than our Privy Archivist Lindhorst. As you know, he lives alone in his old and remote house, and when he is not engaged in working in his office, he is to be found in his library or his laboratory, which, however, he permits no one to enter. He owns, aside from many rare books, a number of manuscripts that are partly in Arabic or Coptic, and some of them are written in exotic letters that belong to no known language. He desires to have the latter meticulously copied, and he needs a man who can draw with the pen and reproduce these markings on parchment in ink with precision and accuracy. This work is done in a separate room in the house, under his supervision; in addition to a free dinner during working hours, he pays a taler every day and promises a considerable reward when the copying is properly completed. The hours are from twelve to six daily; between three and four there is a rest period, and you have your dinner. Having experimented with one or two young people without success, Herr Archivarius Lindhorst has finally requested that I find him a master at ink drawing; and then I thought of you, Anselmus, because I know that you not only write neatly but that you are very expert at drawing with a pen. If, in these grim times, and until you are able to establish yourself permanently, you wish to earn a mint taler a day and, in addition, the gift promised for the job successfully completed, you may call exactly at noon tomorrow upon Herr Archivarius, with whose house you are no doubt familiar. But be on your guard against any inkblot; if a blot stains your copy, you will have to start again, and if ink falls on the original, Herr Archivarius, who is a hotheaded man, is likely to fling you out of the window."

Registrar Heerbrand's proposition made Anselmus very happy because not only did he write and draw beautifully with the pen but he had a passion for the painstaking calligraphy required of this kind of copying. He therefore expressed his grateful thanks and promised not to miss the noon appointment scheduled for the next day.

That night Anselmus saw nothing but shining taler coins and heard their delightful clink. Who could reproach this unfortunate youth, who had been deprived of so many aspirations by a capricious fate and had been forced to deliberate about the expenditure of every penny and to do without all those pleasures desired by a youthful heart? Early in the morning he had already searched out his pencils, his quills, and his India ink—never could the Archivist invent superior materials, he felt. More important than anything else, he gathered and arranged his drawings and his masterpieces of calligraphy, intending to exhibit them to the Archivist as evidence that he was competent to accomplish the work desired by that demanding gentleman. Everything proceeded well; an extraordinary and felicitous star seemed to be watching over him. His cravat was properly arranged at the first attempt; not a seam burst; not a thread tore in his black silken hose; and his hat did not even fall into the dust after he had brushed it clean. In short, at exactly half past eleven Anselmus was standing in Conradi's shop in Castle Street, dressed in his elegant grey coat and black satin trousers, with a roll of calligraphies and pen drawings in his pocket, drinking one—two—glasses of the very best medicinal cordial, for here, he thought, slapping his still-empty pocket, here there will soon be the clinking of talers.

Despite the distance to the remote street where Archivarius Lindhorst's ancient house was located, Anselmus was at the front door before twelve struck. There he stood, looking at the beautiful large bronze knocker; but then, when he raised his hand to grip the knocker, precisely as the last stroke of the clock in the church steeple boomed loudly through the air, the glowing, blue eyes rolled horrifyingly, and the metal face became contorted into a sneering smile. Oh! It was the apple woman from the Black Gate! The sharp teeth clattered together in the flabby jaws, and in the clattering there was a rasping that seemed to say: "You fool—fool—fool! Wait, wait! Why did you run away? Fool!" Terrorstruck, Anselmus tumbled backwards; he tried to grasp the doorpost, but his hand gripped the bell rope and tugged it, and piercingly discordant, the bell rang out more and more loudly while the entire empty house echoed, as if to mock him, "Soon your downfall into the crystal!"

Horror possessed Anselmus and thrilled through his limbs. The bell rope reached downward and changed into a white, diaphanous, enormous serpent that encircled and crushed him, its coils squeezing him more and more tightly until his fragile and paralyzed limbs cracked into pieces and his blood gushed from his veins and into the transparent body of the serpent, dyeing it red. "Kill me! Kill me!" he tried to scream in his terrible agony, but the scream was only a muffled groan. The serpent lifted its head and placed its long, pointed tongue of glistening brass on Anselmus' chest; then a cutting pain pierced the artery of life, and he lost consciousness.

When he regained his senses, he was on his own poor bed, and Dean Paulmann was standing before him, saying: "In heaven's name, what is this madness that possesses you, my dear Anselmus?"

THIRD VIGIL

Accounts Concerning Archivarius Lindhorst's Family. Veronica's Blue Eyes. Registrar Heerbrand.

"The Spirit looked upon the water, and the water moved and churned in frothy waves and, thundering, dashed itself into the abysses, which swallowed it greedily after opening their black throats. Like victorious conquerors, granite rocks lifted their jagged crowns to protect the valley until the sun gathered it to her maternal bosom and cherished and warmed it while embracing it with her rays, as if they were glowing arms. Then a thousand seeds awoke from their profound sleep under the sands of the desert and stretched their leaves of green and their stalks toward the maternal face above; and, like smiling children in cradles of green, the little flowers rested in their buds and blossoms until they were also awakened by the mother, who, in order to please them, tinted the lights with which they bedecked themselves a thousand different hues.

"But there was a black hill in the middle of the valley which rose and fell like the breast of a man inflamed by passion. Vapors billowed up from the abysses and rolled together into stupendous masses in a malevolent effort to hide the face of the mother; but the mother called upon the storm, which, flying to her service, dispersed the vapors. And when the dreary hill was touched again by the rays of the pure light, a superb fire-lily, exulting in its bliss, burst from the hill, its lovely leaves forming like soft lips eager to receive the mother's kiss.

"Now a dazzling light entered the valley; it was the youth Phosphorous. The lily was imbued with warm desire upon seeing him, and besought him: 'Be forever mine, fair youth! I love you and must die if you forsake me!' Phosphorous responded: 'Lovely flower, I will be yours, but then you will, like a naughty child, forsake your father and mother. No longer will you know your playmates, for you will endeavor to be both greater and stronger than those who now share your joy. The salutary desire that now engulfs you will be split into hundreds of rays and will torture and trouble you, for senses will be born of sense, and the ultimate bliss, which will be kindled by the spark I ignite in you, will be the hopeless agony through which you will be destroyed, only to rise again in a different shape. This spark is thought!'

" 'Ah,' the lily lamented, 'can I not be yours in this glow, even as it now flames within me? Can I love you more than now, and if you destroyed me, could I again look upon you as I do at this moment?' Phosphorous kissed her, and the lily, as if pierced through with light, went up in flames, out of which an alien being issued, soaring quickly from the valley and wandering into infinite space, unmindful of childhood playmates or of the loved youth. And, as he had loved her too, so he mourned for the loss of his beloved. Love of the beautiful lily had brought him to the desolate valley. The rocks of granite lowered their heads as they joined him in his anguish. But one of the rocks opened itself, and a dragon with black wings flew from it, saying, 'My brothers, the metals, sleep within, but I am forever awake and active, and I will help you.' Winging to and fro, the dragon finally captured the being which had sprung from the lily, carried it to the hill, and locked it within his wing—then it was the lily again; but thought, which had remained, tore at its heart, and the love for Phosphorous was a cutting pain before which, as if being breathed upon by poisonous vapors, the little flowers, previously rejoicing in the presence of the lovely lily, withered and died.

"Phosphorous dressed himself in a resplendent coat of mail that sported with the light in a thousand hues, and he battled with the dragon, which beat on the mail with his black wing until it rang. And the little flowers sprang to life at this loud clang, and like multihued birds, they fluttered about the dragon. His strength ebbed, and thus vanquished, the dragon hid himself in the bowels of the earth. The lily was freed. Phosphorous, full of glowing desire and heavenly love, embraced her. The flowers and the birds—indeed, even the towering rocks of granite—joined in a jubilant anthem paying homage to her as queen of the valley."

"Forgive me, my worthy Herr Archivarius, but this is Oriental bombast," Registrar Heerbrand said, "and we beg you to offer us, as you frequently have, something about your entirely extraordinary life, something about your adventures while traveling, particularly something true."

"Well, what then?" Lindhorst responded. "What I have been telling you is the truest I can serve up, and, in a certain respect, is part of my life because I come from that valley, and the fire-lily that ultimately reigned there as queen was my great-great-great-great grandmother; thus, I myself am actually a prince." Everyone burst into resounding laughter. "Yes, have a good laugh," Archivarius Lindhorst continued; "what I have told you in a most scanty and abbreviated fashion probably seems to you to be senseless and mad, yet it is nevertheless intended to be anything but incoherent or allegorical; rather, it is literally true. If, however, I had been aware that this beautiful love story, to which I owe my very existence, would have so little pleased you, I would instead have told you something of the news my brother brought me during his visit yesterday."

"What is this? Do you have a brother, Herr Archivarius? Where is he? Where does he live? Is he also in the service of the Crown? Is he perhaps an independent scholar?" they all asked from every side.

"No!" the Archivarius answered, while taking a pinch of snuff very serenely and composedly, "he has joined the bad side and has gone over to the dragons."

"We implore you, dear Herr Archivarius, to tell us what you mean?" Registrar Heerbrand interjected. "Over to the dragons?"

"Over to the dragons?" resounded from all sides, like an echo.

"Yes, over to the dragons," Archivarius Lindhorst continued, "apparently in absolute desperation, I think. Gentlemen, you are aware that my father has only recently died—at the most about three hundred and eighty-five years ago; therefore, I am still in mourning. I was his favorite son, and he left me a beautiful onyx that my brother desired with his whole heart. We argued about it over the corpse of my father, in so unbecoming a manner that the deceased, his patience depleted, arose and threw my evil brother down the stairs. This vexed my brother and he joined the dragons immediately. He now lives near Tunis, in a cypress forest. There he must watch a famous mystic carbuncle, which a devilish necromancer who has set up a summer house in Lapland is after, which is why my brother can get away only for about a quarter of an hour at a time—while the necromancer is taking care of the bed of salamanders in his garden. It is during this period of time that my brother rushes to tell me what is new at the sources of the Nile."

For the second time everyone burst into laughter; but the student Anselmus was growing very uneasy, and he could hardly look into Archivarius Lindhorst's fixed and serious eyes without shuddering internally in a way he himself could not comprehend. Also, there was something about the harsh and strangely metallic tone of Archivarius Lindhorst's voice that was mysteriously penetrating. Anselmus's very bones and marrow tingled as the Archivarius spoke.

The specific purpose Registrar Heerbrand had in mind when he took Anselmus to the café now appeared to be unattainable. Anselmus had steadfastly refused to be induced to attempt a second visit subsequent to the incident at Archivarius Lindhorst's door, because he was utterly convinced that nothing but luck had saved him from death, or at least from madness. Dean Paulmann happened to be strolling through the street at exactly the moment when Anselmus was lying at the door, unconscious, and an old woman who had placed her basket of apples and cakes aside was busily attending to him. The Dean had immediately secured a chaise and, in this manner, had managed to have Anselmus carried home. "You may think anything you like of me," Anselmus said, "you may consider me to be a fool or not, as you wish, but I insist that the accursed face of that witch at the Black Gate was grinning at me from the door knocker. I would rather not talk about what followed, but if I had regained consciousness and seen that execrable apple-hag next to me" (for the old woman was none other), "I would that very instant have suffered a stroke or have gone completely insane." Every effort at persuasion or attempt at rational argument tried by Dean Paulmann and Registrar Heerbrand failed. Not even blue-eyed Veronica herself could extricate him from the profound state of moodiness into which he had sunk. In fact, they considered him mentally ill, and in an attempt to divert his thoughts, Registrar Heerbrand thought nothing could be more effective for him than copying the manuscripts of Archivarius Lindhorst. It was therefore necessary only to introduce Anselmus to Lindhorst, and to this end Registrar Heerbrand, who knew that Archivarius frequented a specific café almost every night, invited Anselmus to accompany him nightly to that very café, there to join him in a glass of beer and a pipe at his expense until the Archivarius Lindhorst would somehow or other get to know him and conclude the deal for the copying—an offer Anselmus had accepted with great gratitude.

"Worthy Registrar, God will reward you if you bring the young man to his senses!" Dean Paulmann said.

"God will reward you!" Veronica echoed as she piously lifted her eyes to heaven, busily thinking that Anselmus was already a most pleasing young man, even without his senses!

Accordingly, as Archivarius Lindhorst, intending to leave, was heading for the door with his hat and cane, Registrar Heerbrand gripped Anselmus by the hand and, obstructing the way, said, "Most revered Herr Archivarius, here is Anselmus the student who has unusual calligraphic and drawing talent and will take the assignment of copying your rare manuscripts."

"I am most delighted to hear this," Archivarius Lindhorst answered quickly, throwing his three-cornered hat on his head, shoving Registrar Heerbrand and Anselmus off to a side, and dashing noisily down the stairs, leaving both the Registrar and the student standing in utter bewilderment, gaping at the door that had been slammed in their faces so that its hinges rattled.

"That is a remarkably eccentric old man," Registrar Heerbrand said.

"Remarkably eccentric old man," Anselmus stammered, feeling that he was being turned into a statue by an icy stream flowing through his veins. But the other guests all laughed, saying, "Archivarius was in an exceptionally whimsical state today, tomorrow he will be as gentle as a lamb, will utter not a word, will watch the smoke clouds raised by his pipe, or read the newspapers. You must not pay attention to such things."

"This is true too," Anselmus thought. "Who would pay attention to such a thing? Didn't Archivarius tell me that he was especially delighted to hear that I would copy his manuscripts? And why did Registrar Heerbrand step right in his way when he wanted to leave for home? No, no, he is basically a good man, this Herr Archivarius Lindhorst, and surprisingly liberal; somewhat strange in his phraseology, but how does this harm me? I will go to see him at the strike of twelve tomorrow, even if a hundred bronze apple-women try to stand in my way!"

FOURTH VIGIL

Anselmus's Melancholy. The Emerald Mirror.
How Archivarius Lindhorst Flew Off in the
Shape of a Vulture and Anselmus Met Nobody.

Gentle reader, may I ask you a question? Have you not had hours, even days and weeks, during which all your accustomed activities caused you nothing but annoyance and dissatisfaction, when everything you normally held to be of worth and significance seemed valueless and trivial? You did not know, at such times, what to do or where to turn. A vague feeling suffused your mind that you had more lofty desires that must be attained, desires that transcended the immediate pleasures of this world but were yet desires which your spirit, like a strictly brought-up, frightened child, dared not even express. In this desire for an unidentifiable something, which hovered over you regardless of where you were, like a diaphanous dream that vanished whenever you sought to examine it, you lost interest in everything around you here. You moped around with the disturbed look of a hopeless lover, and no matter what you saw being tried or gained in the bustle of varied existence, neither sorrow nor joy could be awakened in you—it was as though you no longer belonged to this world.

Gentle reader, if such a mood has ever possessed you, you know the state into which Anselmus had fallen. With all my heart I wish it were in my power to present Anselmus to you with complete vividness, gentle reader, for in these vigils in which I describe his extraordinary story there remains so much more of the marvelous (which jolted the lives of ordinary people into the unknown) that I am fearful that in the end you will believe neither in Anselmus nor in Archivarius Lindhorst; indeed, you may eventually have some doubt as to Registrar Heerbrand and Dean Paulmann, despite the fact that these two honorable people, at least, are still walking the streets of Dresden. Gentle reader, make an effort while you are in the fairy region full of glorious marvels, where both the highest rapture and deepest horror may be evoked, where the earnest goddess herself lifts her veil so that we think we see her face, but a smile often glimmers beneath her glance, a playful, teasing smile that enchants us just as that of a mother playing with her dearest children. While you are in this region that is revealed to us in dreams at least, try, gentle reader, to recognize the familiar shapes that hover around you in the ordinary world. Then you will discover that this glorious kingdom is much closer to you than you ever imagined. It is this kingdom that I now strive with all my heart to reveal to you through the extraordinary story of Anselmus.

Thus, as stated, Anselmus had, ever since that evening when he met Archivarius Lindhorst, been submerged in dreamy musing that made him insensitive to every external contact with the ordinary world. He felt that an ineffable something was awakening within his inmost soul and provoking that pain of rapture which is the longing that promises man the existence of a more exalted Being. His greatest pleasure came when he would wander in solitude through the meadows and the woods; and as if freed from all that chained him to his everyday impoverished existence, he could, so to speak, once more find himself in the manifold images that arose from his soul.

Once, while returning from a long walk, he happened to pass that notable elder tree under which, as if possessed by magic, he had once gazed upon such numerous wonders. He was peculiarly attracted to the familiar green grass, but he had no sooner seated himself upon it than the entire vision, which he had once viewed as if in a heavenly trance and which had, as though through some alien influence, been blotted from his mind, once more floated before him in the most vivid colors, as if he were looking upon it for the second time. Indeed, it was clearer to him than before that the mild blue eyes belonged to the gold-green snake that had slithered its way through the heart of the elder tree and that those marvelous crystal tones that had so filled him with rapture must have emerged from the turnings of its tapering body. Now, as on Ascension Day, he again embraced the elder tree and cried into the branches and leaves, "Oh, once more slide forth and twine and wind yourself amidst the branches so that I may once more see you, you little lovely green snake! Once more cast your gentle eyes upon me! I love you, and if you do not return, I must perish in agony and sorrow!" But everything remained completely mute and still. As before, the branches and the leaves of the elder tree rustled unintelligibly. Anselmus, however, now felt as if he knew what it was that was alive and striving within his heart; he now knew what was lacerating his heart with the agony of infinite desire. "What else can it be," he said, "than that I love you with all my heart and soul, that I love you to the very death, you glorious golden little snake; indeed, that I cannot survive without you and must die in forlorn misery if I fail to find you again, if I don't possess you as my beloved! But I know that you will be mine and that then everything my glorious dreams have promised me of another and loftier world will be fulfilled."

From then on Anselmus could be found every evening, when the sun scattered its sparkling golden rays over the tops of the trees, under the elder, pitiably calling from deep within his heart to the branches and the leaves for a sight of his little beloved gold-green snake. Once when he was behaving in this way, there suddenly appeared before him a tall, thin man wrapped in a wide, light-gray coat who, looking upon him with large flaming eyes, said, "Hey, there! What kind of whining and wailing is going on here? Hey, there! This is Herr Anselmus who is supposed to copy my manuscripts." Anselmus was more than a little frightened upon hearing this powerful voice, because it was the same voice which had on Ascension Day called, "Hey, there! What kind of chattering and gossiping is this?" and so on. Anselmus was so terrified and astounded that he could not utter a word. "What is the matter with you, Herr Anselmus?" Archivarius Lindhorst (the stranger in the light-gray coat was none other) continued. "What do you want from the elder tree, and why haven't you come to me to begin your work?"

In truth, Anselmus had been unable to persuade himself to go to Archivarius Lindhorst's house for a second time, despite the fact that that very evening he had strongly resolved to do so. But, at this moment when his beautiful dreams were being shattered by the hostile voice that once before had snatched his beloved from him, a kind of despair seized him, and he burst out violently: "You, Herr Archivarius, may consider me insane or not—it makes no difference to me—but here in this very tree, on Ascension Day, I saw the gold-green snake, my soul's beloved, and she spoke to me in heavenly crystal tones; but you, you, Herr Archivarius, shouted and called so frighteningly across the water."

"What's this, my dear fellow?" Archivarius Lindhorst interrupted while taking snuff and smiling very oddly.

Anselmus felt an ease coming to his heart now that he had been successful in starting to tell this strange story, and he felt completely right in placing upon the Archivarius the entire blame, because he felt that it was he and no one else who had so thundered from afar. Pulling himself together, he continued: "Well, I will tell you all about the mysterious events that happened to me on Ascension Evening, and then you may say and do and think anything you like about me." He described the marvelous adventure in its entirety, from his unfortunate stumbling into the apple basket to the moment when the three gold-green snakes fled across the river, and how the people after that considered him to be either drunk or mad. Anselmus ended by saying, "I really saw all of this with my own eyes, and deep within my heart those precious voices I heard still echo. It was not a dream; and if I am not to perish of desire, I must believe in these gold-green snakes, though, Herr Archivarius, your smile tells me that you believe that these snakes really are no more than figments of my feverish and overwrought imagination."

"Not at all," Archivarius Lindhorst responded with great serenity and composure, "the gold-green snakes which you saw in the elder were simply my three daughters; and it is now very clear that you have fallen head over heels in love with the blue eyes of Serpentina, the youngest of these. To be sure, I knew it myself on

Ascension Day, and when—at that time I was busily writing at home—I grew annoyed with all the chattering and gossiping going on, I called to the lazy flirts to tell them that it was high time to leave for home because the sun was setting and they had sung enough and had drunk enough of the sunbeams."

Anselmus felt as if he now was hearing articulated something of which he had long dreamed; and although he imagined that the elder and the wall and the grass and everything surrounding him were now beginning to spin slowly around, he pulled himself together and was about to speak again when Archivarius Lindhorst prevented him from doing so by quickly tugging the glove off his left hand and holding before Anselmus's eyes a ring with a stone that glittered with strange sparkles and flames, saying, "Look here, worthy Herr Anselmus, what you can see here may bring you joy."

Anselmus looked in the stone and, wonder of wonders! the stone cast up a cluster of beams as from a burning circle, forming a gleaming crystal mirror in which, now slithering, now fleeing, now twisting together, the three golden snakes were dancing and prancing; and when their tapering shapes, which glittered with a thousand sparkles, touched each other, there came forth from them glorious tones as of crystal bells; and the snake in the middle stretched her little head from the mirror as if possessed by passion and longing, her dark blue eyes saying, "Do you know me? Do you believe in me, Anselmus? Only in belief is there love. Can you indeed love?"

"Oh, Serpentina, Serpentina," Anselmus cried, with insane passion. Archivarius Lindhorst, however, suddenly breathed on the mirror and the rays dissolved with an electric sputter; and on his hand only a little emerald remained, which Archivarius covered by pulling on his glove.

"Did you see the little golden snakes, Herr Anselmus?" asked Archivarius Lindhorst.

"Oh, heavens yes!" the student responded, "and lovely dear Serpentina."

"Quiet!" Archivarius Lindhorst said. "Enough for today. By the way, if you should decide to work for me, you may see my daughters often enough, for I will grant you this true satisfaction if you are well behaved and stick to your task—that is, if you copy every mark with the greatest neatness and accuracy. But, Herr Anselmus, you have not come to me at all despite Registrar Heerbrand assuring me that you would come right away, and I have waited for several days in vain."

As soon as Archivarius Lindhorst mentioned Registrar Heerbrand's name, Anselmus once more felt that he had both feet on the ground, that he really was Anselmus the student, and that the man who stood before him was in fact Archivarius Lindhorst. The stark contrast between the indifference in the tone of Lindhorst's speech and the marvelous visions that the latter had evoked as a true necromancer caused a certain horror in the student, which was only heightened by the piercing look of those fiery eyes that glowed from their bony sockets in the drawn and puckered face, as if from a leather case. Once more the student was inexorably gripped by the same unearthly feeling that had possessed him in the café when Archivarius Lindhorst had told such a wild tale. Anselmus retained his composure through a great effort, and when Archivarius Lindhorst once more asked, "So why is it that you did not come?" the student gathered all his courage and told him what had happened at his door.

"My dear Herr Anselmus," Archivarius Lindhorst said when the student was finished, "my dear Herr Anselmus, I know this apple-woman of whom you speak. She is an evil creature who plays all kinds of ugly tricks on me; but that she would change herself into bronze and into the shape of a door knocker to frighten welcome visitors away is very irritating indeed and not to be tolerated. Worthy Herr Anselmus, if you come at noon tomorrow and again notice anything of this grinning and growling, would you be good enough to put a drop or two of this liquid on her nose. Everything will return to normal immediately. For now, adieu, dear Herr Anselmus. I must hurry, and I cannot, therefore, suggest that you return with me to the city. Adieu, till tomorrow at noon."

Archivarius Lindhorst had given the student Anselmus a small vial with a yellow-golden liquid in it, and he walked quickly away so that he appeared, in the deepening dusk, to be floating down to the valley rather than to be walking. He was already drawing close to Kosel Garden when the wind entered his wide overcoat and caused the coattails to spread out, so that they fluttered in the air like a pair of huge wings. To Anselmus, who was watching Archivarius Lindhorst with a look of utter amazement, it was as if a large bird were spreading its wings for a fast flight. And now, while the student gazed steadfastly into the oncoming dusk, a white-gray vulture soared high into the air with a creaking cry; Anselmus clearly saw that the white flutter he had thought to be the retreating Archivarius Lindhorst must have been this vulture, although he still could not understand where the Archivarius had vanished so abruptly.

"But he may have flown away in person, this Herr Archivarius Lindhorst," Anselmus said to himself, "because I now clearly see and feel that all these strange shapes that have entered my waking life and are having their games with me come from a distant world of marvels which I never before saw except in particularly remarkable dreams. But be that as it may! You, my beautiful, gentle Serpentina, thrive and glow in my heart. Only you can quiet the endless desire which lacerates my soul. Oh, dear, dear Serpentina, when will I again see your lovely eyes!" Anselmus cried aloud.

"That is a despicable, un-Christian name!" mumbled a bass voice nearby which belonged to a man who was returning from a walk. Anselmus, remembering where he was, rushed off while thinking to himself, "Wouldn't it now be a real misfortune if Dean Paulmann or Registrar Heerbrand were to meet me?" But he met neither of them.

FIFTH VIGIL

Frau Court Councillor Anselmus. Cicero de Officiis.
Long-tailed Monkeys and Other Vermin. The Equinox.

"There is nothing in the world that can be done with this Anselmus," Dean Paulmann said. "All my good advice, all my reproofs are fruitless. He does not wish to apply himself to anything, though he has a splendid classical education, which is the basis for everything."

But Registrar Heerbrand, smiling roguishly and mysteriously, replied, "Dear Dean, do allow Anselmus to take his time. He is a peculiar subject, this Anselmus, but there is a great deal in him; and when I say a great deal, I mean a Privy Secretary or even a Court Councillor."

"Court—" Dean Paulmann began, the words sticking in his throat in his astonishment.

"Quiet, quiet!" Registrar Heerbrand went on. "I know what I know. He has these two days been copying manuscripts at Archivarius Lindhorst's, and only last night, upon meeting me at the café, Archivarius Lindhorst said, 'You have recommended me a sound man, worthy sir, something will come of him!' Now think of the connections of Archivarius Lindhorst— Quiet, Quiet! We'll discuss this a year from now." With these words the Registrar left the room, the same roguish smile on his face, leaving behind the Dean, whose astonishment and curiosity had rendered him speechless, and who, as if under a spell, was transfixed in his chair. But on Veronica this conversation made a very special impression. "Haven't I all along known," she thought, "that Herr Anselmus is a very clever and attractive young man who is destined for something great? If only I could be sure that he really cares for me! Didn't he press my hand twice that night when we crossed the Elbe? And during our duet, didn't he look at me with glances which pierced my heart? Yes, yes, he really likes me and I—" As young girls tend to do, Veronica totally surrendered to the sweet dreams of a joyous future. She was Frau Court Councillor; she lived in a magnificent house on Castle Street, or in New Market, or in Moritz Street. Her stylish little hat and her new Turkish shawl were wonderfully becoming; she was having her breakfast on the balcony, dressed in a smart negligee, giving her cook orders for the day: "And please take care that you do not spoil that dish. It is the Court Councillor's favorite." Young dandies who are passing by glance up, and she clearly hears, "Well, isn't that wife of the Court Councillor a divine creature! How well her little lace cap suits her!" Frau Privy Councillor Ypsilon sends her servant to inquire if it would suit the pleasure of Frau Court Councillor Veronica to drive with her to the Linke Baths today. "Many thanks. I am terribly sorry, but I have a previous engagement for tea with Frau President Tz." Then Court Councillor Anselmus, who has gone out early on business, returns. He is dressed in the height of fashion: "Already ten," he declares, looking at his gold watch and bestowing upon his young wife a kiss. "How are you, my little wife? Can you guess what I have for you?" he says teasingly, taking a pair of lovely earrings designed in the latest style from his vest pocket and substituting them for her old ones. "Oh, what lovely, dainty earrings!" Veronica cries aloud, jumping up from her chair and throwing her embroidery aside in order to look at those lovely earrings in the mirror with her own eyes.

"Well, what's all this about?" Dean Paulmann said, deep in his study of *Cicero de Officiis,* and nearly dropping his book. "Are we having fits like Anselmus?" At precisely this moment Anselmus, who, contrary to his habit, had not been seen for several days, entered the room, much to Veronica's amazement and fright because he seemed, in truth, completely changed. Much more precisely than was usual, he spoke of the new possibility life opened to him which had recently become clear to him, and of splendid prospects that were now available to him but which many were quite unable to recognize. Dean Paulmann, remembering the cryptic speech of Registrar Heerbrand, was even more thunderstruck, and barely a syllable could escape his lips before Anselmus had already made his exit, after dropping hints of some important business he had at Archivarius Lindhorst's, and after he had kissed Veronica's hand with foppish facility.

"That was already a Court Councillor," Veronica murmured to herself, "and he kissed my hand without slipping on the floor or stepping on my foot, as he always used to! And he threw me the tenderest look as well. Yes, he truly loves me!"

Once more Veronica surrendered to her reverie, but now it seemed as if a hostile figure was invading these beautiful visions of her future life as Frau Court Councillor, and as if this figure were mocking her, saying to her, "This is all terribly stupid and ordinary business, and false to boot, for Anselmus will never ever be a Court Councillor and your husband. He does not love you even a little, despite your blue eyes and your splendid figure and your lovely hand." An icy stream then froze Veronica's soul, and a profound dismay swept aside the pleasure with which she had imagined herself in her little lace cap and her stylish earrings just a short while before. Tears almost welling in her eyes, she said aloud, "Ah! it is only too true. He does not love me, and I shall never ever be Frau Court Councillor!"

"Romantic rot, romantic rot!" Dean Paulmann cried, and then, snatching up his hat and his cane, he indignantly and hurriedly left the house. "That's the last straw," Veronica sighed; and she was annoyed at her twelve-year-old sister because she sat and kept sewing unconcernedly at her embroidery frame as if nothing had happened.

It was almost three o'clock, time to tidy the room and set the coffee table because the Mademoiselles Oster had sent word that they were coming to call. But from behind every box that Veronica moved, behind the music books that she took from the piano, behind every cup, behind the coffee pot that she brought from the cupboard, peeped the malicious figure, like a little mandrake, laughing mockingly while snapping its tiny spidery tendrils and crying, "He will not be your husband! He will not be your husband!" Finally, when Veronica had fled into the middle of the room, leaving everything, she saw it again with a long nose and colossal bulk behind the stove, and it growled and snarled, "He will not be your husband!"

"Don't you hear or see anything, sister?" Veronica cried, trembling with fright, not daring to touch anything in the room. Fränzchen arose from her embroidering very gravely and quietly, saying, "What troubles you today, sister? You're rattling and banging everything. I see that I must help you."

But at this moment the visitors, gay and laughing briskly, came tripping in; and at the very same instant Veronica saw that she had mistaken the stove top for the figure and the creaking of the poorly shut stove door for those malicious words. She was, nevertheless, beside herself with terror and could not immediately recover her composure, so that her friends could not help seeing her unusual agitation, which her paleness and her expression betrayed. They immediately terminated their cheerful chatter and insisted that she tell them what in heaven's name had happened. She was forced to confess that while she had abandoned herself to quite special thoughts, she had been possessed by an abnormal fear of ghosts, which was quite unlike her. Her description of how a little gray mandrake had peeped out of the corners of the room mocking and torturing her was painted in such vivid colors that the Mademoiselles Oster peered around with timid glances and began to experience all kinds of unearthly feelings. Fränzchen, however, came into the room at this very moment with the steaming coffee pot, and the three, composed again, laughed at their foolishness.

Angelica, the elder of the Osters, was betrothed to an officer. The young man had joined the army, and news of him had so long failed to reach his friends that there was no question but that he was dead, or at the very least critically wounded. This had plunged Angelica into the most profound sorrow; but she was happy today, even exuberant, a condition which so surprised Veronica that she could not help but talk about it quite unreservedly.

"Dear girl," Angelica said, "do you believe that my Victor is out of my heart and out of my thoughts? He is the reason why I am so happy. Oh Lord! So happy, so completely blissful! For my Victor is well and will soon be home, having been promoted to captain, and having been decorated with the honors his heroism earned. He is prevented from writing by a deep but by no means serious wound in his right arm, inflicted upon him by the sword of a French Hussar, and also, the rapid movement of the army— he refuses to leave his regiment—still makes it impossible for him to send me news. But tonight he will be ordered to return home until his wound heals. He will start out for home tomorrow, and at the precise moment when he is stepping into the coach, he will be informed of his promotion."

"But my dear Angelica," Veronica interrupted, "how do you know all this?"

"Do not mock me, my friend," Angelica continued, "and you will certainly not laugh lest you be punished by the little gray mandrake who might peep out at you from behind the mirror there. I cannot relinquish my belief in certain mysterious things, because I have often enough seen them in life. I do not, for example, consider it so remarkable as many others do that there are people who are gifted with a certain clairvoyance. There is an old woman in the city here who has this talent to a great degree. She uses neither cards nor molten lead nor coffee grounds, as do ordinary fortune-tellers, but after taking certain steps in which you yourself participate, she uses a polished metallic mirror, and the weirdest combination of intermingled figures and forms appear in it. These she interprets, and answers your questions. I was with her last night and was told this news of my Victor, which I do not for a moment doubt."

Angelica's story cast a spark into Veronica's soul, which quickly flared to the thought of consulting this same old woman about

Anselmus and her aspirations. She discovered that this old woman was called Frau Rauerin and that she lived on a secluded street near Lake Gate—also, that she could only be seen on Tuesdays, Wednesdays, and Fridays, from seven in the evening, but then, to be sure, during the whole night until sunrise. She also preferred her customers to come unaccompanied. It was Wednesday now, and Veronica resolved, under the pretext of taking the Osters home, to visit this old woman, which she actually did. Thus, she had scarcely said goodbye to her friends, who lived in Neustadt, at the Elbe bridge, when she rushed toward Lake Gate and, before long, had come to that remote and narrow street that had been described to her. There, at the very far end of it, she saw the little red house in which Frau Rauerin was supposed to live. As she approached the door, she could not rid herself of a dread, a kind of horror. Finally, in spite of her reluctance, she summoned her courage and pulled the bell. The door opened and she groped her way through the dark passage toward the stair that lead to the second story, as Angelica had told her to do. "Does Frau Rauerin live here?" she called into the deserted hallway when no one appeared. But instead of an answer there was a long and clear "Meow!" and a large black tomcat, its back arched, its tail whisking back and forth in wavy coils, gravely preceded her to the door of the room, which opened at the sound of a second meow.

"Ah, see—daughter, are you here already? Come in, come in," called an approaching figure whose appearance rooted Veronica to the floor. A tall bony woman covered in black rags!—and while she spoke, her pointed, protruding chin wagged this way and that. Her toothless mouth, overshadowed by a bony hawknose, contorted into a sneering smile, and glowing cat's eyes sparkled behind large eyeglasses; black wiry hair protruded from the motley shawl wrapped around her head; but two large burn scars, which traversed her face from the left cheek across her nose, deformed her face horribly. Veronica's breath stuck in her throat, and the scream that struggled to escape became a profound sigh as the skeletal hand of the witch clutched her and pulled her into the room.

Here everything was awake and astir—there was nothing but noise and tumult and squealing and meowing and croaking and piping, everything at once, and from everywhere. The old witch pounded the table with her fist and screamed, "Peace, you wretches!" And the monkeys whimpered and climbed to the top of the four-poster bed; and the guinea pigs all dashed beneath the stove; and the raven fluttered up to the round mirror; and the black tomcat, as if the rebuke concerned him not at all, sat comfortably on the upholstered chair into which he had jumped immediately after entering the room.

Veronica gained courage as soon as the room grew quiet. She was less frightened now than she had been while in the hall; indeed, the hag herself did not seem so repulsive now, and for the first time Veronica gazed about at the room. All kinds of obnoxious stuffed animals were suspended from the ceiling; weird household implements that she had never seen before were spread in confusion on the floor; there was a meager blue fire burning in the grate which occasionally sputtered and sent forth yellow sparks, and every sputter was accompanied by a rustling noise from above, and monstrous bats with human faces frozen in contorted laughter flew back and forth; and at times the flame leapt up from the grate, onto the sooty wall; and then there arose the sound of piercing, howling tones of anguish that gripped Veronica and shook her with terror. "By your leave, Mam'selle," said the old woman smirking and grabbing a brush with which she sprinkled the grate after having dipped it in a copper skillet. The fire died and the room grew black as pitch, as if filled with thick smoke. The hag, who had gone into a little room, returned with a lighted lamp; and now Veronica saw that there were neither beasts nor household implements around. It was rather a common, coarsely furnished room. The hag approached her and, with a creaking voice, said, "Little daughter, I know what it is that you wish. You would have me tell you whether or not you will be married to Anselmus when he is a Court Councillor."

Veronica froze with astonishment and fear, but the hag continued: "You told me about it all at home, at your father's, when the coffee pot was beside you. I was the coffee pot. Didn't you recognize me? Little daughter, listen to me. Give up this Anselmus, give him up because he is a nasty person. He stepped on my little sons' faces, my dear little sons, and crushed them to pieces—the red-cheeked apples that steal away after people have bought them right out of their pockets and then roll into my basket again. He sides with the old man; only the day before yesterday he poured that damned golden pigment on my face and nearly blinded me with it. You can still see the burn marks. Little daughter, you must give him up, give him up! He does not love you; he loves the gold-green snake; he will never be a Court Councillor because he has gone over to the salamanders and he intends to marry the green snake. Give him up, give him up!"

Veronica, who was possessed of a firm and steadfast spirit, and who could overcome girlish terror, drew back a step and spoke seriously and resolutely: "Old woman, I have heard of your gift for gazing into the future, and I wished—possibly too curiously and too soon—to find out from you whether Anselmus, whom I love and treasure, could ever be mine. If you continue troubling me with your foolish and absurd babble instead of fulfilling my wish, you are doing wrong. For I ask you to do nothing for me that you do not do for others, as I am well aware. Since you are apparently familiar with my deepest thoughts, it should have been a small matter for you to reveal to me much of what now causes me anguish and troubles my mind, but after your pointless slander of the good Anselmus, I no longer wish to find out more from you. Good night!"

Veronica was about to leave quickly, but the crone fell on her knees, crying and lamenting, and holding the girl fast by her dress, and said, "Veronica, Veronica, have you then forgotten old Liese, the nurse who so often carried you in her arms and fondled you?"

Veronica could barely believe her eyes. Then, indeed, she recognized her old nurse who was deformed only by advanced age and the two scars—old Liese who years before had vanished from Dean Paulmann's house, no one knew where. The crone also looked different now. Instead of the patched motley shawl, she wore a presentable cap; instead of the black rags, she wore a gaily printed garment—she was neatly dressed, as she used to be.

She arose from the floor and, taking Veronica in her arms, said, "What I have told you now may seem utterly insane, but it is too true, unfortunately. Anselmus has caused me much harm, though it is not his own fault. He has fallen into the hands of Archivarius Lindhorst, who intends to have him marry his daughter. Archivarius Lindhorst is my greatest enemy, and I could tell you all sorts of things about him, which you would, however, be unable to comprehend, or which would horrify you frightfully. It seems that he is the Wise Man, but I am the Wise Woman—so be it! Now I see that you are in love with Anselmus, and I will help you with all my strength in order that you may find happiness and marry him as you desire."

"But for heaven's sake, Liese, tell me—" Veronica interrupted.

"Hush! Hush, child!" the old woman cried. "I know what you want to say to me. I have become what I am because I had to. I couldn't help it. Well, I know how to cure Anselmus of his foolish love for the green snake and to lead him, the handsomest Court Councillor, directly into your arms, but you must help too."

"Liese, tell me. I love Anselmus with all my heart, and I will do anything and everything!" Veronica whispered, hardly audibly.

"I know you," the crone continued, "to be a courageous child. I could never frighten you to sleep with the bogeyman, for as soon as I tried, you opened your eyes to see the bogeyman. Also, you entered the blackest room without a candle, and many times you terrified the children of the neighbors by wearing your father's dressing gown over your head. So then, if you are serious about using my art to defeat Archivarius Lindhorst and the green snake, if you are serious about calling Anselmus Court Councillor and husband, then at the next equinox, about eleven at night, you are to steal from your father's house and come here. I will accompany you to the crossroads that intersect the field close by. We will do what is necessary, and the marvels you may chance to see will do you no harm at all. And now, little daughter, good night. Papa already waits for you at supper."

Veronica went quickly away. She was firmly determined not to miss the night of the equinox because, she thought, "Old Liese was right. Anselmus has become chained in strange fetters. But I will deliver him from them, and I will call him mine forever. He is mine and he shall be my Court Councillor Anselmus."

SIXTH VIGIL

*Archivarius Lindhorst's Garden, Including Some Mockingbirds.
The Golden Pot. English Script.
Messy Scratchings. The Prince of the Spirits.*

"After all, it may be," Anselmus said to himself, "that the very fine medicinal cordial of which I greedily drank at Monsieur Con-radi's might really be the reason behind all these shocking fantasies that so tortured me at the door of Archivarius Lindhorst. I will, therefore, stay quite sober today and defy whatever additional trouble may attack me."

On this occasion, as before, while preparing for his first visit to Archivarius Lindhorst, Anselmus put into his pocket his pen sketches and his masterpieces of calligraphy, his jars of India ink, and his well-sharpened pens of crows' feathers. He was about to depart, when his eye alighted upon the vial of yellow liquid that Archivarius Lindhorst had given him. There suddenly rose up in his mind, in glowing colors, all of his strange adventures, and an ineffable feeling of rapture and pain shot through his heart. With a piteous voice he involuntarily exclaimed, "Isn't it only for the sight of you, dear lovely Serpentina, that I go to Archivarius Lindhorst's?" At that moment he felt that Serpentina's love might be the prize awarded him for a difficult and hazardous task which he had to undertake, and as if the task were nothing other than that of copying Lindhorst's manuscripts. He expected that at the moment he entered the house or, to be more accurate, even before his entrance into it, all kinds of mysterious things would, as before, occur. No more did he think of Conradi's powerful drink, but instead he quickly put the vial of liquid into his vest pocket so that he could follow Archivarius Lindhorst's directions to the letter should the bronze apple-woman again decide to make faces at him.

At the stroke of twelve, as Anselmus raised his hands to the knocker, didn't the hawk-nose twitch, didn't the cat's-eyes actually glower from it? Now, however, without ado, he sprinkled the liquid on the despicable face and it contracted and immediately remolded itself into the gleaming round knocker. The door opened, the bells sounding delightfully throughout the house—"cling-ling—youngling—in—in—spring—spring—cling-ling." He mounted the beautiful wide steps in good spirits and relished the odor of some exotic incense that wafted through the house. Hesitantly, he stopped in the hall, for he did not know on which of these many fine doors he was supposed to knock. Then Archivarius Lindhorst, dressed in a white damask dressing gown, came out and said, "Well, I am delighted, Herr Anselmus, that you have finally kept your word. Follow me, this way, won't you please. I must take you directly into the laboratory." Saying this, he walked quickly through the hall and opened a small side door that led into a corridor. Anselmus, in good spirits, followed behind Archivarius Lindhorst. From this corridor they entered a hall or, more properly, a majestic greenhouse. All kinds of rare and marvelous flowers grew there on both sides, all the way up to the ceiling; indeed, there were massive trees with exotically shaped blossoms and leaves. A magical dazzling light spread over everything, but it was not possible to determine its source, for there was no visible window. As Anselmus peered through the bushes and flowers, long avenues seemed to open toward remote distances. In the deep shade of thick cypress groves there glistened marble basins from which there arose fantastic figures, spouting crystal jets that gently splashed into the gleaming lily chalices. Strange voices rustled through the forest of marvelous plants, and lovely odors wafted up, then down.

Archivarius Lindhorst had disappeared, and Anselmus saw nothing but a gigantic bush of gleaming fire-lilies. Anselmus was transfixed to the spot, intoxicated by the sight and the delicious odors pervading this fairyland garden. Suddenly, from all sides a giggling and a laughing began, and delicate little voices teased and mocked him: "Herr Studiosus, Herr Studiosus, how did you get here? Why are you so stylishly dressed, Herr Anselmus? Will you chat a minute with us and tell us how Grandmother sat down on the egg and the young master spotted his Sunday vest? Are you able now to play the new tune you learned from Daddy Starling, Herr Anselmus? You look splendid in your glossy wig and thin boots." Thus the little voices chattered and teased from every corner, even immediately next to the student himself. And Anselmus now saw that all varieties of bright-colored birds were fluttering about him and mocking him. At that moment, the fire-lily bush moved toward him, and he saw that it was Archivarius Lindhorst, whose flowered dressing gown, glittering in yellow and red, had deceived him.

"I ask your forgiveness, worthy Herr Anselmus," Archivarius Lindhorst said, "for leaving you alone. I desired, in passing, to take a peep at my beautiful cactus, which is due to blossom tonight—but how do you like my little indoor garden?"

"O Lord! It is unbelievably beautiful," the student said, "but these bright-colored birds have been mocking me a little."

"What kind of chattering is this?" the Archivarius cried angrily into the bushes. Then a huge gray parrot fluttered out and perched itself on a bough of myrtle near the Archivarius and, looking at him with unusual seriousness and gravity through glasses that sat on its hooked bill, creaked, "Don't be offended, Herr Archivarius, my high-spirited children have been a little playful, but the Herr Studiosus is himself to blame because—"

"Be quiet, be quiet!" Archivarius Lindhorst interrupted. "I know the culprits, but you really must keep a tighter rein on them, my friend. Now, let us go on, Herr Anselmus."

The Archivarius stepped through many an exotically decorated room so that Anselmus, in following him, could hardly glance at the gleaming marvelous furniture and other things he had never before seen which filled up all the rooms. They finally entered a large room where the Archivarius, after casting a glance upward, stopped; and Anselmus had time to feast upon the heavenly sight the simple decorations of this hall provided. From the light-blue colored walls there jutted the trunks of stately palm trees with trunks of golden bronze, their colossal leaves, glittering like sparkling emeralds, arching across the ceiling far above them. In the middle of the room, placed on three Egyptian lions cast of dark bronze, there lay a porphyry plate; and on this plate there was a simple golden pot, from which Anselmus could not avert his eyes from the moment he saw it. It seemed as if, in a thousand shimmering reflections, countless shapes were playing on the brilliant polished gold. He often saw his own reflection, arms outstretched in desire—oh! beneath the elder tree—Serpentina darting and winding up and down, looking at him once more with her lovely eyes. Anselmus was beside himself with mad rapture.

"Serpentina!" he cried aloud, and Archivarius Lindhorst suddenly turned around and said, "What is it, worthy Herr Anselmus? I believe you intended to call my daughter, who is at the very opposite side of the house in her room and is having her piano lesson now. Come, let us go on."

Anselmus followed behind, hardly knowing what he was doing. He neither saw nor heard anything more until Archivarius Lindhorst suddenly grasped his hand and said, "Here we are!" Anselmus, awaking as if from a dream, now saw that he was in a high-ceilinged room lined on all sides with bookshelves, a room not different from an ordinary library and study. In the middle of the room there was a large writing table, an upholstered armchair in front of it.

"For the present," Archivarius Lindhorst said, "this is to be your workroom. I cannot yet tell you whether you will at some future time work in the blue library where you suddenly called my daughter's name. I would now like to be convinced of your ability to complete this task you are undertaking in the manner I desire and require."

Anselmus summoned all of his courage and, not without self-satisfaction at his ability to please Archivarius Lindhorst, he took out the drawings and samples of his penmanship from his pocket. But Archivarius Lindhorst had no sooner cast his eye on the first sheet, which contained writing in the finest English style, than he smiled most peculiarly and shook his head. He repeated these actions every time a leaf was presented, and Anselmus could feel the blood rushing to his face until, finally, when the smile had grown utterly sardonic and contemptuous, Anselmus poured out his irritation: "Herr Archivarius does not seem very pleased by my meager talent."

"My dear Herr Anselmus," Archivarius Lindhorst said, "you do in fact have a considerable talent for the calligraphic art, but it is apparent that, for the meantime, I must depend more upon your industry and good intentions than upon your accomplishments. Perhaps it is the fault of the inferior materials you use."

Anselmus spoke at length of his ability in his art, which had so often been acknowledged. He spoke about his fine India ink and the crow quills, which were of the finest quality. Archivarius Lindhorst, however, handed him the sheet containing the English script. "Judge this for yourself!"

When Anselmus saw his handwriting, he felt as if a thunderbolt had struck him. The script was unspeakably wretched. The curves were not rounded, the hairstroke failed to appear where it should have been; capital and small letters could not be distinguished; in truth, the messy scratchings of a schoolboy intruded, frequently ruining the best-drawn lines.

"Also," Archivarius Lindhorst continued, "your ink is not permanent." Dipping his finger into a glass of water, he ran his finger over the lines and they disappeared, leaving not a trace behind.

Anselmus felt as if some monster were choking him; not a word could escape from his throat. With the wretched sheet in his hand, he stood there, but Archivarius Lindhorst laughed out loud and said, "Don't be upset, Herr Anselmus. What you could not do well before you will probably be able to do better here. You will, at any rate, have the use of better supplies than those to which you are accustomed. Just begin confidently."

Archivarius Lindhorst first drew a black fluid out of a locked trunk, from which a very strange odor escaped; he also drew out well-pointed pens of a peculiar color, and a sheet that was extraordinarily white and smooth. Finally, he brought out an Arabic manuscript. As Anselmus sat down to begin his work, Archivarius Lindhorst left the room. Anselmus had frequently had occasion to copy such Arabic writing before. It did not seem to him, therefore, that the first assignment would be difficult to do. "How those scratches got on my fine English script, the Lord and Archivarius Lindhorst know best," he said, "but I will swear to the death that they were not done by *my* hand!"

Each fresh word that now stood beautifully and perfectly on the parchment increased his courage, and as his courage increased, so did his dexterity. In truth, the pens he was using wrote superbly well, and the mysterious ink flowed smoothly, as black as jet, onto the bright white parchment. In addition, as Anselmus worked along industriously and concentrated upon the work before him, he began to feel increasingly comfortable in the remote room; and he had very much adjusted to his work, which he intended to complete successfully, when at the stroke of three he was called by Archivarius Lindhorst to partake of a delicious dinner. At dinner Archivarius Lindhorst was in an especially good mood. He asked about Anselmus's friends, Dean Paulmann and Registrar Heerbrand, and he told many gay stories about the Registrar. Anselmus found the good old Rhine wine particularly delightful, and he grew more talkative than usual. Exactly at the stroke of four he rose from the table to resume his work, and Archivarius Lindhorst was very pleased by this punctuality.

If Anselmus had been doing well in copying these Arabic symbols before dinner, he now did even better. In truth, he could not understand the speed and the ease with which he was able to transcribe the convoluted strokes of these foreign characters. It was as if, deep within him, he could hear a whispering voice: "Ah, could you really work so well if you were not thinking of her, if you did not believe in her and in her love?" Then, throughout the room, whispers floated, as in low undulating crystal tones: "I am near, near, near! I am helping you. Be brave. Be steadfast, dear Anselmus! I am working with you so that you may be mine!" And as soon as Anselmus heard these sounds with inner rapture, the unfamiliar characters grew ever clearer to him, and he hardly needed to look at the original script at all; in fact, it seemed as if the characters were already outlined on the parchment in pale ink and there was nothing more for him to do but fill them in with black. Thus he worked on, surrounded by those precious inspiring sounds, that soft sweet breath, until, at the stroke of six, Archivarius Lindhorst entered the room.

He approached the table with a peculiar smile. Anselmus silently rose, Archivarius Lindhorst continuing to look at him with a derisive smile. But he had no sooner glanced at the copy than this smile was converted to an expression of deep seriousness. No longer did he seem the same. His eyes, which customarily glowed with sparkling fire, now looked at Anselmus with ineffable gentleness; a soft flush colored the pallid cheeks; and instead of the sarcasm that had previously shaped the mouth, his lips, now gently curved and graceful, seemed to be parted to express sententious and persuasive speech. His body seemed taller and statelier, the wide dressing gown spread over his breast and shoulders like a royal mantle unfurling in broad folds, and a narrow streak of gold wound through the white locks that lay on his high brow.

"Young man," Archivarius Lindhorst began solemnly, "I knew before you dreamed of them all the secret relationships binding you to my dearest and holiest concern! Serpentina loves you. An extraordinary destiny spun by the fateful threads of hostile powers will be fulfilled if she becomes yours and when you receive as a necessary dowry the golden pot that properly belongs to her. But your happiness will only arise from struggle and toil; hostile forces will attack you, and only the inner force within you, accustomed to withstand these conflicting powers, can spare you from disgrace and ruination. By working here, you will surmount your apprenticeship. Belief and complete knowledge will lead you to the goal, but only if you keep to that which you have so well begun. Carry her always and faithfully in your thoughts, she who loves you, and then you will see the marvels of the golden pot, and happiness will be yours forever. Farewell. Archivarius Lindhorst expects you in his room tomorrow at noon. Farewell."

And with these words Archivarius Lindhorst gently pushed Anselmus out of the door, which he then locked; and Anselmus found himself in the room where he had enjoyed dinner. One door of the room led into the hallway.

Absolutely bewildered by these cryptic events, Anselmus lingered at the street door. He heard a window opening above him, and he looked up. It was Archivarius Lindhorst, who was once more a very old man, again dressed in his light gray gown, who now looked as he usually did. The Archivarius called to him: "Well, worthy Herr Anselmus, what are you pondering down there? Ah, the Arabic is still on your mind. Extend my compliments to Dean Paulmann if you see him, and come tomorrow exactly at noon. Your wages for this day will be found in the corner of the right-hand pocket of your vest."

Anselmus immediately found the silver taler exactly where he had been told it would be, but he did not derive pleasure from it. "I do not know what will come of all this," he said to himself, "but even if I am in the grasp of some insane delusion and have been seized by a spell, my precious Serpentina will live in my heart even more strongly than before; I will die rather than leave her, for I know that my love and the thought of her are with me forever and that nothing hostile can change that; what else is this thought but Serpentina's love?"

SEVENTH VIGIL

*How Dean Paulmann Knocked the Ashes from His Pipe
and Retired to Bed. Rembrandt and Breughel.
The Magic Mirror and Doctor Eckstein's
Prescription for an Unknown Disease.*

Dean Paulmann finally knocked the ashes out of his pipe and said, "Now it is time to go to bed."

"Absolutely," Veronica replied, frightened by the fact that her father was up so late, the clock long ago having struck ten. Accordingly, no sooner had the Dean withdrawn to his study and bedroom and Fränzchen's heavy breathing indicated that she was asleep, than Veronica, who, to keep up appearances, had also gone to bed, rose softly, very softly, dressed herself, and throwing a coat about her, slipped out of the door.

Anselmus had been continuously before her eyes from the moment she had left old Liese; it was as if a mysterious voice she could not recognize kept repeating in her soul that his resistance resulted from an antagonistic force which kept him prisoner, and that he might be freed through some occult, magical art. Every day her confidence in old Liese increased; and even her earliest impressions of unearthliness and terror had by degrees diminished, so that the mystery and the strangeness of her relationship with the old witch now appeared to her only in the light of something extraordinary and fictional and, hence, not completely unattractive. She had, therefore, firmly stuck to her resolve, even at the risk of being missed at home and encountering a thousand inconveniences, to go on with the adventure of the equinox. And now, at last the fateful night on which old Liese had promised to offer comfort and aid had arrived. Veronica, who had long been accustoming herself to the idea of this night adventure, was infused with courage and hope. She flew through the deserted streets, unmindful of the storm that howled through the air and was already dashing thick raindrops in her face.

The church tower clock struck eleven with a stifled, droning clang as Veronica came to old Liese's house, her clothes soaked through with rain. "Well, my dear! Already here! Wait, my love, wait!" a voice cried from above her; and in a moment the old woman, weighed down with a basket and attended by her cat, was standing at the door.

"Now we will go and do what is proper to do and thrives in the night, which is favorable to our work." Thus speaking, the crone seized the shivering Veronica with her cold hand and gave her the heavy basket to carry while she herself took out a little cauldron, a three-legged iron stand, and a spade. By the time they reached the open field, the rain had stopped, but the wind had grown stronger. It howled all about them with a thousand voices. A horrible, heart-piercing wailing seemed to resound from the black clouds, which rolled together in their speedy flight and veiled everything in the world in densest darkness.

But the hag quickly stepped forward and in a shrill harsh voice cried, "Light! Light, my boy!" Then blue gleams quivered and sputtered before them like forked lightning, and Veronica saw that the sparks were coming from the cat and were leaping forward to light the way while his doleful and ghastly wails punctuated the momentary pauses of the storm. Veronica's heart almost stopped beating. It was as if icy talons were ripping into her soul; but, with enormous effort, she composed herself and, pressing closer to the old hag, said, "It must all be done, come what may!"

"True, true, little daughter!" the hag responded, "stand firm and I will give you something beautiful, and Anselmus to boot."

At last the old hag stopped walking and said, "This is the place!" Using the spade, she dug a hole in the ground and then shook coals into it, placed the iron stand over them, and the cauldron on top of the stand. She did all this while gesturing weirdly, the cat circling around her. Sparkles continued to sputter from its tail, and these sparkles formed a circle of fire. The coals ignited, and finally blue flames leaped up around the cauldron. Veronica was told to remove her coat and her veil and to crouch down beside the old woman, who, seizing her hands, pressed them hard while glaring at the girl with fiery eyes. Before long the exotic materials—and nobody could have determined whether they were flowers, or metals, or herbs, or animals—that the crone had taken from her basket and flung into the cauldron began to seethe and to bubble. The hag now left Veronica and, gripping an iron ladle, plunged it into the glowing mass which she then began to stir, while Veronica, following orders, continued to stare steadily into the cauldron and to focus her thoughts on Anselmus. Now the witch again added shining metals to the cauldron, a lock of hair Veronica had cut from her head, and a little ring she had long worn. Meanwhile she uttered fearful howling noises into the night, and the cat whimpered and whined as it ran around incessantly.

Gentle reader, I sincerely wish that you had been traveling toward Dresden on this twenty-third day of September. The people at the last station had tried futilely to keep you there when night fell, enveloping the earth; the friendly host at the inn had assured you that the storm and the rain were too violent to be dealt with and, further, that for supernatural reasons it was simply not safe to dash away in the dark on the night of the equinox; but you had refused to listen, thinking to yourself, "I will tip the coachman a whole taler and will reach Dresden by one o'clock at the latest; and there in the *Golden Angel* or the *Helmet* or in the *City of Naumburg,* a delicious supper and a soft bed await me."

Now, as you are heading toward the city through the dark, you suddenly see a strange flickering light far off in the distance. Approaching, you can distinguish a ring of fire and in its center, next to a cauldron out of which a thick vapor pours with quivering red flashes and sparks of light, you also see two contrasting figures sitting. Your road cuts directly through the fire, but the horses snort and stomp and rear; the coachman curses and prays and beats the horses with his whip, but they will not move from the spot. Then, without thinking, you leap from the stagecoach and rush toward the fire. Now you can clearly see the dainty, gentle child who, in her thin white night dress, kneels by the cauldron. Her braids have been untied by the storm, and her long, chestnut brown hair flies freely in the wind. Her angelic face hovers in the dazzling light cast by the flickering flame under the trivet, but in the icy terror that has overcome it, the face is as stiff and white as death; and you realize her fear, her complete horror, from the eyebrows which are drawn up, and from the mouth, vainly opened to emit the shriek of anguish that cannot find its way from a heart oppressed with indescribable torment. She holds her soft, small hands aloft; they are pressed together convulsively as if in prayer to her guardian angel to spare her from the monsters of Hell, which, obedient to this all-powerful spell, are about to appear. She kneels there, as still as a marble statue. Opposite her, cowering on the ground, is a tall, shriveled, copper-colored crone with a peaked hawk-nose and glittering cat-eyes; her bony naked arms stick out from the black cloak that is pulled around her, and she stirs the hellish brew while laughing and shrieking through the roaring, bellowing storm with her croaking voice.

I can imagine, gentle reader, that although you are usually unfamiliar with terror and fear, that your hair might have stood on end at the sight of this picture by Rembrandt or Breughel that was actually taking place in true life. But your eyes could not be averted from the gentle child entangled in these hellish pursuits, and the electric shock quivering through all your nerves and fibers with the speed of lightning would kindle in you the courageous thought of standing up to the mysterious powers possessed by the monstrous circle of fire and your terror would disappear at this thought. You would feel as if you yourself were one of those guardian angels to whom this almost mortally frightened girl was praying, even as if you were forced to draw your revolver and blow out the hag's brains without further ceremony. But while you were so clearly thinking about this, you would probably have cried out "Hello!" or "What's going on here?" or "What are you doing?" Then, at a reverberating blast from the coachman's horn, the witch would have somersaulted into her brew and in a flicker all would have disappeared in thick smoke. I cannot tell you whether you would have found the girl for whom you desperately searched in the darkness, but you certainly would have destroyed the spell of the witch and would have broken the magic circle that Veronica had thoughtlessly entered.

Alas, gentle reader, neither you nor anyone else drove or walked this way on the twenty-third of September during that stormy night so favorable to witches; and Veronica was forced to stay by the cauldron, overcome with terror, until the work neared its completion. She did indeed hear all that howled and raged about her, all kinds of despicable voices that bellowed and bleated and howled and hummed, but she did not open her eyes because she felt the very sight of the abominations that encircled her might drive her into an incurable, devastating insanity.

The witch had stopped stirring the brew, and the smoke rising from it grew dimmer and dimmer until, finally, nothing but a light spirit-flame burned in the bottom. Then the crone cried, "Veronica, my child, my dearest, look there into the bottom! What is it you see? What do you see?" But Veronica could not answer, and yet it seemed to her that all kinds of intermingled shapes were whirling in the cauldron. Suddenly, with a friendly look and an outstretched hand, Anselmus rose up from the very depths of the cauldron, and Veronica cried, "It is Anselmus! It is Anselmus!"

The old hag immediately turned the petcock attached to the bottom of the cauldron, and molten metal gushed forth, boiling and bubbling into the tiny mold she had placed beneath it. Now the hag leapt into the air and, darting about wildly and gesturing horribly, shrieked, "It is done, it is done! Thank you, my boy!

You kept guard. Hey—hey—he is coming! Bite him to death! Bite him to death!" But now a loud sweeping sound rushed through the air—as if a gigantic eagle were swooping down and beating all around him with his wings. And a stupendous voice boomed, "Hey there, wretches! It is over, it is over! Get home!" The hag, bitterly bewailing her fate, sank down to the earth. Veronica lost all consciousness.

When she regained her senses, it was bright daylight. She was in her bed; Fränzchen, standing before her with a cup of steaming tea in her hands, was saying, "Tell me, sister, what in the world is wrong with you? I have been standing here for an hour, and you have been unconscious, as if in a fever, moaning and whimpering until we were all scared to death. Father missed his class this morning because of your illness. He will very soon be here with the doctor."

Veronica drank her tea silently; even as she drank it, the tormenting images of the night came vividly before her. "So it was all nothing but a wild dream that tormented me? But surely, I did go to that old woman last night. It certainly was the twenty-third day of September. Well, I must have been terribly sick last night and have imagined all of this. It is my constant thinking about Anselmus and the strange old woman who pretended to be Liese but wasn't and made a fool of me, which is responsible for my illness."

Fränzchen, who had left the room, now returned with Veronica's dripping wet coat in her hand. "But look, sister," she said, "look at the condition of your coat! Last night's storm blew open the shutters and knocked over the chair upon which your coat was hanging, and the rain came in and drenched it." These words weighed heavy on Veronica's heart because now she knew that it was not a dream that had tormented her but that she had, in fact, been with the witch. The very thought caused terror and anguish to seize her, and a feverish chill quivered through her body. Shuddering convulsively, she drew the bedclothes tightly around her, but in so doing she felt something hard pressing on her breast, and when she grasped it it seemed to be a medallion, which as soon as Fränzchen left with the wet coat, she pulled out. It was a small round brightly polished metallic mirror. "This is a gift from the old woman!" she cried eagerly. And it was as if flaming rays were darting from the mirror and penetrating into the deepest recesses of her soul with benevolent warmth. The fever chill left, and through her whole being an inexpressible feeling of serenity and contentment streamed. She could not help but remember Anselmus; and as she thought about him more and more intensely—behold!—his friendly face smiled at her out of the mirror, as if she held in her hand a living miniature portrait.

But before long she felt that it was no longer Anselmus's image she saw, but rather that it was Anselmus himself, alive and in the flesh. He was sitting in a stately room that was peculiarly furnished, and he was industriously writing. Veronica was about to step forward to tap him on the shoulder and to say to him, "Herr Anselmus, turn around; it is me!" but she could not, for it was as though he was surrounded by a circle of fire; yet when she stared more closely, she could see that this circle of fire consisted of nothing but large gilt-edged books. Finally, Veronica managed to catch Anselmus's eye. It seemed as if, while glancing at her, he needed to recall who she was; but at last he smiled at her and said, "Oh, dear Mademoiselle Paulmann, is it you? But why is it that you sometimes desire to appear as a little snake?"

Veronica could not keep from laughing aloud at these peculiar words, and with this she awoke as from a profound dream. She quickly hid the little mirror because the door opened and Dean Paulmann and Doctor Eckstein entered the room. Doctor Eckstein stepped to the side of her bed, felt and long studied her pulse, then said, "Ai! Ai!" and wrote a prescription; once more he felt her pulse, again said "Ai! Ai!" and left his patient. But from this information provided by Doctor Eckstein, Dean Paulmann could not clearly understand what it was that ailed his daughter Veronica.

EIGHTH VIGIL

The Library of Palm Trees. The Fortunes of an Unfortunate Salamander. How a Black Quill Caressed a Beet and Registrar Heerbrand Got Drunk.

Anselmus had now been at work with Archivarius Lindhorst for several days, and these hours were for him the happiest of his life.

Still surrounded by lovely sounds, forever encouraged by Serpentina's voice, he was filled to overflowing by a perfect delight that often mounted to the highest rapture. Every problem, every need of his impoverished existence, had disappeared from his mind, and in this new life that now unfolded before him with its sun-filled brilliance, he understood all of the wonders of a loftier world that had before merely filled him with astonishment, even with fear. His copying work proceeded quickly and easily because he felt more and more as if he were copying characters he had long known, and he hardly needed to glance at the manuscript while he perfectly reproduced it.

Archivarius Lindhorst only appeared occasionally, except at dinner time, and his appearance always exactly coincided with the precise moment when Anselmus had completed the final character of some manuscript. At these times Archivarius Lindhorst would hand him another sheet and, without uttering a word, would immediately leave, after having stirred the ink with a little black stick and having replaced the old pen with newly sharpened ones. One day when, at the stroke of twelve, Anselmus had as usual climbed the stairs, he discovered that the door through which he usually entered was locked. Archivarius Lindhorst approached, dressed in his strange, flowered dressing gown, calling aloud, "Today you are to come this way, good Herr Anselmus, because we must go to the room where *Bhagavad-Gita*'s masters await us."

He walked along the corridor, leading Anselmus through the same rooms and halls the student had passed on the occasion of his first visit. Anselmus was once more astounded by the splendid beauty of the garden, but now he realized that many of the exotic flowers that were suspended on the dark bushes were really marvelously colored insects that fluttered up and down on their little wings, as, dancing and swirling in groups, they caressed each other with their antennae. Again, on the other hand, the pink and azure-colored birds were now seen to be fragrant flowers, and the perfume they scattered about seemed to rise from their cups in low and lilting sounds, which, when mingled with the splashing of fountains in the distance and the sighing of the high groves of trees, merged into mysterious, deep, inexpressible longing. The birds that had unmercifully mocked and jeered him before were again fluttering to and fro over his head and calling incessantly with their sharp little voices, "Herr Studiosus, Herr Studiosus! Don't be in such a hurry! Don't peer into the clouds as you do— you might fall on your nose. Ha, ha, Herr Studiosus! Put on your bathrobe. Cousin screech owl will curl your wig for you!" And thus they continued with all kinds of absurd banter until Anselmus left the garden.

At last Archivarius Lindhorst stepped into the azure room. The porphyry with the golden pot was gone and had been replaced in the middle of the room by a table covered by violet-colored satin; and upon this cover lay the writing equipment familiar to Anselmus. An armchair upholstered with the same material was beside it.

"Dear Herr Anselmus," Archivarius Lindhorst said, "you have now copied a number of manuscripts for me quickly and accurately, to my great satisfaction. You have gained my confidence, but the hardest is still to be done, and that involves the transcription, or rather, the painting of certain works that are written in strange characters. I keep them in this room, and they can only be copied here. You will, therefore, in the future, work here, but I advise you to pay great heed because if you make a false penstroke or—heaven forbid!—if you should allow a blot to fall on the original, you will be plunged into misfortune."

Anselmus saw that small emerald leaves projected from the golden trunks of the palm trees. Archivarius Lindhorst took hold of one of these leaves, and Anselmus perceived that the leaf was, in fact, a roll of parchment, which the Archivarius unfolded and spread out on the table before the student. Anselmus was more than a little struck by these singular intertwined characters, and as he studied the numerous points, strokes, dashes, and twirls in the manuscript, which sometimes represented plants or mosses or animals, he almost despaired of ever copying them accurately.

"Courage, young man!" Archivarius Lindhorst cried. "If you continue to maintain your belief and your true love, Serpentina will help you."

His voice resounded like ringing metal, and as Anselmus, suddenly terrified, glanced up, he saw the Archivarius standing before him in the same majestic form he had assumed during his first visit to the library.

Anselmus felt as if he must sink to his knees in deep reverence, but the Archivarius climbed up the trunk of a palm tree and vanished high among the emerald leaves. Anselmus realized that the Prince of the Spirits had been speaking with him and had left to return to his own study, perhaps intending, by using the beams that had been sent to him as envoys by some of the planets, to send back word about what the fate of Anselmus and Serpentina was to be.

"It might also be," he thought, "that he is awaiting news from the sources of the Nile, or that a magician from Lapland is visiting him. In any case, it is in my interest to begin diligently working." Saying this, he began to study the exotic characters contained on the roll of parchment.

He heard strange music coming from the garden, and he was surrounded by sweet and lovely fragrances; and he could hear the birds too, still mocking and twittering, but he could not make out their words, a state of affairs that pleased him immensely. At times it also seemed to him that the emerald leaves of the palm trees were rustling and that the clear crystal tones Anselmus had heard under the elder tree that eventful Ascension Day were dancing and flitting through the room. Marvelously strengthened by this sparkling and tinkling, Anselmus increasingly and more intensely focused his eyes and his thoughts on the writings on the roll of parchment, and before long, almost as in a vision, he realized that the characters therein could represent nothing other than these words: "About the marriage of the salamander and the green snake." Then the air reverberated with a strong triad of clear crystal bells, and the words "Anselmus, dear Anselmus!" floated down to him from the leaves and—wonder of wonders!—the green snake glided down the palm tree trunk.

"Serpentina, lovely Serpentina!" Anselmus cried in the madness of absolute bliss, because as he gazed more intently, he discovered that he was looking at a lovely and glorious maiden who was coming toward him from the tree, looking at him with ineffable longing with those dark-blue eyes that lived in his heart. The leaves appeared to reach down and to expand; thorns sprouted on every side of the trunk, but Serpentina twisted and twirled herself deftly between them and so skillfully drew her fluttering robe, with its ever-changing colors, along with her, that, clinging to her dainty form, it nowhere was caught on the points and prickles of the palm tree. She sat down on the same chair with Anselmus, clasped him in her arms, and pressed him to her so that he could feel the breath coming from her lips and the electric warmth of her body as it touched his.

"Dear Anselmus," Serpentina began, "now you will be completely mine. You will win me for your bride through your belief and your love, and I will bring you the golden pot, which shall assure our happiness together forever."

"Oh, dearest, lovely Serpentina!" Anselmus cried. "What need have I of anything else if I have you! When you are mine, I will happily surrender to all of these inexplicable mysteries that have beset me ever since the moment I first saw you."

"I know," Serpentina continued, "that the strange and mysterious things which my father—often simply to indulge his mood— has caused to happen to you have provoked in you distrust and fear, but now I hope this will be no more, for at this very moment I have come to tell you, dear Anselmus, everything, from the bottom of my heart and soul, down to the smallest detail you need to know in order to understand my father and so that you may clearly comprehend what our circumstances really are."

Anselmus felt as if he were so completely in the grasp of the gentle and lovely form that he could neither move nor live without her, and as if her beating pulse throbbed within him. He listened to every word she uttered until it resounded in his heart and then, like a burning ray, kindled divine bliss within him. He had put his arms around her very dainty waist, but the strange, ever-changing cloth of her robe was so smooth and slippery that it seemed as though she might writhe out of his arms at any moment and, like a snake, glide away. The thought made him tremble.

"Oh, do not leave me, lovely Serpentina!" he cried involuntarily. "You alone are my life!"

"Not now," said Serpentina, "not until I have told you all that you, because of your love for me, will be able to understand:

"Dearest one, know then that my father is of the marvelous race of salamanders, and that for my existence I am indebted to his love for the green snake. In primeval times, in the fairyland of Atlantis, the powerful Prince of the Spirits, Phosphorous, ruled, whom the other spirits of the elements served. Once upon a time the salamander whom the prince loved more than any of the others (it was my father) happened to be walking in the splendid garden, which had been decorated by Phosphorous's mother in the most marvelous fashion with her finest gifts; and the salamander heard a tall lily softly singing: 'Close your little eyelids until my lover, the morning wind, wakes you.' He approached it, and touched by his glowing breath, the lily spread her leaves, and he saw the lily's daughter, the green snake, lying asleep in the calyx of the flower; then the salamander became enflamed with passionate love for the lovely snake and he took her away from the lily, whose perfumes futilely called for her beloved daughter throughout all of the garden in ineffable anguish. The salamander had carried her off to the palace of Phosphorous and there besought Phosphorous: 'Marry me to my beloved and she shall be mine forever.' 'Madman, what are you asking?' the Prince of the Spirits said. 'Know that the lily was once my mistress and ruled with me, but the spark I cast into her threatened to destroy the lovely lily, and it was only my victory over the black dragon, whom the spirits of the earth keep chained, that preserves her so that her leaves are able to remain strong enough to enclose this spark and to guard it; but if you clasp the green snake, your fire will consume her body and a new being, rapidly springing from her dust, will soar away and leave you!'

"The salamander did not listen to the warning of the Prince of the Spirits. Filled with passion he enfolded the green snake in his arms, and she crumbled into ashes, and a winged being who was born from her dust soared away through the sky. Then the madness of despair gripped the salamander, and he dashed through the garden spouting fire and flame, in his absolute frenzy destroying this lovely garden until the fairest flowers and blossoms it possessed hung limp, black, and scorched, their wailing filling the air. The angry Prince of the Spirits seized the salamander in his wrath and said to him, 'Your fire has burned out. Your flames are extinguished. Your rays are darkened—sink down to the spirits of the earth; let these jeer at you and mock you and keep you their prisoner until such time as the fire element will again be rekindled and will glow with you, a new being, from the earth.'

"Extinguished, the poor salamander sank down, but now the irritable old Earth Spirit, who was Phosphorous's gardener, approached and said, 'Master, is there anyone who has greater cause to complain about the salamander than I do? Had not all the lovely flowers that he has scorched been decorated with my gayest colors? Had I not carefully tended them and nursed them and expanded many a fair color on their leaves? Yet I must take pity upon the poor salamander, for it was nothing but love, in which you, O Master, have often been entangled, which drove him to the despair that resulted in the destruction of the garden. Revoke his punishment; it is too severe!'

" 'For the present,' said the Prince of the Spirits, 'his fire is extinguished, but in a time devoid of happiness, when degenerate man will no longer be able to understand the voice of Nature, when the spirits of the elements, exiled into their own regions, will only speak to him from a great distance, in faint echoes; when banished from the harmonious circle, an infinite desire alone will give him news of the Kingdom of Marvels, which he once inhabited when there was belief and love in his soul—in this hapless time the fire of the salamander will again be ignited. But he will be permitted to rise as a man, and completely entering man's prosaic existence, he will learn how to endure its needs and its oppressions. And not only will he continue to remember his first state, but he will again attain a sacred harmony with all of nature; he will comprehend its wonders, and the power of his fellow spirits will be at his command. He will find the green snake in a lily bush again, and the fruit of his marriage with her will be three daughters that will appear to men in the shape of their mother. In the springtime they will hang in the dark elder tree and will sing with their lovely crystal voices. Then, if during that coarse age a youth is found who understands their song—yes, if one of the little snakes looks at him with gentle eyes; if this look awakens in him an anticipatory vision of distant wondrous lands to which he can courageously soar when he has cast away the onerous lot of commonplace life; if, with his love of the snake, there arises in him vividly a belief in the marvels of nature, rather, a belief in his own existence amid these marvels, the snake will be his. But not until three such youths have been found and married to the three daughters may the salamander cast away his oppressive burden and return to his brothers.'

" 'If I may, Master,' the Earth Spirit said, 'I would bestow a gift upon these three daughters that will make their lives with the husbands they will find glorious. Let each of them receive from me a pot of the most beautiful metal I possess. I will polish each pot with light borrowed from the diamond, and our Kingdom of Marvels will glitter in it as it presently exists in the harmony of universal nature; and on the day of the wedding, from its interior a fire-lily will spring forth that will embrace the worthy youth with its eternal blossoms and sweet wafting perfume. Also, he will soon come to learn the lily's speech and will understand the marvels of our kingdom, and he and his beloved will dwell in Atlantis itself.'

"You understand, dear Anselmus, that the salamander of whom I speak is none other than my father. Despite his lofty nature he has been forced to subject himself to the meanest aspects of everyday existence and, therefore, he is often provoked into that perverse mood that causes troubles to so many. Now and then he has told me that for the temperament the Prince of the Spirits Phosphorous stipulated as a condition of marriage with me and my sisters men have a name, which, to tell the truth, they often enough misapply. They call it a childlike poetic nature. He says that this character is often to be discovered in youths who, because of the extreme simplicity of their way of life and their complete lack of what this world calls worldliness, are mocked at by the common rabble. Oh, dear Anselmus, you understood my glances and my song beneath the elder tree. You loved the green snake and you believe in me; you will be mine forever. From the golden pot the lovely lily will bloom and we, happy, joined together, truly blessed, will dwell in Atlantis together!

"But I must not keep you from knowing that in its mortal battle with the salamanders and the spirits of the earth, the black dragon burst from their grasp and quickly flew off through the air. It is true that Phosphorous once more holds him in bonds, but hostile spirits arose from the black feathers that rained down upon the ground during the struggle, and these spirits have on all sides aligned themselves against the salamanders and the spirits of the earth. That woman who hates you so intensely, dear Anselmus, and who, as is well known to my father, strives to possess the golden pot; that woman owes her very existence to the love of such a feather (plucked from the dragon's wing during the battle) for a certain beet, beside which it dropped. She is aware of her origin and of her power because the secrets of many a mysterious constellation are revealed to her through the moans and convulsions of the captured dragon. She uses every means and makes every effort to work from the outside to the inside, while my father battles her with the beams that shoot forth from the spirit of the salamander. All the destructive powers that exist in deadly herbs and the venom of poisonous beasts are collected by her, and when she mixes these under favorable astrological conditions, she is able thereby to cast many a wicked spell that overwhelms man's soul with trembling and trepidation and makes him vulnerable to the power of those demons produced by the dragon as it was vanquished in battle. Dear Anselmus, beware of that old woman! She loathes you because your childlike innocence and your reverent character have made many of her evil charms impotent. Stay true! Stay true to me! You will soon reach the goal!"

"Oh, my Serpentina, my own Serpentina!" Anselmus cried, "how could I leave you? How would it be possible for me not to love you forever?" A kiss was burning on his lips. He awoke as if from a deep dream. Serpentina had vanished. The hour of six was striking, and he felt oppressed because he had not copied a single letter.

Deeply troubled, fearful of the reproaches of Archivarius Lindhorst, he looked at the sheet before him—Oh wonder!—the copy of the mysterious manuscript was perfectly completed, and upon examining the letters more closely, that which was written was nothing other than the story Serpentina had told about her father, who was the favorite of Phosphorous, the Prince of the Spirits of Atlantis, the Kingdom of Marvels.

Archivarius Lindhorst entered the room now, wearing his light-gray coat and carrying his hat and his cane. He looked at the parchment on which Anselmus had been working, allowed himself a hefty pinch of snuff, and with a smile said, "Exactly as I thought! Well, Herr Anselmus, here is your silver taler. Now if you will only follow me, we will go to the Linke Baths!" Saying this, the Archivarius walked quickly through the garden, which was now so full of the din raised by singing, whistling, and chattering that Anselmus was made completely deaf by the noise and gave thanks when he again found himself on the street.

They had hardly walked twenty paces when they met Registrar Heerbrand, who joined them in a companionable fashion. At the gate they filled their pipes, which they had brought with them, and Registrar Heerbrand complained that he had forgotten his tinderbox and could not strike fire. "A tinderbox!" Archivarius Lindhorst said scornfully. "Here is enough fire, fire to spare!" and he snapped his fingers, from which streams of sparks flew and immediately lit the pipes.

"Do observe the chemical knack of some men!" Registrar Heerbrand said. But, not without inward awe, Anselmus thought of the salamander and his story.

At the Linke Baths Registrar Heerbrand drank so much beer that, despite the fact that he was usually a well-mannered and quiet man, he began singing student songs in a high-pitched tenor voice. Irritably, he asked everyone whether he was his friend or not, and he finally had to be taken home by Anselmus, long after Archivarius Lindhorst had left.

NINTH VIGIL

How Anselmus Gained Some Sense. The Punch Party.
How Anselmus Mistook Dean Paulmann for a
Screech Owl and the Latter Felt Greatly Hurt
Thereby. The Ink Blot and Its Consequences.

Anselmus had completely withdrawn from his normal life because of the strange and mysterious events that happened to him daily. No longer did he visit any of his friends, and he waited with impatience every morning for the hour of noon so that he could unlock the gate to his paradise. But despite the fact that his entire being was focused on gentle Serpentina and the marvels of Archivarius Lindhorst's enchanted kingdom, he could not help thinking occasionally about Veronica; indeed, it often seemed as if she appeared before him and blushingly confessed how she loved him with her whole heart and how desperately she wished to rescue him from the phantoms that ridiculed and confused him.

He felt at times as if some external power that suddenly interrupted his thoughts drew him irresistibly toward the forgotten Veronica, and as if he must pursue her wherever she chose to lead him, as though he were tied to her with an unbreakable bond.

That very night after Serpentina had appeared before him in the shape of a lovely maiden, after the marvelous secret of the salamander's wedding with the green snake had been revealed, Veronica appeared before him more clearly than ever before. In fact, it was not until he awoke that he was fully aware that he had only been dreaming, because he was convinced that Veronica was truly beside him, complaining very sorrowfully to him, in a way that pierced him to the heart because he was sacrificing her profound and faithful love for fantasies that were born only in his distraught mind and that would, moreover, finally prove to be his ruination. Veronica was more beautiful than he had ever seen her, and he could not drive her from his thoughts. It was in this troubled mood that he rushed from the house, hopeful that a morning walk would help him escape his agony.

An occult magical influence directed him to Pirna Gate, and he was about to turn into a cross-street when Dean Paulmann, coming after him, called out, "Ai! Ai! Dear Herr Anselmus—*Amice! Amice!* In heaven's name, where have you buried yourself for so long? We never see you at all. Do you know that Veronica is very anxious to play another duet with you? So, come along now, you are on the street leading to our house anyway."

Anselmus, forced by this friendly aggressiveness, accompanied the Dean. Upon entering the house they were greeted by Veronica, who was dressed so elegantly and with such obvious care that Dean Paulmann, himself amazed, asked, "Why are you so decked out? Were you anticipating visitors? Well then, I bring you Herr Anselmus."

Anselmus, while delicately and elegantly kissing Veronica's hand, felt it exert a gentle pressure that shot through his body like a flash of fire. Veronica was the epitome of gaiety and hospitality, and when Paulmann left them to enter his study, she contrived, using various coquetteries, to encourage Anselmus so that he finally forgot all about his shyness and actually chased the wild girl around the room. But once again his old demon awkwardness possessed him, and he stumbled against the table, Veronica's pretty little sewing box tumbling to the floor. Anselmus picked it up; the lid had fallen open and his attention was attracted by a little round metallic mirror into which he looked now with special pleasure. Veronica, softly walking up to him, placed her hand on his arm and, pressing close to him, looked over his shoulder into the mirror with him. Suddenly, Anselmus felt as if a battle were commencing in his soul. Thoughts and images flashed before his eyes—Archivarius Lindhorst—Serpentina—the green snake. But the tumult finally abated and this chaos was clearly converted into consciousness. Now it seemed obvious to him that he had always thought of no one but Veronica; indeed, that the shape which had appeared before him yesterday in the blue room had been none other than Veronica, and that the wild story of the marriage between the salamander and the green snake had simply been copied by him from the manuscript and was not at all related to what he had heard. He wondered more than a little about all those dreams, and he ultimately attributed them solely to the feverish state of mind into which he had been thrown by Veronica's love, as well as to the work he had done in Archivarius Lindhorst's room where, in addition, there were so many strangely intoxicating odors. He could only laugh heartily at the insane whim that had caused him to fall in love with the little green snake and at mistaking the well-nourished Archivarius Lindhorst for a salamander.

"Yes, yes, it is Veronica!" he cried aloud, and then, upon turning his head, he looked directly into her blue eyes, from which there beamed the warmest love. A soft "Ah!" escaped from between her lips as they now burningly pressed upon his.

"Oh, how fortunate I am!" the blissful student sighed. "Today I have in my possession that which last night was only a dream!"

"But will you really marry me when you are a Court Councillor?" Veronica asked.

"Indeed I will!" Anselmus replied. And at that moment the door creaked open and Dean Paulmann entered. "Now, my dear Anselmus, I will not let you get away today," he said. "You will have dinner with us, and then Veronica will make us delicious coffee, which we will share with Registrar Heerbrand, for he has promised to come here."

"Oh, kind Dean Paulmann," Anselmus answered. "Don't you know that I must go to Archivarius Lindhorst and copy manuscripts?"

"But *amice,* look!" Dean Paulmann said, holding up his watch, which pointed to half-past twelve.

Anselmus realized that it was now much too late to begin working at the Archivarius's and he eagerly complied with the wishes expressed by the Dean, especially because he could now be hopeful of having an opportunity to look at Veronica all day long and to obtain from her many fleeting and meaningful glances and gentle pressures of the hand—even perhaps to succeed in stealing a kiss. Anselmus's desires had now reached these lofty heights, and he grew more and more contented in his heart the more completely he was able to convince himself that he would soon be rescued from all of the fantastic things he had imagined, those things that he now thought might sooner or later have made him quite insane.

As promised, Registrar Heerbrand came after dinner, and when coffee was over and dusk had fallen, puckering up his face and happily rubbing his hands, he announced that he had something with him, which if properly composed and reduced into form— paginated and entitled by the fair hands of Veronica—might entertain them all on this October evening.

"Come on, then, tell us about this mysterious thing you have with you, most valued Registrar!" Dean Paulmann cried. Then Registrar Heerbrand shoved his hand into his deep pocket and, after three such trips, brough forth a bottle of arrack, two lemons, and some sugar; and before half an hour had flown, a savory bowl of hot punch was steaming on Dean Paulmann's table. Veronica drank to their health in a sip of the punch, and before long there was much gaiety and good-natured talk among the friends. But Anselmus, the drink getting to his head, once more felt that the images of those marvels he had experienced these last few weeks were invading his mind. He saw Archivarius Lindhorst in his damask dressing gown, which glowed like phosphorous in the dark; he saw the azure room and the golden palm trees; indeed, now it seemed to him as if he must still believe in Serpentina. A raging ferment of conflict stirred his soul. Veronica handed him a glass of punch, and while taking it from her he gently touched her hand. "Serpentina! Veronica!" he sighed to himself. He surrendered to deep reverie, but Registrar Heerbrand loudly cried, "This Archivarius Lindhorst is a strange old gentleman no one can fathom, and he will always be. Well, long life to him! Your glass, Herr Anselmus!"

It was then that Anselmus awoke from his dreamy state and, as he touched glasses with Registrar Heerbrand, said, "That follows, respected Herr Registrar, from the fact that Archivarius Lindhorst is really a salamander who has in his fury destroyed the garden of Phosphorous, the Prince of the Spirits, because the green snake had fled from him."

"What?" Dean Paulmann asked.

"It is true," Anselmus continued, "and for this reason he is sentenced to be a royal Archivarius and to keep house here in Dresden with his three daughters, who are, after all, nothing more than little gold-green snakes which bask in the elder tree and perfidiously sing and, like so many sirens, seduce very many young people."

"Herr Anselmus! Herr Anselmus!" Dean Paulmann cried. "Are you out of your mind? In heaven's name, what idiocy is this you are babbling?"

"He is right, he is right," Registrar Heerbrand interrupted. "That fellow Archivarius is a damned salamander who strikes fiery flashes from his fingers that burn holes in your coat like red-hot tinder. Yes, absolutely, you are right, my little brother Anselmus, and whoever says 'No!' to you is saying 'No!' to me." And with these words, Registrar Heerbrand hit the table so mighty a blow with his fist that the glasses rang out.

"Registrar, are you crazy too?" the indignant Dean cried. "What is this you are all babbling about?"

"As for you," said the student, "you are nothing but a bird. You are a screech owl who curls toupees, Dean Paulmann!"

"What? I'm a bird? A screech owl? A toupee-curler?" the Dean screamed in rage. "Sir, you are insane, absolutely mad!"

"But the old witch will get her hands on him," Registrar Heerbrand said.

"Yes, she is powerful, that old hag," Anselmus interrupted, "even though she is of low birth. Her father was nothing more than a ragged wing feather, and her mother was only a dirty beet; but she owes most of her powers to all kinds of destructive creatures—poisonous vermin that she keeps in her house."

"What horrible slander!" Veronica cried, her eyes blazing with anger. "Old Liese is a wise woman, and the black cat is not a pernicious creature but is rather a sophisticated young aristocrat possessing elegant manners and is her own blood cousin."

"But can he eat salamanders without singeing his beard and dying like a snuffed-out candle?" Registrar Heerbrand cried.

"No, no!" Anselmus shouted, "he could never do that, never in the world; and the green snake loves me for I have a childlike nature and I have looked into Serpentina's eyes."

"The cat will scratch them out!" Veronica exclaimed.

"Salamander—Salamander—conquers them all, every one of them," Dean Paulmann roared in the height of fury. "But I must be in a lunatic asylum. Have I gone crazy myself? What kind of gibberish am I uttering? Yes, I am mad! I am also insane!" And saying this, Dean Paulmann jumped up, tore his wig from his head and flung it against the ceiling so that the battered locks flew about and, becoming completely entangled and utterly disordered, rained down their powder all over the room. Then Anselmus and Registrar Heerbrand seized the punch bowl and the goblets and, hallooing and shouting, also threw them up against the ceiling, and the pieces of glass jingled and jangled about their ears.

"*Vivat* the salamander! *Pereat, pereat* the witch! Smash the metal mirror! Dig out the cat's eyes! Birds, little birds in the air—*Eheu*—*Eheu*—*Evoe*—*Evoe*—salamander!" the three men shrieked and screamed and bellowed as if they were totally mad. Fränzchen ran out, loudly crying, but Veronica remained behind and sobbed out her pain and sorrow on the sofa.

At this moment the door opened and everything instantly grew still. A little man in a small gray coat entered. His nose, on which a colossal pair of glasses nestled, seemed to be entirely different from any nose that had ever before been seen. He wore a most singular wig, too—one that looked more like a feather cap than a wig.

"Ai, I bid you good evening!" the comical little man crackled. "Is the student Anselmus among you gentlemen? I extend to you the compliments of Archivarius Lindhorst, who today waited vainly for his calligraphist; but he most respectfully requests that you ask Anselmus not to miss his appointment tomorrow."

At this he left, and they all now clearly realized that the serious little man was in fact a gray parrot. Dean Paulmann and Registrar Heerbrand burst into guffaws that echoed through the rooms, punctuated by the sobs and the moans coming from Veronica. As for Anselmus, the madness of an internal horror was pervading his very soul and, unconscious of what he was doing, he rushed out the door and along the street. Mechanically he reached his house, his garret, and before long Veronica came there to see him, in a peaceful and friendly mood, and she asked him why he had so worried her with his tipsiness. She implored him to be on his guard against fantastic hallucinations while working at Archivarius Lindhorst's.

"Good night, good night, my beloved friend," Veronica whispered so softly that she could hardly be heard, and breathed a kiss on his lips. He stretched out his arms in an attempt to clasp her, but the dreamlike shape had disappeared, and Anselmus awoke, cheerful and refreshed.

He could not help but laugh uproariously at the effects of the punch, but when he thought of Veronica, he felt full of a most delicious sense of warm contentment. He said to himself, "To her alone I owe my recovery from mad delusions. In truth, I was little better than the man who believed himself to be made of glass; or the one who would not dare leave his room because he thought he was a barleycorn and was afraid that the hens would eat him! But just as soon as I am a Court Councillor I will marry Mademoiselle Paulmann and be happy; and that will be the end of it!"

And at noon, as he once more walked through the garden of Archivarius Lindhorst, he could not help but wonder at how all of this had once appeared to him to be so exotic and marvelous, because nothing that he now saw seemed at all extraordinary: earthen flower pots, quantities of geraniums, myrtle, and so on. Instead of the gleaming multicolored birds that once teased him, now there were only a few sparrows fluttering about; they broke into a twittering at the sight of him that was both unpleasant and unintelligible. The azure room also looked entirely different now, and he could not understand how that garish blue and those artificial golden trunks of the palm trees with their shapeless glistening leaves could ever have thrilled him for a moment. Archivarius Lindhorst looked at him with a very strange and ironical smile, then asked, "Well, how did you enjoy your punch last night, good Anselmus?"

"Oh, you have no doubt heard from the gray parrot how—" Anselmus answered, completely ashamed; but he hesitated when he remembered that the appearance of the parrot was only a part of his intoxication.

"I was there myself," Archivarius Lindhorst said. "Didn't you see me? But you almost crippled me with those mad pranks because I was sitting in the punch bowl at the precise moment when Registrar Heerbrand got his hands on it to fling it against the ceiling, and I had to retreat quickly into the bowl of the Dean's pipe. Now, adieu, Herr Anselmus! If you are diligent, you will also have a silver coin for the day you missed, because your previous work has been so good."

"How is it that Archivarius Lindhorst can babble such drivel?" Anselmus thought to himself while sitting at the table and preparing to copy the manuscripts, which, as usual, had been spread before him by Lindhorst. But he saw so many strange crabbed strokes and twirls all twisted together in inexplicable confusion, perplexing the eye, that it seemed to him to be almost impossible to transcribe this exactly; indeed, in looking it all over you might have thought that the parchment was in fact nothing but a piece of thickly veined marble, or a stone that had been sprinkled with mosses. He nevertheless resolved to do his very best and boldly dipped his pen in the ink, but regardless of what he tried, the ink would not flow. He impatiently flicked the point of his pen and—O heavens!—a huge blot fell on the outspread original! Hissing and foaming, a blue flash flew up from the blot; crackling and wavering, it shot up through the room to the ceiling; and then a thick vapor rolled from the walls. The leaves began to rustle as if torn by a storm, and glaring basilisks darted down from them in sparkling fire, and these lighted the vapor, the masses of flame then rolling around Anselmus. The golden trunks of the palm trees changed into gigantic snakes, which knocked their frightful heads together with a piercing metallic clang and wound their scaly bodies round the distracted student.

"Madman! Now you must suffer the punishment for that which you have done in your bold irreverence!" cried the terrifying voice of the crowned salamander who, like a glittering beam in the middle of the flame, appeared above the snakes. And now cataracts of fire were poured on Anselmus from the gaping jaws of the snake; but suddenly it seemed as if the cataracts of fire were congealing about his body and turning into a solid icy mass. And while Anselmus's limbs were more and more pressed and contracted together and were hardening into powerlessness, consciousness deserted him. When he came to himself, he could not move a muscle. It seemed to him that he was surrounded by a glistening brilliance that he struck if he so much as tried to lift his hand. Alas! He was sitting in a well-corked crystal bottle on a shelf in the library of Archivarius Lindhorst.

TENTH VIGIL

Sorrows of Anselmus in the Glass Bottle. Happy Life of the Scholars of the Church of the Holy Cross and the Law Clerks. The Battle in the Library of Archivarius Lindhorst. Victory of the Salamander and Deliverance of Anselmus.

Gentle reader, I may rightly doubt whether you ever found yourself sealed up in a glass bottle, unless you have been oppressed in a vivid dream by such magic tricks. If this has been the case, your appreciation of poor Anselmus's woeful situation will be very sharp, but if you have never even dreamed of such things, then for Anselmus's sake and for mine, your imagination may still cooperate enough so that it finds itself enclosed in crystal for a few moments.

You are surrounded by brilliant splendor; everything around you appears illuminated and imbued with the hues of a beaming rainbow; all that you see quivers and shimmers and hums in the magic sheen; you swim, devoid of motion and power in a firmly congealed ether which so presses your limbs together that your mind gives orders in vain to your dead body. The mountainous burden lies upon you with more and more weight, and your every breath consumes more and more of the modicum of air that still drifts in the narrow space around you; your pulse throbs wildly, and cut through with anguish; every nerve tenses and trembles in this mortal agony.

Gentle reader, take pity on Anselmus! This unspeakable torture gripped him in his prison of glass, but he knew only too well that even death could not save him, for did he not recover from the profound unconsciousness into which he had been thrown by excessive pain just as the morning sun brightly shone into the room, and didn't his martyrdom begin again? No limb could he move, but his thoughts bounced against the glass and stunned him with their discordant vibrations. Instead of the words the spirit once spoke from within him, he now could hear only the muffled din of madness. In his agony he exclaimed, "O Serpentina, Serpentina! Save me from this hellish torture!" And it was as if faint sighs breathed around him, spreading over the glass like the translucent green leaves of the elder; the clanging stopped, the dazzling bewildering glitter disappeared. Anselmus was now able to breathe more freely.

"Am I not myself to blame for my unhappiness? O most kind and beloved Serpentina, haven't I sinned against you? Haven't I given way to gross doubts about you? Haven't I lost my belief and, along with it, everything that was going to make me so blissful? Alas! Now you will never ever be mine. And the golden pot is now lost to me as well, and I will never again behold its marvels. Alas, if I might just see you once more; only once more, my lovely Serpentina, hear your sweet and tender voice!" Thus lamented Anselmus, pierced through by this profound sorrow; and then he heard a voice close to him, "I don't know what you want, Herr Studiosus. Why are you lamenting so, beyond all measure?" And now for the first time Anselmus noticed that there were five other bottles on the same shelf, and he could see three Scholars of the Church of the Holy Cross and two Law Clerks.

"Ah, gentlemen, my companions in misery!" he cried. "Tell me how it is possible for you to be so calm, even happy, as I see you are by your cheerful look. You are also sitting here corked up in glass bottles, and you can no more move a finger than I can. Like me, you cannot think a reasonable thought but that there arises such a murderous cacophony of ringing and humming, and such a rumbling and roaring in your head, that it is enough to drive you insane. No doubt you do not believe in the salamander or in the green snake!"

"You are talking drivel, Herr Studiosus," one of the Church scholars replied. "It has never been better for us than it is now, because the silver coins that the insane Archivarius paid us for all kinds of confusing scripts are still in our pockets. Now we no longer have to learn Italian choruses by heart. Each day we go to Joseph's or some other pub where the beer is fine enough, and we can look a pretty girl in the face. So we sing like real students, *Gaudeamus igitur,* and we are absolutely content!"

"That is absolutely correct," a law clerk added. "I am also well provided with coins, as is my dearest colleague beside me. Now we walk about on the Weinberg instead of being occupied by copying nasty briefs within the confines of four walls."

"But my worthiest masters," Anselmus said, "can you not see that all of you are corked up in glass bottles and cannot move, let alone go for walks."

And now the Scholars of the Church of the Holy Cross and the Law Clerks began to guffaw loudly and cry, "The student is out of his mind! He imagines that he is sitting hunched in a glass bottle, and here he is standing on the Elbe bridge, looking right down into the water. Let us leave this madman and continue on our way!"

"Ah," the student sighed, "they have never seen the tender and lovely Serpentina. They do not know what freedom means nor what it is to live with love and belief; therefore, because of their own foolishness and unimaginative natures, they feel no oppression as a result of their imprisonment. But I, miserable I, must perish in want and in woe if she whom I love beyond all words does not save me."

Then, wafting to him in faint tinkles, came Serpentina's voice through the room: "Anselmus! Believe! Love! Hope!" And every sound beamed into Anselmus's prison, and the crystal yielded to his pressure and expanded until the heart of the prisoner once again felt as if it could stir in his breast.

The agony of his situation grew less acute, and he understood now that Serpentina still loved him and that she alone made it possible for him to tolerate his imprisonment. No more did he trouble himself about his foolish companions in misfortune, but instead he concentrated all his thoughts upon gentle Serpentina. Suddenly, however, on the other side of him there arose a muffled, croaking, loathsome murmur, and he could soon observe that it emanated from an old coffee pot, with a lid that was half broken, which stood opposite him on a little shelf. As he looked at it more carefully, the ugly features of a withered old woman were gradually disclosed, and in a few moments the apple-woman of Black Gate stood before him. She smirked and laughed at him, screeching, "Ai! Ai! My handsome boy, must you now suffer? Into the crystal is your downfall. Isn't this what I predicted long ago?"

"Mock and jeer at me, you damned witch!" Anselmus said. "You are responsible for it all, but, the salamander will catch you, you nasty beet."

"Ho ho!" the hag replied, "don't be so proud! You have squashed my little sons; you have scarred my nose—but I still like you, you rascal, for once you were a handsome young fellow; and my little daughter likes you too. You will never escape from the crystal unless I help you, but my friend the rat that lives close behind you will chew the shelf in half. Then you will tumble down, and I will catch you in my apron so that not only will your nose remain unbroken but your splendid face will not be injured in any way; and then I will carry you off to Mam'selle Veronica, to whom you will be married when you become a Court Councillor."

"You offspring of the Devil, get away from me!" Anselmus cried in anger. "It was your hellish tricks that led me to commit the sin for which I now am forced to expiate. But I will patiently bear it all, for I choose to remain here, where gentle Serpentina surrounds me with her love and her consolation. Wretched hag, listen and despair! I defy your power! I love none other than Serpentina; I will not be a Court Councillor; I will not look at Veronica who seduces me to evil through your influence; I will die in sorrow and desire if the green snake cannot be mine. Away with you, you filthy old changeling!"

And the old woman laughed until the room echoed. "Sit and die, then!" she cried, "but now it is time for me to begin my work. I have other business to pursue here." And throwing off her black coat she stood in loathsome nakedness. Then she ran in circles, and large folios tumbled down on her. Out of these she ripped parchment leaves and, quickly piecing them together in an artful combination and attaching them to her body, she was soon dressed in a weird multicolored armor. Out of the inkwell dashed the black cat, fire spitting from its mouth, and it ran meowing toward the hag, who screamed in shrill triumph and disappeared through the door with it. Anselmus saw that she was going toward the azure room, and he immediately heard a hissing and a tumult in the distance. The birds in the garden were crying and the parrot called, "Help! Help! Thieves! Thieves!" At that moment the horrible old woman bounded back into the room carrying the golden pot in her arms and repulsively gesturing all the while. She shrieked fiercely through the air, "Joy! Joy! Little son! Kill the green snake! At her, at her, son!"

Anselmus thought he heard a deep moaning; he thought he heard the voice of Serpentina; then he was seized by despair and, gathering all his strength, he dashed wildly—as if his nerves and arteries were bursting—against the crystal. Suddenly a loud clang resounded through the room, and the Archivarius in his bright damask dressing gown appeared in the door.

"Hey, hey! Wretches! Mad delusion! Witchcraft! Hey, there!" he shouted. Then the hag's black hair stood up like coarse bristles. Her red eyes gleamed with hellish fire; and gnashing the pointed fangs of her hideous jaws together, she sputtered, "Quick, at him! Hiss at him! Hiss!" She laughed and bleated scornfully, pressed the golden pot firmly against her body and from it threw handfuls of sparkling earth on the Archivarius; but as the earth touched his dressing gown, its particles changed into flowers, which rained down on the floor. Then the lilies on the dressing gown flickered and flared, and the Archivarius caught these blazing lilies and flung them on the witch. She howled in agony, but as she leaped into the air and shook her armor of parchment, the lilies' fire was extinguished, and they fell away as ashes.

"Quick, my boy!" the hag screeched again, and the black cat hurtled through the air clear over the Archivarius's head toward the door; but the gray parrot quickly flew out to confront him and, catching him by the nape of the neck with his crooked bill, he tore at him until red fiery blood burst from the cat's neck—and Serpentina's voice cried out, "Saved, saved!"

At this the witch, her mouth foaming with rage and desperation, threw herself at the Archivarius. She threw the golden pot behind her, and baring the long talons of her bony hands, she tried to clutch the Archivarius by the throat. He, however, instantly removed his robe and threw it over her. Then, hissing and sputtering, blue flames leaped from the leaves of parchment that were the armor of the hag, and she rolled on the floor in agony trying desperately to secure fresh earth from the pot and fresh leaves of parchment from the books so that she could suffocate the blazing flames. And whenever earth or leaves touched her body the flames were extinguished. But now from inside Archivarius's body there issued forth fiery crackling tongues of flame that lashed out at the hag.

"Hey, hey! Victory to the salamander!" the Archivarius's voice reverberated through the room, and a hundred fiery bolts whirled in burning circles around the shrieking hag. Ripping and spitting, the cat and the parrot again flew at each other, locked in their ferocious combat; but finally the parrot, using his powerful wings, flung the cat to the ground, and transfixing the cat with his claws, he held his enemy—which, in the agony of death, uttered terrifying meows and shrieks—and pecked out the glowing eyes of the cat with his sharp bill, burning froth spouting from the eyes. Then thick vapor steamed up from the spot where the horrible old hag lay hurled to the ground under the enchanted dressing gown. Her howling, her terrible piercing cries of defeat and woe died away, as in the remote distance. And the smoke that had permeated the room with its stench blew away. The Archivarius lifted his dressing gown; a nasty beet lay beneath it.

"Most honored Archivarius, may I offer you the vanquished enemy?" the parrot said, extending a black hair that he held in his beak to Lindhorst.

"Very good, my dear friend," the Archivarius replied, "and here also lies my vanquished enemy. Be so kind as to take care of that which remains. This very day as a small reward you shall have six coconuts—and a new pair of glasses, because, as I see, the cat has villainously cracked the lenses of your old ones."

"Yours forever, most revered friend and patron," the delighted parrot answered, and then the parrot took the beet in his bill and flew with it out of the window that Lindhorst had opened for him.

And now the Archivarius retrieved the golden pot, and in a powerful voice cried, "Serpentina, Serpentina!" But as Anselmus, rejoicing in the destruction of the loathsome witch who had cast him into misfortune, looked at the Archivarius, he was once more amazed, for here again stood the tall and majestic form of the Prince of the Spirits regarding him with an expression of ineffable grace and dignity.

"Anselmus," the Prince of the Spirits said, "it was not you but a hostile principle that attempted destructively to penetrate your nature and divide you against yourself, and which was to blame for your lack of belief. You have proved your loyalty. You are to be free and happy!"

A brilliant flash quivered through Anselmus's mind; the glorious triad of the crystal bells sounded more powerfully and more loudly than he had ever heard it, and his nerves and his senses quivered. As the melodious tones rang through the room, swelling higher and higher, the glass that enclosed Anselmus shattered, and he dashed into the arms of his dear and gentle Serpentina.

ELEVENTH VIGIL

*Dean Paulmann's Anger at the Madness that Had
Broken Out in His Family. How Registrar Heerbrand Became
a Court Councillor and Walked About in Shoes and
Silk Stockings in the Sharpest Frost. Veronica's Confessions.
Betrothal over the Steaming Soup Tureen.*

"But tell me, worthy Registrar, how could the damned punch last night have gone so to our heads and driven us to all kinds of incredible foolishness?" Dean Paulmann demanded the next morning as he entered his study, which was still full of broken glass, while his hapless wig, separated into its original elements, floated in the punch. After Anselmus had rushed from the house, the Dean and the Registrar had continued running and hobbling up and down the room, shouting like lunatics and bashing their heads together until Fränzchen, with enormous effort, dragged her very tipsy papa off to bed. Then Registrar Heerbrand, utterly exhausted, had collapsed upon the sofa that Veronica had deserted in order to take refuge in her bedroom.

Registrar Heerbrand had tied his blue handkerchief around his head. He looked terribly pale and sad, and he groaned an answer, "Oh, worthy Dean, it was not the punch that Mam'selle Veronica brewed to such perfection. No! It was simply that damned student who is responsible for all the trouble. Have you not observed that he has long been *mente captus*? And are you not aware of the infectious nature of madness? One fool begets twenty—excuse me, that is an old proverb. Especially when you have had a glass or two to drink, you fall easily into madness; then you proceed to perform involuntary capers and go through your exercises exactly as the cracked-brained leader directs. Dean, would you believe that I still get dizzy when I think about that gray parrot?"

"Nonsense!" the Dean interrupted. "It was really nothing but Archivarius Lindhorst's little old librarian who had flung a gray coat over himself and was looking for Anselmus."

"That may be," admitted Registrar Heerbrand, "but I must admit that I feel very wretched. All night long there was a terrible booming of organ notes and whistling in my head."

"That was me," the Dean said, "I snore very loudly."

"Well, that may be so," the Registrar admitted again. "But Dean! Oh Dean! It was not without reason that I tried to convey an atmosphere of good cheer among us last night—and that Anselmus has ruined everything! You don't know—Oh, Dean! Oh Dean!" And with this, Registrar Heerbrand sprang up, snatched the blue handerchief from his head, embraced the Dean warmly, and pressed his hand. Again, in a voice completely heartrending, he cried, "Oh, Dean, Dean!" and quickly taking up his hat and cane, he dashed out of the house.

"This Anselmus will never again cross my threshold!" Dean Paulmann said, "for it is very clear to me that this madness of his robs the best people of their senses. Now the Registrar is stricken with it! Up to now I have escaped, but the devil who knocked so hard last night at the door of our carousal may ultimately get in and play his games with me. So *apage, Satanas!* Away with Anselmus!"

During this conversation Veronica had grown very thoughtful. She spoke not a word, but only smiled occasionally, and then very peculiarly. And as time wore on she persisted in this surprising mood—a gay, gregarious girl who now preferred to be left alone. "She also has Anselmus on her mind!" the Dean said, fuming with indignation. "But it is a good thing that he does not come here. I know that he is afraid of me and that this is why he will not come."

Dean Paulmann had spoken these concluding words aloud, and the tears welled in Veronica's eyes. Sobbing, she said, "Oh, how can Anselmus come here when he has for a long time been corked up in the glass bottle?"

"What's that!" Dean Paulmann cried. "Oh heavens, heavens! She is driveling now just like the Registrar. Soon she will have an attack! Oh, you damned, loathsome Anselmus!"

He dashed quickly out to find Doctor Eckstein, but the physician only smiled and once more said, "Ai! Ai!"

This time, however, he prescribed nothing at all, but merely added the following words to the little he had said. "An attack of nerves! Takes care of itself. Go outdoors; walks; entertainments; theater—go see *Sonntagskind, Schwestern von Prag.* It will take care of itself."

"I have rarely seen the Doctor so eloquent," Dean Paulmann thought. "He is really talkative, I must admit."

And now, days and weeks and months passed. Anselmus had disappeared. Registrar Heerbrand also failed to make an appearance. It was not until the fourth of February that the Registrar, dressed in a stylish new coat made of the finest material, wearing handsome, thin shoes and silk stockings despite the sharp frost, and carrying a large bouquet of fresh flowers in his hand, entered the parlor of Dean Paulmann exactly at noon, the Dean being more than a little astounded upon seeing his friend so grandly attired. Registrar Heerbrand walked up to the Dean most solemnly, embraced him with the most earnest courtesy, and said, "Now at last, on the saint's day of your beloved and most honored Mam'selle Veronica, I will straightforwardly tell you what I have long kept locked in my heart. That evening—that unfortunate evening—when I carried the ingredients of our explosive punch in my pocket, it was my intention to tell you a bit of good news and to celebrate the happy day convivially. I had already learned that I was to be appointed a Court Councillor—and for that promotion I now have the papers, *cum nomine et sigillo Principis,* in my pocket."

"Ah, my dear Registrar—Court Councillor, I mean," the Dean stammered.

"But it is you, you alone, most revered Dean, who can complete my joy," the new Court Councillor continued. "I have for a long time been secretly in love with your daughter, Mam'selle Veronica, and I can boast of many a kind look she has bestowed upon me, obvious proof that she would not reject my attention. In a word, revered Dean, I, Court Councillor Heerbrand, do now entreat you for the hand of your most amiable Mam'selle Veronica, whom I, if you do not oppose it, intend to marry shortly."

Dean Paulmann, immeasurably astounded, clapped his hands together and cried again and again, "Ai! Ai! My good Registrar— Court Councillor I mean. Who would have thought of it! Well, if Veronica really does love you, there are no objections on my part. In truth, it may be that her present moodiness is really nothing but the effect of her secret love for you, Court Councillor! You know what whims can possess girls!"

At this moment, pale and troubled as she now always was, Veronica entered. Court Councillor Heerbrand immediately rose to his feet and went up to her and in a nice little speech said something about her saint's day and gave her the fragrant bouquet, and with it a little package. And when she opened it, a pair of brilliant earrings sparkled up at her. A swiftly fleeting blush colored her cheeks and, her eyes gleaming with happiness, she cried, "Oh, gracious heaven, these are the same earrings I wore several weeks ago, those which pleased me so!"

"But my dearest Mam'selle, how can this be?" the Court Councillor interrupted, rather alarmed and hurt, "when I bought these jewels less than an hour ago for cash in Castle Street?"

But Veronica did not heed his words; she was already before the mirror to look at the trinkets, which she quickly fixed in her lovely little ears. Dean Paulmann, however, grave of countenance and solemn of tone, told her about his friend Heerbrand's promotion and his present proposal, and Veronica turned to the Court Councillor and, with a searching look, said:

"I have known for a long time that you desired to marry me. So be it! I promise you my heart and my hand; but now I must reveal to you—I mean, to both of you, to you, my father, and to you, my promised bridegroom—much of that which is heavy on my heart, and I must tell you now, even if the soup should get cold—which Fränzchen, I see, is now placing on the table."

And without waiting for the Dean or the Court Councillor to reply—although words were clearly forming on the lips of both— Veronica continued:

"Best of fathers, you may believe me. I loved Anselmus from the depths of my heart, and when Registrar Heerbrand, who has himself become a Court Councillor, assured us that Anselmus would very probably reach some such height, I determined that he and none other should be my husband. But then it seemed as if alien, hostile beings were resolved to steal him away from me. At that time I went to old Liese, who had once been my nurse but has since become knowledgeable in necromancy and has become a great enchantress. She promised to help me and to deliver Anselmus completely into my hands. At midnight, on the equinox, we went to the crossroads on the highway. She conjured up hellish spirits, and with the help of the black cat, we produced a little metallic mirror in which I, after focusing my thoughts on Anselmus, had only to look in order to completely dominate his heart and his mind. But now I wholeheartedly repent having done this," Veronica added, "and I now repudiate all satanic arts. The salamander has vanquished old Liese. I heard her shriek, but there was nothing I could do to help her, for as soon as the parrot had eaten the beet, my metallic mirror broke in two."

Veronica took both pieces of the mirror and a lock of hair out of her sewing box and after handing them to Court Councillor Heerbrand, continued:

"Court Councillor, take the fragments of the mirror, and to-night at twelve o'clock throw them into the Elbe from the bridge, at the spot where the cross stands; the steam is not frozen there. Do, however, keep and wear that lock of my hair. I now repudiate all magic," she repeated, "and I wholeheartedly wish Anselmus all joy and good fortune, since he is now married to the green snake who is more beautiful and rich than I am. Dear Court Councillor, I will love you and revere you as befits a true and faithful wife."

"Alas! Alas!" Dean Paulmann cried, full of sorrow. "She is mad, she is mad! She can never be Frau Court Councillor because she is mad!"

"But not in the least," Court Councillor Heerbrand interrupted. "I well know that Mam'selle Veronica has felt some kindness for the bumbling Anselmus; and it may be that she has, during some fit of passion, had recourse to the old witch who, as I realize, can be none other than the cards-and-coffee fortuneteller of Lake Gate—in brief, old Rauerin. Nor can it be denied that there are cryptic arts that exert their all too baleful influence on men. We read of them in the most ancient writings, and no doubt there still are such. As far as what Mam'selle Veronica wishes to say about the victory of the salamander and Anselmus's marriage to the green snake, in truth, I take this to be nothing but a poetic allegory, like a poem in which she celebrates her final complete farewell to the student."

"Take it for what you will, most revered Court Councillor," Veronica said, "perhaps for an extremely stupid dream."

"I will not do that," Court Councillor Heerbrand replied, "for I well know that Anselmus possesses secret powers that torment him and drive him to all the insane capers one can think of."

Dean Paulmann could stand this no longer. He burst out with: "Stop! For the love of heaven, stop! Have we once more imbibed too much of that damned punch, or has Anselmus's lunacy possessed us as well? Court Councillor, what rubbish is this coming from your mouth? I suppose, however, that love haunts your brain. Marriage will soon take care of this. I should otherwise be fearful that you too were plunging into a degree of madness, most revered Court Councillor. What would then become of the future branches of the family, inheriting as they do the *malum* of their parents? But now, I bestow upon this happy union my paternal blessing and permit each of you as future bride and bridegroom a joyous kiss."

Thus they immediately kissed, and so it was that before the soup had a chance to grow cold, the formal betrothal was completed. In a few weeks, Frau Court Councillor Heerbrand was in fact what she had been in her vision—she was sitting on the balcony of a splendid house in Neumarket and, with a smile, was looking down upon the dandies, who in passing turned their glasses up to her and said, "She is a divine creature, the wife of Court Councillor Heerbrand."

TWELFTH VIGIL

Account of the Estate to which Anselmus Withdrew as
Son-in-Law of Archivarius Lindhorst, and How He
Lived There with Serpentina. Conclusion.

How deeply I felt within my spirit the blissful happiness of Anselmus, who was now inwardly united with his gentle Serpentina, and who had withdrawn to the mysterious Kingdom of Marvels that he recognized as the home toward which his heart, filled with strange foreknowledge, had always yearned. In vain I tried, gentle reader, to set before you those glories that surrounded Anselmus, or even to create in the faintest degree an impression of them in words. I was reluctantly obliged to admit to myself the feeble quality of all my attempts at expressing this. The meanness of commonplace life made me feel chained and silent. I grew sick in the torture of my own futility; I wandered about as if in a dream. In brief, I plunged into the identical condition that engulfed Anselmus, and which I tried to describe to you in the Fourth Vigil. When I looked over the eleven vigils, which are now fortunately completed, it grieved me to the heart to think that inserting the Twelfth Vigil, the very keystone of the whole, would never be permitted me, for whenever I tried during the night to complete the work, it was as if mischievous spirits (they might indeed be blood cousins of the slain witch) were holding a polished and gleaming piece of metal before my eyes in which I could behold my own mean self—pale and anxious and melancholy, like Registrar Heerbrand after his bout with the punch. And then, I flung down my pen and got quickly into bed so that I might at least in my dreams once again see happy Anselmus and lovely Serpentina. This had continued for several days and nights when at last, completely unexpectedly, I received the following letter from Archivarius Lindhorst:

Respected Sir: I am familiar with the fact that you have, in eleven vigils, written about the extraordinary fate of my good son-in-law, Anselmus, erstwhile student, now poet, and that you are at present most sorely tormenting yourself so that in the twelfth and final vigil you may write something about his happy life in Atlantis, where he now lives with my daughter on a pleasant estate that I own in that country. Now, notwithstanding my great regret that my own singular nature is hereby revealed to the reading public (seeing that this may expose me to a thousand inconveniences in my office as Privy Archivarius; indeed, it may even, in the Collegium, provoke the question of how far a salamander may justly bind himself through an oath, as a state servant, and how far, generally, he may be entrusted with vital affairs of state since, according to Gabalis and Swedenborg, the Spirits of the elements are not to be trusted at all, and notwithstanding the fact that I realize that my closest friends must now avoid my embrace, fearing that I might in some sudden anger dart out a flash or two and singe their wigs and Sunday coats), notwithstanding all of this, I say, it is my intention to help you complete the work, since much good of me and my dear married daughter (if only the other two were also off my hands!) has been said therein. If you would, therefore, write your Twelfth Vigil, descend your damned five flights of stairs, leave your garret, and come over to me. In the blue palm tree room already known to you, you will find suitable writing materials, and then in a few words you can describe to your readers what you have seen—a better plan for you than any long-winded account of a life about which you know only through hearsay. With esteem,

Your obedient servant,
The Salamander Lindhorst
Pro tempore Royal Privy Archivarius

This somewhat abrupt but, on the whole, friendly note from Archivarius Lindhorst gave me enormous pleasure. In truth, it seemed clear enough that the extraordinary manner in which his son-in-law's good fortune had been revealed to me and which I, sworn to silence, must keep even from you, gentle reader, was well known to this strange old gentleman; yet he did not take it as badly as I might readily have feared. On the contrary, he was here offering me a helping hand to complete my work. And I might, from this, fairly conclude that he was at heart not opposed to having his wondrous existence in the world of spirits revealed through the printed word.

"It may be," I thought, "that through this means he perhaps expects to get his two other daughters married sooner. Who knows but that a spark may fall in the heart of this or that young man and therein kindle a desire for another green snake—whom he will immediately seek out and discover on Ascension Day, under the elder tree? From the woe that was Anselmus's lot when he was held captive in the glass bottle, he will be forewarned to be doubly and trebly on his guard against all doubt and unbelief."

I extinguished the lamp in my study at exactly eleven o'clock and made my way to Archivarius Lindhorst, who was already waiting for me in his hallway.

"Have you arrived, my worthy friend? Well, I am pleased that you have not mistrusted my good intentions. Please follow me."

And saying this he led the way through the garden, which was now filled with lustrous brightness, and into the azure room where I saw the very violet table at which Anselmus had been writing.

Archivarius Lindhorst disappeared, but soon he returned, carrying in his hand a lovely golden goblet out of which there arose a tall, sparkling blue flame. "Here," he said, "I bring you the favorite drink of your friend Kapellmeister Johannes Kreisler. It is burning arrack into which I have thrown a little sugar. Do take a sip or two of it. I will remove my dressing gown, and to amuse myself and enjoy your worthy company while you sit looking and writing, I will just bob up and down a little in the goblet."

"As you wish, honored Herr Archivarius," I answered, "but if I am to keep sipping liquor, there will be none for you."

"You need have no such fear, my good fellow," Archivarius Lindhorst said. Then, quickly throwing off his robe, to my great amazement he climbed into the goblet and vanished in the flames. I enjoyed the drink without fear, softly blowing back the fire. The drink was truly delicious!

Are not the emerald leaves of the palm trees gently moving, softly sighing and rustling, as though kissed by the breath of the morning wind? Awakened from their sleep, they stir and mysteriously whisper of the wonders which, from the far distance, approach like tones of melodious harps! The azure abandons the walls, but dazzling beams shoot through the fragrance. And whirling and dancing in childish happiness, the vapor rises to measureless heights and weaves back and forth above the palm trees; but ever brighter shoots beam on beam until, in boundless expanse, a grove opens before my eyes, and there I behold Anselmus.

Here glowing hyacinths and tulips and roses raise their heads, and their perfumes are like the loveliest of sounds that call to the joyous youth: "Come, wander, wander among us, beloved, for you understand us! Our perfume is the longing of love. We love you and are forever yours!" And then these golden rays seem to chant in vibrant tones: "We are fire, kindled by love. Perfume is longing, but fire is desire; and do we not dwell in your heart? We are your own!" And the dark bushes and the tall trees rustle and whisper, "Come to us, beloved happy one! Fire is desire, but hope is our cool shadow. Lovingly, we rustle round your head, for you understand us because love dwells in your heart." And the brooks and the fountains murmur and patter: "Beloved, do not walk by so quickly; look into our crystal! Your image lives in us, and we preserve it with love, for you have understood us." In the triumphal choir, bright birds are singing: "Listen, listen! We are joy, we are delight, the rapture of love!" But Anselmus eagerly turns his eyes to the glorious temple that rises behind him in the distance. The stately pillars seem to be trees, and the capitals and friezes seem to be acanthus leaves, which, in wondrous wreaths and figures, form splendid decorations. Anselmus walks to the temple, and with inward delight he views the variegated marble, the steps with their strange veins of moss. "Ah, no!" he cries, as if in the excess of bliss. "She is not far from me now; she is near!"

The Serpentina advances, in the fullness of beauty and grace, from the temple. She carries the golden pot, from which a bright lily has sprung, and the inexpressible rapture of infinite longing glows in her gentle eyes. She looks at Anselmus and says, "Oh, my beloved, the lily has sent forth her lovely cupped flower; the highest is now fulfilled. Is there a happiness that is the equal of ours?"

Anselmus clasps her with all the tenderness of passionate devotion. The lily glows in flames over his head; and the happy whispering of the trees and the bushes grows louder; clearer and more happy is the rejoicing of the brooks; the birds and the shining insects dance in the waves of perfume; a gay, joyous tumult in the air, in the water, in the earth, is celebrating the festival of love! Now sparkling gleams dance over the bushes; diamonds peer up from the ground, like shining eyes; high fountains sparkle from the brooks; strange fragrances drift on sounding wing; they are the spirits of the elements who pay tribute to the lily and announce the happiness of Anselmus. And now, Anselmus raises his head as if encircled with a glorious halo. Are they glances? Are they words? Are they songs? Do you hear the sound? "Serpentina! Belief in you, love of you, has unfolded to my soul the inmost spirit of nature! You have brought me the lily that sprang from gold, from the primeval force of the world, before Phosphorous had kindled the spark of thought; this lily is knowledge of the sacred harmony of all beings; and I will live in this knowledge with the greatest bliss forevermore. Yes, I, most fortunate of all, have perceived what is highest: I must indeed love you forever, O Serpentina! Never shall the golden blossoms of the lily grow pale; for, like belief and love, this knowledge is eternal!"

For the vision in which I now beheld Anselmus bodily in his freehold of Atlantis I stand indebted to the arts of the salamander; and it was fortunate that when everything had dissolved in air, I found a paper lying on the violet table with the foregoing account written beautifully and distinctly by my own hand. But now I felt myself as if pierced and lacerated by a sharp sorrow.

Ah, happy Anselmus, who has cast away the burden of everyday life! Who in the love of charming Serpentina flies with bold wings and now lives in rapture and joy on his freehold in Atlantis, while I—poor I—must soon, yes, just in a few moments, leave this beautiful hall, which is itself far from being a freehold in Atlantis, and again be transplanted to my garret, where enthralled by the paltriness of existence, my heart and my sight are so bedimmed by a thousand mischiefs as by a thick fog, that I will never, never behold the lily.

Then Archivarius Lindhorst patted me gently on the shoulder and said, "Be quiet, be quiet, my revered friend. Do not lament so! Were you not yourself just now in Atlantis, and do you not at least have there a lovely little farmstead as a poetic possession of your inner mind? Is the bliss of Anselmus anything else but life in poetry, poetry where the sacred harmony of all things is revealed as the most profound secret of Nature?"

End of the Fairy Tale

Translated by L. J. Kent
and E. C. Knight

Councillor Krespel

Councillor Krespel was one of the most eccentric men I ever met in my life. When I went to H——, where I was to live for a time, the whole town was talking about him because one of his craziest schemes was then in full bloom. Krespel was renowned as both an accomplished jurist and a skilled diplomat. A reigning German Fürst—one of no great significance—requested that he draw up a memorandum for submission to the Imperial Court establishing his legal claim to a certain territory. The suit was crowned with unusual success, and because Krespel had once complained that he could never find a house that properly suited him, the Fürst, who had decided to reward him for services rendered, agreed to assume the cost of building a house that Krespel might erect according to his own desires. The Fürst also offered to purchase any site that pleased Krespel, but Krespel rejected this offer, insisting that the house should be built in his own garden, which was located in a very beautiful area outside the town gates. Then he bought all kinds of building materials and had them delivered there; thereafter, he could be seen all day long, dressed in his peculiar clothes—which he always made himself according to his own specific theories—slaking lime, sifting sand, stacking building stones in neat piles, and so on. He had not consulted an architect, nor had he drawn any formal plan. One fine day, however, he called on a master mason in H—— and asked him to appear at his garden at dawn the next day with all of his journeymen and apprentices, many of his laborers, and so on, to build his house for him. Naturally, the mason requested the architect's plan and was more than a little astonished when Krespel replied that there was no need for a plan and that everything would turn out very well without one.

When the mason and his men arrived the next morning, they discovered that an excavation had been dug in a perfect square. "This is where the foundation of my house is to be laid," Krespel said, "and the four walls are to be built up until I tell you that they are high enough."

"Without windows and doors, without partition walls?" the mason interrupted as if shocked by Krespel's crazy notions.

"Do what I tell you, my good man," Krespel replied very calmly. "The rest will take care of itself."

Only the promise of generous payment induced the builder to proceed with this ridiculous building; but never was there one erected under more merry circumstances. The workmen, who laughed continually, never left the site, as there was an abundance of food and drink on hand. The walls went up with unbelievable speed, until Krespel one day shouted, "Stop!" When trowels and hammers were silenced, the workmen descended from the scaffolding and circled around Krespel, every laughing face seemed to ask, "So, what's next?"

"Make way!" cried Krespel, who then ran to one end of the garden and paced slowly toward his square building. When he came close to the wall, he shook his head in dissatisfaction, ran to the other end of the garden, and again paced toward the wall, with the same result. He repeated this tactic several times until finally, running his sharp nose hard against the wall, he cried, "Come here, come here, men. Make me a door right here!" He specified the exact dimensions to the inch, and his orders were carried out. Then he walked into the house and smiled with pleasure as the builder remarked that the walls were precisely the height of a well-constructed two-story house. Krespel walked thoughtfully back and forth inside. The builders, hammers and picks in hand, followed behind him; and whenever he cried "Put a window here, six by four; and a little window here, three by two!" space was immediately knocked out.

I arrived at H—— at this stage of the operation, and it was very entertaining to see hundreds of people standing around in the garden, all cheering loudly when stones flew out and still another window appeared where it was least expected. Krespel handled the rest of the construction and all other necessary work in the same way. Everything had to be done on the spot, according to his orders of the moment. The comic aspect of the whole project, the growing conviction that everything was turning out better than could possibly have been expected, and above all, Krespel's generosity—which, indeed, cost him nothing—kept everyone in good humor. The difficulties intrinsic in this peculiar method of building were thus overcome, and in a short time a completely finished house was standing, presenting a most unusual appearance from the outside—no two windows being alike, and so on—but whose interior arrangements aroused a very special feeling of ease. Everyone who went there bore testimony to this, and I felt it myself when I grew better acquainted with Krespel and was invited there. Up to that time I had not spoken with this strange man. He had been so preoccupied with his building that he had not even once come to Professor M——'s house for lunch, as had always been his wont on Tuesdays. Indeed, in response to an explicit invitation, he replied that he would not set foot outside his new home before the housewarming took place. All his friends and acquaintances looked forward to a great feast, but Krespel invited no one except the masters, journeymen, apprentices, and laborers who had built his house. He entertained them with the most splendid dishes. Masons' apprentices, without thinking of possible consequences, gorged themselves on partridge pies; carpenters' boys joyfully planed roast pheasants; and hungry laborers for once labored on choicest morsels of *truffes fricassées*. In the evening their wives and daughters arrived, and a great ball began. Krespel waltzed a little with the builders' wives and then sat down with the town musicians, took up his fiddle, and conducted the dance music until daybreak.

On the Tuesday following this festival, which established Krespel as a friend of the people, I finally met him, to my no small pleasure, at Professor M——'s. It would be impossible to imagine anything stranger than Krespel's behavior. His movements were so stiff and awkward that he looked as if he would bump into or damage something at any moment. But he didn't, and it was soon obvious that he wouldn't, for the mistress of the house did not bother to turn a shade paler when he stumbled around the table set with beautiful cups or maneuvered in front of a great full-length mirror, or seized a vase of exquisitely painted porcelain and swung it around in the air as if to let the colors flash. In fact, before lunch Krespel scrutinized everything in the Professor's room most minutely. He even climbed up one of the upholstered chairs to remove a picture from the wall and then rehung it, while chattering incessantly and with great emphasis. Occasionally—it was most especially noticeable at lunch—he jumped from one subject to another; then, unable to abandon some particular idea, he returned to it over and over again, got himself completely enmeshed in it, and could not disentangle his thoughts until some fresh idea caught him. Sometimes his voice was harsh and screeching, sometimes it was slow and singsong; but never was it in harmony with what he was talking about. We were discussing music and praising a new composer when Krespel smiled and said in his musical voice, "I wish that the black-winged Satan would hurl that damned music mutilator ten thousand million fathoms deep into hell's pit!" Then, he burst out wildly and screechingly: "She is heaven's angel, nothing but pure God-given harmony—the light and star of song!" and tears formed in his eyes. One had to recall that an hour before he had been talking about a celebrated soprano.

As we were eating roast hare I noticed that Krespel carefully removed every particle of flesh from the bones on his plate and asked especially for the paws, which the Professor's five-year-old daughter brought to him with a friendly smile. The children had cast many friendly glances at Krespel during dinner, and now they got up and moved near to him, but with a respectful shyness, staying three paces away. "What's going to happen now?" I thought to myself. The dessert was brought in; then Krespel took from his pocket a little box in which there was a tiny steel lathe. This he immediately screwed to the table, and with incredible skill, made all kinds of little boxes and dishes and balls out of the bones, which the children received with cries of delight.

Just as we were rising from the table, the Professor's niece asked, "What is our Antonia doing now, dear Councillor?"

Krespel made a face like someone biting into a sour orange who wants to look as if it were a sweet one; but soon his expression changed into a horrifying mask and his laugh was bitter and fierce as he answered with what seemed to be diabolical scorn: "Our? *Our* dear Antonia?" he asked in his languid, unpleasant singing tone. The Professor quickly intervened; in the reproving glance he threw at his niece, I read that she had touched a chord that must have jarred discordantly within Krespel.

"How is it going with the violins?" the Professor asked gaily, taking the Councillor by both hands.

Then Krespel's face lightened, and he answered in his firm voice: "Splendidly, Professor, only this morning I cut open that marvelous Amati I told you about recently that fell into my hands through a lucky accident. I hope that Antonia has carefully taken the rest of it apart."

"Antonia is a good child," the Professor said.

"Yes, indeed, that she is," Krespel screamed, quickly turning around, simultaneously grabbing his hat and stick, and rushing out through the door. I saw in the mirror that there were tears in his eyes.

As soon as the Councillor had left, I insisted that the Professor tell me immediately what Krespel was doing with violins, and especially about Antonia. "Well," the Professor said, "As the Councillor is in general a very remarkable man, he has his own mad way of constructing violins."

"Constructing violins?" I asked in astonishment.

"Yes," continued the Professor. "In the opinion of those who know what it is all about, Krespel makes the best violins that can be found nowadays. Formerly, if one turned out very well, he would allow others to play it; but that has been over for a long time now. When Krespel has made a violin, he plays it himself with great power and with exquisite expression, for an hour or two, then he hangs it up with the rest and never touches it again, nor does he allow anyone else to touch it. If a violin by any of the eminent old masters is on the market, the Councillor buys it, at any price asked. But, as with his own violins, he plays it only once, then takes it apart in order to examine its inner structure, and if he thinks that he has not found what he has been looking for, he flings the pieces into a large chest that is already full of dismantled violins."

"But what's this about Antonia?" I asked suddenly and impetuously.

"Well, now," continued the Professor. "Well, now, that is something that might make me detest the Councillor if I were not convinced of his basic good nature; indeed, he is so good that he errs on the side of weakness, and there must be some hidden explanation behind it all. When he came here to H—— several years ago, he lived like an anchorite, with an old housekeeper in a gloomy house in —— Street. Soon his eccentricities aroused the curiosity of his neighbors, and as soon as he noticed this, he sought and made acquaintances. Just as in my house, people everywhere grew so accustomed to him that he became indispensable. Despite his coarse appearance, even the children loved him, without becoming pests; for in spite of his friendliness, they retained a certain respect for him that protected him from any undue familiarities. You saw for yourself today how he is able to win the hearts of children with various ingenious tricks. We all took him for a confirmed bachelor, and he never contradicted this impression.

"After he had been here for some time, he went away, no one knew where, and returned after several months. On the evening following his return his windows were lighted up more brightly than usual, and this attracted the attention of the neighbors, who soon heard a surpassingly lovely female voice singing to the accompaniment of a piano. Then the sound of a violin struck up and challenged the voice to a dazzling and fiery contest. One immediately knew that it was Krespel playing. I myself mingled with the large crowd that had gathered in front of the Councillor's house to listen to this wonderful concert; and I must confess that the singing of the most famous soprano I had ever heard seemed feeble and expressionless compared with that voice and the peculiar impression it made, stirring me to the depths of my soul. Never before had I had any conception of such long-sustained notes, of such nightingale trills, of such crescendos and diminuendos, of such surging to organlike stength and such diminution to the faintest whisper. There was no one who was not enthralled by the magic; and when the singer stopped, only gentle sighs interrupted the profound silence.

"It must have been midnight when we heard the Councillor talking violently. Another masculine voice could be heard, which, to judge from its tone, seemed to be reproaching him; and at intervals the voice of a girl complained in disjointed phrases. The Councillor shouted more and more loudly until he finally fell into that familiar singsong voice of his. He was interrupted by a loud scream from the girl, and then all grew deathly silent until, suddenly, there was a commotion on the stairs, and a young man rushed out sobbing, threw himself into a carriage waiting nearby, and drove quickly away.

"The Councillor seemed to be very cheerful the next day, and no one had the courage to question him about what had happened the previous night; but the housekeeper, upon being questioned, said that the Councillor had brought home with him a very young lady, as pretty as a picture, whom he called Antonia, and it was she who had sung so beautifully. A young man, who had treated Antonia very affectionately and must have been her fiancé, had also come along with them. But, because the Councillor had insisted upon it, he had had to leave quickly. The relationship between Antonia and the Councillor is still a secret, but it is certain that he tyrannizes the poor girl in a most hateful fashion. He watches her as Doctor Bartolo watched his ward in *The Barber of Seville;* she hardly dares to be seen at the window. And if she can occasionally prevail upon him to take her into society, his Argus eyes follow her and he will not permit a musical note to be played, let alone allow her to sing. Indeed, she is no longer permitted to sing in his home either. Antonia's singing on that night has become something of a legend, something romantic that stirs the imagination of the townsfolk; and even the people who did not hear her, often say, when a singer performs here, 'What sort of miserable caterwauling is that? Only Antonia knows how to sing.' "

You know that such fantastic events are my special weakness, and you can easily guess how imperative it was for me to become acquainted with Antonia. I had often heard the popular comments about her singing, but I had no idea that the glorious Antonia was living in the town, held captive by the mad Krespel as if by a tyrannical sorcerer. Naturally, I heard Antonia's marvelous singing in my dreams the following night, and when she most touchingly implored me to save her in a superb adagio (which, absurdly enough, I seemed to have composed myself), I determined, like a second Astolpho, to break into Krespel's house as into Alzinen's magic castle, and deliver the queen of song from her shameful bonds.

It all came out differently from what I had imagined. As soon as I had seen the Councillor once or twice and avidly discussed with him the best structure of violins, he himself invited me to call on him at his house. I did so, and he showed me his treasury of violins. At least thirty of them were hanging in a closet, and one of them, conspicuous because it bore the marks of great antiquity (a carved lion's head, and so on), was hanging higher than the rest, crowned with a wreath of flowers that seemed to make it a queen over the others.

"This violin," Krespel said when I asked him about it, "this violin is a very remarkable and wonderful piece by an unknown master, probably of Tartini's time. I am completely convinced that there is something peculiar about its inner construction and that if I take it apart I will discover a secret I have been looking for, but—laugh at me if you like—this dead thing, which depends upon me for its life and its voice, often speaks to me by itself in the strangest manner. When I played it for the first time, it seemed as if I was but the hypnotist who so affects his somnambulist that she verbally reveals what she is able to see within herself. Do not suppose that I am idiotic enough to attribute even the slightest importance to ideas so fantastic in nature, but it is peculiar that I have never succeeded in convincing myself to dismantle that inanimate and dumb object. Now I am pleased that I have never dismantled it; since Antonia's arrival I occasionally use it to play something to her. She is extremely fond of it—extremely."

This was said by Krespel with obvious emotion, and I was encouraged to ask, "My dear Councillor, will you not one day play in my presence?" But his face assumed his sweet-sour expression, and he said in that slow singsong way of his, "No, my dear Herr Studiosus!" And this ended the business; I had to continue looking at all sorts of curiosities, frequently childish ones. Ultimately he thrust his hand in a chest and withdrew from it a folded paper, which he then pressed in my hand, while most seriously saying, "You are a lover of art. Take this present as a true keepsake and value it above all else in the world."

Saying this, he softly clutched both my shoulders and shoved me towards the door, embracing me on the threshold. Actually, I was symbolically thrown out of the house.

When I opened the paper I discovered a piece of an E string, which was about an eighth of an inch in length; and alongside the string was written, "From the E string of the violin used by the deceased Stamitz when he played his last concert."

This unfriendly dismissal at the mention of Antonia suggested that I would never succeed in seeing her; but this was not so, for when I visited the Councillor for the second time I found Antonia in his room, helping him put a violin together. Antonia did not make a strong impression at first sight, but I soon found it impossible to resist her blue eyes, her sweet rosy lips, and her singularly delicate and lovely figure. She was very pale, but if anything was said that was witty and amusing, a fiery blush suffused her cheeks, only to fade to a faint pink glow.

I talked to her without restraint, and I noticed none of those Arguslike glances that the Professor had attributed to Krespel; on the contrary, the Councillor remained absolutely his usual self and even seemed to approve of my conversing with Antonia. And so I often visited the Councillor; and as we grew more familiar, our little circle assumed a warm intimacy that gave the three of us great pleasure. The Councillor continued to entertain me with his eccentricities, but of course it was really Antonia, with her irresistible charm, who drew me there and led me to tolerate a good deal that my impatient nature would otherwise have found unbearable. The Councillor's eccentric behavior was sometimes in bad taste and tedious, and what I found particularly irritating was that as soon as I steered the conversation to music, especially singing, he would interrupt me in his singsong voice, a diabolical smile upon his face, and introduce some irrelevant, often coarse subject. I realized from the great distress in Antonia's eyes at such moments that his sole purpose was to preclude my asking her to sing. I did not give up. The obstacles the Councillor threw in my way only strengthened my resolution to overcome them. If I was to avoid dissolving in fantasies and dreams about her singing, I had to hear her sing.

One evening Krespel was in an especially good mood. He had been taking an old Cremona violin apart and had discovered that the sound post was so fixed that it was about half a line more oblique than was customary—an important discovery of great practical value! I was successful in getting him to talk very fervently about the true art of violin playing. Krespel mentioned that the style of the old masters had been influenced by that of the

truly great singers—Krespel happened just then to be talking about
this—and naturally I commented that the practice was now reversed and that singers imitated the leaps and runs of the instru-
mentalists.

"What is more senseless than this?" I cried, leaping from my
chair, running to the piano, and opening it quickly. "What can be
sillier than such absurd mannerisms, which instead of being music
sound like the noise of peas rattling across the floor!"

I sang several of the modern *fermatas* that run back and forth
and hum like a well-spun top, accompanying myself with a few
chords. Krespel laughed excessively and cried, "Ha, ha! I seem to
hear our German-Italians, or our Italian-Germans, starting some
aria by Pucitta or Portogallo, or by some other *maestro di capella,*
or rather *schiavo d'un primo uomo.*"

"Now," I thought, "is the moment"; and turning to Antonia I
asked, "Isn't that right? Antonia knows nothing of such squealing?" And I immediately began one of the beautiful soul-stirring
songs by old Leonardo Leo. Antonia's cheeks flushed, her eyes
flashed with a newly awakened radiance. She sprang to the piano
and parted her lips. But at that very instant Krespel pushed her
away, seized me by the shoulders, and shrieked in his shrill tenor
voice, "My dear boy, my dear boy!" Then, grasping my hand while
bowing most courteously, he led me immediately away, saying in
his soft singsong way, "In truth, my esteemed and honorable sir,
in truth it would be a breach of courtesy and good manners if I
were to express my wish loudly and clearly that you should have
your neck softly broken by the scorching claws of the devil who
would, one could say, dispose of you quickly; but putting that
aside for the moment, you must admit, my dear, dear sir, that it
is growing very dark, and since there are no lamps lighted today,
you might risk damaging your precious legs, even if I did not kick
you out right now. Be good and go home in safety and think kind
thoughts of me, your true friend, if it so happens that you never—
do you understand me?—if you never happen to find him at home
again."

He thereupon embraced me and, grasping me firmly, slowly
turned me toward the door so that I could not get another look
at Antonia. You must admit that in my situation I could hardly
beat up the Councillor, which he really deserved. The Professor

enjoyed a good laugh at my expense and assured me that my break with the Councillor was absolutely permanent. Antonia was too precious to me, too sacred, I might say, for me to play the part of the languishing *amoroso* who stands gazing up at her window or fills the role of the lovesick adventurer. I left H—— completely shattered, but as usually happens in such cases, the brilliant colors of the picture painted by my imagination grew dim, and Antonia—yes, even her singing, which I had never heard—glimmered in my recollection like a gentle, consoling light.

Two years later, when I settled in B——, I undertook a trip through Southern Germany. The towers of H—— rose up in the hazy red glow of the evening; as I drew nearer, I was oppressed by an indescribable feeling of anxiety that lay upon my heart like a heavy weight. I could not breathe; I had to get out of the carriage and into the open air, but the oppressiveness increased until it became physically agonizing. I soon seemed to hear the strains of a solemn chorale floating on the air. The sound grew more distinct, and I could distinguish men's voices singing a hymn.

"What's that? What's that?" I cried, as it pierced my breast like a burning dagger.

"Can't you see?" said the postillion next to me. "They're burying someone over there in the churchyard."

We were, in fact, close to the churchyard, and I saw a circle of people clad in black standing around a grave that was being filled. Tears welled in my eyes; I felt somehow that all the joy and happiness of my life were being buried in that grave. Moving quickly down the hill, I could no longer see into the churchyard. The hymn was over, and not far from the city gate I could see some of the mourners returning from the funeral. The Professor, his niece on his arm, both in deep mourning, passed close to me without noticing me. The niece had her handkerchief pressed to her eyes and was sobbing convulsively. It was impossible for me to go into town; therefore, I sent my servant with the carriage to the inn where I usually stay, while I hurried off to the neighborhood so familiar to me in an effort to shake off my mood, possibly due to something physical, perhaps the result of becoming overheated on the journey.

When I arrived at the avenue leading to a park, a most extraordinary spectacle took place. Councillor Krespel was being guided by two mourners, from whom he appeared to be trying to escape by making all kinds of strange leaps and turns. As usual, he was dressed in the incredible gray coat he had made himself, but from his small three-cornered hat, which he wore cocked over one ear in a military manner, a mourning ribbon fluttered this way and that in the breeze. A black sword belt was buckled around his waist, but instead of a sword, a long violin bow was tucked beneath it. A cold shiver ran through me. "He is mad," I thought as I slowly followed them. The men conducted him as far as his house, where he embraced them, laughing loudly. They left him, and then his glance fell on me, for I was now standing very close to him. He stared at me fixedly for some time, then called in a hollow voice, "Welcome, Herr Studiosus! You do, of course, understand everything about it." With this he seized me by the arm and dragged me into the house, up the stairs, and into the room where the violins hung. They were all draped in crepe; the violin by the old master was missing; in its place there hung a wreath of cypress. I knew what had happened.

"Antonia! Antonia!" I cried inconsolably. The Councillor, his arms folded, stood beside me as if paralyzed. I pointed to the cypress wreath.

"When she died," he said very solemnly and gloomily, "the sound post of that violin broke with a resounding crack and the soundboard shattered to pieces. That faithful instrument could only live with her and through her; it lies beside her in the coffin; it has been buried with her." Deeply shaken, I sank into a chair, but the Councillor began singing a gay song in a hoarse voice. It was truly horrible to see him hopping about on one foot, the crepe (he was still wearing his hat) flapping about the room and against the violins hanging on the walls; indeed, I could not repress a loud shriek when the crepe hit me during one of his wild turns. It seemed to me that he wanted to envelop me and drag me down into the black pit of madness. Suddenly he stopped gyrating and said in his singsong fashion, "My son, my son, why do you shriek like that? Have you seen the Angel of Death? He's usually seen before the funeral"; and suddenly stepping into the middle of the room, he drew the bow from his belt; and having raised it above his head in both hands, he broke it into a thousand pieces. Then he cried with a loud laugh, "Now you imagine that the death sentence has been passed on me, don't you, my son? But it's not so. Now I am free, free. I am free! I will no longer make violins—no more violins—hurrah! No more violins!" This he sang to a hideously mirthful tune, again jumping about on one foot. Aghast, I tried to get out of the door quickly, but the Councillor held me tightly and said quietly, "Stay here, Herr Studiosus, and don't think I am mad because of this outpouring of agony that tortures me like the pangs of death. It is all because only a short while ago I made a nightshirt for myself in which I wanted to look like Fate or like God."

The Councillor continued his frightening gibberish until he collapsed in utter exhaustion. The ancient housekeeper came to him when I called, and I was glad when I once more found myself in the open air.

Not for a moment did I doubt that Krespel had become insane, but the Professor held to the contrary. "There are men," he said, "from whom nature or some peculiar destiny has removed the cover beneath which we hide our own madness. They are like thin-skinned insects whose visible play of muscles seems to make them deformed, though in fact everything soon returns to its normal shape again. Everything that remains thought within us becomes action in Krespel. Krespel expresses bitter scorn in mad gestures and irrational leaps, even as does the spirit that is embedded in all earthly activity. This is his lightning rod. What comes from the earth, he returns to the earth, but he knows how to preserve the divine. And so I believe that his inner consciousness is well, despite the apparent madness that springs to the surface. Antonia's sudden death weighs very heavily upon him, but I wager that tomorrow he'll be jogging along at his donkey trot as usual."

It happened that the Professor's prediction was almost exactly fulfilled. The next day the Councillor seemed to be completely himself again, but he declared that he would never again construct a violin, or play one. As I later learned, he kept his word.

The Professor's theories strengthened my private conviction that the carefully concealed yet highly intimate nature of the relationship between Antonia and the Councillor, and even her death, had been marked by guilt, which could not be expatiated. I did not want to leave H—— without confronting him with this crime of which I suspected him; I wanted to shake him to the depths of his soul and so compel him to make an open confession of his horrible deed. The more I thought about the matter, the more I convinced myself that Krespel must be a scoundrel, and as the thoughts in my mind grew more fiery and forceful they developed into a genuine rhetorical masterpiece. Thus equipped, and in great agitation, I ran to the Councillor's. I found him calmly smiling, making toys.

"How is it possible," I began the assault, "for you to find a moment's peace in your soul when the memory of your terrible deed must torture you like a serpent's sting?"

Krespel looked at me in astonishment, put his chisel aside, and said, "What do you mean, my dear fellow? Do have a seat please, on that chair."

But I grew more and more heated, and I accused him directly of having murdered Antonia and threatened him with the retribution of the Eternal. In fact, as a recently qualified court official imbued with my profession, I went so far as to assure him that I would do everything possible to bring the matter to light and to deliver him into the hands of an earthly judge. I was considerably taken aback, however, when at the conclusion of my violent and pompous harangue, the Councillor fixed his eyes upon me serenely, without uttering a word, as if waiting for me to continue. Indeed, I did try to do so, but it all sounded so clumsy and so utterly silly that I almost immediately grew silent again.

Krespel luxuriated in my perplexity; a malicious and ironical smile darted across his face. Then he became very serious and spoke to me in a solemn voice: "Young man, you may take me for a madman; I can forgive you for that. We are both confined to the same madhouse, and you accuse me of imagining that I am God the Father because you consider yourself to be God the Son. But how dare you presume to force your way into the life of another person to uncover hidden facts that are unknown to you and must remain so? She is dead now and the secret is revealed."

Krespel rose and paced back and forth across the room several times. I ventured to ask for an explanation; he stared at me with fixed eyes, grasped my hand, and led me to the window. After opening both casements, he propped his arms on the sill, leaned out, and looking down into the garden, he told me the story of his life. When he had finished, I left him, deeply moved and ashamed.

The facts of his relationship with Antonia were as follows: About twenty years ago the Councillor's all-consuming passion for hunting out and buying the best violins by the old masters had led him to Italy. He had not at that time begun to make violins himself, nor, consequently, had he begun to take them apart. In Venice he heard the famous singer Angela ——i, who at that time was triumphantly appearing in the leading roles in the Teatro di S. Benedetto. His enthusiasm was kindled, not only because of her art, which Signora Angela had developed to absolute perfection, but by her angelic beauty as well. The Councillor sought her acquaintance, and despite his uncouthness, he succeeded, primarily by his bold and most expressive violin playing, in winning her entirely for himself.

In a few weeks their close intimacy led to marriage, which was kept a secret because Angela did not wish to part from the theater nor surrender the name under which she had become famous nor add the awkward name of Krespel to it. With the most extravagant irony, the Councillor described the very peculiar way Angela plagued and tortured him as soon as she became his wife. Krespel felt that all the selfishness and all the petulance that resided in all the prima donnas in the world were somehow concentrated in her little body. When he once tried to assert his own position, Angela turned loose on him a whole army of *abbates, maestros, academicos* who, ignorant of his true relationship, found in him a completely intolerable and uncivilized admirer who was beyond adapting himself to the Signora's delightful whims. Right after one of these tumultuous scenes, Krespel fled to Angela's country house, trying to forget the suffering the day had brought by improvising on his Cremona violin. He had not been playing long, however, when the Signora, who had followed hard after him, stepped into the room. She was in the mood for playing the affectionate wife, so she embraced the Councillor with sweet languishing glances and laid her head on his shoulder. But the Councillor, who was lost in the world of his music, continued playing until the walls resounded, and it so happened that he touched the Signora a little urgently with his arm and the bow. Blazing into fury, she sprang back, shrieking *"Bestia tedesca!"* snatched the violin from his hands, and smashed it into a thousand pieces on the marble table. The Councillor stood like a statue before her; but then, as if waking from a dream, he seized the Signora with the strength of a giant and flung her out of the window of her own country house, after which, without troubling himself about the matter any further, he fled to Venice, then Germany.

It was some time before he fully realized what he had done. Although he knew that the window was barely five feet from the ground, and though he was fully convinced that it had been absolutely necessary to fling her from the window, he felt troubled and uneasy about it, especially because the Signora had made it clear to him that she was pregnant. He scarcely had the courage to ask about her, and he was not a little surprised when about eight months later he received a tender letter from his beloved wife that contained no mention of what had happened at the country house, but rather informed him that she had given birth to a lovely little girl and concluded with the heartfelt request that the *marito amato e padre felicissimo* come to Venice at once. Krespel did not go; instead he requested a close friend to supply him with details as to what was really going on. And he learned that the Signora had landed that day on the grass as gently as a bird and that the only consequence of her fall had been emotional. As a result of Krespel's heroic deed, she seemed transformed; no longer was there evidence of her former capriciousness or willfulness or of her old teasing habits, and the *maestro* who had composed the music for the next carnival was the happiest man under the sun, for the Signora was willing to sing his arias without a thousand changes to which he would otherwise have had to consent. All in all, there was every reason for keeping secret the method by which Angela had been cured; otherwise primadonnas would come flying through windows every day.

The Councillor grew very excited, ordered horses, and was seated in the carriage when he suddenly cried, "Stop!" He murmured to himself, "Why, isn't it certain that the evil spirit will again take possession of Angela the moment she sees me again? Since I have already thrown her out of the window, what will I do if the same situation were to occur? What would there be left for me to do?"

He got out of the carriage and wrote his wife an affectionate letter, in which he gracefully alluded to her kindness in expressly detailing the fact that his little daughter had a little mole behind her ear, just as he did, and—remained in Germany. A very spirited exchange of letters ensued. Assurances of love—invitations—regrets over the absence of the loved one—disappointment—hopes—and so on—flew back and forth between Venice and H—— and H—— to Venice. Finally Angela came to Germany, and as is well known, sang triumphantly as prima donna at the great theater in F——. Despite the fact that she was no longer young, she swept all before her with the irresistible charm of her marvelous singing. Her voice at that time had not deteriorated in the slightest degree. Meanwhile Antonia had grown up, and her mother never could write enough to her father about the potential she saw in her daughter, who was blossoming into a first-rate singer. Krespel's friends in F—— confirmed this information and urged him to come to F—— to marvel at the rare experience of hearing two such absolutely sublime singers together. They did not suspect the intimate relationship that existed between Krespel and the ladies. He would have loved seeing his daughter, whom he adored from the depths of his heart, and who often appeared to him in his dreams; but as soon as he thought about his wife he felt very uneasy, and he remained at home among his dismembered violins.

You will have heard of the promising young composer B—— of F—— who suddenly disappeared, no one knows how. (Did you perhaps know him?) He fell desperately in love with Antonia and, Antonia returning his love, he begged her mother to consent to a union that would be sanctified by their art. Angela had no objection to this, and the Councillor gave his consent all the more readily because the young composer's music pleased his critical judgment. Krespel expected to receive news that the wedding had taken place, when instead he received an envelope, sealed in black, addressed in an unfamiliar hand. Dr. R—— informed the Councillor that Angela had fallen seriously ill as a result of a chill she had caught at the theater the evening preceding what was to have been Antonia's wedding day, and had died. Angela had revealed to the doctor that she was Krespel's wife and that Antonia was his daughter. He was therefore to hasten there to assume responsibility for the orphan. Despite the fact that the Councillor was deeply disturbed by this news of Angela's death, he nevertheless soon felt that a disturbing influence had left his life and that now he could breathe freely for the first time.

That very same day he started out for F——. You cannot imagine how dramatically the Councillor described the moment when he first saw Antonia. Even in the very bizarre nature of his language there was a wonderful power of description that I am completely incapable of conveying. Antonia had all her mother's amiability and charm, but she had none of the meanness that was the reverse side of her mother's character. There was no ambiguous cloven hoof to peep out from time to time. The young bridegroom arrived; and Antonia, who was able through her own affectionate nature intuitively to understand her remarkable father, sang one of the old Padre Martini motets, which she knew Angela had had to sing repeatedly to Krespel when their courtship had been in full bloom. Tears flooded the Councillor's cheek; he had never heard Angela sing so beautifully. The timbre of Antonia's voice was quite individual and rare, sometimes like the sound of an Aeolian harp, sometimes like the warbling of a nightingale. It was as if there were no room for such notes within the human breast. Antonia, glowing with love and joy, sang all of her most lovely songs, and B—— in the intervals played as only enraptured inspiration can play. Krespel was at first transported by delight, but then he grew thoughtful—quiet—introspective. Finally he leaped to his feet, pressed Antonia to his breast, and begged her softly and sadly: "If you love me, sing no more—my heart is bursting—the anguish! The anguish! Sing no more."

"No," the Councillor said the next day to Dr. R——. "When she sang, the color gathered into two dark red spots on her pale cheeks, and I knew that it could not be accounted for by any silly family resemblance; it was what I had dreaded."

The doctor, whose face had shown deep concern from the beginning of the conversation, replied, "Whether it results from her having overexerted herself in singing when she was too young, or whether it results from congenital weakness, Antonia suffers from an organic deficiency in her chest from which her voice derives its wonderful power and its strange, I might say, divine timbre and by which it transcends the capabilities of human song. But it will cause her early death; for if she continues to sing, she will live six months at the most."

The Councillor's heart felt as if it were pierced by a hundred daggers. It was as though a lovely tree and its superb blossoms had, for the first time, cast its shadow over him, and now it was to be cut down to the roots so that it could no longer grow green and blossom. His decision was made. He told Antonia everything and presented her with a choice—she could either follow her fiancé and surrender to his and the world's allurements with the certainty of dying young, or give to her father in his old age a happiness and peace that he had never known, and thereby live for many years. Antonia collapsed sobbing into her father's arms, and he, aware of the agony the next few minutes might bring, asked for nothing explicit. He spoke with her fiancé, but despite his assurance that no note would ever cross Antonia's lips, the Councillor was fully aware that B—— himself would never be able to resist the temptation to hear her sing—at least the arias he was composing. The musical world, even though it knew of Antonia's suffering, would surely never surrender its claim to her, for people like this can be selfish and cruel when their own enjoyment is at issue.

The Councillor disappeared from F—— with Antonia and arrived at H——. B—— was in despair when he learned of their departure. He followed their tracks, overtook the Councillor, and arrived at H—— simultaneously.

"Let me see him only once and then die," Antonia entreated.

"Die? Die?" the Councillor cried in wild anger, an icy shudder running through him. His daughter, the only being in the wide world who could kindle in him a bliss he had never known, the one who had reconciled him to life, tore herself violently from his embrace; and he wanted this dreadful event to happen!

B—— went to the piano, Antonia sang, Krespel played the violin merrily until the red spots appeared on Antonia's cheeks. Then he ordered a halt; and when B—— said goodbye to Antonia, she suddenly collapsed with a loud cry.

"I thought," Krespel told me, "I thought that she was really dead, as I had foreseen; but as I had prepared myself to the fullest degree, I remained very calm and controlled. I seized B——, who was staring stupidly like a sheep, by the shoulders and said" (and the Councillor now returned to his singsong voice): " 'Now, my dear and estimable piano master, now that you have, as you wished and desired, succeeded in murdering your beloved bride, you will quietly leave, unless you would be good enough to wait around until I run my bright little dagger through your heart, so that my daughter, who you see has grown rather pale, could use some of your precious blood to restore her color. Get out of here quickly, or I may throw this nimble little knife at you!"

"I must have looked rather terrifying as I said this, for with a cry of the deepest horror, B—— tore himself from my grasp, rushed through the door and down the steps."

As soon as he was gone, Krespel went to lift Antonia, who lay unconscious on the floor, and she opened her eyes with a deep sigh, but soon closed them again as if she were dead. Krespel broke into loud and inconsolable grief. The doctor, who had been fetched meanwhile by the housekeeper, announced that Antonia was suffering from a serious but by no means fatal attack; and she did, in fact, recover more quickly than the Councillor had dared to hope. She now clung to Krespel with a most devoted and daughterly affection and shared with him all of his favorite hobbies, his peculiar schemes and whims. She helped him take old violins apart and put new ones together. "I will not sing anymore, but I will live just for you," she often said to her father, smiling softly, after someone had asked for a song and she had refused. The Councillor tried as hard as possible to spare her from such situations, and therefore he was unwilling to take her out into society and scrupulously shunned all music. He was well aware of how painful it must be for Antonia to forgo completely the art in which she had attained such perfection.

When the Councillor bought the wonderful violin that he later buried with Antonia and was about to take it apart, Antonia looked at him very sadly and, in a gentle, imploring voice, asked, "This one, too?" The Councillor himself couldn't understand what unknown power had impelled him to spare his violin and to play it.

He had barely drawn the first few notes when Antonia cried aloud with joy, "Why, that is me—I am singing again!" In truth, there was something about the silvery bell-like tones of the violin that was very striking; they seemed to come from a human soul. Krespel was so deeply moved that he played more magnificently than ever before, and when he ran up and down the scale with consumate power and expression, Antonia clapped her hands and cried with delight, "I sang that well! I sang that very well!" From this time on a great serenity and happiness came into her life. She often said to Krespel, "I would like to sing something, Father." Then Krespel would take his violin from the wall and play her most beautiful songs, and she was surpassingly happy.

One night, shortly before I arrived in H——, it seemed to Krespel that he heard someone playing the piano in the next room, and soon he distinctly recognized that it was B——, who was improvising in his usual style. He was about to rise, but it was as if there were a heavy weight upon him; he could not so much as stir. Then he heard Antonia's voice singing softly and delicately until it slowly grew into a shattering fortissimo. The wonderful sounds became the moving song that B—— had once composed for her in the devotional style of the old masters. Krespel said that the state in which he found himself was incomprehensible, for an appalling fear was combined with a rapture he had never before experienced.

Suddenly he was overwhelmed by a dazzling lucidity, and he saw B—— and Antonia embracing and gazing at each other rapturously. The notes of the song and the accompaniment of the piano continued, although Antonia was not visibly singing nor B—— playing. The Councillor fell into a profound unconsciousness in which the vision and the music vanished. When he awoke, the terrible anxiety of his dream still possessed him. He rushed into Antonia's room. She lay on the sofa with her eyes shut, her hands devoutly folded, as if she were asleep and dreaming of heavenly bliss and joy. But she was dead.

Translated by L. J. Kent
and E. C. Knight

Mademoiselle de Scudéri

A *Tale of the Times*
of Louis XIV

Thanks to the favor of Louis XIV and the Marquise de Maintenon, Madeleine de Scudéri,* known for her charming poems,
inhabited a small house in the rue Saint Honoré.

One midnight—it might have been in the fall of 1680—someone
knocked on the door of this house so hard and with such violence
that the entire hall echoed loudly. Baptiste, who served as cook,
butler, and doorman in Mademoiselle's small household, had, with
the permission of his mistress, gone to the country to attend his
sister's wedding; and thus it happened that La Martinière, Mademoiselle's personal maid, was the only one awake in the house.
She heard the repeated blows, and it occurred to her that Baptiste
had gone away and that she and her mistress were alone in the
house without any protection. All the crimes of breaking and entering, of robbery, of murder, that had ever taken place in Paris
crossed her mind, and she grew certain that some gang of thugs,

* Madeleine de Scudéri (1607–1701), French author, came to Paris in 1630 and
became connected with Mme. de Rambouillet's salon. Later she formed a literary
circle of her own, their "Saturday gatherings" becoming famous. Her best known
work was the ten-volume novel *Artamène ou le Grand Cyrus* (1649–59); it was
followed by *Clélie* (1654–60). Highly artificial, poorly constructed, flawed by
pointless dialogue, her works were popular at the court, primarily because of their
anecdotes about public personages. They served the parvenu well.

Part of the success of this story results from its combination of realistic scenes,
actual people, and fantastic elements. Almost all of the characters and places de-
picted existed in fact.

aware of the isolation of the house, was raging outside and, if let in, would commit evil against her mistress; and so she remained in her room quaking and quivering, cursing Baptiste and his sister's wedding. Meanwhile, the blows thundered on, and it seemed to her as if a voice were shouting through it all, "Open the door, for God's sake, open the door!" Finally, in growing fear, La Martinière seized a lighted candelabrum and ran into the hall. There she quite clearly heard the voice of a man shouting: "For God's sake, open the door!"

"Well," thought La Martinière, "no robber speaks like that. Who knows, perhaps some persecuted man is seeking refuge with my mistress, who is always charitable. However, let us be cautious." She opened a window and, trying to make her voice sound as masculine as possible, called down and asked who was beating at the door so late at night and waking everybody up.

By the shimmer of the moonbeams, which were just breaking through the dark clouds, she saw a tall figure wrapped in a light gray coat, wearing a large hat pulled down over his eyes. She shouted in a loud voice, so as to be heard by the man below, "Baptiste, Claude, Pierre, get up and see what good-for-nothing wants to break down our house." Then, from below, a soft, almost plaintive voice said, "Oh, La Martinière, I know it is you, dear lady, however much you try to disguise your voice. I know that Baptiste has gone to the country and that you are alone in the house with your mistress. Do not be afraid to open the door. I absolutely must speak with your mistress this very minute."

"What makes you think," La Martinière replied, "that my mistress will speak to you in the middle of the night? Don't you know that she went to bed a long time ago and that nothing on earth could induce me to wake her from her first sweet sleep, which is so necessary at her age?"

"I know," said the person below, "I know that your mistress has just put aside the manuscript of her novel *Clélie*, on which she works so tirelessly, and that she is now writing certain verses that she intends to read tomorrow at Madame de Maintenon's. I beseech you, Madame Martinière, have pity and open the door. I tell you that it is a matter of saving an unfortunate man from ruin, that the honor, freedom, yes, even the very life of a man depend on this moment in which I *must* speak to your mistress. Consider that your mistress's anger would rest on you eternally if she learned that it was you who turned away without mercy the unfortunate man who came to beseech her help."

"But why have you come to appeal to my mistress's compassion at this extraordinary hour? Come again in the morning, at a reasonable time," La Martinière said.

"Does destiny, then," the person below replied, "respect the time of day when it strikes like deadly lightning? When there is but a single moment when it is possible to rescue a man's life, can help be delayed? Open the door for me! You need not fear a defenseless and friendless wretch who is pursued and pressed by a terrible fate, when he wishes to beg your lady to save him from imminent danger!" La Martinière heard him moaning and sobbing with anguish as he uttered those words in a voice at once youthful, soft, gentle, and most touching. Deeply moved, she went to get the keys without further thought.

She had no sooner opened the door when the figure, wrapped in a cloak, burst in violently and, moving past La Martinière into the passage, cried in a wild voice, "Take me to your mistress." In terror, La Martinière lifted the candelabrum she was carrying, and the light fell on the deathly pale, frightfully distorted face of a youth. Terror almost bowled her over when the young man opened his cloak and revealed the shining hilt of a naked stiletto that he was carrying in the open bosom of his doublet. His flashing eyes upon her, he cried, more wildly than before, "Take me to your mistress, I tell you!" La Martinière saw that her mistress was in immediate danger. All her affection for her, whom she honored as if she were her pious, kind mother, inflamed her heart and gave her a courage of which she would not have thought herself capable. Quickly closing the door of her room, which she had left open, she stepped in front of it and said in a voice loud and firm, "Now that you are in the house, your frenzied behavior is very different from your pathetic performance outside. It is clear that my pity misled me. You ought not and shall not speak to my mistress now. If you have no evil intentions, you have nothing to fear from the light of day. Come again tomorrow and state your business. Now, get out of this house!" The young man sighed deeply, glared at La Martinière menacingly, and grasped his stiletto. La Martinière silently commended her soul to God, but she stood firm and boldly returned his glance even as she pressed herself more firmly against the door through which he would have to pass to reach her mistress.

"I tell you to let me go to your mistress!" he cried again.

"Do what you will," La Martinière replied, "I shall not leave this spot. Finish the evil deed already begun. An ignominious death will overtake you on the Place de la Grève, as it did your accursed companions in crime."

"Ha! You are right, La Martinière!" he cried. "I do look like and am armed like an accursed robber and murderer, but my partners are not condemned—they are not condemned!" And glaring at the terrified woman venomously, he drew his stiletto.

"Jesus!" she cried, expecting her deathblow, but at that moment the clatter of arms and the hoofbeats of horses were heard on the street. "The mounted police! The mounted police! Help! Help!" she cried.

"You wish to destroy me, you abominable woman—. All is done for, done for! Take this! Take it, and give it to your mistress today—tomorrow, if you prefer." And with these mumbled words he tore the candelabrum from her, extinguished the candles, and pressed a small casket into her hands. "As you hope for salvation, give this casket to your mistress," he cried and rushed out of the house.

La Martinière had sunk to the floor. With effort she stood up, and groping her way through the darkness to her room, she collapsed into an armchair in a state of complete exhaustion, incapable of uttering a sound. Then she heard the keys that she had left in the front door rattling. The house door was being locked, and soft, hesitant footsteps approached her room. Paralyzed with fear, powerless to move, she awaited the horrible unknown. Imagine her relief when the door opened and, by the light of the night lamp, she immediately recognized honest Baptiste, who looked deathly pale and completely distraught.

"In the name of all the saints," he began. "In the name of all the saints, tell me, Madame Martinière, what has happened? Oh, the fear, oh, the fear I've felt! I don't know what it was, but something drove me violently from the wedding last night. Then I came into our street. Madame Martinière, I thought to myself, sleeps lightly and she will hear me if I tap softly and gently at the door and she will let me in. But when I got to the corner I was confronted by a strong police patrol, on foot and on horseback, armed to the teeth, and they made me stop and refused to let me go on. As luck would have it, Desgrais, the lieutenant of the mounted police, was among them, and he knows me very well. When they thrust a lantern under my nose, he said, 'Where are you coming from in the middle of the night, Baptiste? You should stay home and look after your house. It's not safe to be out here. We expect to be making a good catch tonight.' You wouldn't believe, Madame Martinière, how these words disturbed me. And then, as I stepped on the threshold, a man all muffled up flies out of the house, a naked dagger in his hand, and knocks me down—the house is open, the keys are in the lock—tell me, what does it all mean?"

La Martinière, freed from her terror, told him about everything that had happened. She and Baptiste went into the hall and found the candelabrum on the floor where the stranger had flung it as he fled. "It is only too clear," Baptiste said, "that our mistress was to have been robbed and probably murdered. The man knew, as you told me, that you were alone with her, and he even knew that she was still awake and writing. Undoubtedly he was one of those cursed swindlers and rogues who first ferret out information that will help them carry out their plans and then break into a house. And I think, Madame Martinière, that we had better throw the little casket into the deepest part of the Seine. What assurance do we have that some vile monster is not after our good mistress's life and that when she opens the casket she will not fall dead on the spot, as the old Marquis de Tourney did when he opened the letter that he had received from a stranger?"

After a long discussion, the two faithful servants finally decided to tell their mistress everything the next morning and to give her the mysterious casket, which could, of course, be opened after appropriate precautions had been taken. After considering every circumstance surrounding the appearance of the suspicious stranger, they both decided that there might be some mystery involved in this for which they dared not assume responsibility but which they would have to leave for their mistress to uncover.

Baptiste's fears were well founded. At this time Paris was the scene of the most heinous crimes and, concomitantly, the most diabolical invention of hell offered easy means for the execution of these atrocities.

Glaser, a German druggist and the best chemist of his time, occupied himself, like most members of his profession, with conducting experiments in alchemy. He became obsessed with discovering the Philosopher's Stone. He was joined by an Italian named Exili. But this man practiced alchemy only as a subterfuge. His real purpose was to discover the techniques for mixing, boiling, and sublimating the poisonous compounds by which Glaser sought to make his fortune; and he finally succeeded in producing a subtle poison that was tasteless and odorless, that could kill either instantaneously or gradually, that left no trace behind in the human body, and which, therefore, defied all the talent and art of the physicians who, having no reason to suspect poison, invariably attributed death to natural causes. Despite all of Exili's precautions, he was suspected of selling poison and was taken to the Bastille. Soon afterwards, Captain Godin de Sainte-Croix was locked up in the same cell. This man, who for a long time had been living illicitly with the Marquise de Brinvillier, had brought disgrace to her whole family. The Marquis, however, remained indifferent to his wife's misconduct, and finally her father, Dreux d'Aubray, civil lieutenant of Paris, was forced to break up the criminal liaison by ordering the captain's arrest. Passionate, without principle, hypocritically pious, and inclined to all manner and degree of vice from youth on, jealous, vindictive to the point of madness, the captain could not have welcomed anything more than Exili's diabolical secret, which would give him the power to destroy all his enemies. He became Exili's eager pupil and soon his master's equal, so that when he was released from the Bastille he was able to continue his work on his own.

La Brinvillier was a dissolute woman; through Sainte-Croix she became a monster. He induced her to poison, one after another, first her own father, with whom she was living under the heartlessly hypocritical pretext of nursing him in his old age, then her two brothers, and finally her sister (her father was murdered for revenge, the others for the rich inheritance). This story of multiple poisoning is a horrible example of the way the commission of such crimes grows into an inexorable passion. Aiming for nothing beyond mere pleasure—like the chemist who conducts experiments purely for his own enjoyment—poisoners have often murdered people about whose life or death they were totally indifferent. The sudden death of several indigents in the Hôtel Dieu later aroused the suspicion that the loaves of bread, which La Brinvillier had distributed there every week in order to be seen as the apotheosis of piety and charity, had been poisoned. In any event, it is certain that she served poisoned pigeon pies to her guests. The Chevalier du Guet and several other persons fell victim to these hellish meals. Sainte-Croix, his assistant La Chaussée, and La Brinvillier were long able to mask their terrible crimes behind an impenetrable veil; but regardless of the infamous cunning of abandoned men, the eternal power of heaven had decided to judge the criminals here on earth. The poisons compounded by Sainte-Croix were so subtle that if the powder (*poudre de succession* it was called by the Parisians) was even once inhaled as it was being prepared, instantaneous death resulted. Sainte-Croix therefore wore a mask of fine glass when preparing it. One day this mask fell from his face just as he was shaking the finished poison powder into a phial, and inhaling the fine particles of dust, he instantly dropped dead. Since he died without heirs, the court lost no time in placing his possessions under seal. In his home they found the whole infernal arsenal of poisons that he had had at his command locked in a box, but they also found La Brinvillier's letters, which left no doubt about their evil crimes. She sought refuge in a convent at Liège. Desgrais, an officer of the mounted police, was sent to pursue her. Disguised as a priest, he appeared at the nunnery where she had hidden. He succeeded in engaging in a love affair with his abominable woman and finally, under the pretext of an assignation, enticed her into a deserted garden on the outskirts of town. As soon as the Marquise arrived at the intended rendezvous, she was surrounded by Desgrais' police, while her priestly lover, suddenly converted into an officer of the mounted police, forced her to enter the carriage that was standing ready outside the garden, and surrounded by police, she was driven straight to Paris. La Chaussée had already been beheaded, and La Brinvillier met the same death. After the execution her body was burned and the ashes scattered to the winds.

The Parisians breathed a sigh of relief now that the world was rid of the monster who had used these secret, deadly weapons with impunity against friend and foe. But it soon became evident that the abominable art of Sainte-Croix had been inherited. Like an invisible, malignant ghost, murder insinuated itself into the most intimate circles of love and friendship and surely and swiftly seized the unfortunate victim. He who on one day was blossoming with health, on the next day was tottering about, sick and debilitated, beyond the skill of the physician to save from death. Wealth—a lucrative position—a beautiful, perhaps too youthful wife—any of these were sufficient for persecution to the death. The most sacred bonds were rent by appalling suspicion. The husband trembled before his wife—the father before his son—the sister before her brother. The food and the wine served a friend were left untouched, and where pleasure and gaiety had once prevailed, truculent glances searched for a secret assassin. Fathers of families could be seen anxiously buying provisions in remote districts and preparing the food themselves in some filthy kitchen, afraid of some devilish treachery in their own homes. And yet the greatest precautions were sometimes in vain.

The King, in order to put a stop to this evil state of affairs, which continued to gain ground, established a special court with the sole duty of investigating and punishing these furtive crimes. This was the so-called *Chambre Ardente,* which sat not far from the Bastille, with La Régnie presiding. For a considerable time La Régnie's efforts, as zealous as they were, remained fruitless. It was left to the crafty Desgrais to uncover the most secret haunt of crime.

In the suburb Faubourg Sainte-Germain there lived an old woman, La Voisin by name, who practiced fortune-telling and necromancy and, abetted by her accomplices Le Sage and Le Vigoureux, excited fear and astonishment even in people who were not considered weak or gullible. But this was not all. Like Sainte-Croix a pupil of Exili, she could also brew the subtle poison that left no trace, and in this way she served unscrupulous sons who sought an early inheritance and dissolute wives who sought another and younger husband. Desgrais made his way into her confidence, she confessed everything, and the *Chambre Ardente* condemned her to be burned at the stake; she was executed in the

Place de la Grève. In her house was found a list of everyone who had used her services, and so it was that not only did one execution follow another but that grave suspicion fell upon persons of the highest station. Thus it was that Cardinal Bonzy was believed to have obtained from La Voisin the means of bringing to an early death all those to whom, as archbishop of Narbonne, he was obliged to pay a pension. Thus also the Duchesse de Bouillon and the Comtesse de Soissons, whose names were found on the list, were accused of having dealt with the devilish hag; and even François Henri de Montnorenci-Boudebelle, Duc de Luxembourg, Peer and Marshall of the Realm, was not spared. He too was prosecuted by the dreaded *Chambre Ardente*. He surrendered himself to be imprisoned in the Bastille where the hatred of Louvois and La Régnie resulted in his being incarcerated in a six-foot-long hole. Months passed before it was satisfactorily established that the only crime committed by the Duc was not punishable. He had once had his horoscope cast by Le Sage.

It is clear that the blind zeal of President La Régnie seduced him to acts of terror and brutality. The Tribunal assumed the character of the inquisition; the slightest suspicion was adequate cause for harsh imprisonment, and it was often left to chance to prove the innocence of a man accused of a capital crime. Moreover, La Régnie was of repulsive appearance and malicious temperament, so that he quickly aroused the hatred of those he had been appointed to avenge or protect. The Duchesse de Bouillon, asked by him during her trial if she had seen the Devil, replied, "I think I see him at this very moment."

While the blood of the guilty and the suspected flowed in streams in the Place de la Grève, and murder by poisoning finally grew rarer and rarer, an outrage of another kind made its appearance and again spread alarm in the city. A band of thieves seemed determined to get possession of all the jewels in Paris. As soon as expensive jewelry was bought, it would unaccountably vanish, regardless of how carefully guarded. What was worse, anyone who ventured to wear jewelry in the evening was robbed or even murdered in the public street or in dark hallways of the houses. Those who had escaped with their lives reported that they had been struck on the head by the blow of a fist which hit them like a bolt of lightning and that, regaining consciousness, they had discovered that they had been robbed and were not in a place very different from that in which they had originally been struck. The murder victims, who were found almost every morning lying in the street or inside houses, all bore the same mortal wound—a dagger thrust in the heart, so swiftly and surely delivered that, according to the doctors, the victims must have sunk to the ground without uttering a sound. Was there anyone at the salacious court of Louis XIV who was not involved in some clandestine love affair and who did not surreptitiously make his way to his mistress late at night, often carrying a valuable gift? The band of thieves, as if in league with spirits, knew precisely when anything of this kind was going on. Often the unfortunate victim never reached the house where he hoped to indulge his passion; or often he fell on the threshold, or even at the very door, of the room of his mistress, who, to her horror, would find his bloodstained corpse.

Argenson, the minister of police, ordered the arrest of everyone who was the least suspect, but in vain; La Régnie raged and tried to extort confessions, but in vain; watches and patrols were strengthened, but in vain—the tracks of the criminals were not to be found. Only the precaution of arming to the teeth and being preceded by a torchbearer was to some degree effective; but even then there were instances when the servant was beaten off by stones while the master was murdered and robbed at the same moment.

Remarkably enough, investigations conducted in all of the places where jewelry might possibly be disposed of failed to turn up the tiniest specimen of the stolen goods, so that here too clues could not be followed.

Desgrais foamed at the mouth in fury at the way the criminals evaded even his net. The district of the city in which he happened to be was always spared, while in the other sections, where no crime had been anticipated, murder and robbery claimed their wealthiest victims.

Desgrais hit upon the scheme of using several doubles, so similar in gait, posture, speech, figure, and face, that even the police could not identify the real Desgrais. Meanwhile Desgrais, alone and at the risk of his life, spied in the most secret hideouts and followed at a distance this man or that who, at his suggestion, wore valuable jewelry. *This* man remained unscathed; the thieves, then, knew about *this* technique too. Desgrais was at the end of his wits.

One morning Desgrais came to President La Régnie, pale, agitated, beside himself.

"Is there any news? Are you on their tracks?" the President called to him.

"Ha, Your Excellency," Desgrais began, stammering with rage, "last night—not far from the Louvre—the Marquis de la Fare was attacked in my presence."

"Thank heaven," La Régnie rejoiced, "then we have them!"

"You had better hear me out," Desgrais interrupted with a bitter smile. "You had better hear what happened.

"I was standing near the Louvre, all hell exploding in my chest, watching for these devils who are tormenting me. Then a man who did not see me passed close to me with faltering steps, turning constantly to look back over his shoulder. I recognized the Marquis de la Fare by the light of the moon. I had expected him; I knew where he was sneaking. He was barely ten or twelve paces past me when a figure seemed to spring up from the earth, struck him down, and fell upon him. Astounded, caught off guard by this moment that would have delivered the criminal into my hands, I cried out and leaped from my hiding place to attack him, but I became entangled in my cloak and fell. I saw the man fly away as if on the wings of the wind; I sprang to my feet; I ran after him—blowing my horn as I ran—the policemen's whistles responding to me from the distance—everything burst into life—weapons rattled, horses' hoofs clattered on all sides. 'Here—here—Desgrais—Desgrais!' I cried till the streets echoed, and all the while I could see the man in front of me in the bright moonlight as he dodged here and there to throw me off the track. We came to the Rue Nicaise; his strength apparently failing, I exerted myself to the utmost—he was no more than fifteen paces ahead of me!"

"You caught up to him—you seized him," La Régnie said with flashing eyes, while he seized Desgrais' arm as if *he* were the escaping murderer.

"Fifteen paces," Desgrais continued in a hollow voice, breathing heavily, "fifteen paces from me the man leapt aside into the shadows and vanished through the wall."

"Vanished? Through the wall! Are you mad?" La Régnie cried, taking two steps back and beating his hands together.

"If you like, Your Excellency may call me a madman from here on, or you may accuse me of suffering from hallucinations, but all took place exactly as I told it," Desgrais replied, rubbing his brow like one tormented by evil thoughts. "I stood dumbfounded before the wall when several breathless police came running up. The Marquis de la Fare, who had recovered from the attack, was with them, a naked dagger in his hand. We lit torches and felt along the wall; there was not a trace of a door or a window or of any opening. It is a solid stone wall enclosing a courtyard and attached to a house that is occupied by people who are above the slightest suspicion. Just today I carefully inspected the premises again. The Devil himself is making fools of us."

Desgrais's story became known throughout Paris. Heads were imbued with tales of magic, sorcery, exorcisms, and pacts with the devil made by La Voisin, Le Vigoureur, and the notorious priest Le Sage; and because human nature is such that belief in the miraculous and the supernatural outweighs reason, the public soon began to accept as fact what Desgrais had said in disgruntlement—that the devil himself was protecting the villains who had sold him their souls. As may be imagined, Desgrais's story became fancifully embellished; and an account of it, complete with a woodcut depicting a ghastly devil sinking into the ground before a terrified Desgrais, was printed and sold on every corner. This was enough to terrorize the public and even to destroy the courage of the police, who now fearfully wandered along the streets at night trembling, hung with amulets and soaked in holy water.

Argenson saw that the efforts of the *Chambre Ardente* were ineffective, and he appealed to the King to appoint a new court that would have even more extensive powers to track down and punish criminals. The King, convinced that he had already vested too much power in the *Chambre Ardente* and horrified at the countless executions the bloodthirsty La Régnie had imposed, flatly dismissed the suggestion. Another means of stimulating the King's interest in the matter was selected.

In La Maintenon's apartment, where the King was in the habit of spending the afternoons and also of working late into the night with his ministers, a poem was presented to him in the name of imperiled lovers, complaining that the demands of gallantry that required them to bestow gifts upon their mistresses now entailed risking their lives. While it was at once an honor and a pleasure to shed blood for the beloved in knightly combat, it was altogether something else to confront the treacherous assailant against whom arms were no defense. Louis, the lodestar of love and gallantry, was called upon to use his resplendence to dissipate the darkness of night and uncover the black mystery within it. Let the godlike hero, who had shattered all his enemies, draw his victoriously flashing sword, and as Hercules struck down the Lernaean Hydra, or Theseus the Minotaur, let him strike down the dangerous monster that was consuming love's raptures and turning joy into deepest grief and inconsolable mourning.

As serious as the subject was, this poem was not lacking in witty twists, especially in the passages that described how lovers trembled while sneaking to their beloveds and how their fear nipped in the bud the pleasures to be found in love and gallantry. It need only be added that since the poem concluded with a grandiloquent panegyric to Louis XIV, the King read it with visible satisfaction. This done, he quickly turned to La Maintenon, though without lifting his eyes from the paper, and once more read the poem, this time out loud; and then, with a charming smile, he asked her what she felt about the plea of these endangered lovers. La Maintenon, true to her serious cast of mind with its tinge of piety, replied that those who travel clandestine and forbidden paths do not deserve any special protection but that vile criminals certainly merited being exterminated through special measures. The King, dissatisfied with this inconclusive answer, folded the paper and was about to return to the Secretary of State, who was working in the next room, when his eyes happened to fall on Mademoiselle de Scudéri, who had just taken her place in a small armchair close to La Maintenon. He approached her; the pleasant smile, which had first played about his mouth and cheeks and had then disappeared, regained the upper hand. Standing directly in front of Mademoiselle and unfolding the poem once more, he said gently, "The Marquise does not want to know about the gallantries of our lovelorn gentlemen, and her responses to my question evade me in ways that are nothing short of forbidden. But you, Mademoiselle, what is your opinion of this poetic petition?"

Mademoiselle de Scudéri rose respectfully from her armchair; a fleeting blush like the red of the sunset passed across the pale cheeks of the dignified old lady. She curtsied slightly and, her eyes downcast, said:

"Un amant qui craint les voleurs,
n'est point digne d'amour."

[A lover who is afraid of thieves
Is not at all worthy of love.]

The king, completely astonished by the spirit of chivalry in these few words, which reduced to rubble the endless tirades contained in the poem, exclaimed with flashing eyes, "By Saint Denis, you are right, Mademoiselle! Cowardice shall not be protected through any blind measures which at once affect the innocent and the guilty; let Argenson and La Régnie do their best!"

La Martinière described all of the present horrors in the most vivid colors when, next morning, she told her mistress about what had happened the previous night and tremblingly and timorously gave her the mysterious casket. Both she and Baptiste, who stood in the corner pale with anxiety and nervousness, twisting his nightcap in his hand, barely able to speak, implored Mademoiselle in the most melancholy terms, and in the name of all the saints to exercise every possible precaution in opening the little casket. La Scudéri, weighing and testing the locked enigma in her hands, said with a smile: "You're both seeing ghosts! That I am not rich, and that there is no treasure here worth murder the accursed assassins know as well as you or I, for as you yourselves tell me, they spy out the innermost secrets of houses. You think that my life is endangered? Who can have any interest in the death of a woman of seventy-three, who never harmed anyone but the villains and rioters in her novels; who turns out mediocre verse that can arouse the envy of no one; who will leave behind nothing but the finery of an old spinster who occasionally went to court, and a few dozen well-bound books with gilt edges! And as for you, Martinière, regardless of how frighteningly you describe the stranger, I cannot believe that he had an evil purpose in mind. So then—"

Martinière recoiled three paces; Baptiste sank half to his knees with a hollow "Ah!" as Mademoiselle pressed a projecting steel knob that caused the lid to spring open with a bang.

How astonished Mademoiselle was to see a pair of golden bracelets richly set with jewels and a matching necklace sparkling within the casket! She took the jewelry out, and while praising the exquisite craftsmanship of the necklace as La Martinière eyed the valuable bracelets, she repeatedly exclaimed that not even the vain La Montespan had jewelry such as this. "But what is the meaning of all this?" asked La Scudéri. In that instant she noticed a small folded sheet of paper at the bottom of the casket. She rightly hoped to find in it the solution to the mystery. She had barely read the note when it fell from her trembling hands. She cast an eloquent glance to heaven and sank back in her armchair, as if half swooning. Frightened, La Martinière and Baptiste sprang to her side. "Oh," La Scudéri cried with a voice half choked with tears. "Oh, the insult, oh, the terrible shame! Must I suffer this kind of thing in my old age? Have I been guilty of a foolish, wanton act like some giddy young thing? O God, are words uttered half in jest capable of being so horribly interpreted? And am I, who have remained virtuous and pious since childhood, to be accused to being involved in crime and of being in league with the devil?" Mademoiselle put her handkerchief to her eyes and wept and sobbed bitterly so that La Martinière and Baptiste, completely bewildered and distressed, did not know how to help their good mistress in her profound distress.

La Martinière picked up the fateful note from the floor. It read:

> Un amant qui craint les voleurs,
> n'est point digne d'amour.

Your ingenious wit, honored lady, has saved us—we who exercise the right of the strong over the weak and the cowardly and acquire valuables that were otherwise to be squandered disgracefully—from great persecution. Kindly accept these jewels as a token of our gratitude. They are the most expensive that we have picked up in a long time, though you, worthy lady, should be adorned with jewelry that is much finer. We beseech you not to withdraw your friendship and your gracious remembrance from us.

The Invisibles

"Is it possible," Mademoiselle de Scudéri cried after she had somewhat recovered, "is it possible for shameless insolence and wicked mockery to be carried to such an extreme?"

The sun shone brightly through the curtains of brilliant red silk, and so the gems lying on the table near the open casket blazed with a scarlet gleam. Looking at them, Mademoiselle covered her face in abhorrence and ordered La Martinière immediately to remove the fearsome jewelry to which the blood of murdered men was clinging. La Martinière, after locking the bracelets and necklace in the casket, suggested that the wisest thing to do would be to turn the jewels over to the minister of police and confide in him everything about the terrifying visit of the young man who had delivered the casket.

Mademoiselle de Scudéri rose, slowly and silently paced back and forth in the room, as if only now reflecting upon what should be done. Then she ordered Baptiste to fetch her sedan chair and La Martinière to dress her because she was going to see the Marquise de Maintenon. She had herself carried to the Marquise's apartment at precisely the hour when she knew the Marquise would be alone. She took the casket of jewels with her.

The Marquise was very surprised to see Mademoiselle de Scudéri, usually—despite her age—the personification of dignity and grace and charm, entering pale, disheveled, and with tottering step. "In heaven's name, what has happened to you?" she cried to the poor, frightened lady who, completely beside herself and barely able to stand on her feet, moved as quickly as she could toward the armchair the Marquise pushed towards her. Finally, able to speak again, Mademoiselle told about the insult, still festering within her, which had resulted from the innocent joke with which she had responded to the petition of the imperiled lovers.

After hearing the rest of the story bit by bit, the Marquise expressed the feeling that Mademoiselle de Scudéri was making far too much of the strange experience and that the derision of the nefarious rabble could never touch a mind as pious and noble as hers; and she finally asked to see the jewelry. Mademoiselle de Scudéri handed the open casket to her, and the Marquise could not restrain a loud exclamation of wonderment when she saw the valuable jewelry. She took out the necklace and the bracelets and carried them to the window where she let the sun reflect on the jewels and then held the intricate gold work very close to her eyes so that she could examine the exquisite workmanship with which every little link in the elaborate chain was crafted.

Suddenly the Marquise turned to Mademoiselle and cried: "Do you realize, Mademoiselle, that these bracelets and this necklace could have been crafted by none other than René Cardillac?"

René Cardillac was at that time the most skillful goldsmith in Paris, one of the most talented and extraordinary men of his day. Of something less than medium height, but broad shouldered and of powerful muscular physique, Cardillac, though well over fifty, still possessed the strength and coordination of a young man; and his thick, curly red hair and heavy-set, glistening face bore witness to his exceptional strength. If Cardillac's reputation throughout Paris had been other than that of a most upright and honorable, altruistic, candid, and guileless man, always prepared to help, the very peculiar expression in his small, deep-set, and flashing green eyes might have resulted in his being suspected of hidden malice and viciousness.

As noted, Cardillac was the most skillful craftsman in his field, not only in Paris, but perhaps anywhere at that time. Intimately acquainted with the nature of precious stones, he knew how to treat and set them so that jewelry which originally was without distinction left his workshop in brilliant glory. Every commission was accepted with burning eagerness, and he would set a price so modest that it seemed out of all proportion to the labor involved. Then the work gave him no peace. Day and night he could be heard hammering in his workshop; and often, when the work was almost completed, he would suddenly conceive a dislike for the design and begin to question the daintiness of the setting or of some little link—reason enough for him to throw the entire piece back into the melting pot to begin again. So it was that every piece turned out was a flawless and matchless masterpiece that astounded the patron. But it was therefore almost impossible to regain the completed work from him. Resorting to a thousand pretexts, he would put the customer off week after week, month after month. Offering to pay him double for the work was futile; he would not take a louis more than the price contracted for. When he was finally forced to give up the jewelry, he could not conceal all the signs of profound regret and inner rage that boiled within him. If he had to deliver a piece of singular importance and value, probably worth several thousands because of the costliness of the gems and the superb intricacy of the craftsmanship, he would, as if distracted, rampage madly, cursing his work and everything around him. But as soon as someone would run after him, calling loudly, "René Cardillac, wouldn't you like to make a lovely necklace for my fiancée?—bracelets for my mistress?" and so on, he would freeze in his tracks, look at the customer with his little glittering eyes, and rubbing his hands together ask, "What have you got?" Then the customer would, perhaps, produce a small jewel box and say, "Here are some jewels, nothing much, ordinary things, but in your hands—" Cardillac would not let him finish, but would snatch the jewel box from his hands, take out the jewels, which were really not worth very much, hold them up to the light and cry in delight, "Ha, ha! Ordinary stuff? Not at all! Pretty stones—superb stones—just let me work on them! And if a handful of louis are of little concern to you, I'll add a few little gems that will sparkle in your eyes like the very sun itself." To which the other would reply, "I'll leave it to you, Meister René, and I'll pay whatever you wish." Regardless of whether he was a rich townsman or a prominent gentleman of the court, Cardillac would fling his arms violently around his neck and hug him and kiss him and tell him that he was absolutely happy again and that the work would by finished in a week. He would dash home exuberantly, rush into the workshop, and begin hammering away; and in a week he would have produced a masterpiece. But no sooner would the customer joyfully come to pay the petty sum asked, than Cardillac would become peevish, rude, and obstinate. "But Meister Cardillac, remember that my wedding is tomorrow." "What do I care about your wedding? Come again in two weeks." "The jewelry is ready, here is the money, I must have it." And *I* tell you that I still have to make a lot of changes in it and I can't let you have it today." "And *I* tell you that I wish to pay you double your price, but that if you don't give me the jewelry right now, I will immediately return with Argenson's faithful henchmen." "Then may Satan torture you with a hundred glowing pincers and hang a handerkerchief on the necklace so that it strangles your bride!" With that, Cardillac would ram the jewelry into the bridegroom's breast pocket, seize him by the arm, and throw him out of the door so roughly that he would tumble down the stairs. Then he would lean out of the window and laugh like the devil at the sight of the poor young man limping out of the house, a handkerchief to his bloody nose.

For some inexplicable reason, Cardillac would often, after enthusiastically accepting a commission, suddenly implore the customer, while evincing signs of deep agitation, violently protesting, sobbing, crying, and appealing to the holy Virgin and all the saints, to release him from the work he had undertaken. Many people, highly esteemed by both the King and the public, had vainly offered large sums for even the smallest piece of work by Cardillac. He had thrown himself at the feet of the King and had begged for the favor of being excused from the necessity of working for him. Likewise, he refused to accept any commission from the Marquise de Maintenon; in fact it was with an expression of revulsion and dread that he rejected her proposal that he make a little ring decorated with emblems of the arts, which she intended to present to Racine.

Accordingly, Marquise de Maintenon now said, "I wager that if I send for Cardillac to find out for whom he made this jewelry he would refuse to come here because he would probably fear that I had some commission in mind, and he is determined not to work for me. Although he seems of late to be somewhat less obdurate, according to what I have heard, he is now working more assiduously than ever before and is delivering his work on the spot, though still regretfully and with averted face."

Mademoiselle de Scudéri, very concerned that the jewelry be returned to its rightful owner quickly, if this was at all possible, suggested that Meister Eccentric might consent to come if it were immediately made clear to him that what was sought from him was not a commission but his opinion regarding certain jewels. The Marquise agreed. Cardillac was sent for, and as if he had already been on the way, he very shortly entered the room.

He seemed to be startled when he saw Mademoiselle de Scudéri, and like someone who forgets the demands of etiquette because he is surprised by the totally unexpected, he first bowed deeply and respectfully to the venerable lady, and only then turned to the Marquise. Pointing to the jewelry that now sparkled on the dark green tablecloth, she abruptly asked him if it were his work. Cardillac hardly glanced at it, but staring the Marquise straight in the face, he quickly packed the necklace and the bracelets into the casket that was beside them and pushed it vehemently away from him; and with an ugly smile suffusing his red face, he said:

"Indeed, Madame Marquise, one must be very poorly acquainted with René Cardillac's work to believe for an instant that any other goldsmith in the world was capable of producing such jewelry. Of course it is my work."

"Well, then tell us, for whom did you make it?" continued the Marquise.

"For no one but myself," Cardillac replied. "Yes," he continued, as both the Marquise and Mademoiselle de Scudéri looked at him in amazement, the former full of mistrust, the latter full of fearful expectation to know what sort of turn the affair would now take. "Yes, you may find it strange, Madame Marquise, but that's how it is. For no reason other than to create something beautiful, I gathered my finest stones and, simply for the sheer joy of it, worked on them more diligently and carefully than ever before. A short time ago the jewels vanished from my workshop in some inexplicable way."

"Heaven be praised," cried Mademoiselle de Scudéri, her eyes sparkling with joy; and she jumped from her armchair as quickly and nimbly as a young girl, walked to Cardillac, and placed both hands on his shoulders saying: "Meister René, take back, take back the property the infamous thieves stole from you." Then she related in detail how she had come to possess the jewels.

Cardillac heard it all in silence and with downcast eyes, only now and then uttering an indistinct "Um. So! Ah! Aha!"—now clasping his hands behind his back, now gently stroking his chin and cheeks. When Mademoiselle de Scudéri had finished her story, Cardillac appeared to be struggling with some new idea that had just struck him and that confronted him with a difficult decision. He rubbed his forehead, he sighed, he put his hand over his eyes as if to check a welling of tears. Finally he seized the casket Mademoiselle de Scudéri was offering him, sank slowly on one knee and said, "Destiny decreed that these jewels be yours, noble and worthy lady. Yes, now I realize for the first time that it was of you I thought, for you that I did my work. Do not disdain to accept them nor to wear them. They are among the best things I have made for a long time."

"Oh, oh," Mademoiselle de Scudéri replied in merry playfulness. "What can you be thinking of, Meister René? Would it be right for me at my age to deck myself out with glittering gems? And why should you bestow such an enormously expensive gift upon me? Come, come, Meister René, if I were as beautiful as the Marquise de Fontange and as wealthy, I would not, in fact, let these jewels slip through my hands; but what would these withered arms, this veiled neck offer such glittering gems?"

Cardillac had risen, meanwhile, and speaking as though distracted, with wild eyes, still holding out the casket to Mademoiselle de Scudéri, he said, "Have pity on me, Mademoiselle, and take the jewels. You would not believe how deep a respect for your virtue and your rare qualities I carry in my heart! Accept this meager gift, then, simply as my attempt to express my profound admiration."

But as Mademoiselle de Scudéri still hesitated, the Marquise took the casket from Cardillac's hands, saying, "In the name of heaven, Mademoiselle, you are always talking about your great age, but what have you and I to do with the years and their burdens! Aren't you behaving just like a bashful young thing who longs for the sweet, forbidden fruit that is offered if only she could have it without stretching out hand or finger? Do not reject good Meister René, who freely offers you as a gift what thousands of others cannot obtain despite all of their gold and prayers and entreaties."

The Marquise had, meanwhile, forced the casket on Mademoiselle de Scudéri; and now Cardillac fell to his knees, kissed Mademoiselle's skirt, her hand—groaned, sighed, wept, sobbed, sprang up, ran out like a madman, bowling over chairs and tables in his frenzy, so that china and glasses clattered.

Greatly alarmed, Mademoiselle de Scudéri cried, "May all the saints protect me, what's the matter with the man?" But the Marquise, with an unwonted exuberance born of her gaiety, laughed merrily and said, "There it is, Mademoiselle. Meister René is mortally in love with you and is beginning, according to the proper and ancient custom of true gallantry, to lay siege to your heart with expensive gifts." The Marquise pushed the joke still further, admonishing Mademoiselle not to be too cruel towards her despairing lover; and Mademoiselle, giving full rein to her own inherent spiritedness, was carried away by a flood of witty ideas. She suggested that if this were the true picture of things, she would be unable to avoid being conquered; she would offer the world the unique spectacle of a seventy-three-year-old goldsmith's bride of impeccable nobility. La Maintenon offered to weave the bridal wreath and to instruct her in the duties of a good housewife, since such a young snip of a girl could not, of course, be expected to know much about such things.

When Mademoiselle de Scudéri finally picked up the jewel box and rose to leave the Marquise, she became very serious again, despite all of the spirited raillery. "Madame Marquise," she said, "I will never be able to wear this jewelry. However, come what may, it was once in the hands of those devilish rogues who commit robbery and murder with the audacity of Satan himself, probably even in accursed league with him. I shudder at the sight of the blood that seems to cling to the stones. And also, I must confess, I find even Cardillac's behavior peculiarly disturbing and terrifying. I cannot escape a dark premonition that there is concealed behind all of this some hideous and repulsive secret, but when I consider the matter rationally, in every detail, I still have not the slightest inkling what this secret might be, nor how the honest and upright Meister René, the model of a decent and pious citizen, could be involved in anything that is evil and damnable. But of one thing I am certain—that I will never dare to wear the jewels."

The Marquise felt that this was carrying scruples too far; but when Mademoiselle de Scudéri asked her what her conscience would dictate were their places reversed, the Marquise replied, "I would sooner throw the jewelry into the Seine than ever wear it."

The encounter with Meister René lead Mademoiselle de Scudéri to compose some charming verses, which she read to the King the next evening in La Maintenon's apartment. And it is probable that, conquering her ominous presentiment in regard to Meister René, she painted with vivid colors an amusing picture of the seventy-three-year-old goldsmith's bride of ancient and impeccable nobility. At any rate, the King laughed heartily and declared that Boileau Despréaux had met his master, which led to La Scudéri's poem being regarded as the wittiest ever written.

Several months had passed when Mademoiselle de Scudéri happened to be driving over the Pont-Neuf in the Duchesse de Montansier's glass coach. The appearance of these delicate coaches was so novel that they invariably attracted a crowd of the curious wherever they appeared in the street. Thus it was that a crowd of gaping rabble engulfed La Montansier's glass coach on the Pont-Neuf, almost forcing the horses to halt. Suddenly Mademoiselle de Scudéri, hearing an outburst of cursing and swearing, saw a man fighting his way through the densest part of the crowd with his fists and elbows. As he drew nearer, she met the piercing gaze of his eyes and observed the young man's deathly pale and anguished face. His eyes unwaveringly upon her, he fought his way toward her with elbows and fists until he reached the door of the coach, which he flung open with violent haste; he threw a note into Mademoiselle de Scudéri's lap and disappeared even as he had come, in a flurry of punching and elbowing that he gave and received. As soon as the man appeared at the coach door, La Martinière, who was sitting beside Mademoiselle de Scudéri, screamed out in terror and sank unconscious into the cushions. In vain Mademoiselle de Scudéri tugged the cord and called out to the coachman; he, as if driven by an evil spirit, whipped up the horses, who, spraying foam from their mouths, reared and kicked their hoofs and finally thundered across the bridge at a fast trot. Mademoiselle de Scudéri poured the contents of her bottle of smelling salts over the unconscious woman, who at last opened her eyes and, trembling and shaking and clinging convulsively to her mistress, fear and shock reflected in her pale face, moaned with effort, "In the name of the blessed Virgin, what did that terrible man want? He is the one—yes, the one who brought you the casket on that dreadful night!"

Mademoiselle de Scudéri calmed the poor woman, assuring her that nothing harmful had happened, and that the sensible thing to do would be to find out what the note contained. She unfolded the paper and found these words:

> A malicious fate, which you could avert, forces me into an abyss. I beseech you as a son would a mother from whom he cannot part, whom he loves with childish fervor, to return the necklace and bracelets that you received from me to Meister René Cardillac under any pretext—to have them im-

proved—altered—something of the sort. Your well-being, your
very life depends upon it. If you have not done this by the
day after tomorrow, I will force my way into your house and
kill myself before your eyes!

"Now it is certain," Mademoiselle de Scudéri said when she had
read this, "that this mysterious stranger, even if he does belong to
the band of accursed thieves and murderers, intends no evil against
me. Perhaps, if he had succeeded in speaking to me that night,
who knows but that I might have learned of strange events and
dark mysteries about which I now have not the slightest inkling
and for which I vainly search in my soul. Be that as it may, I will
do as the letter commands, even if it is only to be rid of these
accursed jewels, which seem to me like a hellish charm of the Devil
himself. Cardillac, true to his old habits, will not let them out of
his hands so easily again."

Mademoiselle de Scudéri intended to return the jewelry to the
goldsmith the very next day. But somehow it seemed as if all the
wits in Paris had conspired to assail Mademoiselle that morning
with their verses, plays, and anecdotes. La Chapelle had barely
finished a scene from a tragedy, with the sly assurance that he
would outdo Racine, when Racine himself entered and shattered
him with an elevated tirade about some king or other. Then, to
escape from an endless disquisition on the colonnade of the Louvre, which Dr. Perrault, the architect, was inflicting upon him,
Boileau launched his meteor and sent it soaring into the black sky
of tragedy.

It was high noon by now, and Mademoiselle had an appointment to visit the Duchesse de Montansier; thus the visit to Meister
René Cardillac was postponed until the next morning. Mademoiselle de Scudéri, however, was tormented by a feeling of extraordinary restlessness. The young man appeared continually before
her eyes, and from deep within her a dim recollection sought to
rouse itself as though she had seen this face, these features before.
Her light sleep was disturbed by frightening dreams in which it
seemed that her failure to grasp the hand the unhappy wretch had
stretched out to her as he sank into the abyss had been rash, even
criminal; indeed, as if it had been within her power to prevent
some terrible disaster, some hellish crime! As soon as the sun rose

she had herself dressed and set off for the goldsmith's, taking the jewel box with her.

Masses of people were streaming into the rue Nicaise, where Cardillac lived, gathering outside his door, screaming, ranting, raving, trying to storm their way in and prevented from doing so only by the mounted police who surrounded the house. From the midst of the frantic confusion angry voices shouted, "Tear him to pieces, pulverize the damned murderer!" Finally Desgrais appeared with a sizable force of his men, who made a passage for him through the thick crowd. The door of the house sprang open, and a man weighed down with chains was brought out and dragged off, accompanied by the most hideous curses of the enraged mob. No sooner had Mademoiselle de Scudéri, half dead from shock and terrible forebodings, witnessed this than a shrill cry of distress pierced her ears. "Forward! Keep moving!" she cried, quite beside herself, to her coachman, who scattered the dense crowd with a skillful and quick turn and pulled up directly in front of Cardillac's door. Here Mademoiselle de Scudéri saw Desgrais and, at his feet, a young girl as lovely as day, half naked, her hair hanging freely, an expression of wild anxiety and inconsolable despair on her face, who was clinging to his knees and crying in a voice of heartrending despair, "He is innocent! He is innocent!" The efforts of Desgrais and his men to tear her away and lift her from the ground were futile. Finally a powerful brute grabbed her with his great hands and tore her forcefully from Desgrais, then clumsily stumbled and dropped the girl, who rolled down the stone steps and lay without a whimper in the street, as if dead.

Mademoiselle de Scudéri could restrain herself no longer. "In the name of Christ, what has happened? What is going on here?" she cried, quickly opening the coach door and stepping out.

The crowd respectfully made way for the worthy lady, who saw that a few compassionate women had picked the girl up and placed her on the step and were rubbing her forehead with spirits. She approached Desgrais and emphatically repeated her question.

"Something terrible has happened," Desgrais said. "René Cardillac was found stabbed to death this morning. His associate, Olivier Brusson, is the murderer. He has just been taken away to prison."

"And the girl?" cried Mademoiselle de Scudéri.

"She is Cardillac's daughter, Madelon," answered Desgrais. "The vile man was her lover. Now she weeps and wails over and over again that he is innocent. She really knows about the deed, and I must also have her taken away to the Conciergerie." As he said this, Desgrais glanced at the girl so slyly and maliciously that Mademoiselle de Scudéri trembled. The girl was beginning to breathe softly now; but unable to make a sound or to move, she lay there with closed eyes, so that no one knew what to do, whether to carry her into the house or to remain with her until she regained consciousness. With tears of sympathy in her eyes, Mademoiselle de Scudéri looked at the innocent angel, and she felt horror for Desgrais and his men. Then the sound of muffled footsteps could be heard on the stairs—Cardillac's corpse was being carried down. Quickly making a decision, Mademoiselle de Scudéri cried in a loud voice, "I am taking the girl with me. You take care of the rest, Desgrais!" A low murmur of approval swept through the crowd. The women lifted the girl up; everyone pressed toward her; a hundred hands came to her aid, and as though floating through the air, she was carried to the coach while blessings from all showered down upon the worthy lady who had snatched an innocent from the bloodthirsty tribunal. The efforts of Seron, the most famous doctor in Paris, were finally successful in bringing Madelon back to consciousness after she had lain in a profound coma for hours. What the physician had begun, Mademoiselle de Scudéri completed by kindling some gentle rays of hope in Madelon's soul until a violent outburst of tears poured from her eyes and brought relief. Then she was able to tell everything that had happened, although she was from time to time overcome by her poignant grief and her words stuck in her throat.

She had been awakened about midnight by a faint knocking at the door of her room and had heard Olivier's voice entreating her to get up at once because her father was dying. Startled, she sprang from her bed and opened the door. Olivier, pale, his face contorted, dripping with sweat, a light in his hand, staggered to the workshop, she following him. There her father lay struggling with death, eyes staring blankly, a death rattle in his throat. Wailing, she rushed toward him, and only then noticed bloodstains on his shirt. Olivier gently drew her away and then busied himself with a wound in the left side of her father's chest, washing it with balsam and bandaging it. While this was taking place, the father regained consciousness; the death rattle ceased; he looked tenderly at Madelon, then at Olivier, took her hand, and placing it in Olivier's, fervently pressed them together. Both Olivier and she had fallen on their knees at her father's bed when he sat up with a piercing cry, but immediately sank back, sighed deeply, and died. Then they both wept and wailed loudly. Olivier told her that he had, at his master's request, accompanied him on his walk in the night; that he had been murdered in his presence, and that he had carried home the heavy man, whose injury he did not think was fatal, with the greatest difficulty. At daybreak the others occupying the house, who had heard the din, the weeping, and the lamenting during the night, had come upstairs and found them still kneeling inconsolably by her father's corpse. Then an uproar broke out, the police forced their way in, and Olivier was dragged off to prison as his master's murderer. Madelon now added the most touching account of her beloved Olivier's virtue, piety, and faithfulness. She told how he had respected his master as if he had been his own father, and how this affection was fully reciprocated, her father choosing him for his son-in-law despite his poverty, because his skill and fidelity were equal to his nobility. Madelon told all this with the greatest sincerity, and concluded that if Olivier had thrust the dagger into her father's breast in her presence she would more easily have believed it to be an illusion created by Satan than to have believed that Olivier was capable of such a terrible and gruesome crime.

Mademoiselle de Scudéri, most deeply touched by the unspeakable suffering of Madelon and completely disposed to believe in the innocence of poor Olivier, conducted inquiries and confirmed everything Madelon had said about the personal relationship between the master and his journeyman. The occupants of the house and the neighbors unanimously praised Olivier as the model of virtuous, devout, faithful, and industrious behavior, not one having anything bad to say about him; and yet, when the atrocious deed was alluded to, everyone shrugged his shoulders and thought that there was something incomprehensible about that.

Brought before the *Chambre Ardente,* Olivier, as Mademoiselle de Scudéri learned, denied the deed of which he was accused with the utmost steadfastness and candor, maintaining that his master had been attacked and struck down in the street in his presence, that he had carried him back to his home while he was still alive, where he very soon died. This also agreed with Madelon's account.

Mademoiselle de Scudéri had the most minute details of the terrible event repeated over and over again. She carefully sought to determine whether there had been any dispute between master and journeyman, whether Olivier was not sometimes afflicted by sudden violent fits that often affect even the most good-natured people like a blind madness and cause them to commit acts quite involuntarily. But the more she heard Madelon enthusiastically describing the serene domestic happiness in which these three people lived, bound by the most sincere affection, the more did every trace of suspicion against Olivier, who was now on trial for his life, disappear. Meticulously weighing all the circumstances, and proceeding on the assumption that Olivier, despite all that so loudly spoke for his innocence, was nevertheless Cardillac's murderer, Mademoiselle de Scudéri could not discover any possible motive for the horrible deed, which in any case could do nothing but shatter Olivier's happiness.

"He is poor, but skillful. He succeeded in winning the affection of the most famous of all master goldsmiths. He loves the daughter. The master approved of this love. Happiness and prosperity for all his life awaited him. But supposing that—only God knows how—he was overcome by anger and actually committed this murderous attack upon his benefactor, his father, what diabolical hypocrisy would have been required for Olivier to behave as he had behaved after the murder!" Firmly convinced of Olivier's innocence, Mademoiselle de Scudéri determined to save the innocent young man at any cost.

Before appealing for clemency to the King himself, it seemed to her that it would be best to approach President La Régnie and call to his attention all the facts that indicated Olivier's innocence, and thereby arouse in him a conviction of the accused's innocence, which he might then communicate to the judges.

La Régnie received Mademoiselle de Scudérie with all the respect that the worthy, who are highly honored by the King himself, might expect. He listened in silence to everything she had to say concerning the terrible event and Olivier's life and character, but the only indication that her words were not falling on completely deaf ears was a faint and almost malicious smile with which he heard her protestations and tearful admonitions that, like every judge, he should not be the enemy of the accused but be ready to consider any evidence in his behalf. When Mademoiselle de Scudéri was at last utterly exhausted and had dried her tears and grown silent, La Régnie began:

"It does credit to the kindness of your heart, Mademoiselle, that you, touched by the tears of a young girl in love, believe everything she tells you and that, in fact, you find the terrible crime completely inconceivable; but it is different for the judge, who is accustomed to ripping the mask from insolent hypocrisy. It is not incumbent upon me to reveal the course of a criminal trial to anyone who chooses to inquire. Mademoiselle, I do my duty, and I concern myself little with world opinion. Let those who commit evil tremble before the *Chambre Ardente,* which knows no punishment other than blood and fire. But, Mademoiselle de Scudéri, I do not wish you to look upon me as a monster of severity and cruelty; therefore, permit me to demonstrate in a few words the bloodguilt of this young scoundrel upon whom, heaven be praised, vengeance has fallen. Your acute intelligence will then repudiate the generosity that does you honor but which would be unsuitable in me.

"Well, then: René Cardillac was found stabbed to death in the morning. Nobody is with him except his journeyman, Olivier Brusson, and the daughter. In Olivier's room there is found, among other things, a dagger covered with fresh blood that exactly fits into the wound. Olivier says 'Cardillac was struck down before my eyes during the night.' 'Was the intention to rob him?' 'I do not know.' 'You were walking with him and you were not able to drive off the murderer, to seize him, to call for help?' 'The master was walking fifteen, probably twenty paces in front of me; I was following him.' 'Why in the world were you so far behind him?' 'The master wished it so.' 'What was Meister Cardillac doing in the street so late at night?' 'That I cannot say.' 'But he ordinarily never left the house after nine o'clock, did he?' At this point Olivier hesitates, becomes confused, sighs, cries, protests by everything holy that Cardillac did go out that night and met death in the street. Now, Mademoiselle, note this carefully. It has been established with complete certainty that Cardillac did not leave his house that night; consequently, Olivier's assertion that he went out with him is a barefaced lie. The front door of the house is fitted with a heavy lock that makes a piercing noise when it is opened and shut; further, the door creaks and groans on its hinges, making a noise that, as experiments have proved, even reaches to the top story of the house. Now, on the ground floor, that is to say, next to the front door, there lives old Meister Claude Patru with his housekeeper, a person almost eighty years of age, but still vigorous and active. Both of them heard Cardillac come downstairs, according to his habit, at precisely nine o'clock, lock and bolt the door with a great deal of noise, go upstairs again, read aloud the evening prayer, and then, as could be presumed from the banging of the doors, go into his bedroom. Meister Claude, like many old people, suffers from insomnia. And on that night he could not close an eye; therefore, at about nine-thirty the housekeeper, crossing the entrance hall, struck a light in the kitchen and sat down at the table with Meister Claude and read aloud from an ancient chronicle while the old man mused, sometimes sitting in his armchair, sometimes walking slowly back and forth in the room, trying to invite weariness and sleep. Everything was quiet until after midnight. Then they heard quick steps overhead, a hard fall as though something heavy had dropped to the floor, and immediately afterwards a muffled groaning. They were both filled with a strange anxiety and dread. The horror of the heinous deed that had just been committed swept over them. With daybreak, the light revealed what had been committed in the dark."

"But in the name of all the saints," Mademoiselle de Scudéri broke in, "after considering everything that I told you at such length, can you think of any motive for this diabolical deed?"

"Hm," La Régnie replied. "Cardillac was not poor—he possessed splendid jewels."

"But would it not all have reverted, would it not have reverted to the daughter?" Mademoiselle de Scudéri continued. "You forget that Olivier was to become Cardillac's son-in-law."

"Perhaps he was forced to share, even to murder for others," La Régnie said.

"Share, murder for others?" Mademoiselle de Scudéri asked in complete astonishment.

"You must know, Mademoiselle," La Régnie continued, "that if Olivier's crime were not connected with the thickly veiled mystery that has till now so broodingly lain over Paris, his blood would long ago have flowed in the Place de la Grève. Olivier is obviously a member of that accursed band that carries out its crimes with perfect impunity, in contempt of all scrutiny and all the investigative efforts expended. Cardillac's wound is identical with those inflicted on all the people who have been murdered and robbed in the streets and in the houses. Most conclusively, since the arrest of Olivier Brusson, all the murders and robberies have ceased. The streets are as secure at night as they are during the day, proof enough that Olivier was perhaps the leader of the band of murderers. He has not yet confessed, but there are ways to make one talk against one's will."

"And Madelon," cried Mademoiselle de Scudéri, "Madelon, the true innocent dove?"

"Ah," La Régnie said with a venomous smile. "Ah, who can assure me that she was not involved in the plot? What does she feel for her father? Her tears are reserved for the murderer."

"What are you saying?" cried Mademoiselle de Scudéri. "It is impossible. Not for her father! That girl!"

"Oh," La Régnie continued, "just remember the Brinvilliers. You must forgive me if I must soon tear your protégée away from you and have her thrown into the Conciergerie."

Mademoiselle de Scudéri shuddered at this dreadful suspicion. It seemed to her that neither truth nor virtue existed for this terrible man, as if he detected murder and bloodguilt in man's deepest and most hidden thoughts. She rose. "Be humane!" was all that she could say as she left, breathing with difficulty because of her distress. As she was about to descend the stairs, to which the President had accompanied her with ceremonious courtesy, a strange idea came to her—she herself knew not how. "May I be allowed to see this unfortunate Olivier Brusson?" she asked the President, turning around quickly. He scrutinized her thoughtfully, then his face became distorted with the repulsive smile characteristic of him.

"No doubt," he said, "no doubt you have in mind, my worthy Mademoiselle, to investigate Olivier's guilt or innocence for yourself because you have more faith in your feelings and in your inner voice than you have in what has taken place before our eyes. If you are not averse to the dismal sanctum of crime, if you are not repelled by the sight of depravity in all its stages, the gates of the Conciergerie shall be opened to you in two hours. This Olivier whose fate arouses your sympathy will be brought before you."

In truth, Mademoiselle de Scudéri was incapable of convincing herself of the young man's guilt. Everything spoke against him; indeed, confronted by the evidence at hand, no judge in the world would have acted differently from La Régnie. Yet the picture of domestic bliss that Madelon had so vividly painted for her outshone all evil suspicion, so that she preferred to accept the existence of an inscrutable mystery rather than believe something against which her entire inner being revolted. It was her intention to hear Olivier relate again all that had taken place on that fateful night, and thereby, as far as possible, penetrate into a mystery that judges had been unable to solve because they considered it unworthy of additional investigation.

On her arrival at the Conciergerie, Mademoiselle de Scudéri was taken into a large, well-lighted room. Soon she heard the clanking of chains, and Olivier Brusson was brought in. But as soon as he appeared in the doorway Mademoiselle de Scudéri fainted. When she regained consciousness, Olivier was gone. She vehemently demanded that she be taken to her carriage. She would not for another instant remain in that den of malicious depravity. At the first glance she recognized in Olivier Brusson the young man who had thrown a note into her carriage on the Pont-Neuf, and who had brought her the casket that contained the jewels. Now all doubt was gone; La Régnie's frightful suspicions were completely confirmed. Olivier Brusson was a member of that fearful band of murderers, and he had no doubt also murdered his master! And Madelon? Deluded by her emotions more bitterly than ever before in her life, mortally shattered by the power of hell on earth, in whose very existence she had not believed, Mademoiselle de Scudéri despaired of ever again recognizing truth. The terrible suspicion that Madelon might be implicated and share the heinous bloodguilt was given free rein, for it is the nature of the human mind, once a picture has been admitted, to search diligently and find colors with which to heighten it; and so it was that Mademoiselle de Scudéri, weighing all the circumstances of the crime and the most minute details of Madelon's behavior, found a great deal with which to nourish her suspicion. Many things that had previously been regarded as evidence of innocence and purity now became proof of wanton maliciousness and studied hypocrisy. The heartrending lamentations, the tears of anguish, might well have been pressed from her, not by her mortal dread of seeing her sweetheart bleed—no!—but at her own death at the hands of the executioner.

Resolving that she must immediately cast away the serpent feeding in her bosom, she alighted from her carriage. Madelon threw herself at her feet as she entered the room. Her heavenly eyes— there is not an angel of God whose eyes are more truthful—raised, her hands clasped to her heaving breast, she lamented and implored help and consolation. Mademoiselle de Scudéri, controlling herself with difficulty, trying to give the tone of her voice as much gravity and serenity as possible, said, "Go—go—rejoice that the murderer awaits the just punishment for his shameful crime. May the holy Virgin grant that bloodguilt does not burden you, yourself!"

"Oh, then all is lost!" Madelon cried shrilly and fell unconscious to the ground. Mademoiselle de Scudéri, requesting La Martinière to see to the girl, went to another room.

Completely torn apart inwardly, filled with loathing for everything earthly, Mademoiselle de Scudéri desired to depart from a world so infested with diabolical deception. She cursed the destiny that had granted her so many years in which to strengthen her belief in truth and virtue, only, in her old age, to destroy the beautiful picture that had illuminated her life.

As La Martinière was leading the girl out, Mademoiselle de Scudéri heard Madelon sigh softly and lament, "Oh, *she, she* too has been deceived by the cruel ones. Oh, wretched me—poor, miserable Olivier!"

Mademoiselle de Scudéri was pierced to the heart by Madelon's voice and once again deep within the inmost depths of her soul there dawned the feeling that there was a mystery involved and that Olivier was innocent. Beside herself, torn by the most contra-

dictory emotions, Mademoiselle de Scudéri cried out in desperation, "What hellish spirit has entangled me in this horrible affair
that will cost me my life?"

Baptiste entered at this moment, pale and frightened, with the
news that Desgrais was outside. Since the despicable trial of La
Voisin, the appearance of Desgrais in a house had been an absolute precursor of some terrible accusation; hence, Baptiste's terror,
about which Mademoiselle simply asked him with a gentle smile,
"What is the matter, Baptiste? Has the name Scudéri been discovered on La Voisin's list?"

"Oh, in the name of Christ," Baptiste cried, his entire body
trembling, "how can you say such a thing; but Desgrais—the horrible Desgrais is behaving so mysteriously and with such urgency
that it seems as if he can hardly wait to see you!"

"Well, Baptiste," said Mademoiselle de Scudéri, "bring in at once
this man of whom you are so terrified and who does not terrify
me at all."

"President La Régnie," Desgrais said when he had stepped into
the room, "President La Régnie sends me to you with a request
that he would not dare expect to see fulfilled if he did not know
your goodness and your courage and if the last hope of shedding
light upon an atrocious murder did not lie in your hands, and if
you had not already taken part in the terrible trial that is now
keeping the *Chambre Ardente* and all of us in breathless suspense.
Olivier Brusson, since he saw you, is half mad. Once almost ready
to confess, he now swears by Christ and everything sacred that he
is completely innocent of Cardillac's murder, although he wishes
to suffer the death he has deserved. Note, Mademoiselle, that the
last remark clearly suggests that he is guilty of other crimes. But
all efforts to force one more word from him have been in vain.
He entreats and implores us to arrange for him to talk to you. To
you, to you alone, he will confess everything. Mademoiselle, con-
descend to hear Brusson's confession."

"What?" cried Mademoiselle de Scudéri indignantly. "Am I to
become an organ of the tribunal, am I to abuse the trust of this
unfortunate man and bring him to the scaffold? No, Desgrais! Even
if Brusson were an accursed murderer, I could never so deceive
him. I wish to know nothing of his secrets, which would anyway
remain locked in my breast like a holy confession."

"Perhaps," Desgrais answered with a subtle smile, "perhaps, Mademoiselle, you will change your mind after hearing Brusson. Did you not entreat the President himself to be humane? He is being humane by yielding to Brusson's fantastic request and thus making one final attempt to avoid resorting to the torture for which Brusson has long been ripe."

Mademoiselle de Scudéri trembled involuntarily.

"Understand," Desgrais continued, "understand, worthy lady, that no one expects you to return again to those gloomy dungeons that so filled you with horror and loathing. In the still of night Olivier will be brought to your house like a free man. What he says to you will be overheard by no one, though, to be sure, there will be guards in the house; and he may thus freely tell you everything he wishes to confess. I guarantee with my life that you have nothing to fear from that wretched man. He speaks of you with the most profound veneration. He swears that only the grim fate that prevented his seeing you earlier drives him towards his death. Moreover, how much you will tell us of what Brusson confesses to you depends upon you. Can we compel you to do more?"

Mademoiselle de Scudéri stared straight ahead, in deep reflection. It seemed to her that she must obey that higher power that had marked her for the solution of some terrible mystery—as if she could no longer escape the web—in which she had unwittingly become entangled. Making up her mind suddenly, she said with dignity, "God will grant me composure and fortitude. Bring Brusson here. I will speak to him."

As when Brusson had brought the casket, at midnight there was a knock at Mademoiselle de Scudéri's door. Baptiste, who had been alerted to the nocturnal visit, opened the door. An icy shudder leapt through Mademoiselle de Scudéri as she heard from the soft footsteps and the muffled murmur that the guards who had brought Brusson were stationing themselves in the passages of the house. Finally the door of her room quietly opened. Desgrais entered, behind him Olivier Brusson, free of chains and respectfully dressed. "Here," said Desgrais, bowing respectfully, "here is Brusson, worthy lady"; and he left the room.

Brusson sank on both knees before Mademoiselle de Scudéri and raised his folded hands imploringly, a rush of tears streaming from his eyes. Mademoiselle de Scudéri, pale of face and unable to speak, looked down at him. Though his face was distorted by grief and anguish, it radiated true goodness. The longer Mademoiselle allowed her eyes to rest upon his face, the more vivid became her recollection of some person she had loved, but whom she could not see. When her horror left her, she forgot that it was Cardillac's murderer kneeling before her, and speaking in the pleasant tone of serene benevolence that was characteristic of her, she said, "Well, Brusson, what have you to say to me?"

Brusson, still on his knees, sighed deeply with profound melancholy and said, "Oh, noble lady, is there no trace of recollection of me in your mind?"

Mademoiselle de Scudéri, looking at him still more attentively, answered that she certainly recognized in his features a resemblance to someone she had loved and that her ability to overcome her deep repugnance to the murderer and to be able to listen to him quietly was due to this fact. Brusson, heavily wounded by these words, rose quickly to his feet and, looking gloomily at the floor, took a step backwards. Then he asked in a hollow voice, "Have you completely forgotten Ann Guiot? Her son Olivier, the boy whom you often dandled on your knee, it is he who now stands before you."

"Oh, in the name of all saints!" Mademoiselle de Scudéri cried, covering her face with both hands and sinking back into the cushions. There was reason enough for her being so horrified. Ann Guiot, the daughter of an impecunious citizen, had lived with Mademoiselle de Scudéri from her childhood; she had raised her, the dear child, with all affection and loving care. When she grew up, she was courted by a handsome, well-mannered young man named Claude Brusson. Because he was a first-rate watchmaker who was certain to earn a good wage in Paris, and because Ann had fallen completely in love with him, Mademoiselle de Scudéri was not at all hesitant about approving the marriage of her foster daughter. The young couple set up house and lived in serene and happy domesticity, love's bond being tied even more tightly by the birth of a most beautiful boy, the very image of his lovely mother.

Mademoiselle de Scudéri idolized little Olivier, whom she would take from his mother for hours and days at a time so that she could pet and fondle him. Therefore the boy grew attached to her and liked to be with her as much as with his mother. Three years

later, the professional envy of Brusson's fellow craftsmen account-
ing for the diminution in the quantity of work that came his way,
Brusson was barely able to provide for his family. In addition,
there was Brusson's homesickness for his beautiful birthplace, Geneva. And so, despite Mademoiselle de Scudéri's opposition, and
despite her promises of every kind of support, the little family
ultimately moved there. Ann wrote a few times to her foster mother
and then stopped; Mademoiselle de Scudéri imagined that she had
been forgotten in the happiness experienced by the Brussons.

It was now exactly twenty-three years since Brusson had left
Paris for Geneva with his wife and child.

"Oh, horror," Mademoiselle de Scudéri cried when she was
somewhat recovered. "Are you Olivier? My Ann's son? And now?
Like this!"

Quietly and in a composed manner, Olivier replied, "You probably never thought, worthy lady, that the boy whom you dandled
on your knee, whom you gave the sweetest names, having grown
to become a young man, would stand before you accused of a
horrible murder! I am not completely innocent, and the *Chambre
Ardente* can justly charge me with a crime; but, as truly as I wish
to die blessed, even though executed, I am innocent of any bloodguilt. It was not through me, it was not my fault that the unfortunate Cardillac met his death." As he uttered these words Olivier
began to tremble and sway. Silently, Mademoiselle de Scudéri mo-
tioned him to a small chair standing beside him. He slowly sat
down.

"I have had enough time," he went on, "in which to prepare
for this interview with you—which I consider the final favor of a
merciful heaven—and to gain the calm and composure necessary
to tell you the story of my terrible, unique misfortune. Be so compassionate as to hear me out calmly, regardless of how much the
disclosure of a secret of which you assuredly have no inkling may
amaze, in fact, horrify you. If only my poor father had never left
Paris! As far as my earliest recollections of Geneva are concerned,
I remember being sprinkled by the tears of my inconsolable parents and myself crying because of the lamentations that I did not
understand. Later there came a clear sense, a full awareness of the
oppressiveness in which they lived. All my father's hopes were disappointed. Bowed down, crushed by sorrow, he died just when he

succeeded in placing me as an apprentice to a goldsmith. My mother spoke a great deal of you; she wanted to tell you of her misfortunes but was prevented from doing this because of a hopelessness born of poverty. That, and probably also a false shame that often gnaws at mortally wounded spirits, kept her from carrying out her resolution. A few months after the death of my father, she followed him to the grave."

"Poor Ann! Poor Ann!" Mademoiselle de Scudéri cried, overwhelmed by grief.

"Thanks and praise to the eternal power of heaven that she has passed where she cannot see her beloved son fall under the executioner's hand, branded with disgrace!" Olivier cried loudly, looking wildly toward the skies. There was a restlessness outside, the sound of men moving about was heard. "Aha," said Olivier with a bitter smile, "Desgrais is waking his compatriots, as though I could possibly escape from *here*! But to go on: My master treated me harshly, even though I worked hard and was soon one of the best workmen and finally much better than he himself. One day a foreigner happened to come to our workshop to purchase some jewelry. Seeing a necklace I had made, he gave me a friendly slap on the back, eyed the piece of jewelry, and said, 'Well, well, my young friend, this is really a fine piece of work. I know of no one who could outdo you except René Cardillac, who is the finest goldsmith in the world. You should go to him; he would be glad to admit you into his workshop, for no one but you could help him in his superb art, and from no one but him can you learn.' The words of the stranger sank deep into my soul. Geneva offered me no more peace; I felt myself forced from her. Finally I succeeded in freeing myself from my master. I came to Paris, where René Cardillac received me coldly and harshly. I refused to give up. He had to give me work, regardless of how trivial it might be. He told me to make a small ring. When I finished it and brought it back to him, he stared at me with his glistening eyes as though trying to see right through me, then said, 'You are a first-rate journeyman; you may move in with me and help in the workshop. I will pay you well and you will be happy with me.'

"Cardillac kept his word. I had been with him for several weeks without having seen Madelon, who, if I am not mistaken, was staying in the country with one of his cousins. At last she came.

Oh, eternal power of heaven, what happened to me when I saw that angelic creature! Has anyone ever loved as I love! And now! Oh, Madelon!"

Olivier was overcome by sorrow and could say no more. He held both hands over his face and sobbed violently. At last, subduing his wild anguish with a mighty effort, he continued.

"Madelon looked on me with friendly eyes. She came more and more often to the workshop. With delight I saw that she loved me. Although her father kept a close watch on us, we stole many hand clasps in token of our bond. Cardillac did not seem to notice anything. I planned to ask his consent to our marriage when I had succeeded in gaining his favor and my mastership. One morning, when I was about to begin work, Cardillac, anger and contempt in his dark gaze, said, 'I need your work no more. You are to be out of this house before the hour is passed, and my eyes are never to rest on you again. There is no need for me to tell you why your presence here is now intolerable. The sweet fruit after which you long hangs too high for you, poor beggar!' I tried to say something, but he seized me with his powerful hand and flung me out of the door. I fell and seriously injured my head and my arm. Furious, torn by deadly pain, I finally found my way to a kindhearted acquaintance who lived at the far end of the Faubourg Saint-Martin and who found room for me in his garret. I had neither peace nor rest. At night I prowled round Cardillac's house hoping that Madelon might hear my sighs and my lamentations and that she might be able to speak to me from the window without being observed. All kinds of desperate plans which I hoped to convince her to carry out crossed my mind. There is a high wall with niches and old, partly crumbling statues next to Cardillac's house in the rue Nicaise. One night I was standing near one of these statues, looking up at the windows of the house which open to the courtyard that the wall encloses. Suddenly I saw a light in Cardillac's workshop. It was midnight and he was normally never awake at that time, usually going to bed precisely at the stroke of nine. My heart pounded with a terrifying premonition. I imagined that something might take place which would provide me with entry into the house. But the light immediately disappeared again. I pressed myself tightly against the statue and into the niche, but recoiled in horror when I felt the pressure being returned, as if the statue had come to life. In the dim dusk of night I saw the statue rotate slowly and a dark figure slip out from behind it and stealthily make its way down the street. I sprang to the statue. It was again standing close to the wall. Involuntarily, as if driven by a force within me, I crept after the figure. The full light of a bright lamp burning before the statue of the Virgin fell upon its face. It was Cardillac! An incomprehensible terror, an eerie shudder ran through me. As though under a spell, I was compelled to pursue this ghostlike sleepwalker—for that was what I felt my master to be, although it was not the time of the full moon when sleepers are so afflicted. Finally Cardillac vanished into a deep shadow. From a familiar sound he made as he cleared his throat, I knew that he had gone into the entrance of a house. 'What is the meaning of this? What is he up to?' I asked myself in astonishment, pressing myself close against the houses. Not long after this, a man singing and warbling, wearing a white plumed hat, spurs jangling, came out. Like a tiger on his prey, Cardillac pounced upon the man from his dark hiding place. The man immediately sank gasping to the ground. I sprang forward with a cry of horror. Cardillac was bending over the man as he lay on the ground. 'Meister Cardillac, what are you doing?' I screamed. 'Damn you!' Cardillac bellowed, running past me with lightning speed and vanishing. Completely beside myself, barely able to walk a step, I approached the fallen man. I knelt down beside him, thinking it was still possible to save him; but not a trace of life was left in him. In my desperation I barely noticed that I had been surrounded by the mounted police. 'Another one struck down by the devils! Hey, young man, what are you doing here? Are you one of the gang? Away with you!' This is how they cried out in confusion and seized me. I was barely able to stammer that I was incapable of committing such a dastardly crime and that they must release me. Then one of them held a light to my face and called with a laugh, 'This is Olivier Brusson, the goldsmith who works with our worthy and honest Meister René Cardillac! Sure—he's the kind to murder people in the street! Just the type—and, of course, one would expect a murderer to lament over the corpse and allow himself to be nabbed. Come, young man, tell us about what happened.'

" 'Right before my eyes,' I said to them, 'a man pounced upon this man, struck him down, and ran away as fast as lightning when I shouted. I wanted to see whether I could still save the victim.'

" 'No, my son,' one of the men who lifted up the corpse called, 'he's finished, stabbed through the heart as usual.' 'Damn it,' said another, 'again we are too late, just as we were the day before yesterday.' And with this they left with the corpse.

"I really cannot tell you what I felt about all of this. I pinched myself to see whether I was not being deceived by an evil dream; it was as if I would awake almost at once, amazed at this crazy figment of my imagination. Cardillac—the father of my Madelon—a villainous murderer! I sank feebly down on the stone steps of the house. The morning grew ever brighter. A finely plumed officer's hat lay before me on the pavement. Cardillac's bloody crime, committed on the very spot where I sat, appeared to me vividly. And I fled in terror.

"Completely bewildered, almost unconscious, I was sitting in my garret when the door opened and René Cardillac entered. 'In the name of Christ, what do you want?' I cried. Paying no attention to my question, he approached me, smiling at me with a tranquility and serenity that only heightened my inner revulsion. Because I was unable to get up from my straw bed where I had flung myself, he pulled up an old rickety stool and sat down beside me. 'Well now, Olivier,' he began, 'how are you, my poor boy? I really was much too hasty in throwing you out of the house; I miss you at every turn. Just now I have a job to do that I will not be able to complete without you. How would it be if you came back to work with me again? No answer? Yes, I know, I have insulted you. I do not want to hide from you the fact that I was angry about your flirtation with my Madelon, but afterwards I thought things over and concluded that, given your talent, your conscientiousness, and your honesty, I could not hope to have a better son-in-law than you. Then come with me and see if you can win Madelon for your wife.'

"Cardillac's words pierced my heart; I shuddered at his wickedness. I could not utter a word. 'You hesitate,' he said sharply, boring through me with his glittering eyes. 'You hesitate? Perhaps you have other things to do today and therefore cannot come to me. Perhaps you wish to visit Desgrais or perhaps even D'Argenson or La Régnie. Be careful, fellow, lest the claws you would unsheath to destroy others seize and tear you yourself.' At this my utter indignation suddenly found expression. 'Let those,' I cried, 'who have a horrible crime on their conscience tremble at the names you have uttered. I need not—I have nothing to do with them.' 'In fact,' Cardillac continued, 'you should be honored to work with me! I am the most renowned contemporary master craftsman, and everywhere I am highly esteemed for my honesty and directness, so that any evil slander uttered would fall back heavily upon the head of the accuser. As for Madelon, I must confess that she alone is responsible for my indulgence. She loves you with a passion with which I would not have credited the gentle child. As soon as you were gone she fell at my feet, embraced my knees, and with a thousand tears declared that she could never live without you. I thought that this was merely her imagination—those infatuated young things are always ready to die when the first pale-faced youth looks at them in friendly fashion—but, in fact, my Madelon did really grow ill; and when I tried to talk her out of all this nonsense, she cried out your name a thousand times. Ultimately, what could I do if I did not want to see her surrender to despair? Yesterday evening I told her that I agreed to everything and that today I would go to fetch you. Overnight she bloomed like a rose; and now, beside herself with lovesickness, she awaits you.'

"May the eternal power of heaven forgive me, for I myself do not know how it happened; I was suddenly standing in Cardillac's house, and Madelon was exuberantly shouting 'Olivier—my Olivier—my beloved—my husband!' and pressing me to her breast, her arms around my neck, so that I, in supreme happiness, swore by the Virgin and all the saints that I would never leave her."

Olivier was overwhelmed by the remembrance of this decisive moment, and he had to pause. Mademoiselle de Scudéri, overcome by horror at the crime of a man whom she had looked upon as the personification of virtue and goodness, cried, "Terrible! René Cardillac is a member of the gang of murderers who have for so long turned our good city into a den of thieves?"

"Mademoiselle, did you say 'gang'? There never was any gang; it was Cardillac alone who diabolically sought and found his victims throughout the city. The fact that he was alone accounts for his impunity and is the reason that the police could never track the murderer. But let me go on. What follows will clear up the mystery and reveal the secrets of this man who is at once the most evil and wretched of all men. The situation in which I now found myself in relation to my master anyone can imagine. The step had been taken and there was no going back. At times it seemed to me as if I had become Cardillac's accomplice in murder, and only in Madelon's love was I able to forget for a time the inner pain that tortured me; only when with her could I throw off all the outward signs of the unspeakable horror that burdened me. When I worked with the old man in the shop, I could barely trade a word with him because of the terror that made me shiver just to be in the presence of this abominable man, who displayed all the merits of the tender father and the upright citizen while the night shrouded his crimes. Madelon, pure angelic child that she is, worshiped him. It cut me to the heart to think that she, who had been so deceived by all the diabolical craft of Satan, would find herself the victim of the most abysmal despair if ever vengeance were to fall upon the unmasked villain. This in itself sealed my lips and would have kept them sealed even if my silence were to result in my dying a criminal's death. Although I had heard a good deal from the *maréchaussée*, Cardillac's crimes—their motive and the manner in which he carried them out—were a riddle to me. I did not have to wait long for the solution.

"One day Cardillac, who, to my utter disgust, usually was very lighthearted while at work and laughed and joked, was very serious and withdrawn. He suddenly flung away the piece of jewelry on which he was working, pearls and gems scattering in all directions, leapt to his feet, and said, 'Olivier, things cannot go on between us this way. The situation is unbearable. What the most ingenious cunning of Desgrais and his henchmen failed to discover, chance has placed in your hands. You have seen me at the nocturnal work to which I am compelled by my evil star—denial is beyond me. But it was also your evil star that compelled you to follow me and that wrapped you in a mantle of invisibility and gave to your footsteps such lightness that you moved as noiselessly as the smallest animal; so that I, who like the tiger can see in the darkest of nights and can hear the slightest sound, the humming of the flies a street away, did not observe you. Your evil star has made you my accomplice. You cannot betray me in your present situation; therefore, you shall know all.'

" 'I shall never ever again be your accomplice, you hypocritical villain!' was what I wanted to cry out, but the horror that overwhelmed me when I heard his words paralyzed my tongue. Instead of words, I could only utter an unintelligible sound.

"Cardillac again sat down on his workbench. He wiped the sweat from his brow and seemed deeply shaken by the recollection of the past and appeared to find it difficult to pull himself together. Finally he began: 'Wise men have much to say about the susceptibility of pregnant women to strange impressions, and about the curious influences that these vivid and involuntary impressions, which stem from the external, may exercise upon the child. A singular story was told to me about my mother. During the first month of pregnancy she and other women watched a superb court pageant at the Trianon, and she saw a cavalier in Spanish dress wearing a sparkling jeweled necklace from which she could not thereafter remove her eyes. Her entire being longed for the dazzling gems, which seemed to her to be supernaturally valuable. This same cavalier, several years earlier, when my mother was not yet married, had made an attempt upon her virtue, but he had been rejected with loathing. My mother recognized him; but now, bathed by the light of the gems, he seemed to her to belong to a higher sphere, to be the very embodiment of beauty. The cavalier noticed my mother's desirous, fiery look and thought that he would be more successful now than he had been before. He contrived to get close to her, to separate her from her friends, and even to lure her to a lonely place. There he passionately clasped her in his arms. My mother grabbed at the beautiful necklace; but at that moment he fell to the earth, dragging my mother along with him. I do not know whether he had suffered a stroke or whether it was for some other reason, but he was dead. In vain did my mother attempt to free herself from the dead man's rigid arms which embraced her. With eyes that were hollow and devoid of light fixed on her, the corpse rolled this way and that with her upon the ground. Her shrieks for help finally reached people who were passing in the distance, and they rushed to her aid and released her from the arms of her gruesome lover. The shock of all this made my mother seriously ill. She and I were given up for lost; but she recovered, and the birth was easier than anyone had expected. But the terrors of that awful moment had marked me. My evil star had risen and flung down sparks that ignited in me a most strange and fatal passion. From my earliest childhood I valued glittering diamonds and the products of the goldsmith above everything else. This was looked upon simply as a childish fancy for lovely things. But it was otherwise, for as a boy I stole gold and jewels wherever I could lay my hands on them. And like the most accomplished connoisseur, I could instinctively distinguish paste jewelry from the genuine. Only the genuine attracted me; I ignored false jewels and rolled gold. This inborn craving was ultimately repressed by my father's severe punishments. But so that I might always be able to handle gold and precious stones, I entered the goldsmith's profession, and working at it with passionate enthusiasm, I soon became the leading craftsman in this field. Then there began a period when my impulse, which had so long been repressed, forced itself to the surface and, growing mightily, consumed everything else. As soon as I had completed and delivered a piece of jewelry, I fell into a state of restlessness and desperation that kept me from my sleep, wrecked my health, and drained my will to live. The person for whom I had made the work haunted me day and night like a ghost—I saw him continually, bedecked in my jewelry, and a voice whispered in my ear, "It's yours! Take it, it's yours, it's yours, take it! What use are diamonds to the dead?" Ultimately I began to steal. I had access to the houses of the great, and I quickly took advantage of every opportunity. No lock resisted my skill, and soon my jewelry was back in my hands again. But even this was not sufficient to calm my uneasiness. The eerie voice made itself heard again, jeering at me and saying, "Aha, a dead man wears your jewels!" I did not know how it happened, but I began to harbor an indescribable hatred toward those for whom I had made jewelry. Even more, in the depths of my soul there began to seethe an impulse to murder before which I myself shuddered. It was then that I bought this house. I had concluded the terms with the owner, and we were sitting together in this room, drinking a bottle of wine in honor of the completed transaction. Night had fallen; he was about to leave when he said to me, "Listen, Meister René; before I go, I must inform you of a secret about this house." He opened the cupboard built into the wall, pushed the back of it aside, stepped through into a small closet, where he bent down and raised a trap door. We descended a steep and narrow staircase, arrived at a narrow gate, which he opened and which let us out into the open courtyard. Then the old gentleman went up to the encircling wall, pushed at a piece of iron that slightly projected from the wall; immediately a part of the wall revolved so that a man could step out through the opening into the street. You must see this device, Olivier. It must have been made by the cunning monks of the monastery that once existed here so that they were able to slip in and out secretly. It is wood, but mortared and whitewashed on the outside; and a statue, also of wood, but that looks as if it were made of stone, is fitted into the side; the wall and the statue rotate together on hidden hinges. When I saw this device, dark thoughts surged up in me. It seemed a presentiment of deeds that were as yet hidden even from myself. I had just delivered an opulent ornament to a gentleman of the court, which I knew was to be presented to a dancer at the opera. I was terribly tortured—the ghost haunted my steps—the whispering devil was in my ear! I went back into the house. Drenched in the sweat of anguish, I tossed and turned on my bed, sleepless. In my mind's eye I saw the man slipping off to the dancer with my beautiful jewelry. Infuriated, I sprang up—threw on my coat—climbed the secret staircase—went out through the wall into the rue Nicaise. He came, I fell upon him, he screamed, but I seized him from behind and plunged my dagger into his heart—the jewelry was mine! This done, I felt a peace and contentment in my soul such as I had never known before. The ghost had disappeared, Satan's voice was no more. Now I knew what it was that my evil star demanded. I had to obey or perish!'

" 'Now you understand my actions and that which drives me, Olivier. Do not think that because I do that which I am compelled to do I am devoid of all feelings of pity or of compassion, which are said to be intrinsic in man's nature. You know how difficult it is for me to deliver a piece of jewelry; that there are some for whom I will not work at all because I do not wish them to die; that sometimes, knowing that my ghost will be exorcised with blood the next day, I forestall this with a powerful blow of my fist, which flattens the owner of my jewels on the ground so that I can get them back into my hands!'

"Having said all this, Cardillac led me into his secret vault and allowed me to look at his jewel cabinet. The King does not own a finer one. Each article had attached to it a small label stating exactly for whom it had been made and when it had been taken back by theft, robbery, or violence. 'On your wedding day, Olivier,' Cardillac said in a hollow, solemn voice, 'you will swear a sacred oath with your hand on the crucifix that as soon as I am dead you will immediately reduce this opulence to dust with a technique I will teach you. I want no human being, least of all Madelon and you, to come into possession of this blood-bought hoard.'

"Trapped and snared in this labyrinth of crime, torn by love and revulsion, I was like the accursed soul whom a beautiful, softly smiling angel beckons aloft, while Satan holds him back with red-hot claws, and the holy angel's loving smile, in which is reflected all of the bliss of paradise, becomes the most agonizing of his tortures. I thought of flight, even of suicide—but Madelon! Blame me, blame me, worthy lady, for having been too weak to smash forcefully a passion that chained me to crime, but am I not to atone for it by a shameful death?

"One day Cardillac came home in unusually good spirits. He caressed Madelon, cast a most friendly look at me, drank a bottle of vintage wine at dinner—something he only did on special occasions and holidays—sang, and was merry. Madelon had left us, and I was about to go into the workshop. 'Sit still, boy,' Cardillac cried, 'no more work today. Let us drink to the welfare of the most worthy and excellent lady in all of Paris.' After we had clinked glasses and he had emptied his at a gulp, he said, 'Tell me, Olivier, how do you like these lines?

> Un amant qui craint les voleurs
> N'est point digne d'amour.'

"He then told me what had happened between you and the King in the Marquise de Maintenon's apartment, adding that he had always revered you above any other human being and that before your lofty virtue his evil spirit would never arouse in him any vile thoughts of murder, even were you to wear the finest piece of jewelry he had ever made. 'Listen, Olivier,' he said, 'to what I have decided to do. A long time ago I was commissioned to make a necklace and bracelet for Henrietta of England, supplying the gems myself. This work turned out to surpass anything I had ever done before, and it broke my heart to think that I must part with these ornaments, which had become treasures of my soul. You know of the Princess's unfortunate death by assassination. I kept the jewelry, and now I will send it to Mademoiselle de Scudéri, in the name of the persecuted gang, as a token of my respect and gratitude. Besides, if I deliver these jewels to Mademoiselle de Scudéri as a symbol of her triumph, it will be heaping upon Desgrais and his men the contempt they deserve. You shall take the jewelry to her.' Mademoiselle, as soon as Cardillac mentioned your name, it was as if black veils had been pulled aside, and the beautiful bright picture of my happy early childhood rose again before me in gay and glowing colors; a wonderful sense of consolation came into my soul, a ray of hope before which the gloomy shadows vanished. Cardillac must have seen the effect that his words had upon me, and he interpreted this in his own way.

" 'My plan,' he said, 'seems to please you. I may confess that in doing this I was responding to a voice deep within me which was so very unlike the voice that demanded of me blood sacrifice as if from a voracious beast of prey. At times a strange feeling comes over me—an inner anxiety, the dread of something malicious, the terror of which seems to float across the earth from the world beyond, seizes me. At such times I feel that those things that are committed through me by my evil star may be charged to my immortal soul, which plays no part in it. In one of these moods I determined that I would make a stunning diamond crown for the holy Virgin in the church of Saint-Eustache. But whenever I attempted to start making it, I was filled with an ever-increasing, incomprehensible anxiety, until I finally gave up. But now it seems to me that in sending to Mademoiselle de Scudéri the most splendid jewelry I have ever crafted I will be humbly bringing a sacrifice to the very model of virtue and piety and imploring effective intercession.' "

"Cardillac, who was familiar with every detail of your mode of life, Mademoiselle, told me precisely how and when I was to deliver to you the jewelry, which he had encased in a rich jewel box. My entire soul was imbued with happiness, for heaven itself seemed to be showing me, through the sacrilegious Cardillac, a way to escape from the hell in which I, a banished sinner, was languishing. This is what I thought. Completely against Cardillac's wishes, it was my intention to meet with you personally. As Ann Brusson's son and your foster child, I intended to throw myself at your feet and to tell you all, everything. Moved by the unspeakable misery that the disclosure of the secret would have brought upon poor, innocent Madelon, you would have maintained the secret, but your brilliant mind would surely have been able to find the way to control the accursed wickedness of Cardillac without revealing it. Do not ask me through what means this could have been done, I do not know. But the conviction that you would rescue Madelon and me was as deeply ingrained in my soul as my belief in the consoling help of the holy Virgin.

"You know, Mademoiselle, that my plan fell through that night. I did not abandon hope that I would be more fortunate another time. But then Cardillac suddenly lost all his gaiety. He crept around gloomily, stared into space, muttering unintelligible words, and hit the air with his hands as if he were fighting off something hostile; his mind seemed full of evil thoughts. This continued for a whole morning. At last he sat down at the workbench, peevishly sprang up to his feet again, looked out of the window, said in a grave and gloomy voice, 'I wish Henrietta of England had worn my jewelry.'

"These words filled me with terror. I knew now that his insane mind was once more possessed by the specter of malignant murder and that the voice of the Devil was again loud in his ears. I saw that your life was threatened by the accursed demon. If Cardillac could only regain possession of his jewels, you would be safe. Every instant increased the danger. Then I met you on the Pont-Neuf, broke my way into your carriage, and threw you the note in which I implored you to return the jewelry you had received from Cardillac. You did not come. My anxiety mounted to despair when, the next day, Cardillac spoke of nothing but the priceless jewelry that had appeared before his eyes during the night. I could only surmise that this was a reference to your jewelry, and I was certain that he was brooding upon a murderous attack, which he undoubtedly had determined to pursue that night. I had to save you even were it to cost me Cardillac's life. When Cardillac, as usual, shut himself up in his room after evening prayers, I entered the courtyard by climbing out of the window, slipped out through the opening in the wall, stationed myself close by in deep shadow. It was not long before Cardillac came out and softly crept down the street. I followed him. He went towards the rue Saint Honoré. My heart quivered. All at once he vanished. I determined to station myself at your door. Then, just as chance had once made me witness to Cardillac's murderous attack, it intervened again, and an officer who was singing and warbling passed by without seeing me. But at that very instant a black form sprang out and attacked him. It was Cardillac. I wanted to prevent this murder. Shouting loudly, I was on the spot in two or three bounds—it was not the officer—it was Cardillac who sank to the earth mortally wounded, the death rattle in his throat. The officer dropped his dagger, and under the impression that I was the murderer's accomplice, unsheathed his sword and assumed a fighting stance; but he quickly left when he noticed that I paid him no attention but merely examined the corpse. Cardillac was still alive. After retrieving the dagger that the officer had dropped, I lifted Cardillac to my shoulders and, with difficulty, carried him home and up the secret passage to the workshop.

"You know the rest. You see, Mademoiselle, that my only crime consists of my not having betrayed Madelon's father to the courts, thereby ending his crimes. I am innocent of any bloodguilt. No martyrdom will tear from me the secret of Cardillac's outrages. I do not wish that now, contrary to the everlasting power that concealed from the virtuous daughter her father's atrocious crimes, I should be responsible for unleashing upon her all of the misery of the past which would mean her death, nor that the world's vengeance shall exhume the corpse from the soil that covers it and that the executioner shall brand the moldering bones with shame. No, my soul's beloved will mourn for me as an innocent victim. Time will assuage her grief and her sorrow, but her anguish for her father's atrocious crimes could never be assuaged!"

Olivier grew silent, but then suddenly a torrent of tears burst from his eyes; he threw himself at Mademoiselle de Scudéri's feet and implored, "You are convinced that I am innocent—I'm sure you are! Have pity on me, tell me how Madelon is."

Mademoiselle de Scudéri summoned La Martinière, and a few minutes later Madelon flung her arms about Olivier's neck.

"Everything is well now that you are here—I knew that this

noble-hearted lady would save you!" cried Madelon over and over again; and Olivier forgot the fate that awaited him and all that threatened him. He was free and blissful. In the most moving way they both lamented what each had suffered for the other and then embraced each other again and wept for joy at having once more found each other.

Had Mademoiselle de Scudéri not already been convinced of Olivier's innocence, she must have been convinced of this now as she saw them both forgetting, in the rapture of profound and sincere love, the world, their misery, and their indescribable torment. "No," she called, "only a pure heart is capable of such blissful forgetfulness."

The bright rays of morning broke through the window. Desgrais knocked softly on the door and reminded them that it was time for Olivier Brusson to be taken away because it could not be done later without attracting attention. The lovers had to part. The dim presentiments that had possessed Mademoiselle de Scudéri when Brusson first appeared in her house now assumed a fearful actuality. She saw the son of her beloved Ann as being innocent, but as being so enmeshed by events that there was no apparent way of saving him from a shameful death. She honored the young man's heroism which led him to prefer dying with the burden of apparent guilt rather than to betray a secret that would result in Madelon's death. In the entire realm of possibility she could think of no way to tear the unfortunate youth from the cruel court. And yet, firmly imbedded in her soul was the conviction that no sacrifice should be spared to prevent the crying injustice that was being committed. She tortured herself with all sorts of projects and plans, some of which were completely impractical and all of which were rejected as soon as they were formed. Every glimmer of hope grew more and more faint until she was but a step from despair. But Madelon's unhesitating, pious, childlike trust, and the change that came over her when she spoke of her beloved—who, a freed man, she would soon embrace as a wife—touched Mademoiselle de Scudéri's heart and inspired her to new efforts.

In order to do something, Mademoiselle de Scudéri wrote a long letter to La Régnie, in which she informed him that Olivier Brusson had proved to her absolute satisfaction his complete innocence in the death of Cardillac, and that only his heroic resolution to carry to his grave a secret whose disclosure would result in the ruin of true innocence and virtue prevented him from offering to the court a statement that would not only absolve him from the terrible suspicion of having murdered Cardillac, but also of having been a member of the accursed gang of murderers. In her effort to soften La Régnie's hard heart, she put into her letter all the burning zeal and brilliant eloquence at her command. A few hours later La Régnie replied, saying that he was sincerely pleased that Olivier had succeeded in convincing his noble and worthy patroness of his innocence. As for Olivier's heroic resolution to carry into the grave a secret relating to the murder with which he was charged, he regretted that the *Chambre Ardente* could not honor such heroism but must, rather, attempt to break it by the most powerful means necessary. Within three days he hoped to possess the amazing secret which would result in light being cast on miraculous events.

Only too well did Mademoiselle de Scudéri know what the terrible La Régnie meant by the means that would be used to break Olivier's heroic silence. It was now clear that the unfortunate young man was to be tortured. In her mortal anguish, it at last occurred to Mademoiselle de Scudéri that the advice of a lawyer would be helpful, even if it were only to obtain a postponement. Pierre Arnaud d'Andilly was at that time the most celebrated lawyer in Paris. His profound knowledge and his comprehensive intelligence were equal to his integrity and virtue. She went to him and told him everything she could without divulging Olivier's secret. She thought that d'Andilly would enthusiastically accept the innocent man's defense, but her hopes were bitterly smashed. D'Andilly listened calmly to all that she had to say and then, smiling, responded with Boileau's words: "Truth may sometimes look improbable." He showed that the evidence against Brusson was of a most powerful kind, that the procedure followed by La Régnie was neither brutal nor precipitous, but, on the contrary, entirely within the bounds of law, and that, in fact, he could respond in no other way if he were not to neglect his responsibility as a judge. D'Andilly did not believe that even the most skillful defense could spare Brusson from torture. Only Brusson could accomplish that, either by fully confessing or, at the least, by accurately relating the circumstances surrounding Cardillac's murder, which might then result in fresh facts being brought to the surface.

"Then I shall throw myself at the King's feet and plead for mercy," Mademoiselle de Scudéri said, beside herself, in a voice half choked with tears.

"Do not do that, for heaven's sake do not do that, Mademoiselle," d'Andilly cried. "That should be reserved as a last resort. If you attempt it prematurely and do not succeed, it will be lost to you forever. The King would never pardon such a criminal at this point, for if he did he would expose himself to the most bitter reproaches of the people who feel themselves to be endangered. It is possible that Brusson, by revealing his secret, or by some other means, may succeed in exonerating himself in the eyes of the populace. Then would be the time to beg the King for mercy, who would not ask what had or had not been established legally but would be guided by his own inner conviction."

Mademoiselle de Scudéri could not but agree with what d'Andilly's broad experience suggested. Deeply worried, brooding without end about what she could do—in the name of the Virgin and all the saints—to save Brusson, she was sitting in her room late that evening when La Martinière entered and announced that the Comte de Miossens, a colonel of the King's Guard, urgently wished to speak to Mademoiselle.

"Pardon me, Mademoiselle," said Miossens, after bowing with soldierly courtesy, "for disturbing you so late; we soldiers do things that way; moreover, just a few words will excuse my behavior. I am here on behalf of Olivier Brusson."

Extremely interested in what she was going to hear, Mademoiselle de Scudéri cried out, "Olivier Brusson? The most unfortunate of all men? What have you to do with Brusson?"

"I thought," said Miossens, laughing again, "that your protégé's name would assure me a sympathetic hearing. The whole world is convinced of Brusson's guilt. I know that you think otherwise, although I have been told that your opinion is supported only by what the accused has told you. In my case it is different. No one can be more certain than I am that Brusson had nothing to do with Cardillac's death."

"Speak, oh, speak!" cried Mademoiselle de Scudéri, her eyes glistening with delight.

"I," Miossens said emphatically, "it was I who struck down the old goldsmith in the rue Saint Honoré, close to your house."

"In the name of all of the saints, you? You!" cried Mademoiselle de Scudéri.

"And I swear to you, Mademoiselle," he continued, "that I am proud of my deed. Know that Cardillac was the most detestable and hypocritical villain, and that it was he who cunningly murdered and robbed at night and for so long escaped every snare. I myself do not know what aroused my suspicion of the old villain when, obviously distressed, he brought me the jewelry I had ordered, asked in great detail for whom I intended it, and most shrewdly asked my valet about when I was in the habit of visiting a certain lady. It had long ago occurred to me that the unfortunate victims of this repulsive robber all had the same mortal wound, and I understood that the murderer had practiced a particular thrust that killed instantaneously and on which he depended. If he failed in this, it would mean a fight. I therefore took a precaution so simple that I am astounded others had not thought of it before and saved themselves from the cowardly murderer. I wore a light breastplate beneath my vest. Cardillac attacked me from behind. He grasped me with the strength of a giant, but his deadly accurate thrust glanced off the iron. I broke free from his grasp at the same instant and stabbed him in the breast with a dagger I held ready."

"And you have said nothing?" asked Mademoiselle de Scudéri. "You have not made a statement to the authorities regarding what happened?"

"Allow me," said Miossens, "allow me to remark that such a statement, even if it did not cause my ruin, would at least involve me in a most loathsome trial. Would La Régnie, who scents crime everywhere, immediately believe me if I accused the honest Cardillac, the very embodiment of complete piety and virtue, of attempted murder? What if the sword of justice were pointed at me?"

"That would not be possible," cried Mademoiselle de Scudéri, "your birth, your rank—"

"Ah," Miossens interrupted, "remember the Maréchal of Luxembourg, who was locked in the Bastille because he was suspected of poisoning, as a result of having his horoscope read by Le Sage?

Know, by Saint Denis, neither one hour of my freedom nor the lobe of my ear would I sacrifice to the raving La Régnie, who would be delighted to put his knife to all our throats."

"But in this way you will bring the innocent Brusson to the scaffold," interrupted Mademoiselle de Scudéri.

"Innocent?" Miossens responded. "Are you calling the accursed Cardillac's accomplice innocent, Mademoiselle? He who assisted him in his crimes and who has deserved death a hundred times over? No, in truth, he will justifiably bleed; and if I have related to you the actual facts of the case, Mademoiselle, it was on the presumption that you would somehow know how to make use of my secret in the interests of your protégé without delivering me into the clutches of the *Chambre Ardente*."

Mademoiselle de Scudéri, completely delighted at the convincing confirmation of her conviction of Olivier's innocence, was not at all reticent about telling the Comte everything, since he already knew of Cardillac's crimes, and she requested that he accompany her to d'Andilly who would, when the entire story had been told to him under the seal of secrecy, advise them on what was next to be done.

D'Andilly, after Mademoiselle de Scudéri had told him as precisely as possible what had happened, asked again about the most minute particulars. He especially asked Comte Miossens if he was absolutely positive that it was Cardillac who had attacked him and whether he would be able to identify Olivier Brusson as the one who had carried the corpse away.

"Aside from the fact that I distinctly recognized the goldsmith in the moonlit night," Miossens replied, "I have also seen at La Régnie's the dagger with which Cardillac was stabbed. It is mine; it is distinguished by delicate work on the handle. I was standing only a pace from the young man, whose hat had fallen from his head, and I saw every feature distinctly. I would have no difficulty recognizing him."

D'Andilly sat in silence for a few moments, staring into space, then said, "There is absolutely no way to snatch Brusson from the hands of justice by ordinary methods. Because of Madelon, he refuses to name Cardillac as a robber and murderer. He may keep to this because even if he were to succeed in proving this accusation by revealing the secret entrance and the hoard of stolen jewels, he would nevertheless be condemned to die as an accomplice. The same would occur if Miossens were to inform the judges about what truly happened to the goldsmith. All that we can look forward to accomplishing for the time being is delay. Let Comte Miossens go to the Conciergerie and be confronted by Brusson so that he may identify him as the man who carried Cardillac's corpse away. Let him then hasten to La Régnie and say, 'I saw a man struck down in the rue Saint Honoré, and while I was standing next to the corpse, I saw another man dart forward and bend down over the body and, finding that there was still life in it, lift it over his shoulders and carry it away. In Olivier Brusson I recognize that man.' This statement will result in Brusson's once more being questioned by La Régnie in the presence of Miossens. Brusson will not be tortured and additional investigations will be conducted. Then will be the time to approach the King himself. Mademoiselle, doing this in the most diplomatic manner possible will be left to your discretion. It is my opinion that it would be best to reveal everything to the King. Comte Miossen's statement will support Brusson's confession, which may additionally be confirmed by a secret investigation of Cardillac's house. The matter cannot be handled through the Court's verdict, but must rather be resolved through a decision of the King, who, drawing upon intrinsic feeling, will grant pardon where a judge would mete out punishment."

Comte Miossens precisely followed the advice of d'Andilly, and everything took place precisely as he had predicted it would.

The next step was to approach the King. This was the major difficulty because he had such an intense aversion to Brusson, whom he believed to be singly responsible for the atrocious robberies and murders that had for so long held all of Paris in a reign of terror that the slightest allusion to the infamous trial enraged him. Madame de Maintenon, consistent with her principle of never speaking to the King of unpleasant subjects, refused to act as an intermediary. Brusson's fate was, therefore, utterly in the hands of Mademoiselle. After extended reflection she came to a decision upon which she immediately acted. She put on a black dress made of heavy silk, bedecked herself in Cardillac's magnificent jewelry, added a long black veil, and attired in this fashion, appeared at La Maintenon's at the hour when the King would be there. Dressed in this solemn manner, the venerable lady had about her an air that was designed to kindle reverential respect even from those jaded people who are wont to expend their trivial existences in the royal antechambers. Everyone made way for her; and even the King, in great surprise, rose when she entered and came forward to meet her. The stunning diamonds in her necklace and bracelets dazzled him, and he exclaimed, "By heaven, that is Cardillac's jewelry!" Turning to La Maintenon, he then smiled charmingly and said, "See, Madame La Marquise, how our lovely bride mourns her bridegroom."

"Oh, gracious Sire," Mademoiselle de Scudéri said, as though following up the jest, "how would it become an agonized bride to bedeck herself in such magnificence? No, I have totally abandoned the goldsmith, and were it not that the terrifying image of his corpse being borne close before me keeps appearing before my eyes, he would be absent from my thought."

"What," the King asked, "you saw the poor devil?"

Mademoiselle de Scudéri then told him in a few words (not mentioning Brusson's role in the business) how chance had brought her to Cardillac's house immediately following the discovery of the murder. She described Madelon's frantic grief, the deep impression made upon her by the heavenly child, and how she had rescued the poor girl from the grasp of Desgrais amid the cheers of the populace. With continually heightening effect, she described the scenes with La Régnie, Desgrais, and Olivier himself. The King, transported by the very great vividness with which Mademoiselle de Scudéri told the tale, did not notice that they were talking about the notorious trial of that very Brusson whom he found so repulsive, and he listened wordlessly, only occasionally expressing his involvement through an exclamation. Before he was aware of what was going on, while still in a turmoil from the fantastic story just told to him, Mademoiselle lay at his feet begging mercy for Olivier Brusson.

"What are you doing?" the King exclaimed, taking both her hands and seating her in an armchair. "What are you doing, Mademoiselle? You have astonished me. It is a terrifying story. Who can vouch for the accuracy of Brusson's story?"

"Miossens's statement—the search of Cardillac's house—an inner conviction—oh, Madelon's virtuous heart that recognized the identical virtue in the unfortunate Brusson!" Mademoiselle de Scudéri responded.

The King was about to reply when he was distracted by a noise coming from near the door. Louvois, who had been at work in the next room, entered with a troubled expression. The King rose and left, Louvois following. Both Mademoiselle de Scudéri and La Maintenon considered this interruption to be dangerous because the King, having been caught by surprise once, might avoid falling into the trap again. But he returned in a few minutes, walked quickly back and forth two or three times, then, his hands behind his back, he stood before Mademoiselle de Scudéri and, without looking at her, said in a soft voice, "I would like to see your Madelon!"

To this, Mademoiselle de Scudéri replied, "Oh, gracious Sire, what great, great joy you are bestowing upon this poor, unfortunate child. You have only to give a sign, and the little one will be at your feet." Saying this, she tripped to the door as quickly as her heavy clothing permitted, called out that the King wished to have Madelon Cardillac admitted to his presence, and returned, weeping and sobbing with joy and gratitude. Having anticipated this favor, Mademoiselle de Scudéri had had Madelon accompany her, leaving her to wait with the chambermaid of the Marquise, with a short petition drawn up by d'Andilly in her hands. A few moments later she was lying prostrate at the King's feet. Fear, confusion, shyness, love, and anguish forced the boiling blood of the poor girl to surge through her veins ever more quickly. Her cheeks glowed red, her eyes sparkled with pearlike teardrops, which now and then fell from her silky lashes onto her lovely lily-white bosom.

The King seemed to be moved by the wonderful beauty of the angelic child. He gently raised the girl and moved as if to kiss the hand he was holding. He let it fall and looked at the precious child through eyes wet with tears that testified to deep emotion. La Maintenon whispered softly to Mademoiselle, "Isn't the little thing the very image of La Vallière. The King revels in the sweetest memories. Your game is won!"

Despite La Maintenon's having spoken softly, the King appeared to have heard. A blush came to his face; he cast a glance at La Maintenon; he read the petition that Madelon had given to him and then said, gently and kindly, "I find it easy to believe, dear child, that you should be certain of the innocence of your beloved, but let us hear what the *Chambre Ardente* has to say about it."

A light movement of the hand dismissed the little one, who was swimming in tears.

To her terror, Mademoiselle de Scudéri noted that the recollection of La Vallière, as propitious as it had appeared at first, had changed the King's intention as soon as the name had been mentioned by La Maintenon. It was perhaps felt by the King that he had been rudely reminded that he was about to sacrifice stern justice to beauty, or that he was like a dreamer who discovers that the beautiful image created by sleep quickly disappears even as he prepared to embrace it when he is awakened by a loud call. Perhaps he no longer could see his La Vallière before him, but thought only of Soeur Louise de la Miséricorde (La Vallière's cloister name among the Carmelite nuns), whose piety and penitence tortured him. There was nothing that could now be done other than to await the decision of the King.

Meanwhile, the statement made by Comte de Miossens to the *Chambre Ardente* had become known, and as often happens, public opinion being easily swayed from one extreme to the other, the man who had so recently been cursed by the mob as the vilest of murderers and threatened with being torn to pieces before reaching the scaffold, was now lamented as the innocent victim of a barbarous justice. His neighbors only now recalled his decorous behavior, his great love for Madelon, his faithfulness and complete devotion to the old goldsmith. Masses of people began assembling in front of La Régnie's palace and shouted threateningly, "Release Olivier Brusson, he is innocent"; and they even flung stones at the windows so that La Régnie was forced to seek protection from the incensed rabble with the mounted police.

Several days passed without Mademoiselle de Scudéri hearing anything new about Olivier Brusson's trial. Very disconsolate, she went to see La Maintenon, who assured her that the King was keeping absolutely silent on the subject and that it did not seem advisable to remind him of it. When she then, with a peculiar smile, asked how the little La Vallière was doing, Mademoiselle de Scudéri became convinced that inwardly the proud lady was grieved by the affair that threatened to entice the susceptible King into a realm whose magic spell was beyond her control. Consequently, nothing was to be hoped from La Maintenon.

With d'Andilly's help, Mademoiselle de Scudéri was ultimately able to discover that the King had had a long discussion with Comte de Miossens; also, that Bontems, the King's most trusted valet and deputy, had been to the Conciergerie and had spoken to Brusson; and finally, that the same Bontems had, in the company of several men, been to Cardillac's house and had spent a long time there. Claude Patru, the ground floor tenant, assured them that there had been rumbling noises overhead throughout the night and that he was certain that Olivier Brusson had been there because he had clearly recognized his voice. That the King was himself attempting to discover what the facts were was thus far clear, but what remained puzzling was the long delay in reaching a decision. La Régnie must have been exhausting every means to preclude his victim's being torn from his grasp. This nipped all hope in the bud.

Nearly a month had elapsed when La Maintenon sent word to Mademoiselle de Scudéri that the King desired to see her that evening in her, La Maintenon's, rooms.

Mademoiselle de Scudéri's heart beat furiously. She knew that Brusson's case was about to be decided. She informed poor Madelon, who fervently prayed to the Virgin and all the saints that they succeed in convincing the King of Brusson's innocence.

And yet it seemed as if the King had forgotten the entire matter; as usual, he passed the time engaged in pleasant conversation with La Maintenon and Mademoiselle de Scudéri, not directing a single syllable to poor Brusson. Finally Bontems appeared, approached the King, said a few words to him so softly that neither of the ladies understood any of it. Mademoiselle trembled inwardly. Then the King rose, walked to Mademoiselle de Scudéri and, his eyes radiant, said, "I congratulate you, Mademoiselle! Your protégé Olivier Brusson is free!" Mademoiselle de Scudéri, tears streaming from her eyes, unable to utter a word, was about to throw herself at the feet of the King. He prevented her from doing this, saying, "Now, now, Mademoiselle, you should be Lawyer of the Court and argue lawsuits on my behalf, since by Saint Denis, no one on earth is able to resist your eloquence. But," he added with greater seriousness, "but is not he who is protected by virtue not secure from every evil accusation, from the *Chambre Ardente* and from every court in the world?"

Mademoiselle de Scudéri now found words again, and glowing gratitude poured forth. The King interrupted her, told her that far more enthusiastic thanks awaited her at home than he could claim from her, because the happy Olivier was, at that very instant, undoubtedly embracing his Madelon. "Bontems," the King concluded, "is to pay you one thousand louis; present them to the little one in my name, as a dowry. Let her marry her Brusson, who does not deserve such a treasure, but then they are both to leave Paris. This is my wish."

La Martinière rushed to meet Mademoiselle de Scudéri, followed by Baptiste, both with faces beaming with joy, both triumphantly crying, "He is here—he is free! Oh, the dear young people!"

The ecstatic couple fell at the feet of Mademoiselle de Scudéri.

"Oh, I knew that you, only you, would rescue my husband," Madelon cried.

"Oh, my faith in you, my mother, stood firm in my soul," Olivier cried, and both kissed the hands of the worthy lady and shed a thousand burning tears. And then they embraced again and declared that the divine bliss of this moment outweighed all the unspeakable sufferings of the past, and they swore never to part till death.

A few days later a priest's blessing bound them to each other. Even if it had not been the King's wish, Brusson could not have remained in Paris, where everything reminded him of the heinous period of Cardillac's outrages, and where his tranquil existence might at any moment be shattered forever by some accidental disclosure of the evil secret now known to but a few. Immediately following the wedding, he and his young wife moved to Geneva, accompanied by the blessings of Mademoiselle de Scudéri. Handsomely equipped with Madelon's dowry, highly gifted in his profession, endowed with every civic virtue, he soon established a happy and carefree life there. In him were fulfilled the hopes whose frustration had led his father to the grave.

A year had passed since the departure of Brusson when a public proclamation signed by Harloy de Chauvalon, Archbishop of Paris, and Pierre Arnaud d'Andilly, Lawyer of the Court, appeared, stating that a repentant sinner had, under the seal of confession, turned over to the church a hoard of stolen jewelry. All who had, up until about the year 1680, been robbed of jewelry, particularly through a murderous attack in the open street, were invited to make a claim to d'Andilly, and if the description provided by the claimant precisely tallied with any of the jewelry and there was no reason to doubt the legitimacy of the claim, it would be returned to him.

Many who were described in Cardillac's list as having been merely struck down with a fist, rather than having been murdered, gradually came to d'Andilly and, to their amazement, received the jewelry that had been stolen from them. What remained went to the treasury of the Church of Saint-Eustache.

Translated by L. J. Kent and
E. C. Knight

The Mines of Falun

All the people of Göteborg had gathered at the harbor one cheerful sunny day in July. A rich East Indiaman, which had happily returned from distant lands, lay at anchor in Klippa Harbor; the Swedish flags waved gaily in the azure sky while hundreds of boats of all kinds, overflowing with jubilant seamen, drifted back and forth on the crystal waves of the Götaelf, and the cannon on the Masthuggetorg thundered forth resounding greetings toward the sea. The gentlemen of the East India Company were strolling back and forth along the harbor, estimating their handsome profits with happy smiles and rejoicing that their daring enterprises flourished increasingly with the years and that Göteborg's trade was blooming marvelously.

The East Indiaman's crew, about a hundred and fifty men strong, were landing in many boats and were preparing to hold their *Hönsning*—that is the name of the festival that is celebrated on such occasions by the crew and which often lasts several days. Musicians in curious, gay-colored costumes led the way with violins, fifes, oboes, and drums, which they played with vigor while singing all kinds of merry songs. The sailors followed them two by two, some with gaily beribboned jackets and caps from which fluttering pennants streamed, while others danced and leaped and all shouted with such exuberance that the sound echoed far and wide.

The joyful throng paraded across the wharf and through the outskirts of the city to Haga, where there was to be feasting and drinking in a large inn.

The finest beer flowed in rivers, and mug after mug was emptied. As is always the case when seamen return from a lengthy voyage, all sorts of pretty girls soon joined them. A dance began; the fun grew wilder and wilder, and the rejoicing louder and madder.

Only one lone seaman, a slim, handsome youth, scarcely twenty years old, had slipped away from the turmoil and was sitting alone on a bench by the door of the tavern.

A couple of sailors stepped up to him, and one of them called out, laughing loudly, "Elis Fröbom! Elis Fröbom! Are you being a wretched fool again and wasting these lovely moments with silly thoughts? Listen, Elis. If you are going to stay away from our *Hönsning,* then keep away from our ship. You will never be a decent, proper sailor. You have courage enough and are brave in times of danger, but you don't know how to drink and would rather keep your money in your pockets than throw it away on landlubbers. Drink, boy, or may the sea devil, Näck, that old troll, take you!"

Elis Fröbom jumped up quickly from the bench, looked at the sailors with glowing eyes, took the goblet that was filled to the brim with brandy, and emptied it at one gulp. Then he said, "You see, Joens, that I can drink like one of you, and the captain will decide whether I am a worthy seaman. But now shut your filthy mouths and get out! I hate your wildness. It is none of your business what I am doing out here."

"Well, well," replied Joens. "I know you are a Neriker man, and they're all sad and dreary and don't really enjoy the good life of a seaman. Just wait, Elis, I'll send someone out to you. You must be cut adrift from that confounded bench that you were tied to by the Näck."

Within a short time a very pretty girl came out of the inn and slid down beside the melancholy Elis, who was again sitting on the bench, silent and withdrawn. It was evident from her finery, from the whole manner of the girl, that she unfortunately sacrificed herself to evil pleasures; but the wild life had not yet exerted its destructive power on the unusual, gentle features of her charming face. There was not a trace of suppressed insolence; instead, a quiet, yearning sadness glowed in her dark eyes.

"Elis! Don't you want to share your comrades' joy? Don't you feel a little happy that you have come home again and have escaped the terrible dangers of the treacherous ocean?"

The girl spoke thus in a soft, gentle voice while she put her arm around the youth. Elis Fröbom, as though awakening from a deep dream, looked into the girl's eyes and, taking her hand, pressed it to his breast. One could see that the girl's sweet whisperings had found an echo in his heart.

"Alas," he began finally, as if considering what to say. "Alas—as to any gladness there is nothing there. At least I can't share my comrades' revelry. Go back inside, my dear child, and be gay with the others if you can, but leave the dreary, miserable Elis out here alone. He would only spoil all your fun. But wait! I like you very much, and you must think well of me when I am again at sea."

He took two bright ducats from his pocket, pulled a beautiful East Indian scarf from his breast, and gave them both to the girl. Bright tears came to her eyes as she rose, placed the ducats on the bench, and said, "Oh, keep your ducats. They only make me sad; but I will wear the beautiful scarf in remembrance of you. You probably will not find me here at the *Hönsning* next year when you stop in Haga."

The girl slipped away, her hands covering her face, not into the tavern but across the street in the other direction.

Elis Fröbom sank into melancholy reverie again and finally, when the celebration in the tavern became very loud and wild, exclaimed: "If only I lay buried at the very bottom of the sea! There is no one left in this life with whom I can be happy."

Then right behind him a deep, rough voice said, "You must have experienced a very great misfortune, young man, that you should wish for death just when your life should be beginning."

Elis looked around and saw an old miner who was leaning against the wooden wall of the tavern with his arms crossed and observing him with a serious, penetrating glance.

As Elis continued to look at the old man, it seemed to him as if a familiar figure were approaching him offering friendly comfort in the wild loneliness in which he believed himself lost. He pulled himself together and recounted how his father had been a fine helmsman but had been drowned in the same storm from which he himself had been rescued in a remarkable way. His two brothers, both soldiers, had been killed in battle; and he, all by himself, had supported his poor deserted mother from the excellent pay he received after each voyage to the East Indies. He had had to remain a sailor, since he had been destined for that calling since childhood, and it had seemed to him to be a great piece of luck to have been able to enter the service of the East India Company. The profit had turned out to be higher than ever this time, and each sailor had received a good sum of money in addition to his wages; so, with his pockets full of ducats, he had run to the little house where his mother lived happily. But unknown faces had looked out the window at him; and a young woman, who finally opened the door and to whom he explained himself, told him in a rough voice that his mother had died three months ago and that he could collect at the town hall the few rags that were left after the burial had been paid for. His mother's death had lacerated his heart; he felt abandoned by the whole world, as alone as if shipwrecked on a desolate reef—helpless, wretched. His whole life on the sea seemed to him like mad, pointless activity. In fact, when he thought that his mother had perhaps been badly cared for by strangers and had thus died without comfort, it seemed to him wicked that he had gone to sea at all and had not stayed at home to care for his poor mother. His comrades had dragged him by force to the *Hönsning,* and he had thought that the gaiety and strong liquor would deaden his sorrow, but instead, it had soon seemed to him as if the arteries in his breast were bursting and that he would bleed to death.

"Well," said the old miner. "Well, you will soon put to sea again, Elis, and your sorrow will be over in a short time. Old people die. That can't be changed, and your mother has departed a poor, laborious life, as you yourself said."

"Alas," replied Elis. "Alas, that no one believes in my sorrow! That I am ridiculed for being foolish and stupid is what alienates me from the world. I don't want to go to sea any more. The life there is hateful to me. My heart used to leap when the ship sailed forth on the sea, the sails spreading like stately wings, the waves splashing with gay music, the wind whistling through the rattling rigging. Then I rejoiced with my comrades on deck, and then—if I had the watch on a still, dark night—then I thought of the return home and of my good, old mother, of how she would rejoice again when Elis had returned! Then I was able to enjoy myself at the *Hönsning,* when I poured my ducats into my mother's lap; when I handed her the beautiful cloths and many strange objects from foreign lands; when joy flashed in her eyes; when she clapped her hands again and again, quite filled with happiness; when she tripped busily back and forth and fetched the best ale that she had saved for Elis. And when I sat with the old lady evenings, I would tell her about the strange people I had met, of their customs, of all the marvelous things that had happened to me on my long voyage. She enjoyed that greatly and would tell me of my father's remarkable voyages far up north and would serve up many frightening sailors' legends that I had already heard a hundred times and which I could never tire of hearing. Alas! Who can bring me these joys again! No, never again to sea. What should I do among comrades who would only mock me, and how could I take pleasure in the kind of work that would now seem only a tiresome effort without purpose?"

"I listen to you," said the old man when Elis grew silent. "I listen to you with pleasure, young man, just as I have had pleasure watching you for a couple of hours without your having seen me. Everything you did, what you said, proves that you have a pious, childlike nature that is turned inward, and heaven could not bestow a better gift on you. But never in all your life have you been suited to be a sailor. How can the wild, inconstant life at sea agree with you, a quiet Neriker inclined to melancholy?—that you are a Neriker I can see from the features of your face and from your whole bearing. You would do well to give up that life forever. But you won't remain idle? Follow my advice, Elis Fröbom! Go to Falun, become a miner. You are young, energetic. You will make a fine apprentice, then pickman, then miner. You will keep on moving up. You have some good number of ducats in your pocket that you can invest and which you can add to from earnings, and eventually you can acquire a small house and some land and have your own shares in a mine. Follow my advice, Elis Fröbom, become a miner."

Elis Fröbom was almost frightened at the old man's words.

"What are you advising me?" he cried. "Do you want me to leave the beautiful free earth, the cheerful sunny sky that surrounds me and quickens and refreshes me—I am to go down into the fearful depths of hell and like a mole grub around for ores and metal for a miserable pittance?"

"That," cried the old man angrily, "sounds like the common folk who despise what they can't appreciate. Miserable pittance! As if all the fearful torment on the surface of the earth that results from trading was nobler than the miner's work, whose skill and unflagging labor unlock nature's most secret treasures. You speak of a miserable pittance, Elis Fröbom! But perhaps there is something of higher value here. When the blind mole grubs in the earth out of blind instinct, it may well be that in the deepest tunnel, by the feeble light of the mine lamp, man's eyes see more clearly; indeed, in becoming stronger and stronger the eyes may be able to recognize in the marvelous minerals the reflection of that which is hidden above the clouds. You know nothing about mining, Elis Fröbom. Let me tell you about it."

With these words the old man sat down on the bench beside Elis and began to describe in great detail what went on in a mine and tried to give the ignorant boy a clear and vivid picture of everything. He talked about the mines of Falun, in which, he said, he had worked since childhood. He described the huge opening with the blackish-brown walls, and he spoke of the immeasurable wealth of the mine with its beautiful stones. His account became more and more vivid, his eyes glowed brighter and brighter. He roamed through the shafts as if through the paths of a magic garden. The minerals came to life, the fossils stirred, the marvelous iron pyrites and almandine flashed in the gleam of the miner's lights; the rock crystals sparkled and shimmered.

Elis listened intently. The old man's strange way of talking about the marvels under the earth as if he were in their midst engaged his whole being. He felt oppressed. It seemed to him as if he had already descended to the depths with the old man and that a powerful magic was holding him fast so that he would never again see the friendly light of day. And then it seemed to him again as if the old man had opened up to him an unknown world in which he belonged and that all the enchantment of this world had long ago been revealed to him in his earliest boyhood as strange, mysterious presentiments.

"I have," the old man finally said, "I have revealed to you, Elis Fröbom, all the splendors of a calling for which nature has actually destined you. Take counsel with yourself, and then do what your mind prompts you to do."

With that the old man jumped quickly up from the bench and strode away without saying goodbye or looking around again. He soon vanished from sight.

Meanwhile it had become quiet in the inn. The power of the strong ale and brandy had triumphed. Many of the sailors had slipped away with their girls; others lay in corners and snored. Elis could not go to his accustomed home, and at his request he was given a little room for the night.

Tired and weary as he was, he had scarcely stretched out on his bed when a dream touched him with her wings. It seemed to him that he was drifting in a beautiful ship in full sail on a crystal-clear sea, a heaven of dark clouds arching above him. But when he looked down into the waves, he realized that what he had thought was the sea was a solid, transparent, sparkling mass in the shimmer of which the whole ship dissolved in a marvelous manner so that he was standing on a crystal floor; and above him he saw a dome of darkly gleaming minerals, which he had at first thought were clouds in the sky. Driven by an unknown power, he strode on; but at that moment everything around him began to stir and, like curling waves, there shot up all around him marvelous flowers and plants of glittering metal, the blossoms and leaves of which curled upward from the depths and became intertwined in a most pleasing manner. The ground was so transparent that Elis could clearly see the roots of the plants; but when he looked down deeper and ever deeper, he saw in the depths innumerable, charming female forms who held each other locked in embrace with white, gleaming arms, and from their hearts there sprouted forth those roots and flowers and plants; when the maidens smiled, sweet harmony echoed through the dome, and the wondrous metal flowers thrust ever higher and became ever more gay. An indescribable feeling of pain and rapture seized the youth. A world of love, of desire, and of passionate longing expanded within him. "Down—down to you!" he cried, and he threw himself down with outspread arms onto the crystal ground. But it dissolved beneath him and he hovered in the shimmering air.

"Well, Elis Fröbom, how do you like it here among these splendors?" a hearty voice called. Elis saw the old miner beside him;

but as he stared at him, the miner changed into a gigantic shape, as if cast of glowing metal. Before Elis had time to be afraid, there was a sudden flash of lightning from the depths, and the solemn visage of a majestic woman became visible. Elis felt the rapture in his breast turn increasingly into crushing fear. The old man seized him and cried, "Take care, Elis Fröbom. That is the Queen. You may look up now."

Unconsciously he turned his head and saw that the stars in the night sky were shining through a crack in the dome. A gentle voice called his name in hopeless sorrow. It was his mother's voice. He thought he saw her figure through the cleft. But it was a charming young woman who stretched out her hand toward the dome and called his name.

"Carry me up there," he cried to the old man. "I belong to the upper world and its friendly sky."

"Take care," said the old man somberly, "take care, Fröbom! Be faithful to the Queen to whom you have given yourself."

But as soon as the youth looked down again into the majestic woman's rigid face, he felt his being dissolve into the shining minerals. He screamed in nameless fear and awoke from the strange dream, the rapture and horror of which resounded deep within his heart.

"That was inevitable," said Elis when he had pulled himself together with an effort. "That was inevitable. I had to dream such strange stuff. After all, the old miner told me so much about the splendor of the subterranean world that my whole head was full of it. But never in my whole life have I felt as I do now. Perhaps I am still dreaming—no, no—I am probably ill. I'll go outdoors. A breath of fresh sea air will cure me."

He pulled himself together and ran to Klippa Harbor where the revels of the *Hönsning* were beginning again. But he noticed that he did not feel happy, that he could not hang on firmly to any thoughts, and that presentiments and wishes that he could not name crisscrossed his mind. He thought sorrowfully of his deceased mother; then it seemed to him as if he were longing to meet that girl again who had spoken to him yesterday in such a friendly way. And then he feared that if the girl should appear in this or that little street, it would really only be the old miner whom he feared, although he could not say why. And yet he would have liked to have had the old man tell him more about the marvels of mining.

Tossed about by all these impelling thoughts, he looked down into the water. Then it seemed to him as if the silver waves were being transformed into a sparkling solid in which lovely, large ships were dissolving, and as if the dark clouds that were rising into the pleasant sky were massing and solidifying into a dome of stone. He was dreaming again; he saw the majestic woman's solemn visage, and that destructive yearning desire seized him anew.

His comrades shook him out of his reverie; he had to go along with them. But now it seemed to him as if an unknown voice were whispering constantly in his ear: "What do you still want here! Away! Away! Your home is in the mines of Falun. There all the splendors that you dreamed of will be revealed to you. Away! Away to Falun!"

For three days Elis Fröbom roamed around the streets of Göteborg, constantly pursued by the strange figments of his dreams, constantly admonished by the unknown voice.

On the fourth day Elis was standing by the gate through which the road to Gefle led. A large man was just passing through ahead of him. Elis thought he recognized the old miner, and irresistibly driven, he hurried after him but was unable to catch up with him.

On and on Elis went without stopping.

He knew very well that he was on the road to Falun, and it was this knowledge that calmed him in a special way, for he was certain that the voice of destiny had spoken to him through the old miner who was now leading him toward his true vocation.

Actually, particularly when he was uncertain of the way, he quite often saw the old man suddenly step out from a ravine or a thick copse or from behind the dark boulders and stride on ahead of him without looking around and then suddenly disappear again.

Finally, after many days of tedious wandering, Elis saw in the distance two large lakes, between which a thick mist was rising. As he climbed higher and higher to the heights on the west, he distinguished a couple of towers and some black roofs in the mist. The old man was standing like a giant in front of him, pointing with outstretched arms toward the mist, and then he vanished again among the rocks.

"That is Falun!" cried Elis. "That is Falun, the goal of my journey!" He was right, for people who were following behind him confirmed that the town of Falun was situated there between Lake Runn and Lake Warpann and that he was just climbing the Guffris mountain where the great *Pinge* or main entrance to the mine was situated.

Elis Fröbom walked on in high spirits, but when he stood before the huge jaw of hell, his blood froze in his veins and he became numb at the sight of the fearful, blighted desolation.

As is well known, the great entrance to the mine of Falun is about twelve hundred feet long, six hundred feet wide, and one hundred and eighty feet deep. The blackish-brown sidewalls at first extend down more or less vertically; about halfway down, however, they are less steep because of the tremendous piles of rubble. Here and there in the banks and walls can be seen timbers of old shafts that were constructed of strong trunks laid closely together and joined at the ends in the way block houses are usually constructed. Not a tree, not a blade of grass was living in the barren, crumbled, rocky abyss. The jagged rock masses loomed up in curious shapes, sometimes like gigantic petrified animals, sometimes like human colossi. In the abyss there were stones—slag, or burned-out ores—lying around in a wild jumble, and sulfurous gases rose steadily from the depths as if a hellish brew were boiling, the vapors of which were poisoning all of nature's green delights. One could believe that Dante had descended from here and had seen the Inferno with all its wretched misery and horror.

When Elis Fröbom looked down into the monstrous abyss, he thought of what the old helmsman on his ship had told him long ago. Once, when he was lying in bed with a fever, it had suddenly seemed to the helmsman that the waves of the sea had receded and that the immeasurable abyss had yawned beneath him so that he could see the frightful monsters of the depths in horrible embraces, writhing in and out among thousands of strange mussels and coral plants and curious minerals until, with their jaws open, they turned rigid as death. Such a vision, the old seaman said, meant imminent death in the ocean, and he actually fell from the deck into the sea accidentally shortly thereafter and vanished. Elis was reminded of the helmsman's story, for indeed the abyss seemed to him like the ocean depths when drained of the sea; the black minerals and the bluish-red metallic slag seemed like revolting monsters that were stretching out their tentacles toward him. It so happened that several miners were just climbing up from the depths, dressed in dark work clothes and with dark burned faces; they looked like ugly creatures who were creeping out of the earth with difficulty and were trying to make their way to the surface.

Elis felt himself trembling with horror, and a giddiness that he had never experienced as a sailor seized him. It seemed to him as if invisible hands were pulling him down into the abyss.

Shutting his eyes, he ran away, and not until he was far from the entrance and was climbing down Mt. Guffris again, and could look up at the cheerful sunny sky, was all his fear of that dreadful sight banished from his mind. He breathed freely once more and cried from the bottom of his soul, "O Lord of my life, what are all the horrors of the ocean compared to the frightfulness that dwells in that barren rocky abyss! Let the storm rage, let the black clouds dip down into the foaming flood, the glorious sun will soon reign again and the violent storm grow silent before its friendly face; but the sun's rays will never penetrate that stygian hell, and not a breath of spring air will ever refresh the heart down there. No, I do not wish to join you, you black earthworms; I could never accustom myself to your dreary life."

Elis thought he would spend the night at Falun and then start his journey back to Göteborg at daybreak.

When he came to the marketplace, which is called Helsintorget, he found a crowd gathered there.

A long parade of miners in full array, their lamps in their hands, musicians in the lead, had just halted in front of a stately house. A tall, slender, middle-aged man stepped out and looked around with a gentle smile. One could see that he was a true Dalkarl from his easy manners, his open expression, and the dark blue, sparkling eyes. The miners formed a circle around him; he shook everyone's hand cordially and spoke a few friendly words with each.

Elis Fröbom found out on inquiry that the man was Pehrson Dahlsjö, the chief official of the district and owner of a fine *Bergfrälse*. Estates in Sweden that are rented for their copper and silver works are called *Bergfrälse*. The owners of such estates have shares in the mines and are responsible for their operation.

Elis was also informed that the court session had just ended on that day and that the miners would then go to the houses of the mine owner, the foundry master, and the senior foreman and would be entertained hospitably.

When Elis observed the handsome, dignified people with their friendly, open faces, he was no longer able to recall those earthworms in the great entrance. The gaiety that inflamed the whole group when Pehrson Dahlsjö came out was quite different from the frenzied revelries of the sailors at the *Hönsning*.

The miners' kind of pleasure appealed directly to the quiet, serious Elis. He felt indescribably at ease, and he could scarcely keep back his tears when several of the younger lads began an old song that sounded the praises of mining in a simple melody that went straight to the heart.

When the song was over, Pehrson Dahlsjö opened the door of his house, and all the miners went inside. Elis followed automatically and stopped at the threshold so that he could see all around the spacious hall where the miners were sitting down on benches. A hearty meal was set out on a table.

Then the rear door opposite Elis opened, and a charming, beautifully attired young girl entered. Tall and slender, her dark hair wound in braids around her head, her neat little bodice fastened with rich brooches, she walked with all the grace of glowing maidenhood. All the miners rose and a happy, subdued murmur ran through the ranks: "Ulla Dahlsjö—Ulla Dahlsjö! God has indeed blessed our valiant chief with this lovely, innocent child of heaven!" Even the eyes of the oldest miners sparkled when Ulla shook their hands in friendly greeting. Then she brought in beautiful silver pitchers, poured out the excellent ale that is brewed at Falun, and served it to the happy company, her charming face aglow with the radiant innocence of heaven.

As soon as Elis Fröbom saw the girl, it seemed to him that a lightning bolt had struck his heart and ignited all the divine joy and all the pain and rapture of love that were enclosed in it. It was Ulla Dahlsjö who had offered him her hand to save him in that fateful dream. He now believed that he had guessed the dream's deeper meaning, and forgetting the old miner, blessed the fate that led him to Falun.

But then, standing on the threshold, he felt like a neglected stranger—wretched, miserable, abandoned. He wished he had died before he had even seen Ulla Dahlsjö, since he must now die of love and yearning. He was not able to turn his eyes away from the charming girl, and when she passed quite close to him, he called out her name in a gentle, trembling voice. Ulla looked around and saw poor Elis, who was standing there with a scarlet face and downcast eyes, rigid, incapable of words.

Ulla walked up to him and said with a sweet smile, "Oh, you are a stranger here, dear friend. I can see that by your seaman's clothing. Well, why are you standing there on the threshold? Do come in and be merry with us." She took his hand and pulled him into the hall and handed him a full mug of ale. "Drink!" she said. "Drink, my dear friend, to a warm welcome."

It seemed to Elis as if he were lying in a blissful dream of paradise from which he would shortly awaken and feel indescribably wretched. Mechanically he emptied the mug. At that moment Pehrson Dahlsjö stepped up to him, shook his hand in friendly greeting, and asked him where he came from and what had brought him to Falun.

Elis felt the warming strength of the noble drink course through his veins. Looking the worthy Pehrson in the eye, he became cheerful and bold. He related how he, the son of a sailor, had been at sea since a child; how he had just returned from East India and had found his mother, whom he had cherished and supported, no longer alive; how he now felt completely abandoned in this world; how the wild life on the sea was now quite repugnant to him; how his deepest inclinations were for mining; and how he wanted to try to be taken on as an apprentice miner in Falun. This last remark, which was just the opposite of everything he had decided to do just a few minutes before, came out quite automatically; it seemed to him that he couldn't have told the manager anything different, as if he had expressed his innermost desire, of which he had till now been unconscious.

With a serious expression, Pehrson Dahlsjö looked at the youth as if he wished to see into his heart, and then said, "I do not assume, Elis Fröbom, that mere frivolity has driven you from your previous occupation and that you have not considered carefully all the tedium and difficulties of mining before you made the decision to come here. There is an ancient belief among us that the mighty elements, among which the miner boldly reigns, will annihilate him unless he exerts his whole self in maintaining his mastery over them and gives thought to nothing else, for that would diminish the power that he should expend exclusively on his work in the earth and the fire. But if you have considered your true calling adequately and found it has stood the test, then you have come at a good time. I lack workers in my mine. If you wish, you can stay with me right now and, tomorrow morning, go with the foreman, who will show you your work."

Elis's heart was lifted at Pehrson Dahlsjö's words. He no longer thought about the horrors of that frightful hellish abyss into which he had looked. He was filled with rapture and delight that he would now see the lovely Ulla every day and would live under the same roof with her. He allowed himself the sweetest hopes.

Pehrson Dahlsjö informed the miners that a young apprentice had just reported in, and he introduced Elis Fröbom to them.

All looked approvingly at the sturdy youth and thought that he was a born miner with his slender, powerful build and that he was surely not lacking in industry or application.

One of the miners, already well along in years, approached him and shook his hand heartily, saying that he was the chief foreman in Pehrson Dahlsjö's mine and that he would make it a point to instruct him thoroughly in everything that he needed to know. Elis had to sit down beside him, and the old man began to speak at length—over a mug of ale—about the first duties of the apprentices.

The old miner from Göteborg came to Elis's mind again, and in some special way he was able to repeat almost everything that had been said to him.

"Why, Elis Fröbom," cried the chief foreman with astonishment. "Where did you get all that information? You really can't miss. In no time at all you will be the best apprentice in the mine."

The lovely Ulla, who was wandering among the guests and serving them, often nodded at Elis in a friendly way and urged him to enjoy himself. She said to him that he was no longer a stranger but belonged in the house and not to the deceitful sea. Falun with its rich mountains was now his homeland. A heaven full of rapture and bliss opened up to the youth at her words. It was noticed indeed that Ulla liked to linger with him, and even Pehrson Dahlsjö, in his quiet, serious way, observed him with approval.

But Elis's heart beat violently when he stood again by the steaming abyss of hell and, clothed in the miner's uniform, the heavy nailed boots on his feet, went down with the foreman into the deep shaft. At times hot vapors that encircled his breast threatened to choke him; at times the mine lights flared up from the cuttingly cold draughts that streamed through the abysses. They descended deeper and deeper, finally climbing down iron ladders scarcely a foot wide, and Elis Fröbom noticed that all the skill in climbing that he had acquired as a sailor did not help him here.

They finally reached the deepest bore, and the foreman assigned Elis the work that he was to do there.

Elis thought of the fair Ulla. He saw her form hovering like a shining angel above him, and he forgot all the horrors of the abyss, all the difficulties of the toilsome work. It was now clear in his mind that only if he dedicated himself to mining at Pehrson Dahlsjö's with all the strength of his mind and all the exertions that his body could endure would his sweetest hopes perhaps one day be fulfilled, and thus it was that in an incredibly short time he rivaled in work the most skilled miner.

With every day the worthy Pehrson Dahlsjö grew more and more fond of the industrious, pious youth and frequently said quite frankly to him that he had acquired in the young man not so much a worthy apprentice as a beloved son. Ulla's liking for him also became more open. Frequently, when Elis went to work and some danger was involved, she begged him, pleaded with him, bright tears in her eyes, to guard himself against accidents. And when he returned, she rushed out happily to meet him and always had the best ale or some tasty snack ready to refresh him.

Elis's heart beat with joy when Pehrson Dahlsjö once said that with his diligence and thrift, since he had already a good bit of money that he had brought with him, he would surely get a small house and some land or even a *Bergfrälse,* and then there would not be a property owner in Falun who would reject him when he came wooing a daughter. Elis should have said at once how indescribably much he loved Ulla and how all his hopes rested on possessing her, but a shyness he could not overcome kept him silent, although probably it was still the fearful uncertainty about whether Ulla, as he often suspected, truly loved him.

Once Elis Fröbom was working in the deepest bore, wrapped in such sulfurous fumes that his miner's light flickered dimly and he was scarcely able to distinguish the lodes in the rock, when he heard a knocking that seemed to be coming from a still deeper shaft and sounded as if someone were working with a hammer. Since that kind of work was impossible in the bore and since Elis knew that no one besides himself was down there, because the foreman had put his workers in the winding shaft, the knocking and hammering seemed quite uncanny. He put down his hammer and spike and listened to the hollow sounds that seemed to be coming nearer and nearer. All at once he saw a black shadow beside him, and as a cutting blast of air scattered the sulfur fumes, he recognized the old miner of Göteborg, who was standing at his side. "Good luck getting back up!" cried the old man. "Good luck to you, Elis Fröbom, down here among the rocks. How do you like the life, comrade?"

Elis wanted to ask by what marvelous means the old man had come to the shaft, but the latter struck the stone such a powerful blow with his hammer that sparks flew and a noise like thunder echoed through the shaft; and he called out in a terrible voice, "That is a marvelous lode, but you despicable, miserable rogue see nothing but a seam that is scarcely worth a straw. Down here you are a blind mole whom the *Metallfürst* [Metal Prince] will never favor, and up above you are also unable to accomplish anything and pursue the *Garkönig* [Refined Prince] in vain. Oh yes, you want to win Pehrson Dahlsjö's daughter Ulla for your wife, and therefore you are working here without love or interest. Beware, you cheat, that the *Metallfürst,* whom you mock, doesn't seize you and hurl you into the abyss so that all your bones are smashed on the rocks. And never will Ulla be your wife; that I say to you."

Anger welled up in Elis at the old man's insolent words. "What are you doing," he cried, "what are you doing in the shaft of my master, Pehrson Dahlsjö, where I am working with all my strength and as is proper to my calling? Get out as you have come, or we will see which one of us can bash in the other's skull."

Elis stood defiantly in front of the old man and raised the iron hammer with which he had been working. The old man laughed mockingly, and Elis saw with horror how he scrambled up the narrow rungs of the ladder as nimbly as a squirrel and vanished in the black cleft.

Elis felt paralyzed in all his limbs; the work would not progress, so he climbed up and out. When the old chief foreman, who was just climbing out of the winding shaft, saw him, he cried, "For God's sake, what happened to you, Elis? You look pale as death. It was the sulfur fumes, which you are not yet used to, that did it, wasn't it? Well, have a drink, boy. That will do you good."

Elis took a good swig of brandy from the bottle the chief foreman offered him, and then, feeling revived, told him everything that had happened in the shaft, as well as the mysterious way he had made the acquaintance of the uncanny miner in Göteborg.

The chief foreman listened quietly but then shook his head thoughtfully and said, "Elis Fröbom, that was old Torbern whom you met, and now I realize that what we relate about him here is more than a legend. More than a hundred years ago there was a miner here in Falun by the name of Torbern. He is said to have been one of the first who really made mining flourish in Falun, and in his time the profits were much greater than now. Nobody else knew as much about mining as Torbern, who with his thorough knowledge was in charge of all aspects of mining in Falun. The richest lodes were revealed to him as if he possessed a special, higher power. In addition, he was a gloomy, melancholy man, without wife, child, or his own home; and he almost never came into the daylight, but grubbed around unceasingly in the shafts; and so it was inevitable that a story arose that he was in league with secret powers who reign in the bowels of the earth and fuse metals. No one paid any attention to Torbern's warnings—he constantly prophesied that a disaster would occur if it were not true love for marvelous rocks and metals that impelled the miner to work. Out of greed, the mines were constantly enlarged until finally, on St. John's day of the year one thousand six hundred and eighty-seven, a frightful cave-in occurred that created our huge entrance and destroyed the whole structure to such an extent that many of the shafts could only be repaired with tremendous effort and great skill. Nothing more was seen or heard of Torbern, and it seemed certain that he had been killed by the cave-in, for he had been working in the deep bore. Soon after, when the work was going along better and better, the pickmen claimed that they had seen old Torbern, who had given them all kinds of good advice and had shown them the best lodes. Others had seen the old man walking around the main shaft, now complaining sadly, now raging angrily. Other youths came here as you did and maintained that an old miner had urged them into mining and had directed them here. That happened whenever there was a shortage of workers, and it may well be that Torbern looked after the mine in this way. If it really was old Torbern with whom you quarreled in the shaft, and if he spoke to you about a wonderful lode, then it is certain that there is a rich vein of iron in the rock, for as you know, iron-bearing veins are called trap-runs, and a trum is a vein of the lode that divides into a number of parts and probably runs out completely."

When Elis Fröbom, torn in his mind by various thoughts, came into Pehrson Dahlsjö's house, Ulla did not come to meet him in her friendly way as formerly. With her eyes cast down and tear-stained as Elis thought he observed, Ulla was sitting in the house beside a fine young man, who held her hand tightly in his and was trying to make all sorts of humorous remarks, which Ulla was not particularly listening to. Pehrson Dahlsjö took Elis, who was staring at the couple and was filled with apprehension, into another room and said, "Well, Elis Fröbom, you will soon be able to prove your love and loyalty to me, for even if I have always considered you as a son, now you will be a son in all ways. The man whom you see at my house is the rich merchant Eric Olawsen from Göteborg. I am giving him my daughter, whom he has wooed. He is going to take her back to Göteborg, and then you will stay here alone with me, Elis, the only support of my old age. Well, Elis, you are silent? You have turned pale. I hope that my decision does not displease you and that now that my daughter must leave me, you will not also want to leave. But I hear Herr Olawsen calling my name—I must go back."

With that Pehrson went back into the other room.

Elis felt his soul slashed by a thousand glowing knives. He had no words—no tears. He dashed out of the house in wild despair— away—away—to the huge entrance. If the enormous abyss presented a frightful sight in the daylight, now that night had arrived and the moon's disc was just beginning to gleam, the desolate rocks had a truly terrible appearance, as if an unnumbered crowd of fearful monsters, the frightful offspring of hell, were writhing and twisting together on the smoking ground, their eyes flashing fire, and stretching out their monstrous claws toward a wretched humanity.

"Torbern! Torbern!" Elis cried in such a fearful voice that the desolate abyss resounded. "Torbern, I am here! You were right. I was a vile fellow to yield to the foolish hope of life on the surface of the earth. My treasure, my life, my all lies below. Torbern! Climb up to me; show me the richest trap-runs. I will grub and bore and work there and never more see the light of day. Torbern! Torbern! Climb up to me!"

Elis took his flint and steel from his pocket and lighted his miner's lamp and went down into the shaft which he had yesterday been in without having seen the old man. How strange he felt when he clearly saw the seam in the deepest bore and could recognize the direction of the strata and the edge of the gouge.

But as he directed his eyes more and more sharply at the vein in the rock, it seemed as if a blinding light were passing through the whole shaft, and its walls became as transparent as the purest crystal. That fateful dream which he had dreamed in Göteborg returned. He looked into the fields of paradise filled with marvelous metal flowers and plants on which gems flashing fire were hanging like fruit, blossoms, and flowers. He saw the maidens; he saw the lofty face of the majestic Queen. She seized him, pulled him down, pressed him to her breast, and there flashed through his soul a glowing ray—he was conscious of only a feeling of drifting in a blue, transparent, sparkling mist.

"Elis Fröbom! Elis Fröbom!" cried a strong voice from above, and the light of torches was reflected in the shaft. It was Pehrson Dahlsjö himself who was coming down with the foreman to look for the youth whom they had seen running towards the main shaft in complete madness.

They found him standing rigid, his face pressed against the cold rock.

"What," cried Pehrson to him, "what are you doing down here at night, you foolish young man! Pull yourself together and climb up with us. Who knows what good news you will hear up above?"

Elis climbed up in complete silence, and in complete silence he followed Pehrson Dahlsjö, who did not cease from scolding him firmly for putting himself in such danger.

It was full daylight when they came to the house. Ulla rushed toward Elis's embrace with a loud cry and called him the most endearing names. But Pehrson Dahlsjö spoke to Elis. "You fool. Didn't I long know that you loved Ulla and that you work in the mine with such industry and zeal only for Ulla's sake? Didn't I long notice that Ulla also loved you from the very bottom of her heart? Could I wish for a better son-in-law than a fine, industrious, decent miner like you, my dear Elis? But it angered me, it offended me that you remained silent."

"Didn't we," Ulla interrupted her father, "didn't we ourselves know that we loved each other inexpressibly?"

"That," continued Pehrson Dahlsjö, "that may well be so. It suffices to say that I was angered that Elis did not speak openly and honorably to me of his love, and therefore, because I also wanted to test your heart, I served up the story with Herr Eric Olawsen, which nearly caused your destruction. You foolish young man! Herr Eric Olawsen has been married for a long time, and it is to you, dear Elis Fröbom, that I give my daughter in marriage, for I repeat, I could not wish myself a better son-in-law."

Tears of pure joy ran down Elis's cheeks. All of life's happiness had quite unexpectedly descended on him, and it almost seemed to him that he was again in the midst of a sweet dream.

At Pehrson Dahlsjö's command all the miners gathered for a festive meal.

Ulla was wearing her most beautiful dress and looked more charming than ever. Everyone cried, almost simultaneously, "Oh, what a magnificent bride our good Elis Fröbom has won! May heaven bless them both in their goodness and virtue."

The horror of the past night could still be seen on Elis Fröbom's face, and he frequently stared in front of him as if remote from everything around him.

"What is the matter with you, my Elis?" asked Ulla. Elis pressed her to his breast and spoke, "Yes, yes—You are really mine and now everything is well."

In the midst of all his bliss it sometimes seemed to Elis as if an icy hand were gripping his heart and a dark voice were speaking,

"Is this your highest ideal, winning Ulla? You poor fool! Have you not seen the Queen's face?"

He felt almost overcome by an indescribable fear. The thought tortured him that one of the miners would suddenly loom up as tall as a giant and that, to his horror, he would recognize Torbern who had come to remind him reprovingly of the subterranean kingdom of precious stones and metals to which he had surrendered himself.

And yet he did not know at all why the ghostly old man was hostile to him or what the connection was between his love and his work as a miner.

Pehrson indeed noticed Elis Fröbom's disturbed behavior and ascribed to it to the unhappiness he had endured and to the trip into the shaft on the previous night. But not Ulla, who was filled with a secret presentiment and pressed her beloved to tell her what horrible thing had happened to him that was tearing him away from her. Elis's heart was about to break. In vain he strove to tell his beloved of the marvelous face that had revealed itself to him in the shaft. It was as if an unknown power held his mouth closed by force, as if the fearful face of the Queen were looking out of his inner being, and that if he should call her by name, everything around him would be turned to dreary, black stone, as occurs when Medusa's dreadful head is viewed. All the splendor that had filled him with the deepest rapture down in the shaft now seemed like a hell full of wretched agony, deceitfully adorned for the purpose of enticing him to his destruction.

Pehrson Dahlsjö commanded that Elis Fröbom stay at home for several days to recover completely from the illness to which he seemed to have succumbed. During this time, Ulla's love, which flowed bright and clear from her childish, innocent heart, dispelled all recollections of that fateful adventure in the shaft. Elis lived in bliss and joy and believed in his good fortune which no evil power could destroy.

When he went down again into the shaft, everything seemed quite different. The most marvelous lodes lay revealed before his eyes; he worked with redoubled zeal; he forgot everything; when he returned to the surface, he had to recall Pehrson Dahlsjö and his Ulla; he felt split in half; it seemed to him that his better, his true being, was climbing down into the center of the earth and was resting in the Queen's arms, while he was seeking his dreary bed in Falun. When Ulla spoke to him of her love and how they would live together happily, then he began to speak of the splendor of the shaft, of the immeasurably rich treasures that lay concealed there, and he became entangled in such strange, incomprehensible speeches that fear and anxiety seized the poor child and she did not know at all how Elis could have changed so suddenly into a quite different person.

With the greatest delight, Elis kept reporting to the foreman, and to Pehrson Dahlsjö himself, how he had discovered the richest veins and the most marvelous trap-runs; and when they found nothing but barren rock, he would laugh disdainfully and say that he alone understood the secret signs, the meaningful writing that the Queen's hand itself had inscribed in the rock and that it was actually enough to understand these signs without bringing their meaning into the light of day.

The old foreman looked sadly at the youth, who with wildly sparkling eyes was speaking of the radiant paradise that flared up in the depths of the earth.

"Alas, sir," the old man whispered in Pehrson Dahlsjö's ear. "Alas, sir, evil Tornbern has bewitched the poor youth."

"Don't believe in such superstitions, old man," replied Pehrson Dahlsjö. "Love has turned the head of the melancholy Neriker—that is all. Just let the marriage take place, and trap-runs and treasures and subterranean kingdoms will all be done with."

The wedding day set by Pehrson Dahlsjö finally arrived. Several days before, Elis Fröbom had become quieter, more serious, and more withdrawn than ever, but never had he been so devoted in his love to charming Ulla as he was at this time. He did not wish to be separated for a moment from her, and therefore he did not go to the mine. He did not seem to be thinking at all of his troubled activity as a miner, for not a word about the subterranean kingdom crossed his lips. Ulla was utterly blissful. All her fears that the threatening powers of the subterranean abyss, of which she had often heard the miners speak, would lure Elis to his destruction had disappeared. Pehrson Dahlsjö also spoke to the old foreman: "Surely you see that Elis Fröbom had only become giddy in the head out of love for my Ulla."

Early in the morning on his wedding day—it was Saint John's day—Elis knocked at the door of his bride's chamber. She opened it and reeled back when she saw Elis already dressed in his wedding suit, pale as death, dark, flashing fire in his eyes.

"I only wish," he said in a soft, hesitant voice, "I only wish to tell you, my dearly beloved Ulla, that we are standing near the peak of the greatest happiness that is granted to men on earth. Everything has been revealed to me in the past night. Down in the shaft the cherry red sparkling almadine lies enclosed in chlorite and mica, on which is inscribed the chart of our life. You must receive it from me as a wedding present. It is more beautiful than the most splendid blood-red carbuncle; and when we, united in true love, look into its radiant light, we can clearly see how our inner beings are intertwined with the marvelous branch that is growing from the Queen's heart in the center of the earth. It is only necessary that I fetch this stone up to the daylight, and that I will do now. Farewell for now, my dearly beloved Ulla. I will be here again shortly."

Ulla begged her beloved with hot tears to desist from this visionary undertaking, since she had a foreboding of the greatest misfortune. But Elis Fröbom assured her that without that gem he would never more have a peaceful moment and that there was no reason to fear that any danger threatened. He pressed his bride to his breast with fervor, and departed.

The guests had already assembled to escort the bridal couple to the Kopparberg Church, where the marriage was to be performed after divine service. A whole crowd of elegantly clad young girls, who were to march in front of the bride as bridesmaids according to the customs of the country, were laughing and joking around Ulla. The musicians were tuning their instruments and were practicing a gay wedding march. It was already nearly midday, and Elis Fröbom had not yet appeared. Suddenly some miners, with fear and horror on their pale faces, came rushing in and announced that a frightful cave-in had destroyed the entire excavation at Dahlsjö's mine.

"Elis—my Elis! You are gone! Gone!" Ulla shrieked loudly and fell down as if dead. Pehrson Dahlsjö learned for the first time from the mine inspector that Elis had gone to the great entrance early in the morning and had gone down into it; but no one else had been working in the shaft, since all the apprentices and miners had been invited to the wedding. Pehrson Dahlsjö and all the miners hurried to the main entrance; but their search, which was carried on only at great risk, was in vain. Elis Fröbom was not found. It was certain that the cave-in had buried the unfortunate youth in the rocks. And so misfortune and misery came to the house of Pehrson Dahlsjö at the very moment when he thought he had achieved repose and peace for his old age.

The good owner and overseer Pehrson Dahlsjö had long since died; his daughter Ulla had vanished. No one in Falun remembered anything about them, for a good fifty years had passed since that calamitous wedding day. Then one day miners who were investigating an opening between two shafts found the corpse of a young miner lying in sulfuric acid in a bore nine hundred feet deep. When they brought the body to the surface, it appeared to be petrified.

The body looked as if the youth were lying in a deep sleep, so well preserved were the features on his face and so without trace of decomposition were the elegant miner's clothes, even the flowers on his breast. All the people of the area gathered around the youth who had been carried up from the main shaft, but no one recognized the features of the corpse, and none of the miners could recall that any of their comrades had been buried alive. They were about to carry the corpse to Falun when a hoary woman, ancient as the hills, appeared, hobbling along on her crutches.

"Here comes Saint John's Granny!" cried several of the miners. They had given this name to the old woman because they had long since noticed that she would appear every year on Saint John's day and would look down into the depths, wringing her hands, groaning sadly and lamenting as she crept around the main shaft; and then she would vanish again.

Scarcely had the old woman seen the petrified youth than she dropped her crutches, stretched her arms toward heaven, and uttered wretched sounds of lamentation. "Oh, Elis Fröbom—oh, my Elis—my darling bridegroom!"

She squatted down beside the body and seized the stiffened hands and pressed them to her withered breast beneath the icy sheath of which, like a holy naptha flame, a heart filled with ardent love was burning.

"Alas," she spoke then, looking around in a circle. "Alas, no one, not one of you, knows poor Ulla Dahlsjö any longer, this young man's happy bride of fifty years ago. When I moved to Ornäs full of grief and sorrow, old Torbern comforted me and said that once again on this earth I would see my Elis, whom the rocks buried on my wedding day, and so I have come here every year and have looked down into the abyss with longing and true love. This blissful reunion has been granted to me this day. Oh, my Elis—my beloved bridegroom!"

Again she put her withered arms around the youth as if she would never leave him, and all those standing around were deeply moved.

The old woman's sighs and sobs became quieter and quieter until they died away into silence.

The miners stepped forward. They wanted to raise poor Ulla up, but she had breathed out her life on the body of her petrified bridegroom. They noticed that the corpse of the unfortunate man, which they had thought was petrified, was beginning to turn to dust.

The youth's ashes, along with the body of his bride, who had been faithful unto death, were placed in the Kopparberg Church, where the couple were to have been wed fifty years before.

Translated by L. J. Kent
and E. C. Knight

The Fermata

On the Significance
of an Interrupted Cadence

Hummel's amusing and vivacious picture, "Company in an Italian Inn," won immediate renown when it was shown in the autumn of 1814 at the Art Exhibition in Berlin, where it delighted everyone who looked at it. Under an arbor almost hidden in foliage, the painting shows a table well furbished with wine flasks and fruit, and seated facing each other on the opposite sides two Italian ladies, one singing, the other playing a guitar; standing somewhat in the background between them, an abbot acts as music director. With baton raised, he is awaiting the moment when the Signora, with a long trill, shall end the cadence in the midst of which—as her eyes are directed toward Heaven—the artist has just caught her; looking at the picture, one knows that the abbot's hand will then descend sharply, while the guitarist gaily dashes off the dominant chord. The abbot is filled with admiration—indeed, with exquisite delight; yet his attention, at the same time, is tautly concentrated. It is plain that not for the world would he miss the proper downward beat. He hardly dares to breathe. If he could, he would stop every bee's buzzing, the movement of every fly. So much the more, then, is he irritated by the bustling intrusion of the host, who must needs choose just this decisive and supreme moment to come in with the wine! Beyond the arbor, one can see a tree-arched avenue, where a horseman has just pulled up for a refreshing drink, which is at this moment being handed up to him, so that he can enjoy it without dismounting.

"The more I look at this singer," said Edward, "who, it is true, seems a bit old for her gay costume but, nonetheless, is obviously fired with the true inspiration of her art; the more I am delighted by the grave but truly Roman profile and lovely form of the guitarist, and the more amused I become by the earnest mien of my estimable friend the abbot, the more the whole painting seems to me instinct with the freedom and vitality of actual life. It is plainly a caricature, in the higher sense of that term; but it also suggests a certain charm and joy. I should like to step into that arbor and open one of those little wine bottles that are tempting me on the table. I tell you more—I fancy that I can already catch something of the bouquet of that rare vintage! And I feel—come, now, it would be a sin if this cheerful solicitation were wasted on the cold, insensitive atmosphere that surrounds us here! Let us go and drain a flask of Italian wine in honor of this fine picture, in honor of art, and in honor of merry Italy, where life is exhilarating and pleasure is given its due!"

While Edward was thus running on in lively—if somewhat disconnected—sentences, Theodore stood silent, deeply absorbed in his own sober reflection. "Yes, that is what we will do. Come along," he said at last, starting up as if he were waking from a dream. It was plain, nevertheless, that he had some difficulty in tearing himself away from the picture. And as, almost mechanically, he followed his friend, he had to stop at the door, and turn around for another lingering and longing look at the singer and the guitarist, and the abbot who was directing their performance. . . .

Edward's proposal, however, was very easy to execute! The friends crossed the street diagonally, and very soon they were seated in the little blue room of the Sala Tarone, before a flask of wine that was the very image of those in the painting they had just left.

"It seems to me," said Edward—as Theodore remained thoughtful and silent, even after several glasses of wine—"it seems to me that you are more deeply impressed by that painting than I am; and that your impression is not so agreeable as mine."

Theodore still did not break his silence for a moment. "I assure you that I did not lose anything of the brightness and grace of that animated composition," he said at last. "And yet," he added, slowly, "it is very strange: that picture is a true and accurate representation of a scene out of my own life. The faithful portraits of the individuals concerned are nothing short of startling. And you will agree with me that such swift memories themselves, unexpectedly and extraordinarily brought to life as if by the stroke of a magician's wand, must exert a sudden and remarkable power over the mind. That is how it stands with me at this moment."

"What!" exclaimed Edward, in astonishment. "A scene out of your own life? Do you mean to say that the picture represents an episode that you have actually seen and can actually remember? I saw at once that the two ladies and the priest were eminently successful pieces of portraiture; but I could never for one moment have dreamed that you had met them in the flesh, in the course of your own personal experience! My dear friend, do tell me about it! We are entirely alone here. Nobody else will come into the café at this hour. Tell me what happened, who they are, how it all came about."

"I will gladly do that," Theodore responded. "But I must go a long way back. You must bear with me if I carry you back to my childhood!"

"Never mind that! Go ahead!" rejoined Edward. "As a matter of fact, I don't know as much as I'd like to about your early youth. And if the story lasts a long time, the worst that can happen is that we shall have to empty a bottle more than we'd bargained for. To that, I know, nobody will have any objections: neither ourselves nor Signor Tarone."

Thus encouraged, Theodore embarked upon his recital. "It can surprise nobody," he began, "that in planning my future I threw everything else aside and devoted myself entirely to the noble art of music. For even as a little boy I would rather play the piano than do anything else; and I spent hours and hours strumming upon my uncle's creaking, jarring, tuneless old instrument. The little town where I lived was badly off for music: there was nobody who could teach an aspiring student except one opinionated old organist, who made a religion of tempo and plagued me almost to death with obscure and unmelodious toccatas and fugues. I would not let myself be daunted, however; I held on like grim death. In fact, although the old fellow was crabbed and faultfind-

ing, he was in his own way something of a master: he had only to
play a good piece in his own powerful style, to reconcile me to the
man and his art.

"It thus happened that I would often be thrown into a curious
state of mind. Especially, many pieces by old Johann Sebastian
Bach would seem to me almost like harrowing ghost stories, and
I would give myself up to that mood of pleasurable awe to which
we are so prone in the days of our fantastic youth. But I entered
within the gates of a real Eden when, as sometimes happened in
winter, the town bandmaster and his colleagues, supported by a
few amateurs of moderate ability, would give a concert, and I
would be permitted to play the kettledrum in the symphony. It
was not until long afterwards that I realized how extravagant—
indeed, how ridiculous—these concerts were. My teacher usually
played two piano concerti by Wolff or Karl Philipp Emanuel Bach,
a member of the town band would be struggling with Stamitz,
while the local tax collector worked away at the flute with un-
bounded energy, and took in such an immense supply of breath
that he blew out both the candles on his music stand, and someone always had to relight them for him.

"As for singing, that wasn't given much attention among us.
My uncle, who was a friend of the arts and a great patron of
music, always disparaged local talent along this line. His mind still
dwelt with exuberant delight upon those days, now long gone by,
when the four choristers of the town's four churches would join
forces in a performance of *Lottchen am Hofe.* Above all, he was
wont, in this connection, to extol the mutual tolerance that united
the singers in this work of art—for, you understand, not only were
the Catholic and the Evangelical bodies separate and hostile, but
the Reformed Community was itself split in two sections: those
who spoke German and those who spoke French. The French
chorister was not daunted by the *Lottchen,* but, my uncle maintained, sang his part, spectacles on nose, in the finest falsetto that
ever proceeded from the human throat!

"Now there was among us at this time—I mean in our town—
a spinster named Meibel, whose age was about fifty-five years, and
whose only means of livelihood was the scanty pension she received as a former court singer at the Residenz. And my uncle was
rightly of the opinion that Miss Meibel might still do something

to earn money in the concert hall. She assumed airs of importance when she was approached on this question, and she required a great deal of coaxing; but at last she consented to appear on our stage, and so we came to have *aria di bravura* at our concerts. She was a singular creature, this Miss Meibel. I still retain the lively recollection of her thin little figure, as, dressed in a particolored gown, holding her roll of music in her hand, and looking inexpressibly solemn, she was wont to step to the front of the stage and acknowledge the presence of the audience with a slight inclination of the upper part of her body. Her headdress, especially, was remarkable: I remember that it had a bouquet of china flowers fastened in front, and as she sang these would keep up a continual trembling and nodding, distracting to see. At the end of her song, when the audience had greeted her with unstinted applause, she would first hand her music roll, somewhat haughtily, to my uncle, and would then permit him to dip his thumb and finger into a little porcelain snuffbox, fashioned in the shape of a pug dog, out of which she took a pinch herself with obvious pleasure.

"You will better understand my telling you that we did not pay much attention to singing, when I add that this prima donna of our concert stage had a horrible squeaky voice, with which she indulged in all sorts of ludicrous flourishes and roulades. And you can imagine the effect of all this—combined with her ridiculous manners and style of dress—upon a sensitive, music-loving lad like myself. My uncle lost no opportunity to shower praise upon Miss Meibel's performance. And I, who could not understand this at all, turned naturally to my organist; he looked with contempt upon vocal efforts in general, and he delighted me down to the ground by parodying the absurd old spinster's antics, with a certain hypochondriac malice that I found irresistibly amusing.

"The more emphatically I came to share my master's scorn for singing, the higher he rated my musical abilities. He took a great and zealous interest in instructing me in counterpoint, so that I was soon composing the most ingenious toccatas and fugues. And it happened that on my nineteenth birthday I was entertaining my uncle with one of these adroit specimens of my skill, when the head porter of our town's leading hotel stepped into the room to announce the visit of two foreign ladies who had just arrived at his establishment.

"Before my uncle could throw off his dressing gown—its material was of a large flower pattern—and don his coat and waistcoat, his callers entered the room. You know what an electrifying effect every unusual event has upon almost any individual brought up in the narrow confines of a small country town; this sudden encounter was, preeminently, of a sort to work a complete revolution in my mind. Picture to yourself two tall and slender Italian ladies, dressed in bright-colored costumes that seemed fantastic to me (though as a matter of fact they were of the latest mode), who approached my uncle with the freedom of professional *artistes,* yet with considerable charm of manner, and addressed him in firm and resonant tones. What the deuce, I asked myself, was that strange language they were speaking? Only now and then was there a sound that bore the slightest resemblance to German. And it was plain that my uncle didn't understand a word. Embarrassed, incapable of intelligible human utterance, he stepped back and pointed to the sofa. The two ladies sat down and talked together—and their voices were like music itself. At length they succeeded in making my good uncle understand that they were singers on tour. They wished to give a concert in our town, and so they had come to him, as the proper man with whom to conduct musical negotiations.

"As they were talking together I picked up their Christian names; and soon I was able to distinguish one from the other. In the confusion of their first overwhelming appearance that had been impossible! Now I noticed that Lauretta, apparently the older of the two, looked about her with sparkling eyes, and talked away at my embarrassed old uncle with an effervescent vivacity that had its natural accompaniment in demonstrative gestures. Teresina, taller, more slender, and with a much more serious face, spoke very little; but what she said was intelligible. Now and then a rather peculiar smile flitted across her face. It almost seemed as if she were amused by my respected uncle, who had withdrawn into his gay silk dressing gown like a snail into its shell, and was desperately preoccupied with the vain effort to push a treacherous yellow string out of sight within its folds: it was the cord of his nightshirt, and it kept falling out from under his dressing gown, apparently yards and yards long.

"At length the ladies rose to take their leave. My uncle promised to make all arrangements for their concert to be given on the third day following. Then the sisters (we knew now that they were sisters) gave him, and me, a most courteous invitation to take chocolate with them in the afternoon. My uncle, in the meantime, had introduced me as a young musician, which naturally pleased me very much.

"That afternoon, then, we went to the hotel restaurant—but I must confess that we made our way up the steps with a solemn and awkward gait. We both felt odd and out of place, as if we were going to meet some adventure to which we were not equal. As a result of careful preparation for the occasion, my uncle had at his tongue's end a great many fine things to say about art, which nobody understood—neither he himself nor any of the rest of us. When these impressive pronouncements had been made (and when I, smiling through my pain with the stoical fortitude of a Scaevola, had thrice burned my tongue with the scalding hot chocolate), Lauretta said that she would sing for us. Teresina took up her guitar, tuned it, and struck a few full chords. It was the first time I had ever heard that instrument, and the characteristic mysterious sounds of the trembling strings made a deep and remarkable impression upon me.

"Lauretta began to sing very softly; but soon she held a note to *fortissimo*, and then quickly broke into a crisp and complicated run through an octave and a half. I can still remember the words with which her song began: '*Sento l'amica speme.*' My heart was as if gripped—and even oppressed—by wonder. I had never had an idea of anything of this kind! But as Lauretta's voice continued to soar, in bolder and higher flights, and as the musical notes fell upon me like the sun's sparkling rays, I was roused from any sense of oppression to, indeed, its liveliest opposite. I felt that all the music within my own spirit, which had lain mute and sleeping all my life, had now been awakened and enkindled, so that it could burst forth in strong and splendid flame. Ah, I had never before heard music; in all my nineteen years, I had never known what music was. . . .

"After this, the sisters sang one of those great imposing duets of Abbot Steffani, which confine themselves to notes of low register. My whole soul was stirred by Teresina's alto, sonorous and pure as silver bells. I couldn't for the life of me restrain my emotion; tears started to my eyes. My uncle coughed warningly and cast indignant glances in my direction, but it was no use: I was really quite beside myself. This seemed to please the sisters. They began to inquire into the nature and extent of my musical studies. I was ashamed, now, of my labors and performances in that line; and with the hardihood born of enthusiastic admiration I bluntly declared aloud what I had already said to myself—that I had to-day heard music for the first time in my life. . . .

" 'The dear, good boy!' lisped Lauretta, so sweetly and bewitchingly that my head was more than ever in a whirl.

"When I reached home, I was seized with a sort of fury. I pounced upon all the clever toccatas and fugues that I had hammered out, and threw them in the fire; and not only my own compositions, but with them a beautiful copy of forty-five variations on a canonical theme that the organist had written and had done me the honor of presenting to me. And as the double counterpoint smoked and crackled in the flames I laughed with spiteful glee. Then I sat down at the piano, and tried first to imitate the tones of the guitar, then to play the sisters' melodies; I climaxed my efforts by attempting to sing them. My uncle put an end to this at last, about midnight, when he came out of his bedroom and called to me, 'My boy, you'd better stop that screeching and troop off to bed!' Then he put out both candles, and went back to his own room.

"I had no alternative but to obey. But the mysterious power of song came to me in my dreams—at least I thought it did—and I sang *'Sento l'amica speme'* in excellent style!

"The next morning my uncle hunted up everybody who could fiddle and blow, and gathered them together for the rehearsal. He was filled with pride over the idea of showing the visiting *artistes* what good musicians our town possessed; but everything seemed, in stubborn perversity, to go wrong. Lauretta set to work on a fine *scena,* but very soon the orchestra was all at sixes and sevens in the recitative: not one of the players had any idea of the accompaniment. Lauretta screamed, raved, wept with impatience and anger. She poured the bitterest reproaches upon the organist, who was presiding at the piano; silent and obdurate, he got up and marched out of the hall. The orchestra leader (our town bandmaster), whom she had just been railing at as an *'assino tedesco,'*

196 · E. T. A. Hoffmann

tucked his violin under his arm, slammed his hat down on his head with an air of defiance, and likewise made for the door. The members of his company, respectively sticking their bows under the strings of their violins and unscrewing the mouthpieces of their brass instruments, followed him.

"Only the dilettanti were left in the hall; and they gazed about them disconsolately, while the local tax collector expressed the feelings of them all as he exclaimed, with an air of overwhelming tragedy, 'Gracious Heaven! How mortifying I find all this!'

"All my natural diffidence vanished. I could not let our great occasion fail this way! I could not let this promise of real music go unfulfilled! I jumped right in front of the orchestra leader: I begged, I pleaded, in my desperation I promised him six new minuets with double trios for the town's annual ball! And so I succeeded in appeasing him. He went back to his place; his companions followed suit; and soon the orchestra was reconstituted, with the single exception of the organist, who was already outside the building and crossing the marketplace, and could not be moved, by any shouting or beckoning, to turn back.

"Teresina had looked on at this whole scene with smothered laughter. And Lauretta was now as full of merriment and delight as she had been, a few moments before, of anger. She was lavish in her praise of my efforts; and, since we had now no one at the piano, she asked me if I could play that instrument. Before I knew what I was about, I was sitting in the organist's place, with the music before me. Never in my life had I accompanied a singer, to say nothing of assisting in the direction of an orchestra! But the sisters were kindness itself. Teresina sat down beside me at the piano, and gave me every beat. Lauretta encouraged me with repeated 'Bravos!' The orchestra proved to be cooperative. And things continued to improve. At the second rehearsal everything went off satisfactorily. And when the townspeople crowded the hall for the great concert, the effect of the sisters' singing was something not to be described.

"The Prince's return to the Residenz was soon to be celebrated with a number of festive demonstrations in the capital, and the sisters had been summoned to sing in the theater and at concerts then. But until the time came for these command performances they decided to remain in our little town, and so it happened that they gave us several more concerts. The admiration of the public reached the point of frenzy. But old Miss Meibel took a pinch of snuff out of her porcelain pug, and gave it as her opinion that 'such impudent caterwauling was not singing; singing,' she added, 'should be low and melodious.' And my old friend the organist never showed himself once, either among the musicians or in the audience.

"But, to tell the truth, I did not miss him! I was the happiest fellow in the world. I spent all of every day with the sisters, copying out the vocal scores of what they were to sing at the capital. Lauretta was my ideal. I endured with patience her unpredictable—not to say outrageous—caprices, her outbursts of passionate violence, the torments she inflicted upon me as her pianist. What did all that matter? She alone had unsealed for me the springs of true music. . . . I began to study Italian, and I tried my hand at a few canzonets. And in what heavenly rapture was I plunged when Lauretta sang one of my compositions, or even praised it! Often it seemed to me that it was not I who had thought out and set to music what she was singing, but that the creative impulse itself only shone forth for the first time as she sang.

"With Teresina, on the other hand, I somehow could not get on familiar terms. She seldom sang. And she did not seem to take much account of all I was doing. Sometimes I even imagined that she was laughing at me behind my back.

"It was indeed different with Lauretta; and when the time came for them to leave the town, I realized for the first time how dear she was to me, and how unendurable it would be to be separated from her. Often, when she was in a mood of tender playfulness, she had touched my cheek, or stroked my head, in a fashion that was nonetheless caressing because it was also completely artless. And at such times only the realization of her ordinary coolness toward me would restrain my ardent impulse to clasp her in my arms. But now, as I was about to lose her forever, my passion was heightened by despair.

"I possessed a tolerably good tenor voice, which, however, I had never tried to cultivate. Under the spur of my association with the sisters I began to practice assiduously; and frequently Lauretta and I would sing some tender Italian duet (you know them—there are so many!) together. Now it happened that as the hour of departure was drawing near we were singing one of these pieces: *'Senza di te ben mio, vivere non poss' io!'* (Without thee, my own, I cannot live!) And—can you blame me that I could not resist it? In desperation I threw myself at Lauretta's feet. And she gently pulled me up again.

" 'But, my friend,' she said, in tones that moved me through and through, 'need we part?'

"And as I stood there, thunderstruck with amazement, she quietly proposed that I should accompany Teresina and herself to the capital. If I intended to devote myself wholly to music, she continued, I must certainly leave this wretched little town sometime or other. What time could be better than now?

"My friend, can you picture to yourself a man struggling in the dark depths of boundless despair, a man who has given up all hope of happiness and fulfillment in this life, and who now—in the very moment when he awaits the blow that is to crush him forever—suddenly finds himself transported to some gloriously bright rose arbor, where unseen but loving spirits whisper to him, 'You are still alive, and we cherish you—you are still alive!'? I repeat—can you imagine this, my good friend? If so, you will know how I felt at this moment. To go along with Lauretta and Teresina to the capital! The dream came to life as an ineradicable resolution. . . .

"But I won't bore you now with the recital of all the details of my procedure: how I set to work to convince my uncle that I ought by all means to go, and now, to the capital—which, as a matter of fact, was not very far away. At length he gave his consent. And, furthermore, he announced his intention of going with me. I did not dare to state my purpose of traveling in company with the two sisters. Again, I was distracted. But at just the right moment my uncle caught a violent cold; he had to stay at home, and I was free!

"I left the town by the stagecoach, but I went only as far as the first stopping place. There I awaited my divinity. My purse, happily, was well lined. I had thus been able to make all proper preparations for my journey. And I had been seized with the romantic notion of accompanying the ladies in the character of a protecting paladin, and as such a knight should—on horseback. I procured a horse, which its owner assured me was quiet and docile—though

I must admit it was not romantically handsome—and I rode back at the appointed time to meet the two fair singers. I soon saw their little carriage coming toward me. It had two seats: Lauretta and Teresina occupied the principal one, while on the other, with her back to the horses, sat their maid, the fat and brown-cheeked little Neapolitan Gianna. In addition, the carriage was packed with boxes, satchels, and baskets, of all shapes and sizes, such as always accompany ladies on their travels. And there were also two pug dogs, which Gianna was holding in her lap, and which began to bark when I gaily saluted the company.

"All had gone very well, and we were completing the last section of the journey, when my steed all at once conceived the idea that it was high time to be returning homeward. Being aware that stern measures were not always blessed with a high degree of success in such cases, I felt advised to have recourse to milder means of persuasion; but the obstinate brute remained insensible to all my well-meant exhortations. I wanted to go forward. He wanted to go backward. And all the advantage that my efforts gave me was that, instead of taking to his heels for home, he ran around in circles. Teresina leaned out of the carriage and had a hearty laugh. Lauretta held her hands before her face and screamed as if my life were in danger.

"Together, these responses served to give me the courage of despair. I drove the spurs into the brute's ribs. But the result was not what I had hoped for. I was abruptly hurled from his back, and found myself sprawling on the ground. The horse, now, stood perfectly still; and, stretching out his long neck, he regarded me with what I could only take to be a look of derision. I, alas, was unable to rise to my feet: the driver of the carriage had to come and help me. Lauretta, meanwhile, had jumped out, and was weeping and lamenting. Teresina did nothing but laugh. As for me, I had sprained my ankle in my fall: it was impossible for me to mount the horse and ride again. What was I to do? Well, my erstwhile steed was tied to the carriage, while I, perforce, got into it. . . .

"So now, my friend, you can imagine us all—two rather robust young women, a fat servant girl, two pug dogs, a dozen boxes, satchels, and baskets, and myself as well, all packed into a small vehicle. Imagine Lauretta's complaints over her lack of comfort, crowded in as she was; the maid's witless Neapolitan chattering, the yapping of the dogs, Teresina's sulky silence, and the inexpressible pain I had now begun to feel in my foot, and you will have some idea of my enviable situation!

"Before long, Teresina declared that she could not stand it any longer. The driver stopped the carriage. In a trice she was out on the road, had untied my horse, and was up in the saddle, prancing and curvetting around us. I must indeed admit that she cut a fine figure. The dignity and carriage that marked her ordinary bearing were still more pronounced when she was on horseback. In a few moments she asked for her guitar, and, dropping the reins on her arm, she began to sing proud Spanish ballads with a full-toned accompaniment. Her thin silk dress fluttered in the wind, and light played in sparkling sheen upon its folds, while the white feathers of her hat waved and quivered as if in accompaniment to the air she sang. Altogether, she made such a romantic picture that I could not take my eyes off her, even though Lauretta was scolding her for making herself look like a fantastic simpleton, and was predicting that she would suffer for her senseless daring.

"But no accident occurred. Either the horse had lost his stubbornness, or else he preferred the fair singer to the would-be paladin. Be that as it may, Teresina did not dismount from the horse and reenter the carriage until we were almost at the city gates.

"If you had seen me then at concerts and operas, if you had observed my joyous concentration on music of all sorts, if you had heard me as a diligent accompanist at work at the piano on arias, duets, and I don't know what besides—if you had been a witness of all this, my friend, you would have realized, by the complete change in my behavior, that my being itself had been completely changed. Indeed, there was a new and rich spirit within me. I had conquered, cast off, forgotten, all my rustic shyness; and now I sat at the piano with my score before me like an experienced professional, directing my prima donna's performance. My mind was filled with happy melodies. And it was with a reckless disregard of all those laboriously studied rules of counterpoint that I composed for Lauretta a vast variety of canzonets and arias.

"She sang them all: but only in her own room. Why would she never sing any of my pieces at a concert? I could not understand it. And, while Lauretta continued to inspire me, the eyes of my imagination would suddenly be filled also with the sight of Teresina curvetting on her proud steed, with her lute in her hands, like the figure of Art itself in some romantic disguise. Without consciously thinking of Teresina, without having any aim in view, I wrote several songs of a high and serious nature. And something of the difference between the two sisters permeated my mind, although at the time I scarcely realized it. Lauretta played with her notes like some capricious fairy queen, forever regal and forever blessed: there was nothing upon which she ventured that was not crowned with success. But never did a roulade cross Teresina's lips. Nothing more than a simple interpolated note, at most a *mordent,* sounded from her throat when the sisters sang together. Yet her long-sustained notes gleamed like meteors through the darkness of night, and awakened strange spirits who came and gazed with earnest eyes into the very depths of my heart. I do not know, now as I look back upon it, how I remained in ignorance so long!

"The sisters were granted a benefit concert, and in it I joined with Lauretta in a long *scena* from *Anfossi.* As usual, I presided at the piano. We came to the last *fermata,* and Lauretta was exerting all her skill, demonstrating all her art; she warbled trill after trill, like a nightingale; she executed sustained notes, and then long elaborate roulades—a whole *solfeggio.* In fact, I thought that this time she was almost carrying the thing too far. As I was musing to this effect, I felt a soft breath on my cheek: Teresina stood behind me. And at this moment Lauretta took a good start with the intention of swelling up to a 'harmonic shake,' and so passing back into *a tempo.* The Devil entered into me: I jammed down the keys with both hands; the orchestra followed suit; and it was all over with Lauretta's trill, just at the supreme moment when she was to sweep her audience to the highest pitch of astonishment.

"She turned to me with such a look of fury that I felt almost annihilated, crushed her roll of music in her hand, and threw it at my head; then she rushed, as if smitten by madness, through the orchestra, and into the offstage waiting room. As soon as we had played through the piece, I followed her.

"She wept and raved. 'Out of my sight, you blackguard!' she screamed, as soon as she saw me. 'You devil, you've completely ruined me! Ruined my reputation, my honor—and my trill. Out of my sight, you devil's brood!'

"She made a rush as if to attack me physically, but I escaped through the door. And while someone else was performing on the stage, Teresina and the music director succeeded in so far pacifying her as to win her consent to coming out again. But she made one condition: I was not to be allowed to touch the piano.

"Then, in the last duet that the sisters sang, Lauretta did contrive to introduce the swelling 'harmonic shake,' and was rewarded with a storm of applause. Whereupon she settled down into the best of humors.

"But I could not get over the outrageous treatment that I had received at her hands in the presence of a large audience; and I made up my mind that I would leave her the next morning, and return to my native town. I was actually engaged in packing my things when Teresina came into my room. Observing what I was about, she exclaimed in astonishment, 'What! Are you going to leave us?' And I gave her to understand that after the affront Lauretta had put upon me I could not think of remaining any longer in her society.

" 'And so,' responded Teresina, 'you are going to let yourself be driven away by the preposterous conduct of a little fool, who is now heartily sorry for what she has done? I ask you, where else than with us can you better live in your art? And let me tell you, too, that it only depends on yourself and your behavior, to keep her from such pranks as this. You are too pliable, too soft, too gentle. What is more, you rate her powers too highly. It is true that her voice is not bad, and it has a wide range. But those fantastic warblings and flourishes, those extravagant runs, those never-ending shakes—what are they but delusive artifices of style, which people admire in the same way that they admire the foolhardy agility of a tightrope walker? Do you really think that such things as that can make any deep impression, that they can stir the heart? The "harmonic shake" which you spoiled,' she continued with emphasis, 'is a thing I cannot tolerate. When she attempts it, I always feel anxious and pained. And then this scaling up into the region of the third line above the stave—what is that but a violent straining of the natural voice? And the natural voice, after all, dear friend, is the only thing that really moves the heart. . . . I like the middle notes and the low notes; a sound that goes through to the heart, a quiet and easy transition from note to note—those are the things I love above all. No useless ornamentation; a firm, clear, strong note; a definite expression, which reaches and transports the mind and the soul—that's real, true singing, and that's how I sing.

" 'If you can't be reconciled to Lauretta,' she added, a little wistfully, 'then think of Teresina, who indeed likes you so much that you shall, in your own way, be her musical composer. Don't be cross—but all your elegant canzonets and arias cannot match this single piece. . . .' And in her lovely, resonant voice she sang a simple devotion canzona that I had written a few days before.

"I had never dreamed that it could sound like that. I felt the power of the music going through and through me. Tears of joy and rapture stood in my eyes. I grasped Teresina's hand, and as I pressed it to my lips I swore, over and over and over again, that I would never leave her.

"Lauretta showed a certain envious attitude toward my intimacy with her sister, but she suppressed any obvious sign of vexation; for the fact was, as I soon realized, that she could not do without me. In spite of her skill in singing, she read badly, and she was uncertain in time and beat. Teresina, on the contrary, sang everything at sight, and her ear for time was perfect in its accuracy. Never did Lauretta give such free rein to her capricious and violent temper as when her accompaniments were being practiced: they were never right; they were nothing but a necessary evil anyway; the piano ought not to be heard at all; it must always be *pianissimo*. So there was nothing to do but give way to her again and again, and alter the time just as the whim happened to strike her at the moment. Now, however, I took a firm stand against her. I combatted her impertinences. I taught her that an accompaniment devoid of energy was nothing short of inconceivable, and that there was a marked difference between supporting the song—carrying it along—and letting it run riot, without time and without form. Teresina faithfully lent her assistance in all this. And now I composed nothing but church pieces, and wrote all the solos for a voice of low register. It is true that Teresina also tyrannized over me not a little, but I submitted to her despotism with a good grace. She had, I assured myself, more knowledge of good

German seriousness, and (so at least I thought) deeper appreciation of it, than her sister could possess.

"When we were touring in south Germany, some time after the incident I have just recalled, we met, in a little town, an Italian tenor who was making his way from Milan to Berlin. My fair companions were delighted with their fellow countryman. And he, for his part, attached himself closely to them, and cultivated Teresina's acquaintance, especially, with such eagerness and success that to my great vexation I soon came to feel that my role among them was only secondary. At last affairs came to a sudden climax. One day, as I was about to enter the sisters' sitting room with a roll of music under my arm, the voices of my companions and the tenor, engaged in an animated conversation, fell upon my ear. My name was mentioned. I pricked up my ears. Unashamed, I listened. Lauretta was telling the whole tragic story of the concert in which I had cut short her trill by prematurely striking the concluding notes of the bar. '*Assino tedesco!*' the tenor exclaimed.

"I felt as if I must rush into the room and throw the flighty hero out of the window; but I restrained myself. I continued to listen, however. And I heard Lauretta go on to say that she had been minded to send me about my business immediately, but had been so moved to compassion by my clamorous entreaties as to tolerate me for some time longer, since I was studying singing under her. This, to my utter amazement, Teresina confirmed.

" 'Yes, he's a good child,' I heard the latter add. 'He's in love with me now, and he sets everything for the alto. He is not without talent, but he must rub off that stiffness and awkwardness that are so characteristic of the Germans. I hope to make a capable composer out of him. Then he shall write me some good things—for as yet there is very little written for the alto voice—and after that I shall let him go his way. He's a terrible bore,' she went on, 'with his billing and cooing and lovesick sighing; and he bothers me much too much with his tedious compositions, which so far have been poor stuff.'

" 'I at least got rid of him,' Lauretta interrupted. 'And you know, Teresina, how the fellow pestered me with his arias and duets.'

"And now she began to sing a duet of my composing, which formerly she had praised very highly. The other sister took up the second voice; and both in tone and in execution they burlesqued me in the most shameful manner. The tenor laughed until the walls rang with the echo of his mirth. My limbs seemed frozen. But at once I came to an irrevocable decision. I quietly slipped away from the door and back to my own room, the windows of which looked out upon a side street. Opposite was the post office. The post-coach for Bamberg had just driven up to take on the mails and passengers. The latter were standing ready waiting in the gateway, but I still had an hour to spare. . . .

"Hastily packing my things, I generously paid the whole of the bill at the hotel, and hurried over to catch the post-chaise. As I crossed the broad street I saw the fair sisters and the Italian standing at the window, and leaning out to hear the sound of the post-horn. I leaned back in the corner of the chaise, and dwelt with a good deal of satisfaction upon the crushing effect of the bitter and scathing letter that I had left behind for Lauretta and Teresina at the hotel."

With evident gratification, Theodore tossed off the rest of the fiery Aleatico that Edward had poured into his glass. The latter, opening a new bottle and skillfully shaking off the drops of oil that floated on top of the wine, remarked, "I should not have dreamed Teresina capable of such artfulness and falsity. I cannot banish from my mind the recollection of the charming picture she made— on your mind and through you on mine—as she sat singing Spanish ballads on horseback, while the steed gracefully pranced and curvetted along the road."

"That was her climactic point," Theodore interrupted. "I still remember the strange impression the scene made upon me. I forgot my pain. She seemed to me like a creature of some higher race. It is indeed true that such moments are turning points in one's life, and that in them images arise that time is powerless to dim. Whenever I have succeeded in any fine *romanza,* it has always been when Teresina's image has stepped forth from the treasure house of memory, in clear bright colors, at the moment of writing it."

"At the same time," said Edward, "let us not forget the artistic, and 'temperamental,' Lauretta. And, casting all rancor to the winds, let us drink to the health of the two sisters."

They did so. And as he raised his glass Theodore exclaimed,

"Oh, how the fragrant breezes of Italy rise from this wine and fan my cheeks! My blood courses through my veins with quickened energy. Oh, why was I obliged so soon to leave that glorious land?"

"As yet," interrupted Edward, "as yet, in all that you have told me, there has been no connection, so far as I can see, with the delightful painting we were looking at. And so I believe that you still have something to tell me about these two sisters. Of course I perceive that the two ladies in the picture are none other than Lauretta and Teresina—but come, you must have something more to say."

"You are right," replied Theodore. "They are Lauretta and Teresina; and I still have something more to say, to which my sighs and ejaculations, my longing for the lovely land of Italy, will form a fitting introduction. . . .

"A short time ago," he now plunged again into his narrative, "perhaps two years since, as I was about to leave Rome, I made a little excursion on horseback. Before a village inn, as I went riding along, I saw a charming young girl; and the thought came to me, how pleasant it would be to receive a glass of wine from the hands of that pretty child. I pulled up before the door, in an avenue so thickly planted with shrubs that only patches of sunlight could make their way through the leaves. In the distance I heard sounds of singing, and the tinkling of a guitar. And I pricked up my ears and listened, as I became conscious that the two female voices were affecting me in quite a singular way.

"Strange recollections were stirring dimly in my mind, but they refused to take definite shape. By this time, however, I was so interested that I got down from my horse, and slowly approached the vine-covered arbor from which the music seemed to proceed— eagerly listening, meanwhile, to catch every sound. The second voice had fallen silent. The first sang a canzonet alone. As I drew nearer, the sense of familiarity faded; the initial attraction ceased to beckon me; but I was still interested. The singer was now in the midst of an elaborate and florid *fermata*. Up and down she warbled, and down and up; at length, holding one note for a long time, she stopped. Then all at once a woman's voice broke out in a torrent of abuse, maledictions, vituperations, curses. A man protested. Another man laughed. The second female voice joined in the altercation. The quarrel waxed louder and more violent, with true Italian fury. At last I stood directly in front of the arbor, and an abbot rushed out and almost knocked me down. As he turned his head to look at me, I recognized my good friend Signor Lodovico, my musical newsmonger from Rome."

" 'What in the name of wonder—' I exclaimed. But he interrupted me, screaming.

" 'Oh, sir, sir!' he cried. 'Save me! Protect me from this mad fury, this crocodile, this hyena, this tiger, this devil of a woman! It is true that I did what I did: I was beating time for her to Anfossi's canzonet, and I brought down my baton too soon while she was in the midst of the *fermata*. I cut short her trill. I admit it. But why did I meet her eyes, the devil-goddess! Deuce take all *fermate*, I say!'

"In a most curious state of mind, I hastened into the arbor, taking the priest back with me. And at first glance I recognized the sisters Lauretta and Teresina. The former was still shrieking and raging. Her sister was still earnestly remonstrating with her. The host of the inn, his bare arms crossed over his chest, was looking on and laughing, while a serving girl was placing fresh flasks of wine on the table. And now my entrance still more strangely complicated the scene.

"For both sisters knew me at once. No sooner had they caught sight of me than they literally threw themselves upon me, apparently in a transport of affection. 'Ah, Signor Teodoro!' they exclaimed, and both embraced me. The quarrel of a moment before was totally forgotten.

" 'Here you have a composer,' said Lauretta to the abbot, 'who is as charming as an Italian, and as strong as a German.' Then both sisters, continually interrupting each other, began to recount the happy days we had spent together, to tell how they had discovered my musical abilities while I was still a youth, to praise my compositions, to recall our hours of practice together; never did they enjoy singing anything, they said, but what I had arranged or composed.

"Teresina at length informed me that a manager had engaged her as his first singer in tragic parts for his next music festival; but now, she said, she would give him to understand that she would sing for him only on condition that the composition of at least one tragic opera was entrusted to me. The tragic was above all others my special field, she averred, and so on, and so on.

"But now Lauretta maintained that it would be a great pity if I did not follow my bent for the light and the graceful—in a word, for *opera buffa*. She had been engaged as prima donna for this type of composition; and it was simply a matter of course—it went without saying—that no one but I should write the piece in which she was to appear. . . .

"You may imagine what my feelings were, as I stood there between the two! In short, you perceive that the company I had just joined was the one that Hummel painted, and that the painting shows the group at precisely the moment when the priest is about to cut short Lauretta's *fermata*."

"But," Edward broke in, "did they not make any allusion to your departure, or to the scathing letter you left behind?"

"Not with so much as a syllable," Theodore answered. "And you may be very sure that I said nothing about any of that. The fact is, I had long ago banished all animosity from my heart, and had come to look upon my adventure with the two sisters in the light of a merry prank. I did, however, make one oblique reference to the subject, not addressing them, but speaking to the priest. I told him that, several years before, the same mischance had befallen me, in one of Anfossi's arias, as had been his ill luck today; I painted the period of my association with the sisters in tragicomic colors, and, throwing off many a keen side-blow, I gave them an unmistakable understanding of the superiority that the ripe experience of the intervening years had given me, both in life and in art.

" 'And a good thing it was,' I concluded, 'that I cut that *fermata* short. For it was evidently meant to last through eternity. And I am firmly of the opinion that if I had left the singer alone I should be sitting at the piano now.'

" 'But, Signor,' said the priest, 'what director is there who would dare to lay down rules for the prima donna? Your offense was much more heinous than mine, for you were in the concert hall, and I was here in a leafy arbor. Besides, I was director in imagination only; what I did was of no importance whatever. And if the sweet fiery glance of those heavenly eyes had not fascinated me, moreover, I should not have made an ass of myself.'

"The abbot's last words had a calming effect; for although Lauretta's 'heavenly eyes' had begun to flash with anger as he was speaking, she was quite appeased by the time he had finished with his pretty compliment.

"We spent the evening together. It was fourteen years since I had left my fair friends, and many changes had taken place in that time. Lauretta, though she looked somewhat older, had by no means lost her charm. Teresina had worn somewhat better, and her figure was as graceful as before. Both were dressed in rather gay colors, and their manners were exactly as I remembered them— that is, they were, let us say, fourteen years younger than the ladies themselves. At my request, Teresina sang some of the serious songs that had once so deeply affected me, but I fancied that they did not sound quite the same as when I had first heard them. And Lauretta's singing, also, seemed to me to be quite different from my recollection of it, even though her voice had not appreciably lost anything in power or range.

"The sisters' behavior to me, their feigned ecstasies, their crude praise—even though this last took the form of gracious patronage—had done much to put me in a bad humor; and now my mood deteriorated still further in the obtrusiveness of this comparison between the romantic images in my mind and the not overly pleasing reality. I was restored to a more amiable temper at last by the drolleries of the priest—who in the most saccharine phrases imaginable was playing the *amoroso* to both sisters at once—as well as by numerous glasses of the good wine. And we ended by spending a very pleasant evening in perfect concord and companionable gaiety. The sisters were most pressing in urging me to accompany them to their home, so that we might at once discuss the parts that I was to write for them and begin to make our plans without delay. But, needless to say, I did not accept their invitation. And I left Rome without making any effort to find out where they lived."

"And yet, after all," Edward reflected, "it is to them that you owe the awakening of your musical genius. . . ."

"That I know well!" Theodore replied. "I admit that I owe this to them, and many good melodies besides. And that is just the reason why I did not want to see them again. Every composer, as I said a minute ago, has experienced certain impressions which time does not obliterate. The spirit of music spoke, and the artist heard the creative word that suddenly awoke the answering spirit within himself; and that inner spirit was never to sleep again. Thus it is unquestionably true that when a melody has been called in this way from the depths of the composer's being, it seems to belong to the singer who fanned the artist's first inner spark. It is as if one heard her voice, and merely recorded what she had sung.

"But it is in the human heritage of us weak mortals," Theodore continued, "that we are all too prone to drag what is superearthly down within the narrow enclosure of this earthly life where we, poor clods, dwell. And so it comes to pass that the singer becomes the lover, or even the wife. The spell is broken. And all that melody of her nature, which was formerly the revelation of glorious things, is now voiced in complaints about broken soup plates or the ink stains on fresh linen. Happy is the composer who never again, as long as he lives, sets eyes upon the woman who by some mysterious power kindled the flame of music within him! Even though the young artist's heart may be rent by anguish and despair when he must part from his lovely enchantress, nevertheless it is precisely so that she will continue to exist for him as a divinely beautiful strain of music itself: it is so that she will live on and on in his heart and mind, never losing her youth or her loveliness, and forever engendering harmonies in which he forever feels the presence of his love. For what is she, now, but the Highest Ideal which, working its way from within outward, is at last reflected in external form?"

"A strange theory, but not impossible," Edward commented. And the two friends, arm in arm, made their way from the Sala Tarone, and out into the street.

Translated by Ch. Lazare

The Deed of Entail

Rossitten castle, the ancestral seat of the Barons von Ross, lies close to the shores of the Baltic sea. It is in a wild, desolate region with scarcely a blade of grass pushing up out of its bottomless drift sands; and whereas in other districts a baronial castle is generally surrounded by fine gardens, here a sparse wood grows right up to the building's naked walls upon the landward side. The funereal gloom of its Scotch pines makes even spring a mockery. For here are no gay songs of waking birds; all the noises this woodland hears are the horrid cawing of ravens and the confused screechings of gulls. But only a quarter of a mile away the whole scenery changes; and one is transported, as if by magic, into flowering fields, rich pasture, and ploughland. Before one lies a prosperous village with one large house belonging to the bailiff, while at the head of a slope covered with alders stand the foundations of another castle, planned by one of the former Barons. His successors, however, let his project drop, and dwelt not here but on their estates in Courland; and even Baron Roderick von Ross, who resumed residence on these ancestral lands, did not go on with the new building. He found living in the old lonely castle by the shore more agreeable to his gloomy misanthropic nature, and had such repairs as were possible done to it, before shutting himself up there with one morose steward and a few servants.

Baron Roderick was seldom seen in the village, though he often walked or rode out along the shore, and the villagers told tales of having heard him from a distance loudly addressing the waves, and of having seen him listening to their hiss and roar, as if to hear the answering voice of the sea spirit. He had a little room built for himself at the top of the watchtower, and equipped it with telescopes and astronomical instruments; and there he would stand by day, looking out to sea and watching the frequent ships that passed like white-winged birds across the far horizon. Clear nights he spent in astronomical—or, it was alleged, astrological—observations, in the company of his ancient steward.

Moreover, rumor had it that he had given himself over to the occult sciences—to the so-called black arts—and that he had been banished from Courland for some unsuccessful practices which had seriously injured the reigning house of that province. The slightest reminder of his life there certainly filled him with horror, but whatever misfortunes had befallen him he ascribed to his ancestors' wicked desertion of their castle at Rossitten. So, to compel the heads of the family to reside there for the future, he affixed an entail to the estates—an arrangement that met with his overlord's approval, since it retained on his lands a family of some military distinction, which had begun to stray abroad.

Nevertheless, neither Roderick's son Hubert nor the present owner of the property, named Roderick also after his grandfather, consented to live in the family castle. Both preferred to stay in Courland, perhaps because, being of a more cheerful disposition than their gloomy forebear, they shunned residence in such desolate surroundings. By Lord Roderick's permission, two old unmarried sisters of his father's, who had been left ill provided for, lived with one aged woman servant in some small sheltered rooms in one wing; and besides them and their cook, who had a large ground-floor room beside the kitchen, there was also one aged huntsman. He filled the post of steward, and tottered about the high rooms and reception halls of the main building. The rest of the servants lived down in the village at the bailiff's.

It was only in the autumn, when the early snow began to fall and the season for wolf and boar hunts came round, that the empty, abandoned castle came alive. Then relatives and friends with their huntsmen came over from Courland, and the main building and wings were scarcely large enough to house the influx of guests. High-piled fires crackled in every stove and on every hearth; the meat jacks hummed from early morning till night, and the stairs were thronged with a bustling, jovial crowd of masters and servants. Wine glasses clinked, hunting songs rang out, there was shrill music and dancing, loud laughter and merriment, and for four to six weeks the castle was more like a fine inn on a much-frequented road than the residence of a landed gentleman.

Baron Roderick gave up as much time as he could to serious business and, withdrawing from the tumult of entertainment, attended to the affairs of his estate. He had a full account of its revenues put before him, listened to all proposals for improvements, and did his utmost to remedy any wrongs or injustices. In all these matters he had the able assistance of Herr Voetheri, an old lawyer of a family that had been legal advisers to the Rossitten estates from father to son. It was Herr Voetheri's habit to leave for the castle about a week before the owner's expected arrival.

Now, in the year 1790 the time had come round for his visit. But though the old man felt very strong at sixty, he must have thought that some assistance would be helpful. For, half in jest perhaps, he said to me one day: "Nephew"—I was actually his great-nephew—"A little sea air might do you good. Why don't you come with me to Rossitten and lend me a hand with the business—it's often very intricate—and you can have a taste of rough hunting as well. Spend one morning drawing up a report for me in your best hand, and the next you can go out after wild game— the shaggy gray wolf and the long-tusked boar. You can see then whether you have the courage to stare such creatures in the eye, and perhaps if you shoot straight enough you may bring one down." I had heard rare stories of the hunting at Rossitten, and I was deeply attached to my excellent old uncle; and so, quite delighted by the invitation and fairly practiced in his legal work, I accepted, promising to take all the work I could off his shoulders.

Next day, swathed in thick furs, we were driving in a coach through a snowstorm that warned us of the approach of winter, on our way to Rossitten. On the way my uncle told me some strange tales about the Baron Roderick, who had drawn up the entail and, to his great surprise—for he was still a young man— taken him as legal adviser and executor of his will. He spoke of the old nobleman's uncouth and violent nature, which seemed to have descended right through the family. For even the present Baron, whom he had first known as a mild, somewhat weak-willed young man, seemed to inherit more of it as the years went by. He warned me that I must speak up for myself boldly, if I wanted his

Lordship to take any notice of me. Then he described the rooms in the castle which he had chosen for himself long ago, for their warmth and comfort, and because they were sufficiently removed for him to be able to withdraw at will from the noisy society of the guests. They were a couple of small tapestry-hung apartments leading off the great audience chamber, in the opposite wing to the two old ladies' quarters.

Our journey was quick but most fatiguing, and it was late at night that we drove through Rossitten village. As it was Sunday, dance music and laughter rang out from the inn, and there was a sound of singing from the bailiff's house, which was lit up from garret to cellar. All of which made the wasteland into which we now drove appear the more horrible by contrast. A cutting sea wind howled dolefully across it, and the gloomy pines groaned in dull complaint as if it had just woken them from an enchanted sleep. Soon the black castle walls loomed up against a background of snow, and we pulled up at the closed gates. But though we shouted and cracked the whip, hammered and knocked, it was in vain. Everything seemed dead. There was no light in any window.

Then my uncle raised his strong, booming voice. "Franz, Franz!" he cried. "Get stirring, the devil take you! We're freezing here at the gate and our faces are chapped with the cold. Devil take you, get stirring!"

At that a watchdog began to whimper, and we saw a light moving on the ground floor. Soon we heard a jangling of keys and the heavy gates creaked open. "Ah, welcome, welcome, your worship," cried Franz, raising his lantern so high that the light fell on his shriveled face, strangely contorted into a friendly smile. The coach drove into the courtyard, and it was not till I got out that I noticed the old servant's odd appearance. He was enveloped in a capacious old-fashioned huntsman's uniform, most marvelously trimmed and braided. His broad forehead was pale, with just two gray locks falling across it, while the lower part of his face had a healthy huntsman's tan; and though his contorted smile seemed to have transformed his face into a queer mask, the stupid good nature that shone from his eyes and played about his lips gave quite a contrary impression.

"Now, Franz, old man," began my great-uncle, knocking the snow from his furs in the lobby, "is everything ready? Have the tapestries been beaten in my room, and the beds set up? Have you kept a good fire going there yesterday and today?"

"No," replied Franz. "No, your worship, nothing has been done."

"For goodness' sake!" began my great-uncle. "I wrote early enough, and I always come on time. This is churlish behavior. Am I to live in ice-cold rooms, then?"

"Yes, your worship," replied the huntsman, very carefully snipping a glowing "thief" from the candlewick with his snuffers and stamping it out on the floor. "You see, nothing would have helped much, not even heating. The wind's driving the snow in too hard through the broken windows. So . . ."

"What!" interrupted my great-uncle, throwing open his furs and putting his arms akimbo. "The windows are broken, and you, the steward, have done nothing about it?"

"Yes, your worship," answered the old man quietly and calmly. "You can't get at them for all the rubble and stones lying about the room."

"How the blazes have rubble and stones got into my rooms?" shouted my great-uncle.

"Bless you, young gentleman," cried the old man with a polite bow, for I had just sneezed. "It's the stones and plaster from the partition wall that fell in at the great crash," he went on to explain.

"Have you had an earthquake?" burst out my great-uncle in a fury.

"No, not an earthquake," answered the old man, smiling all over his face, "but three days ago the great coffered ceiling of the audience hall fell down with a tremendous crash."

"May the . . ." My great-uncle was on the point of breaking into a mighty oath; but just as he was raising his right hand and pushing his fur cap back from his forehead with his left, he suddenly mastered himself and said, turning to me with a loud laugh, "Nephew, we had better hold our tongues. One more question and we shall hear of even worse disaster. The whole castle may fall in on our heads. But, Franz," he asked, "couldn't you have had the sense to clean another room for us and light a fire in it? Couldn't you have quickly fitted up some apartment in the main building for my audience chamber?"

"That has all been done," answered the old man, obligingly leading us to the stairs and beginning to mount.

"Now there's a queer customer for you," exclaimed my uncle, as he followed him up.

We walked through long vaulted corridors, Franz's flickering light throwing strange gleams into the pitch darkness. Pillars, capitals, and arches, momentarily lit, seemed to be floating unsupported in the air. Our gigantic shadows stalked beside us, gliding over grotesque portraits on the walls, which seemed to waver and tremble as we passed, and to whisper in the booming echo of our steps: "Do not wake us. But let us sleep our enchanted sleep within these old stones."

At last, after leading us through a series of cold dark chambers, Franz threw open the door of a great hall, where a bright, glowing open fire greeted us with a cheerful crackle. I felt at home as soon as I went in, but my uncle remained standing in the middle of the room. "Well," said he, solemnly looking around him. "So this is to be our audience chamber, is it?"

"It won't be the first time that justice has been done here," answered Franz in a gloomy voice, raising his lantern at that moment to reveal a light patch the shape of a door on the huge, dark wall.

"What do you mean?" cried my uncle, hastily throwing off his furs as he drew near to the fire.

"Oh, it just slipped out," replied the old servant, lighting the lamps and throwing open an adjoining room which had been most comfortably furnished for our reception.

It was not long before a table was laid beside the fire and Franz brought us up a well-cooked supper, followed, to our great satisfaction, by a good bowl of punch brewed according to the northern recipe. My uncle was exhausted by the journey and went to bed immediately after his meal, but I was too excited by my new and strange surroundings—not to mention the punch—to think of sleep. Franz cleared the table, made up the fire, bowed in most friendly fashion, and left me.

I sat alone in the high feudal hall. The snow was giving over and the wind had ceased to howl. The sky had cleared, and a bright full moon shone through the wide bow windows, casting its magic beams into all the dark corners of this strange room, which the weak light of my candle and the glimmering fire had failed to penetrate. The walls and ceiling were decorated in the queer old style peculiar to ancient castles, the ceiling heavily coffered and the walls hung with fantastic paintings in carved gilt and colored frames. Most of the pictures were of wild boar and wolf hunts, with the heads of the men and animals carved in relief, and so perfectly were they applied to the painted bodies that, in the flickering light of the moon and fire at least, the scenes had a certain living and ghastly reality. Among them were some life-sized portraits of gentlemen in hunting dress, those ancestors of the Baron's, no doubt, who were so enthusiastic for the chase. All the paintings and carvings bore the dark color of age, and threw into greater relief, therefore, that light bare patch on the wall, between two doors leading into our neighboring rooms. Here I soon realized must once have been a third door, now walled up; this alone would account for this fresh patch, which had neither been painted in with the rest nor decorated with carving.

Who does not know how a chance stay in some strange place may seize upon the mind? Even the most sluggish imagination receives intimations of something as yet unknown, in a valley enclosed by strange crags perhaps, or in some gloomy and deserted church. I was twenty and had drunk several glasses of strong punch. It is not surprising, therefore, that in this audience chamber I fell into a strange frame of mind, which I had never known before. The night was utterly quiet, except for the dull roar of the sea and the weird whistling of the wind, like the sound of some huge organ played by supernatural hands. The flying clouds seemed to peer, bright and shining, like passing giants, through the rattling bow window. It is hardly strange that a slight shudder ran through me. I felt that a strange realm was about to open, visibly and palpably before me. I was seized with that pleasurable shiver of fear that goes through one as one listens to a well-told ghost story.

I could not be in a better frame of mind, I thought, for reading the book that, like all amateurs of the romantic, I was carrying in my pocket. It was Schiller's *Ghost-seer*. I read on and on, in a state of growing excitement, till I came to that gripping and miraculous description of the wedding at Count von V's. The bloodstained figure of Jeronimo had just made its appearance—when the door leading from the antechamber opened with a loud noise. I started in fear and the book fell from my hands. But the next moment everything was still and I felt ashamed of my childish panic. It was probably a gust of wind, or something of the sort, that had blown the door open. It was nothing, only my excited imagination making an ordinary occurrence seem supernatural. Thus calming myself, I picked up my book and leaned back again in my armchair.

Then I heard the sound of light, smooth, even steps crossing the hall, and at the same time something sighing and groaning as if in the most dire pain, the most appalling grief. Oh, it must be a sick animal shut up in a room downstairs, I thought. Night plays strange tricks with acoustics and makes faraway things sound near. There's nothing to be frightened about in that. Thus I reassured myself once more. But this time I heard a scratching and a loud deep sighing, as of someone in instant peril of death, and it seemed to come from that fresh patch on the wall. A poor imprisoned animal, of course, I reasoned. I have only to shout or stamp on the floor, and either everything will be quiet or the creature below will make a more natural, recognizable sound.

Those were my thoughts, but the blood ran cold in my veins, an icy sweat started on my forehead, and I sat rigid in my chair, afraid to stand up, let alone to call out. At last that awful scratching ceased, and the steps began again. Then life and movement seemed to wake within me. I sprang up and took two steps forward, but an icy draught blew through the hall; and at the same time bright moonbeams fell on the portrait of a very sinister cruel-looking man upon the wall. It might have been his voice whose whisper I heard above the roar of the waves and the shrill howling of the night wind. "Not a step further," it threatened. "Not a step further, or you will fall into the dread chasm of the spirit world."

The hall door slammed to as loudly as it had opened. I distinctly heard the steps crossing the antechamber. They descended the stairs. The main gate of the castle clattered open and was shut. It sounded as if a horse were being taken out of its stall and after a while led back. Then everything was still.

I heard my great-uncle stirring in the next room. Coming to my senses, I grasped the candlestick and hurried in to him. He seemed to be battling with a terrible nightmare. "Wake up! Wake up!" I shouted, gently taking his arm and shining the candle on to his face.

He started up with a muffled cry. "It was kind of you to wake me, nephew," he observed with a smile. "I had a dreadful dream. It must have been these rooms, I think, that reminded me of the past and all the strange things that have happened here. But now let us sleep the night out." Pulling the covers round him, my uncle seemed to doze off immediately, but when I had put out the candles and lain down on the bed beside him, I heard him softly saying his prayers.

Our business began next morning, when the bailiff arrived with the accounts, and various people called with disputes for settlement or other matters to be dealt with. At midday my uncle took me over to pay a formal call on the two old Baronesses. We were kept waiting for some minutes after Franz had announced us, before being led by a bent old body of sixty in a bright silk dress, who called herself their maid of honor, into the holy place. Here we were received with comical ceremonial by the two old ladies, who were rigged out in the fashions of a bygone age. My uncle introduced me, in his waggish way, as a young lawyer come to assist him; and from then on I was the object of their special attention. To judge by their looks, they considered the well-being of the Rossitten tenants in grave danger from my youth. There was something quite ludicrous about the whole visit, but my fears of the previous night still lay chilly upon me. I felt that I had been in contact with unknown powers, or had reached a frontier to overstep which by a single yard would bring me to irremediable disaster; and it took me all the strength I had to combat that terror, which seldom yields to any other state but stark madness. So I was not so much amused as scared by the old Baronesses with their queer towering headdresses and their odd clothes all bedizened with flowers and ribbons. There was something ghostlike about their shriveled faces, about their blinking and their bad French, which they spoke half through their skinny blue lips and half through their sharp noses. I thought that they must at least be on good terms with the spook that walked the castle, and might even be capable of sinister behavior themselves. My uncle, in high good humor, encouraged their ridiculous chatter, however, and in any other mood I should have been powerless to choke back my laughter. But, as I have said, they and all their nonsense continued to give me an uncanny feeling, and my uncle, disappointed at his failure to amuse me, stared at me in astonishment. But it was not until the meal was over and we were alone together again that he broke out: "Will you be so good as to explain to me, nephew, just what is the matter with you? You don't laugh. You don't speak. You don't eat. You don't drink. Why, if you please? Are you ill, or is something wrong?"

I had no hesitation in telling him my whole hideous experience of the previous night. I kept nothing back, but confessed the quantity of punch I had drunk and what book I had been reading. "I must mention these points," I said, "for they provide a possible explanation; perhaps it was all the creation of my overexcited imagination, and had no existence outside my own brain."

I expected my uncle to chaff me unmercifully for seeing ghosts, but he became very serious and gazed down upon the floor. Then, looking up and piercing me with his glance, he replied, "I don't know your book, nephew, but it's not the story or the spirits of the punch that you have to blame for your uncanny visitation. What you describe, let me tell you, appeared to me in my dream. I was sitting just as you were—or so I dreamed—in an easy chair by the fire. But what you only heard, I saw—and clearly—with the eye of the spirit. I saw that monster, saw him come in and slink across to the walled-up door, and saw him scratch desperately at it till the blood dripped from his torn nails. I saw him go down the stairs and lead the horse out of its stall. I saw him bring it back. Did you hear the cock crow in the farmyard away at the village? It was just then that you woke me, and I soon shook off the evil ghost of that creature that still has power to disturb our peace."

The old gentleman ceased, and I asked him for no further explanations, knowing very well that he would tell me more if he thought fit. After a few moments of deep thought, however, he spoke again: "Have you the courage, nephew, now that you know something of the matter, to face the ghost again—in my company this time?" I, of course, answered that I felt strong enough now. "In that case," he resumed, "we will watch together tonight. Something tells me that the evil spirit will quail, if not before my courage, before certain powers in which I trust. It won't be tempting Providence. I shall be risking body and soul in a just cause if I try to exorcise this monster that is driving the Barons von Ross from their ancestral castle. Right is on my side, and I shall surely conquer, but should it be God's will that the evil powers touch me, then you shall proclaim, nephew, that I perished in right Christian combat with the spirit of hell that haunts this place. As for you, you must keep in the background, and no harm will come to you."

Evening found us deep in business. Franz cleared away our dinner as before and brought us our punch. The full moon shone clear through gleaming clouds, the breakers roared, and the night wind howled, shaking the rattling windowpanes. Inwardly excited, we compelled ourselves to indifferent conversation. But just as my uncle's repeater watch, which lay on the table, struck twelve, the door opened with the same terrifying noise as on the previous night, and we heard the same light, slow steps crossing the hall, the same groans and sighs from the walled-up door. The old gentleman blanched and an unaccustomed light burned in his eyes. Rising from his chair, he drew himself up to his full height, placed his left hand on his hip, and pointed with his right into the center of the hall with a commanding gesture.

The sighing and groaning, however, became louder and more distinct; and the scratching on the wall was even more terrifying than on the night before. Then my uncle advanced to the walled-up door with a steady tread that made the floor resound. Reaching the spot where the scratching continued wilder than ever, he stopped still and, in a firm and solemn voice that I had never heard before, he said, "Daniel, Daniel, what are you doing here at this hour?" There was an unearthly, terrifying shriek, followed by a dull thud, as if something had fallen to the floor. "Pray for pity and grace before the Almighty's throne," cried my uncle in powerful tones. "There's no place for you here. Away with you out of this life. You belong here no more." A gentle whimper seemed to pass through the air and die in the roaring of the storm, which was beginning to rise. Then the old gentleman strode to the door and slammed it to with such violence that the echo rang through the empty antechamber. There was a superhuman quality about his voice and his gestures that filled me with awe. He returned to his chair with his face transfigured, and folded his hands in silent prayer. It must have been some minutes before he observed in that mild, penetrating voice of his: 'Well, nephew?' With feelings of mingled awe, fear, astonishment, love, and admiration, I fell on my knees and wet his outstretched hand with my tears. He clasped me in his arms and, holding me to his breast, remarked very tenderly: "Now we shall sleep sound, my dear nephew." Indeed we did and, nothing untoward occurring on the next night, we soon regained our high spirits, unfortunately for the old Baronesses. For though their rig-out still seemed a little uncanny, their eccentricities were at least entertaining, and my uncle knew how to draw them out in the drollest way.

Several days later the Baron arrived with his wife and a great number of huntsmen, the guests assembled, and the castle came suddenly alive with all the din I have already described. The master of the house paid us an immediate visit, and seemed much surprised at our change of quarters. Casting a gloomy glance at the walled-up door and turning quickly away, he passed his hand over his brow as if to dismiss an unpleasant memory. My great-uncle spoke of the damage to the audience chamber, and the Baron blamed Franz for not having lodged us better. He begged my uncle most earnestly to order anything he needed for his comfort, regretting that the new apartments were so much poorer than the old ones.

The Baron's attitude to the old gentleman was more than cordial; he treated him with almost filial respect, as if he were an old relative. This, in my eyes, was the Baron's only redeeming quality, for his domineering manner seemed to be growing worse and worse. He took very little notice of me; to him I was just an ordinary secretary. The first time I drew up a document, however, he chose to find something wrong with the wording. This made my blood boil, and I was on the point of answering rudely when my uncle interposed with the remark that I had followed his instructions, and that nothing was ever done without them.

When we were alone I complained bitterly of the Baron, whom I found increasingly antipathetic. "Really," replied the old gentleman, "the Baron's the most excellent and kindly fellow in the world for all his unfriendly ways. He has only been like this, as I've told you, since he inherited the property; up to that time he was a mild, modest young man. Besides, he's not as bad as you make out. I wonder why you dislike him so much."

With this he gave me a mocking smile, and the blood mounted to my cheeks. For my heart clearly told me that this strange hatred arose from my love—or rather my passion—for the loveliest and purest creature that ever walked, for none other than the Baroness herself. The very moment she walked into the castle, with her Russian sables fitting tightly to her slender figure and her head in a fine veil, she had enchanted me with her irresistible spell. I watched the old aunts, in yet odder dresses and hair fashions, come tripping on either side of her, gabbling away their welcome in French, while she looked around her and smiled first at one and then at another, speaking a few words of German with a Courlandish accent. It was a strange and enchanting scene, yet involuntarily it called that uncanny apparition to my mind; the Baroness was the angel of light before whom the ghostly powers of evil must bow. As my uncle spoke, the lovely creature stood vividly before my eyes. She was scarcely nineteen, and her features, which were as delicate as her figure, bore an expression of angelic goodness; in the glance of her dark eyes dwelt an indescribable magic, a melancholy desire like dewy moonlight; and in her smile was a whole heaven of rapture and delight. Often, though, she seemed lost in thought, and then shadows clouded her face. It was as if she suffered from some transient pain, but I read in her sudden gloom a melancholy foreboding of a future heavy with misfortune; and that thought brought me back in some strange and inexplicable way to the ghost in the castle.

At breakfast on the morning of the Baron's arrival my uncle presented me to the Baroness and not unexpectedly, considering my state of mind, I behaved with indescribable stupidity. For when she asked me how I was enjoying my stay at the castle, I babbled some confused nonsense, which the old aunts must have attributed to my humble respect for the lady. Thinking to encourage me, anyhow, they began to sing my praises in French, describing me as a very nice and clever young man, *"un garçon très joli."* This so annoyed me that I pulled myself together and came out with a sharp retort in better French than they spoke; which caused them to stare at me open-eyed and raise a large pinch of snuff to their long, thin noses. To judge by the Baroness's serious expression, which changed her whole face for me, I had said something pretty foolish. Still more annoyed, therefore, I wished the old ladies in the lowest pit of hell.

My great-uncle had long ago mocked me out of the delusions of calf-love, and so I well knew that the Baroness had roused deeper feelings in me than any woman before. I saw, I heard, only her, but I was resolutely aware that to speak to her of love would not only be tasteless but downright crazy. On the other hand, I could not stare and worship her from a distance like a lovesick boy; that would have been shameful. No, I would draw near to my beloved, yet never let her suspect my secret feelings. I would drink the sweet poison of her eyes and voice and bear it far away, for years, or perhaps forever, treasured in my heart: so much was permissible.

So exhilarated was I by my romantic and chivalrous passion that I lay awake all night, childishly composing the most pathetic addresses, and finally sighing out in lugubrious tones, "Seraphine! Ah, Seraphine!" till at last my uncle awoke and called out, "Nephew, nephew, you're talking in your dreams. Keep your chatter for the daytime, if you can, and let me sleep."

I was afraid that the old gentleman had heard me speak her name. He had already noticed my agitation upon her arrival, and I feared that he would overwhelm me with his sarcasm. But he said nothing next morning. Only, as we entered the audience chamber he loudly observed, "God grant us all a good understanding and resolution to stick to our business. It's a very bad thing for a man to make a fool of himself." Whereupon he took his seat at the great table and added, in an aside to me, "Write clearly, my dear nephew, so that I have no trouble in reading your script."

The Baron showed his respect or filial feelings toward my uncle in all his actions. At meals the old gentleman was placed in the seat of honor beside the Baroness, and I sat wherever chance might put me, usually between a couple of officers from the nearby capital, who liked to regale me with the garrison gossip and the latest jokes; in my company they felt free to drink as much as they liked. So it was that for several days I was at the lower end of the table, far away from the Baroness, though finally fate brought me near her. When the dining hall was thrown open I was deep in conversation with the Baroness's companion, a lady no longer young but by no means plain or unintelligent. As she was enjoying our talk, I had, of course, to offer her my arm and, to my great pleasure, she led me to a place at table quite close to her mistress. The Baroness welcomed me with a friendly nod and, as can be imagined, my words were no longer addressed solely to my neighbor, but aimed at her mistress's ears. Perhaps my excitement lent a particular liveliness to all I said; but, whatever the reason, the Lady Adelheid—that was the companion's name—listened most attentively and was soon drawn into the bright, kaleidoscopic world I drew before her eyes. She was, as I said, not unintelligent, and our conversation, despite the restless chatter of the guests, took on a life of its own, even sending a few sparks in the direction I intended. I saw my partner glance meaningly toward the Baroness, and saw that her mistress was at some pains to overhear us, especially when I turned the conversation to the subject of music. I talked enthusiastically of that rare art, and finally proclaimed that, for all my dry and boring profession, I was a pretty good performer on the piano, could sing and had composed several songs.

We had moved into the other room for coffee and liqueurs and, inadvertently—I don't know quite how—I found myself facing the Baroness. She had been talking to her companion but, upon my approach, turned to me and repeated, more intimately, the question she had asked me on our first meeting. I replied that for the first few days I had found the old castle and its lonely situation strangely depressing, but even in that mood I had felt its grandeur, and now all I wanted was to be excused from the hunting, to which I was unaccustomed.

"I can well imagine," replied the Baroness with a smile, "that riotous expeditions into our forests are not much to your taste. You're a musician and, if I'm not mistaken, a poet as well. I am passionately devoted to both arts, and can play a little on the harp. But I have to do without it here at Rossitten, as my husband does not like me to bring the instrument. Its sound is too gentle to harmonize with the wild "view-hallos" and shrill hunting horns, which are all the tunes we have in this place. My goodness, how I should enjoy some real music!"

I promised to try and grant her her wish, saying that surely there must be some instrument in the castle, if only an old clavichord. The Lady Adelheid, however, observed with a laugh, "All the music that's been heard in this castle within the memory of man has been the braying of trumpets and lugubrious calls on the hunting horn, except when wandering musicians pay us an occasional visit with their harsh fiddles, their rumbling basses, and bleating hautboys. Surely you know that?" The Baroness, however, persisted in her request for music and to hear me play, and the two ladies taxed their invention devising plans for obtaining a passable pianoforte.

Just then old Franz walked into the room. "Here is the man for good advice," cried Lady Adelheid. "He supplies all our wants. Even the most unheard-of things he can find." And calling him over, she explained our needs. The Baroness stood by with folded hands, looking into the old man's face, and her smile was a joy to see. She was like a sweet and pretty child who feels the toy it longs for already in its hands. Long-winded as usual, Franz at first brought out several reasons why it was absolutely impossible to obtain so rare an instrument at such short notice. But finally, scratching his chin with a satisfied grin, he remarked: "But the bailiff's wife down in the village is an uncommon good player on the clavicembalo or whatever outlandish name they call it. She sings such pretty sad things to it, too, that it brings tears to your eyes—just like onions—and your legs begin to twitch."

"She has got a piano, in fact," exclaimed Lady Adelheid, cutting him short.

"Oh yes," said the old man. "It came straight from Dresden."

"That's marvelous," broke in the Baroness.

"A lovely instrument," the old man went on, "but rather delicate. Because when the organist tried to play 'O God, our help' on it, he brought the whole thing to the ground and . . ."

"Oh, my goodness," cried the Baroness and Lady Adelheid together.

"And," pursued the old man, "it had to be taken to Königsberg at great expense and repaired."

"Is it back again now?" asked Lady Adelheid impatiently.

"Oh yes, miss, and the bailiff's wife will be most flattered."

Here we were interrupted by the Baron, who strolled over, surveyed our group in some surprise, and whispered mockingly in the Baroness's ear, "Has Franz been called in for more good advice?" The Baroness blushed and lowered her eyes, and old Franz broke off to leap suddenly to attention. Then the old aunts floated over in their old-fashioned dresses and led the Baroness away, Lady Adelheid followed her, and I was left standing stock still as if nailed to the spot, my delight at my conversation with my adored Baroness conflicting in my heart with anger against the hateful Baron, who seemed to me a barbarous despot. Why else should the old gray-haired servant behave to him with such servility?

"Can't you hear me?" called my great-uncle, tapping me on the shoulder. "Come along now!" We went up to our room. "Don't force yourself upon the Baroness," he said when we arrived. "What good can it do you? Leave it to the young sparks to play the courtier. They enjoy it, and there's no shortage of them."

I explained how the situation had arisen, and asked if I had earned his reproaches, but all the reply I got was "H'm, h'm!" which he followed by lying back in his armchair, lighting his pipe and teasing me about the shots I had missed on the previous day's hunting.

The ladies and gentlemen were in their rooms dressing for the evening and all was quiet in the castle. The musicians Lady Adelheid had spoken of had arrived with their harsh fiddles, their rumbling basses and bleating hautboys, and there was to be a regular ball that night in the grand style. My uncle, preferring a quiet sleep to such frivolous goings-on, was to stay in his room. But I had just dressed in my best, when there came a knock on our door and Franz entered to announce with a satisfied grin that the clavicembalo had just arrived on a sledge from the bailiff's and was to be taken to the Baroness's room. Lady Adelheid would be glad if I would come straight over.

It can be guessed how my blood coursed in my veins and my heart pounded as I opened the Baroness's door to find her there. Lady Adelheid got up to greet me, but her mistress, already dressed for the dance, was sitting pensively before the mysterious case, from which I was to call forth its slumbering music. She rose, radiant in such beauty that I could only stare dumbfounded. "Now, Theodore"—she called everyone by his Christian name in that comfortable northern way, that one finds also in the extreme south—"Now, Theodore," she said in a most friendly way, "the instrument's here, and I hope it won't prove unworthy of your skill."

As I opened the lid I was greeted with the twang of broken wires, and the first chord I struck sounded abominable, for such wires as were unbroken were out of tune. "The organist has been touching it again in his gentle way," laughed Lady Adelheid, but the Baroness remarked with annoyance, "Now that's really too bad. Am I to have no pleasures at all in this place?" I searched the drawer and fortunately found some spare coils of wire, but no tuning-key. More lamentations. "Perhaps some other key will fit," I suggested, upon which the Baroness and Lady Adelheid ran joyfully around, and it was not long before a whole store of bright keys lay before me on the sounding board.

Then I got to work, with Lady Adelheid—and even the Baroness—busily helping me to try each one. "This one will do," they both eagerly cried at the first turn, but the wire snapped as it was drawn tight and they both jumped back in fright. The Baroness plunged her delicate fingers among the brittle wires, and handed me the numbers I asked for, holding the coil carefully till I had unwound it. Suddenly, however, one would spring back, the Baroness would groan, and Lady Adelheid would follow the tangled coil with a laugh to the corner of the room where it had jumped. Then we would all try to cut out a straight, undamaged length, which to our mortification would then snap again. But finally we did find enough good coils, the wires began to stay in place, and instead of tuneless thrumming we gradually got clear notes.

"Oh, good, good! The instrument's all right," cried the Baroness, smiling charmingly at me, so quickly had our common task abolished all distance and conventional reserve. There was a secret intimacy between us, which glowed through me like an electric current, dispelling the uneasy shyness that had lain like ice on my heart. The strange pathos, common to such infatuations, had left me, and as soon as the piano was sufficiently tuned, far from expressing my feelings in passionate improvisations I struck up one of those charming songs that come to us from the south. At all my *Senza di te's, Sentimi idol mio's, Al men se non poss'io's, Morir me sento's, Addio's* and *Oh dio's,* Seraphine's eyes grew brighter. She stood close beside me at the piano, I felt her breath on my cheeks, her arm rested on the chair back behind me, and a white ribbon that had come loose from her lovely ball-dress fell onto my shoulder, fluttering like a love token to the sound of my music or the breath of her sighs. It was a wonder that I kept my senses.

I was just striking some chords, searching my memory for another song, when Lady Adelheid, who had been sitting in the corner, suddenly jumped up and fell on her knees before the Baroness. Seizing her mistress's hands, and pressing them to her breast, she exclaimed: "Oh, my dear Baroness! Seraphine darling, you must sing too."

"What are you thinking of, Adelheid?" protested the Baroness. "How can I sing, with my poor voice, before our virtuoso here?" It was a delight to see her blush and cast down her eyes like a bashful child, torn between shyness and desire. Needless to say, I too implored her to sing; and once she had mentioned some Courlandish folk songs, I did not give up till she had struck a little prelude with her left hand. I wanted to make way for her at the piano, but she would not let me, insisting that she could not play a single note and that her singing would sound very thin and wavering without my accompaniment.

At length she began in a delicate voice, as pure as a bell, which rang straight from her heart. It was one of those simple melodies that shine with their own inner light, and reveal to us our own poetic nature. There is a hidden magic in their simple words, which expresses in a sort of hieroglyphic the ineffable truth that fills our hearts. One has only to think of that Spanish song which says no more than, "I sailed out to sea with my beloved. The storm began to rise. The ship began to rock. No, I'll never sail out to sea with my beloved again." The Baroness only said, "I danced with my beloved at a wedding. A flower fell out of my hair. He picked it up, gave it to me and said: 'When shall we two go to a wedding again, my dear?'" Since by the second verse I was accompanying her in arpeggios and was able in my exhilaration to pick up the tunes of her later songs straight from her lips, no doubt I seemed to them a very master of the art. At all events, they smothered me with praises.

But soon the newly lit candles of the ballroom in the wing shone into the Baroness's room, and the dissonant notes of trumpets and horns announced the opening of the ball. "I must go now, alas," cried the Baroness, and I sprang up from the piano. "You have given me a marvelous hour," she went on. "The happiest I have known here at Rossitten."

She held out her hand and, as in my delight I pressed it to my lips, I felt her fingers throbbing upon my palm. I do not know how I reached my great-uncle's room, or got from there to the ballroom. A Gascon must fear battle, for any wound will prove fatal to a man who is all heart. In such case was I, in such case is any man in my state of mind; the slightest touch is fatal. The Baroness's hand, the pulse in her fingers, had wounded me like poisoned arrows; my blood burned in my veins.

Without a single question, my great-uncle soon had from me next morning the whole story of my evening with the Baroness, and I was not a little taken aback when his gay and smiling tones suddenly changed to seriousness. "Nephew," he began, "I beg of you, resist this folly that has got such a hold on you. Don't you see that harmless beginnings may lead to most dreadful consequences? In your headstrong madness you're standing on thin ice, which may break, most unexpectedly, beneath you. Then you'll fall in, and I shall take good care not to hang on to your coattails. You'll quickly struggle out, of course, and when you're mortally sick you'll say that you caught a little cold while you were dreaming. But the fever will burn you to the marrow, and it will be years before you recover your strength. The devil take your music if you can't put it to better use than upsetting sensitive young ladies with it."

"But," I interrupted, "do you think I should have the effrontery to flirt with the Baroness?"

"If I thought you had, you idiot," cried the old gentleman, "I'd pitch you out of this window." Our painful conversation was interrupted by the Baron's arrival, and the opening of proceedings broke my infatuated dream, in which I saw and thought of nothing but Seraphine.

In company the Baroness dropped me only an occasional friendly word, but scarcely an evening passed in which I did not receive a private message by Lady Adelheid summoning me to her room. Soon conversation on a variety of subjects alternated with our music, Lady Adelheid introducing all sorts of trivial and facetious nonsense, hardly befitting her years. Seraphine and I began to plunge into sentimental speculations and fancies, and much that she said confirmed me in my belief that she had something on her mind. I had read it in her glance when first I saw her, and now I clearly detected in her uneasiness the hostile influence of the castle ghost. Some terrible disaster had occurred or was imminent. Only too often I felt impelled to tell Seraphine of my own adventure with the invisible enemy, and of my uncle's final exorcism of the creature. But some inexplicable timidity fettered my tongue each time that I was about to speak.

One day the Baroness was missing from the dinner table; she was said to be indisposed and confined to her room. Someone asked the Baron in some concern whether the complaint was serious. He smiled disagreeably and answered, "Nothing but a slight catarrh, the effect of the raw sea air. It is not kind to sweet voices. All the music it allows here is the harsh calls of the chase." I was not sitting opposite to the Baron, but as he spoke he threw me a piercing glance that was clearly not intended for the guest who had asked him the question.

Lady Adelheid, who was sitting beside me, blushed scarlet, looked down on her plate and scratched on it with her fork. "Still you *shall* see Seraphine today," she said. "Your singing will do her sick heart good."

The words were intended for my ears alone, and I felt as if I were engaged in a sordid love intrigue that could only end in disaster. My uncle's warning gripped my heart. What should I do? See her no more? For so long as I stayed at the castle that was impossible, and even if I might go back to Königsberg, I had not the strength. Now, indeed, I realized that I was powerless to shake myself out of this dream that deluded me with fantastic hopes. Adelheid seemed no more than a common go-between. I longed to despise her, but on second thoughts was ashamed of my own stupidity. There was nothing about those delightful evenings that could bring me any closer to Seraphine than convention allowed. I could scarcely suppose that the Baroness had any feeling for me, yet I was convinced that my position was dangerous.

The table was cleared early, for there was to be an evening wolf hunt; some beasts had been seen among the pines quite close to the castle. The hunt was just the thing for my overexcited mood, and when I told my uncle that I wanted to join in, he remarked with a contented smile, "That's fine, for you to get out for once. I shall stay behind, so you can take my gun. Strap my hunting knife to your belt as well. It's a good weapon in an emergency, provided you keep your head."

The covert was surrounded by huntsmen. It was piercingly cold, the wind howled through the pines, and the bright snowflakes drove in my face, so that when dusk fell I could scarcely see six paces ahead. Quite numb with the frost, I left the post assigned to me to look for shelter deeper in the wood. There I leaned against a tree, my gun under my arm and, forgetting the hunt, let my thoughts wander back to Seraphine in her room in the castle. Suddenly I heard distant shots, and at that same instant there was a rustling in the thicket. Not ten paces away I saw a wolf trying to break way. I aimed and fired, but I missed. Then the beast rushed at me with glowing eyes, and I should have been lost if I had not had the presence of mind to draw my hunting knife and plunge it into the creature's throat, just as it was about to spring. Its blood spurted over my hand and arm. One of the Baron's huntsmen had not been far off, and he ran up to me shouting. Others came in answer to his cries, and with them the Baron, who hurried toward me. "Good heavens, man! You're bleeding," he exclaimed. "Are you hurt?"

I assured him that I was not. But this did not prevent his turning on the huntsman who had been posted next to me and reproaching him angrily for not having fired after I missed. That would have been impossible, the poor man insisted, since the wolf had sprung on me instantaneously and a shot might have hit me. The Baron answered, however, that as I was the less experienced hunter he should have kept an eye on me.

Meanwhile the huntsmen had picked up the dead wolf, which was the biggest that had been seen for many a year. Everyone praised my courage and presence of mind, though what I had done seemed natural enough to me, and I had not actually given a thought to my danger. The Baron was most concerned and, even though I was not hurt, could not leave off asking me whether I did not feel some ill effects from my fright. As we walked back to the castle he took my arm in the most friendly way, and went on talking about my heroic act until I began to believe in it myself. A huntsman walked behind me carrying my gun and, feeling established in the Baron's eyes as a man of resolute courage, I threw off all embarrassment. The schoolboy had passed his examination—and was no longer a schoolboy. Gone was my nervous diffidence. I felt that I had earned the right to court Seraphine's favors. Such are the foolish reasonings of a lovesick youth! Back in the castle, beside the fire and over the steaming punch, I was still the hero of the hour. Except for myself, only the Baron had brought down a wolf; the others had to content themselves with blaming their misses on the weather or the poor light, and with telling stories of previous hunting triumphs and hairbreadth escapes. I imagined myself entitled even to my uncle's praise and admiration, and so made a long narrative of my adventure, not omitting a lurid description of the savage beast's bloodthirsty appearance. But the old gentleman just laughed in my face. "God reveals His power even through the weakest implements," was his only comment.

Weary of the drinking and the guests, I was slipping along the corridor back to the audience chamber when I caught sight of a shape gliding ahead of me and carrying a light. On entering the room, I recognized Lady Adelheid. "Must one wander like a ghost or a sleepwalker to find you, my bold hunter?" she whispered, taking me by the hand. The words *ghost* and *sleepwalker,* spoken in that place, fell heavily on my heart, instantly calling to my mind the ghostly apparitions of those two hideous nights. I heard again the howling wind's deep organ notes, the whistling and rattling at the bow windows; again the moon threw her pale light onto that mysterious wall; again I heard that eerie scratching, and I imagined I could see bloodstains upon the plaster. Lady Adelheid must have felt the chill run through me, for she was leading me by the hand. "What's the matter? What's wrong?" she whispered. "If you're frozen, I'll soon revive you. Listen, do you realize that the Baroness is all impatience to see you? She can't believe that dreadful wolf didn't bite you. She is greatly alarmed. Oh, my dear friend, what have you done to Seraphine? I have never seen her like this before. Now that's set your pulse ticking again! The dead man is suddenly coming to life. Quickly now, we must go to our dear Baroness."

I silently allowed her to lead me. I did not care for the way she spoke of her mistress, and I was shocked at her hints of a relationship between us. As we entered, Seraphine ran to meet us with a gentle "Oh." Then, as if thinking better of it, she stood still in the middle of the room. I dared to seize her hand and carry it to my lips. She left it in mine and said, "What business have you to meddle with wolves? The legendary days of Orpheus and Amphion are long since passed, you know, and savage beasts have lost all respect for singers, even for great singers."

Her charming turn of phrase assured me past all doubts of her interest in me, and put me immediately into the right vein. I do not know how it was, but instead of taking my place at the piano I sat down on the sofa beside her. One question—"How did you come into danger?"—showed that we were agreed: this was a night not for music but conversation. I related my adventure in the wood, referring to the Baron's concern for me with the passing remark that I had not thought him capable of it. Whereupon she began gently, almost sadly, "Indeed, the Baron must seem to you a very violent, rough man. But his whole character, or at least his outward behavior, changes when he stays here. Within these dark uncanny walls and while he hunts in the wild and desolate pinewoods, he is oppressed by a single obsessive thought, that something dreadful is going to happen in this place. That is why he was so upset by your accident, although it had no serious consequences. He won't have the meanest of his servants exposed to the slightest danger, much less a new and valued friend. That fellow Gottlieb whom he blames for leaving you in the lurch may not be jailed, but he will receive the huntsman's punishment, to follow the hunt in disgrace, unarmed and with only a stick in his hand. Such hunts as these are never without danger, and the Baron, for all his fears, gaily tempts the evil powers to do their worst; but the strain upon him is terrible, and this affects me too. There are some strange tales of his ancestor who drew up the entail. I'm sure there's some gloomy family secret shut up in these walls, that like some dreadful ghost drives its owners away, and makes it impossible for them to stay here except for a short time and in a wild turmoil. You can imagine how lonely I feel amidst all this hurly-burly. The uncanniness that seeps out of every wall weighs on my heart. Your music, my dear friend, has given me the first happy moments I have known in this place. How can I thank you enough?"

I kissed her hand, and confessed my own terror on the first

day—or rather the first night—of my stay in this uncanny place. She did not take her eyes from my face as I ascribed the baleful atmosphere of the castle to the paintings in the audience chamber, the howling of the sea wind and all the rest. But something in my voice and manner must have shown that I had something more on my mind. For she cried impetuously when I stopped: "No! no! Something dreadful happened to you in that hall. I am terrified each time I go in. Tell me the whole story, I beg of you."

Her face was deathly white, and I saw that it would be better to tell her the whole story than leave it to her excited imagination to conjure up a ghost, which might in some unknown way be even more terrible than the one I had encountered. Her fears mounted as my tale proceeded. Finally, when I told her of the scratching on the wall, she cried out: "That's ghastly. Yes, I'm certain. The terrible secret is concealed in that wall." When I went on to describe my uncle's greater power of spirit that had laid the ghost, she gave a deep sigh as if a heavy load had been lifted from her breast. Leaning back on the sofa, she put both hands before her eyes. Not till then did I notice that Adelheid had left us. I had long finished my story and Seraphine was still silent. So getting up and going to the piano, I played a series of major chords in the hope of calling up a comforting spirit to lead her out of the dark realm into which my tale had plunged her. Soon I began to sing softly one of Abbé Steffan's *Sacred Songs*. On the sad notes of *Occhi perche piangete*, she woke from her reverie and listened with a gentle smile and with glistening pearls in her eyes.

I found myself on my knees before her. She leaned down to me, and I took her in my arms. A long burning kiss scorched my lips. I do not know why I did not faint away when I felt her draw me softly to her. Then I let her out of my arms, swiftly rose and went to the piano. Turning from me, she moved toward the window; but turning back with a certain stiffness that was foreign to her, she exclaimed, looking into my eyes, "Your uncle is the finest man I've ever known. He's our family's guardian angel. Ask him to remember me in his prayers."

I was powerless to utter a word. The fatal poison I had imbibed in that kiss seethed and burned in all my veins and nerves. Lady Adelheid came in. The violence of my inner conflict broke out in hot tears. Lady Adelheid looked at me in astonishment and gave a dubious smile. I could have murdered her. The Baroness held out her hand to me and said with indescribable tenderness: "Farewell, my good friend, and good fortune go with you. Remember that perhaps no one has understood your music better than I. Your songs will ring in my head for many a day." I contrived to speak a few senseless words and ran to our room.

My uncle had already gone to bed. I stayed in the audience hall. I fell on my knees and wept aloud, crying out my beloved's name. In short, I gave myself over to all the mad frenzies of a lover, and might have gone on all night had I not woken the old gentleman with my clamor.

"Have you gone out of your wits, nephew?" he cried. "Or are you having another scuffle with a wolf? Clear off to bed, if you don't mind." So it was that I was driven to my room to lie down in the firm resolve to dream only of Seraphine.

It must have been after midnight and I was still awake, when I fancied I heard distant voices, a running up and down and the opening and closing of doors. I listened and heard steps approaching along the corridor, the audience-hall door was opened, and soon there was a knocking at ours: "Who is there?" I shouted.

Then came a voice from outside. "Your worship! Your worship! Wake up!"

I recognized Franz's voice and, as I cried "Is the castle on fire?" the old gentleman woke up and called.

"Where is the fire? Where's that devilish ghost got loose this time?"

"Oh, get up, your worship," cried Franz. "The Baron is asking for you."

"What does the Baron want with me?" asked my uncle. "What does he want at this time of night? Doesn't he know that the law goes to bed with the lawyer and sleeps just as sound?"

"Oh," called Franz nervously, "your worship. Oh, my dear sir, please get up! The Baroness is on her death-bed."

With a cry of horror I jumped up. "Open the door for Franz!" my uncle shouted to me, as I staggered about the room in a daze, so powerless to find the door or the lock that my uncle had to help me. Pale and with drawn features, Franz entered and lit the candles.

We had scarcely thrown on our clothes before we heard the

Baron shouting in the courtroom: "May I speak to you, my dear Voetheri?"

"Why have you dressed, nephew?" asked the old gentleman, on the point of going out. "The Baron only asked for me."

"I must go down and see her too," I answered dully, in the depths of grief. "Then I shall die."

"Oh yes, you're right there, nephew!" replied my uncle, banging the door in my face with a violence that shook the hinges, and locking it from outside. In my first moment of indignation at this treatment, I wanted to break it down. But coming quickly to my senses, I realized that such uncontrolled madness would have fatal consequences. So I decided to await my uncle's return, and then, at whatever cost, elude his vigilance. I heard him in vehement conversation with the Baron outside. I heard them repeat my name several times, but could understand no more. Every second my position became more intolerable. Finally someone brought the Baron a message, and I heard him hurry away. My uncle came back into the room.

"She is dead!" I cried, rushing to meet him.

"And you're crazy," he calmly answered, taking hold of me and forcing me into a chair.

"I must go down," I shouted. "I must go down and see her, even if it means my death."

"Very well, my dear nephew," said he, locking the door, removing the key, and putting it into his pocket.

Then I burst into a mad fit of rage, seized the loaded rifle and cried, "If you don't open the door at once, I'll blow my brains out before your face."

The old man came right up to me and stared into my eyes with a glance that pierced me to the depths. "Do you think you can frighten me with your miserable threats, boy?" he asked. "Do you think I set any store by your life, if you're willing to throw it away in childish idiocy like a worn-out plaything? What have you to do with the Baron's wife? Who has given you the right to poke your nose, like a tiresome ninny, where you don't belong and no one wants you? Do you intend to roll your sheep's eyes on a death-bed?"

I sank back, speechless, into my chair, and after a while my uncle went on in a milder tone: "And for your information, there's probably nothing in this alleged danger of the Baroness's death. Lady Adelheid gets beside herself over everything. If a drop of rain falls on her nose, she talks about a fearful storm. Unfortunately the cry of fire alarmed the two old aunts, and they turned up in floods of tears, with a whole arsenal of invigorating drops and elixirs of life and goodness knows what else. A severe fit of fainting, that's all it is." My uncle stopped. He could see the violence of the struggle within me. He took a pace or two up and down the room. Then he sat down again facing me, and laughed heartily. "Nephew, nephew," he said. "What is this foolish game you're playing? Satan, let me tell you, walks this place in more forms than one. You've fallen nicely into his clutches, and he's leading you a pretty dance." He took several more paces up and down the room before resuming: "There's no more hope of sleep. So I think we might while away the last hours of darkness with a pipe."

With these words my uncle took a clay pipe from the cupboard, and filled it, humming a tune as he did so. Then he rummaged among some papers, tore out a sheet, folded it into a spill and lit it. After which, blowing the thick clouds of smoke before him, he said through his clenched teeth, "Now, nephew, tell me about the wolf."

I cannot describe the strange effect upon me of the old gentleman's calmness. I might no longer have been at Rossitten. The Baroness might have been far, far away, only to be reached on imagination's wings. But my uncle's last question put me out. "Do you find my hunting accident so comical?" I asked, "so fit for your mockery?"

"Not a bit," replied the old gentleman. "Not a bit, my dear nephew. But you've no idea what a ridiculous figure a coxcomb like you cuts if something really remarkable does happen to him. He looks quite absurd. I had a learned friend once, a quiet, reflective, self-sufficient sort of fellow. Now, through no fault of his own he happened to get mixed up in an affair of honor; and though most of the lads thought of him as a weakling and a duffer, he behaved with such resolute courage in the matter as to earn their genuine admiration. From that moment, however, he was a completely changed man. From an industrious, thoughtful youngster he became an intolerable and boastful bully. He indulged in drunken orgies and celebrations, and picked all sorts of childish quarrels until one day the president of a student association, whom he had grievously insulted, killed him in a duel. Draw your own conclusions from my story, nephew. But to revert to the Baroness and her illness—"

At this moment a sound of light steps came from the audience hall, and I seemed to hear a terrible groan ring through the air. "It's all over"—the thought ran through me like a lightning flash. But my uncle got up and called, "Franz! Franz!"

"Yes, your worship," came the answer from outside.

"Franz," said my uncle, "rake the fire on the hearth together, and make us two cups of strong tea, if you can. It's devilish cold," he added, turning to me, "but we've one or two things to talk about over the fire."

My uncle opened the door and I followed him mechanically. "How are things downstairs?" he asked.

"Oh," answered Franz, "there wasn't very much wrong. Her ladyship's got her spirits back again. She was taken a bit faint, she says, because of a bad dream."

I wanted to shout for joy and delight, but a warning look from my uncle reduced me to silence. "I think," said he, "it might really be better for us to lie down for the next couple of hours. Never mind about that tea, Franz."

"As you wish, your worship," answered Franz, and left the room, in hopes of a quiet night, although the cocks were crowing already.

"See here, nephew," said my uncle, knocking out his pipe in the grate. "It's a good thing that you have met with no accident— from wolves or loaded guns." I understood everything and was ashamed that I had given my uncle cause to treat me like a spoiled child.

"Be so kind, my dear nephew," said the old gentleman next morning, "as to go down and find out how the Baroness is. You can ask Lady Adelheid. She will give you a full report."

You can imagine the speed with which I hastened down. But just as I was going to knock at the Baroness's antechamber door, the Baron came hurrying out. On seeing me, he stopped as if surprised, and looked me up and down with his sinister, piercing stare. "What do you want here?" he burst out.

Violently though my heart beat in my breast, I pulled myself sufficiently together to answer firmly: "I have my uncle's instructions to ask after her ladyship's health."

"Oh, it was nothing, one of her usual nervous attacks," he answered. "She is sleeping quietly, and will of course appear at lunch, well and in good spirits. Tell him that. Just that."

The Baron spoke with a certain emotional intensity that told me he was more concerned for the Baroness than he wished to show, and I was turning to go back when he suddenly gripped me by the arm. "I have something to say to you, young man," he cried, staring at me fiercely. Here I had the wronged husband before me, and it was hardly surprising that I feared an incident that might end in my disgrace. I was unarmed, but I instantly bethought me of the fine hunting knife that my uncle had given me, and that I carried in my pocket. I followed the rapidly advancing Baron, resolved to spare no life if I were in danger of shameful treatment. As we entered his room, he closed the door behind him. For a few moments he paced violently up and down with folded arms. Then, stopping before me, he repeated: "I have something to say to you, young man."

Filled with foolhardy courage, I answered loudly, "I hope it is something I can hear without detriment to my honor."

The Baron stared at me in astonishment, as if he failed to grasp my meaning. Then, looking balefully on the ground, he clasped his hands behind his back and began to stride up and down the room again. Suddenly he took down a gun and inserted the ramrod, as if to try whether it were loaded or not. The blood boiled in my veins, I felt for my knife, and approached so near to him that it would have been impossible for him to take aim. "A lovely piece," he remarked, putting the gun back in its corner. I retreated several paces, but he followed me, and tapping me on the shoulder with more than necessary emphasis, observed, "I must seem to you distracted and overwrought, Theodore. Indeed I am, with all the countless worries of this sleepless night. My wife's nervous attack was not at all dangerous. That I realize now. But this castle is haunted by an evil spirit, and I am always in dread of some terrible disaster. This is the first time that she has fallen ill here, and you—you are the sole cause."

"How that can be I haven't the least idea," I answered calmly.

"Oh," exclaimed the Baron, "I wish that wretched instrument

had been shivered into a thousand pieces, and you—I wish you
. . . But no, no! It was bound to be, it had to happen, and the
whole fault is mine. From the moment you began to make music
in my wife's room it was my duty to warn you of my wife's condition, of the whole state of affairs." I made as if to speak. "Let
me go on," cried the Baron, "I must prevent your coming to hasty
conclusions. You will consider me a rough man, and insensitive to
the arts. But that I certainly am not. Certain most necessary con-
siderations, however, compel me to exclude from here, in so far
as I can, all music that may affect anyone, myself included. My
wife, I must inform you, suffers from an abnormal excitability,
which will end by robbing her of all joy in life. Here, within these
strange walls, her nervous state never leaves her, though it affects
her only momentarily elsewhere, and seldom except as the prelude
to a serious illness. You may well wonder why, considering her
delicate health, I do not spare her this dreadful visit and the wild
turmoil of the hunting season. You may call it weakness in me,
but I find it impossible to leave her alone. I should be racked by
anxieties and incapable of all serious action, for my mind would
always be filled, in the hunting field or the audience hall, with
pictures of the appalling disasters that might be befalling her. I
also believe that a stay here may act as a powerful tonic upon a
weak woman. The wild sea wind roaring through the pinewoods,
the baying of the hounds, and the bold crashing notes of our hunting horns are the proper music for such a place, as your weak
effeminate tinklings on the piano are not; it is no instrument for
a man. But you seem determined methodically to torture my wife
to death." The Baron raised his voice and his eyes sparkled wildly.
The blood mounted to my head, I lifted my hand violently against
him, I tried to speak, but he would not let me. "I know what you
want to say," he began. "But I tell you once more that you were
on the way toward killing my wife. I cannot affix the least blame
upon you, of course, though you will understand that I must bring
the danger to an end. To be brief, you worked upon her with your
singing and playing; and once you had set her helplessly adrift
among the visions and forebodings that your music calls up like a
black spell, you plunged her into the depths with your eerie tale
about some ghost, that played tricks on you, you say, up there in
the audience hall. Your great-uncle has told me the whole story,

but I should be glad if you would repeat to me now all that you saw—or didn't see—all that you heard, felt or sensed.

Pulling myself together, I quietly told him the whole story from beginning to end, and he interrupted me with no more than an occasional expression of astonishment. But when I spoke of my old uncle's godly fortitude, of his standing up to the ghost and laying it with a few resolute words, he put his hands together, raised them towards Heaven, and rapturously cried, "Yes, he's our family's guardian angel! His mortal remains shall be buried in our ancestral vault." I had finished my tale. "Daniel, Daniel, what are you doing here at this hour?" muttered the Baron, pacing up and down the room with folded arms.

"So her ladyship's illness was no worse than that, your Lordship?" I asked loudly, making a move toward the door.

He started out of his dream, took me amicably by the hand and said, "The Baroness is now beneath the magic spell of your music; it would be foolish and terrible to wrench her suddenly from it. Go on with your playing. You will always be welcome in the evenings in my wife's rooms. Bud gradually you must change over to more vigorous tunes. You must skillfully blend gay airs with serious—and, most important of all, you must frequently repeat your tale of the ghost. The Baroness will grow used to it; she will forget that it is within these walls that it walks, and finally the tale will have no more effect on her than a ghost story in a novel or mystery book. That is what I require of you, my dear friend."

The Baron let me go, and I went, reduced in my own eyes to an insignificant creature, a mere foolish child. How mad I had been to imagine he harbored jealousy in his heart; he had sent me to Seraphine himself, seeing in me no more than an inert tool that he could pick up and throw down at will. A few minutes ago I had feared the Baron; deep in my heart was a consciousness of my guilt, and this guilt had given me a taste of the higher, grander life for which I was now ripe. But at that moment everything was plunged in darkness, and all I saw was a silly child, who in his foolishness had taken the paper crown he had crammed upon his heated brow for real gold. I hurried to my uncle, who was waiting for me. "Where have you been, nephew? Where have you been?" he called as I approached. "I have been talking to the Baron," I replied quickly and quietly, unable to face the old man's gaze.

"The devil you have!" he remarked in astonishment. "The devil you have! I thought as much. Then the Baron sent for you, did he?"

The burst of laughter with which my uncle followed this question told me that he had seen through me once more, as he always did. I clenched my teeth and could not answer; for I knew that one word would be enough to set off the stream of mockery that was rising to the old man's tongue.

The Baroness came to table in a beautiful morning dress, whiter than new-fallen snow. She looked limp and strained, but when she raised her dark eyes and spoke, a sweet sad desire glowed in their gloomy depths, and a passing blush clouded her lily-pale cheeks. She was lovelier than ever and her voice even more melodious. The stupidities of a youngster with overheated blood in his head and heart are indeed boundless. I turned the bitter resentment that the Baron had roused in me upon the Baroness. Now everything seemed an unholy mystification, and I wanted to show them the keenness of my judgment and my extraordinary powers of perception. Like a silly child, I avoided the Baroness—and Adelheid too when she came after me. Consequently at the end of the meal I was left sitting, as I had planned, between the two officers, and with them I began on a drinking bout. Over dessert we studiously clinked our glasses and I, not unexpectedly, behaved with riotous gaiety. I was interrupted, however, by a servant, who as he handed me a plate of sweets whispered in my ear, "From Lady Adelheid." On taking one I quickly noticed that upon it had been scratched with a knife point "And Seraphine?"

The blood coursed in my veins. I looked over to Adelheid, who was gazing at me with a sly, cunning look. Almost involuntarily I murmured "Seraphine!," picked up my glass and emptied it at a gulp. My glance flew over to her. I saw that she had drunk at that same moment and was putting down her glass. Her eyes met mine, and a malicious devil whispered in my ear, "You fatal fellow, she's in love with you." Then one of the guests got up and, according to the northern custom, drank to the lady of the house. The glasses loudly clinked. Rapture and despair cleft my heart in two. The glow of the wine leapt up within me; everything was going round. I felt I must throw myself at her feet before all eyes, and there breathe out my last breath. "What's the matter, my good friend?"

244 · E. T. A. Hoffmann

My neighbor's question brought me to my senses. Seraphine had disappeared. The table was cleared. I tried to go out, but Adelheid held me fast. She was talking a great deal, but I did not hear or understand a word. She took me by both hands, and said something laughingly into my ear. I stood mute and motionless as if stricken with a catalepsy. All I know is that finally I took a glass of liqueur from Adelheid's hand and drank it down. Later I found myself alone at a window, rushed out of the hall and down the stairs, and ran into the wood. The snow was falling in large flakes, the pines sighed as they tossed in the storm. I ran like a madman in wide circles, and laughed and wildly cried, "Look, look! Hurrah! The devil's leading the youngster a dance, who thought he could eat of strictly forbidden fruit!"

Who knows how my mad prank would have ended had I not heard my name called loudly in the wood. The storm had died down, the moon shone bright through the broken clouds and somewhere the hounds were baying. I recognized a dark figure approaching me. It was the old huntsman. "Hi, hi, Master Theodore," he shouted. "What made you wander out into such a shocking snowstorm? His worship is waiting for you most impatiently."

I followed the old man in silence, and found my great-uncle working in the audience hall. "That was very sensible of you," he called. "Very sensible indeed to get a little fresh air to cool your brain. You needed it. Don't drink so much wine. You're much too young, and it doesn't agree with you." I did not answer a word, but sat down silently at the desk. "But tell me now, my dear nephew, what was it the Baron wanted with you?" he asked. I told him the whole story, and ended by saying that I would not lend myself to the dubious cure the Baron had proposed. "It wouldn't be possible, anyhow," interrupted my uncle. "We are leaving very early tomorrow, my dear nephew." So it was that I never saw Seraphine again.

Immediately upon our arrival at Königsberg my uncle complained of being more upset than usual by the journey. Disagreeable silences, broken only by violent bouts of bad temper, announced the return of his gout. One day, after being hurriedly sent for, I found the old gentleman stretched speechless on his bed by a stroke. In his rigidly clenched hands was a crumpled letter on which I recognized the handwriting of the bailiff of Rossitten. But

I was so distressed that I dared not wrench the paper from his grasp. I had no doubt that he was near his death. But before the doctor arrived his seventy-year-old pulse was beating again; his amazing constitution had resisted the fatal attack, and next day he was proclaimed out of danger. It was a particularly hard winter, and a raw, gloomy spring followed. So what with the gout and the bad weather, which made it worse, the old gentleman lay a long time on his sickbed. During his illness he decided to retire from his business, and transferred his legal agencies into other hands. So it was that any hope I had of ever revisiting Rossitten disappeared.

The old man would allow no one but me to attend him, and it was I who had to entertain and amuse him. But though in his painless moments his gaiety returned and we had no lack of harsh fun; though we even told hunting stories, and I hourly expected my heroic act of killing the huge wolf with a hunting knife to contribute to our mirth, he never mentioned our stay at Rossitten and, of course, I was too ashamed of myself to introduce the subject. My anxieties for my uncle and the labor of nursing him had pushed Seraphine's picture into the background. But when the old gentleman began to recover, that moment in the Baroness's room shone more brightly in my mind once more, like a star that had sunk forever below the horizon. One single incident vividly recalled all the grief I had suffered, and seized me with an ice-cold shudder like an apparition from the spirit world. One evening, as I opened the writing case that I had used at Rossitten, there fell out of the papers I was sorting a lock of dark hair tied in a white ribbon which I immediately recognized as Seraphine's; and when I examined the ribbon more closely, I clearly saw upon it the mark of a blood spot. Perhaps Adelheid had contrived to deliver me this keepsake, I thought, during the momentary madness that had seized me on the last day. But why the blood spot? I was filled with fearful forebodings, and what had seemed a moment ago a charming memento became the portent of a tragedy that might have cost a heart's blood. This was the white ribbon that had fluttered lightly and playfully on my shoulder the first time I was beside Seraphine; and now the dark powers had transformed it into the omen of a death wound. Boys should not play with weapons more dangerous than they understand.

At length the spring storms began to give over, summer came into its own and, instead of being unbearably cold, by the beginning of July it was unbearably hot. The old gentleman, now visibly recovering, moved, as he generally did, to a country house in the suburbs; and one still, warm evening, as we were sitting in the fragrant shade of the jasmine, he was filled with unexpected high spirits. His habitual sarcastic irony had left him, and he was in a benevolent, almost a tender mood. "Nephew," he began, "I don't know how it is, but today I feel better than I have felt for years. There's a sense of well-being flowing through me like an electric current. I think it's a portent of my approaching death." I tried to shake him out of his gloomy mood, but in vain. "Let me be," he said. "I shall not stay long down here below, and I have a debt I want to pay you. Do you still think about that autumn in Rossitten?" My uncle's question went through me like a lightning flash. But before I could reply he continued, "It was the will of heaven that you should stumble upon the secrets of the house in a strange way, and become involved in them against your will. Now is the time when everything must be made plain to you. Often enough, nephew, we have spoken of things that you have rather sensed than understood. In the procession of the seasons nature gives a symbolic representation of the cycle of man's life. That's a common saying, but I mean it in a quite different sense. The mists of spring come down, the hazes of summer rise, only the clear air of autumn reveals the distant landscape, before everything here below descends into winter's night. I mean that the sway of the occult powers is most clearly revealed to the clairvoyance of old age. It is like a glimpse into the promised land, into which the pilgrim begins his journey at the moment of temporal death. So at this moment the dark destiny of that house, to which I am bound by closer ties than kinship, rises clearly before me. Everything lies open before the eyes of my spirit. But though I see it all outspread before me, I cannot express the reality to you in words; it is beyond the power of man's tongue. Listen, my son, to so much as I can tell you; it may sound no more than a strange tale that any man might tell. But accept deep within your soul the knowledge that the mystery, into which you, not perhaps quite fortuitously, ventured, might well have destroyed you. But that is all over now."

The history of the Rossitten entail, which my uncle then told me, remains so clear in my memory that I can almost repeat it in his own words (he spoke of himself in the third person).

One stormy night in 1760 a terrifying noise woke the household of Rossitten from their sleep; it was as if the whole huge castle had been shattered in pieces. Everyone was up in an instant—candles were lit—white as a corpse with terror and apprehension, the steward panted by with the keys; but to everyone's great astonishment a deathly silence ensued, broken only by the creak and rattle of laboriously opened doors, and the ghastly echo of every footstep taken through the undamaged corridors, halls, and rooms of the castle. There was not the slightest trace of the disaster. Dark forebodings seized the old steward. He climbed to the great feudal hall, from which led the room where Baron Roderick von Ross used to sleep after his midnight astronomical observations. There were two doors in the wall of this huge apartment, leading to bedrooms, and between them was a postern, opening through a narrow passage straight into his observatory tower. But when Daniel (that was the steward's name) opened this door the howling storm blew debris and broken chips of building stone into his face. He jumped back in horror, letting the candlestick fall. The candles guttered and went out. "Lord God in Heaven!" he shouted. "The Baron has been dashed to pieces!"

At that moment, however, a wailing was heard from the Baron's bedroom, and Daniel found the rest of the servants gathered round their master's body. They had discovered him completely dressed in his best clothes, sitting in his great, finely upholstered armchair, with a calm, serious look on his undistorted features, as if he were resting after some exacting work. But his calm was the calm of death.

When day dawned it was seen that the crownlike roof of the tower had collapsed. Its great square stones had driven in the ceiling and floor of the astronomical observatory, and with the added weight of the huge beams, which were wrenched outwards, had carried away part of the castle wall and the narrow passage to the tower with it. A single step through the postern from the hall would mean death; there was at least an eighty-foot drop into a deep chasm.

The old Baron had foreseen his death to the hour and duly informed his sons. Consequently upon the following day Wolfgang von Ross arrived, the eldest son of the deceased and heir to the entail. Trusting his father's premonition, he had left Vienna, where he had been on his travels, immediately on receiving the fatal letter, and hurried with all possible speed to Rossitten. The steward had hung the great hall with black, and had the Baron laid out on a magnificent state bed, dressed in the clothes in which they had found him. Wolfgang climbed the staircase in silence, crossed the hall and approached his father's body. There he stood, his arms folded, and gazed fixedly into his father's pale face, gloomily knitting his brows. He stood like a statue, without a tear in his eye, till at last, raising his right arm with an almost convulsive movement toward the corpse, he murmured dully, "Did the stars decree that you should reduce the son you love to misery?" Then throwing up his hands, he took a step backwards and, gazing towards the ceiling, said in a subdued voice, almost softly, "Poor deluded old man! Now your masquerade with all its childish mystifications is over. Now you must acknowledge that the scanty wealth we enjoy here below bears no relation to that which lies above the stars. What will or power can reach beyond the grave?" Baron Wolfgang was silent for a few seconds, only to cry out more violently, "No, your stubbornness shan't rob me of a tithe of that earthly fortune which you sought to destroy." Then he pulled a folded paper out of his pocket, and held it between two fingers in the flame of a candle that was burning beside the corpse. The paper caught fire, and flared up. But as the light of the flame shimmered and played in the corpse's face, the old man's muscles appeared to twitch as if he were speaking soundless words; so strong was the illusion indeed, that the servants, who were some way off, rushed up in fear and consternation. Baron Wolfgang completed his task, however, carefully stamping out the last corner of the paper, which he had dropped still burning onto the floor. Then he threw one more baleful glance at his father and hurried from the hall.

Next day Daniel informed the Baron of the recent destruction of the tower, giving him a long account of all the events on the night of the late Baron's death, and concluding with the recommendation that the tower should be immediately repaired; for should there be any further fall the whole castle would be in danger, if not of complete collapse at least of very serious damage.

"Repair the tower?" exclaimed Baron Wolfgang, turning on the old servant with anger blazing from his eyes. "Repair the tower? Never. Don't you realize, fellow," he continued more calmly, "that the tower couldn't have collapsed without due cause? What if my father himself desired the destruction of the place where he practiced his unholy astrology? What if he himself made certain preparations that enabled him to bring down the roof of the tower at any moment he would, and smash the contents of his observatory to pieces? But, be that as it may, the whole castle can tumble down, for all I care. Do you think I shall ever live in this curious owl's nest? No. My worthy ancestor who laid the foundations of a new castle down there in the valley started a work that I am going to continue."

"And so," said Daniel dejectedly, "your faithful old servants must take the pilgrim's staff and depart."

"Naturally, I have no use for the services of a lot of useless tottering graybeards," replied the Baron. "But I shall turn no one off. The bread of charity will taste pretty good, if you have no work to do for it."

"Me, the steward," cried the old man in grief, "you'd relieve me of my post?"

The Baron had turned his back on the old servant, and was about to leave the hall when suddenly he rounded on the old man, his whole face red with anger and his fists clenched, and shouted in a terrifying voice, "You, you hypocritical old rascal, who took part in that unholy business of my father's up there! You that sucked his heart's blood like a vampire. Why, you probably made criminal use of the old man's madness, and planted those hellish ideas in his head that brought me to the edge of the abyss. I ought to kick you out like a mangy dog."

The Baron's fearful threat reduced the old servant to such terror that he fell down on his knees before him, and it was perhaps involuntarily—for in anger the body often acts mechanically upon a mere thought—that his master raised his left foot and kicked the old man so hard in the chest that he collapsed with a dull cry. Slowly pulling himself up, the servant uttered a single strange sound, like the whining howl of a dying dog, and casting his master a burning glance of mingled fury and despair, walked away. The Baron threw a purse of gold after him as he went, but the old servant left it lying on the floor where it had fallen.

In due course all the local family connections assembled, and the old Baron was interred in the family vault in Rossitten church. Once the guests had dispersed the heir seemed to emerge from his gloom and to enjoy his newly inherited property. He made a complete survey of the estate revenue with Voetheri, the old Baron's legal adviser, to whom he gave his full confidence, confirming him in his office after a single conversation. He considered how much could be set aside for improvements and how much for the building of the new castle. Voetheri was of the opinion that the old Baron must have left some money hidden somewhere, since he could not possibly have spent his yearly revenue, and only a couple of small bundles of banknotes had been found, while the cash in the strongbox amounted to no more than a thousand thalers. Who was more likely to know where than the stubborn Daniel, who was no doubt only waiting to be asked? The Baron was rather afraid that Daniel might be allowing the treasure to moulder in its hiding place rather than reveal its existence; not for his own profit—for what could any fortune do for a childless old man whose only wish was to end his days in the old castle?—but out of revenge for the insult he had suffered. He gave Voetheri a full account of the incident, concluding that from various reports that had reached him he felt certain that it was Daniel who had fostered the old man's inexplicable distaste for receiving his sons at Rossitten. His legal adviser assured him that the rumors were false; for no one in the world was capable of influencing the old Baron's decisions in any way, let alone of making up his mind for him. Furthermore, he promised to wheedle the secret of the hidden hoard out of the old servant.

Daniel needed no wheedling. No sooner was he asked, "How comes it, Daniel, that the old gentleman left so little cash behind?" than he answered with a distrustful smile, "Are you thinking of the miserable thaler or two you found in the small strongbox? All the rest lies in the vaulted closet beside his Lordship's little bedroom. But the most valuable part," he went on, his smile changing into an evil grin, and red fire blazing in his eyes, "that is buried down there in the chasm."

The lawyer immediately called for the Baron and they went into the bedroom. There Daniel fumbled in a corner of the wall paneling to reveal a lock. The Baron looked greedily at that lock and began to try the keys on the great bunch that he had pulled with a great jangling out of his pocket; while Daniel stood there looking down with malicious pride at his master, who crouched low to get a better look at the lock. The old servant's face was deathly white, as he said in a trembling voice, "You called me a dog, your Lordship. You'll find that I'm as faithful as a dog." Whereupon he handed the Baron a little steel key, which his master snatched greedily out of his hand. It turned in the lock without much effort, and they entered a little low closet in which stood a great iron chest with its lid open. Inside were several bags of gold, and on them lay a slip of paper, with writing in the old Baron's familiar, large, old-fashioned hand:

> One hundred and fifty thousand thalers in Prussian guineas: money saved from the revenue of the Rossitten entail: this sum to be devoted to the castle building. Further, he that shall succeed me in the entail and in the possession of this money shall erect on the highest hill to the east of this castle tower, which he will find in ruins, a tall lighthouse for the benefit of seamen, and keep it burning every night. . . .
> Rossitten, St. Michael's Eve, 1760.
> Roderick, Baron von Ross.

Having lifted the bags, one after another, and dropped them back into the chest, rejoicing in the chink of the gold, he turned briskly to the old servant, thanked him for his faithfulness, and assured him that but for libelous rumors he would have trusted him from the first. Now not only should he retain the post of steward, but he should receive double pay. "I owe you full compensation," he concluded, lowering his gaze. "If you want gold take one of these bags." Standing before the old man, he pointed to the chest, then went over to it again and examined the bags.

The steward suddenly went a fiery red, and uttered that fearful cry that the lawyer had compared to the whining howl of a dying dog. Voetheri trembled, for what the old man had muttered between his teeth sounded like "Blood for gold!"

The Baron had been too absorbed in contemplating his treasure to notice anything. Daniel, however, trembling in every limb as if in some spasmodic fever, approached his master with humbly bowed head and kissed his hand. He spoke in a tearful voice, rubbing his handkerchief over his eyes, as if to wipe away his tears. "Oh, my dear gracious Lord, what good is gold to a childless old man like me? But double wages I gladly accept, and I will do my duty actively and untiringly."

The Baron paid no particular attention to the old man's words, but let the heavy lid of the chest fall with such a crash that the whole vault echoed and rang. Then, locking it and carefully taking the key, he remarked casually, "Good, fellow! Good! But you said something, something about a great deal of gold lying in the ruined tower."

Daniel crossed silently to that fatal postern and laboriously tugged it open. Whereupon the storm blew great snowflakes into the hall, and a scared raven circled cawing and screaming beneath the roof, beat its black wings against the window, and, regaining the open door, threw itself into the abyss. The Baron went out into the passage but stumbled back, after casting barely a glance into the chasm. "A terrible sight," he stammered. "I am dizzy," and fell half fainting into the lawyer's arms. He immediately pulled himself together, however, and fixed the old servant with a sharp glance. "Down there?" he asked. Meanwhile Daniel had shut the door, and was pressing against it with all his strength, panting and groaning in his efforts to draw the heavy key out of the rusty lock. Finally succeeding, he turned to the Baron and, jerking the great key to and fro in his hand, observed with a strange smile, 'Down there lie thousands and thousands and thousands—all the late Baron's fine instruments—telescopes—quadrants—globes—lenses—all lying there shattered among the stones and the timber."

"But cash," interrupted the Baron. "Cash. Didn't you speak of gold coins, fellow?"

"I only meant," replied the old man, "things that cost thousands in gold," and they could get nothing more out of him.

The Baron was highly delighted to have once and for all the

necessary means for carrying out his darling plan of building a fine new castle. His legal adviser was of the opinion that the deceased's will envisaged only the repair or complete reconstruction of the old castle, and indeed that a new building could hardly achieve the venerable size or the imposing yet simple character of the old family seat. But the Baron persisted in his intention, claiming that in such provisions as were not sanctioned by the deed of foundation, the will of the dead man must be overridden. He added further that it was his duty to improve the residence of Rossitten in so far as the climate, soil, and surroundings would allow, particularly as he intended shortly to bring back as his beloved bride a being in every respect worthy of the very greatest sacrifices.

The mysterious way in which the Baron spoke of an alliance, perhaps already secretly concluded, prevented his adviser from asking further questions. He found some comfort in the Baron's matrimonial plans, since he could now ascribe the Lord of Rossitten's cupidity not so much to greed as to a desire to compensate someone he dearly loved for leaving a more genial climate to live with him in these barren wastes. Still, if the Baron was not intolerably avaricious, he could not help admitting that he was at least very grasping for money. For though he was wallowing in gold and forever feasting his eyes on the Prussian guineas, he could not refrain from observing morosely, "The old scoundrel has certainly kept the secret of the richest treasure to himself, but next spring I'll have the tower cleared under my own eyes."

Builders arrived and held long conversations with the Baron as to the most practical way of proceeding with the building. He rejected drawing after drawing. No architecture was sufficiently rich and imposing for him. Then he began to make drawings himself. This employment constantly conjured up before him the sunny picture of a happy future, and this put him in a cheerful mood often bordering on high spirits. The mood was infectious. His openhandedness and the luxury of the household at least contradicted all suspicion of avarice. Even Daniel seemed to have forgotten his wrongs. His behavior toward the Baron was quiet and humble; though, mindful of the treasure in the chasm, his master often cast a distrustful eye upon him. But the most amazing thing was that the old man seemed to be growing younger every day. Perhaps he had been broken by grief for the old Baron and was now beginning to get over his loss; it may have been because he had no longer to spend cold sleepless nights on the tower and could now enjoy his fill of better food and good wine; whatever the reason, the old graybeard seemed to be turning into an active man with red cheeks and a well-nourished body, a man with a firm step, who laughed aloud whenever a joke was made.

The cheerful life of Rossitten, however, was interrupted by the coming of a man whom one would have expected to be welcome. This was Wolfgang's younger brother, Hubert, upon whose appearance Wolfgang turned white as death, and cried, "What do you want here, wretch?" Hubert rushed into his brother's arms, but the Baron seized him and led him off to a distant room upstairs, where he shut himself in with him. The pair remained together for several hours, at the end of which time Hubert came down in a most agitated state and called for his horse. The legal adviser intercepted him; he tried to pass. Hoping that perhaps a fratricidal quarrel might here be repaired, Voetheri begged him to remain for at least a couple of hours, and at that same moment Wolfgang also came down crying, "Stay, Hubert. You'll think better of it." Hubert's eyes lighted up, he gained control of himself and, quickly taking off his rich furs, threw them to the servant behind him. Then taking Voetheri by the hand and leading him into a quiet room, he said with a mocking smile, "So the master of the entail will allow me to stay here, after all." Voetheri replied that this unfortunate misunderstanding could certainly be resolved, since it had only arisen from long separation. Hubert picked up the steel poker from beside the hearth and, splitting a gnarled and smoking log to make the fire burn brighter, replied, "Observe, my dear sir, that I am a good-natured man and skilled in the domestic arts. But Wolfgang is full of the strangest prejudices and— he's a little miserly." Voetheri thought it wiser to pry no further into the brothers' relationship, though Wolfgang's face, behavior, and tone of voice clearly revealed a man racked by conflicting passions.

Later in the evening, when he went up to the Baron's room to get his decision on some matter concerning the estate, the lawyer found him pacing up and down, with his arms clasped behind his back, in a state of great agitation. Finally noticing the agent's presence, however, he stopped, took him by the hands and, peering gloomily into his eyes, said in a broken voice, "My brother has arrived. I know," he continued, before Voetheri could open his mouth to question him, "I know what you are going to say. But you don't understand. You don't know that my wretched brother—yes, wretched I must call him—is always standing in my way like an evil ghost; he disturbs my peace of mind. It is not his fault that I am not in the depths of misery; he has done his best to bring me there, but Heaven has willed it otherwise. Ever since the deed of entail was drawn up, he has persecuted me with a deadly hatred. He envies me the estate, which in his hands would fly like chaff. He is the maddest wastrel in the world. His debts amount to far more than the half of the unentailed property in Courland that is his share, and now that he is followed and harrassed by creditors, he has come to beg for money."

"And you, his brother, refuse him," Voetheri was about to interpose.

But dropping his adviser's hands and taking a step backwards, the Baron shouted violently, "Stop! Yes, I refused. I won't give him a penny from the revenue of the property. But listen to the proposal I made him a few hours ago and that the madman refused, before you judge my sense of duty. Our unentailed possessions in Courland are, as you know, considerable, and I am willing to give up the half share that falls to me, but in favor of his family. Hubert married in Courland a poor young beauty, who has borne him children and is starving with them. The property must be held in trust, and the necessary monies paid to him out of the revenue, for his support; an agreement must be made with the creditors. But he sets no store by a quiet, easy existence or by his wife and children. What he wants is money, great sums of money that he can squander on his accursed frivolities. I don't know what devil has let him into the secret of the hundred and fifty thousand thalers, but he demands a half share. He insists in his insane way that the money is no part of the entail but must count as liquid capital. This request I must and will refuse—but I have a suspicion that secretly he is brooding on my destruction."

Voetheri tried to reason with the Baron on the subject of his brother. But, being ignorant of the more intimate circumstances, he had to resort to general, moral, and seemingly obvious arguments. He was, however, completely unsuccessful. The Baron gave him the task of dealing with the hostile and greedy Hubert; and this he performed with all possible tact. He was, indeed, not a little delighted when Hubert finally declared, "Very well. I accept the proposals of the master of the entail, but upon condition that, as I am in danger of losing my honor and good name forever through my creditors' harshness, he advances me a thousand guineas and allows me, at least for a while, to reside at Rossitten as my kind brother's guest."

"Never," cried the Baron, when Voetheri brought him Hubert's proposals. "I will never permit him to spend an hour in my house from the moment I have brought my wife here. Go to him, my dear friend, and tell that disturber of my peace that he shall have two thousand guineas, not as an advance but as a present. But away with him—he must go." Voetheri realized in a flash that the Baron had married without his father's knowledge, and that this marriage must also have been the cause of the brothers' quarrel. Hubert listened proudly and calmly to the lawyer, and when he had finished, sullenly observed, "I'll think it over, and for the present I'll stay here a few days." Voetheri did his best to persuade the discontented Hubert that the Baron was really doing everything he could to compensate him by renouncing his share of the unentailed property, and that he had absolutely no cause for complaint. But he had to admit that there was something hateful about this deed of entail that so favored the firstborn at the expense of the other children.

For reply Hubert tore open his waistcoat, as if to admit the air to his stifled breast, and with one hand on his ruffle and the other on his hip, swung round on one foot with the light movement of a dancer and exclaimed in cutting tones, "Pah! Hateful things are born of hatred." Then, bursting into a shrill laugh, he continued, "How kind the master of the entail thinks he is when he throws his gold to the poor beggar!" Voetheri well understood that there could be no question of a full reconciliation between the brothers.

Hubert, much to the Baron's displeasure, settled into the room assigned him in the wing of the castle, for a long stay. He was observed to be in frequent and lengthy conversation with the steward, and sometimes the pair of them went out hunting wolves. For the rest, he made infrequent appearances and utterly avoided any interview with his brother; a state of things that suited the Baron.

Voetheri felt the oppressive nature of the relationship, but had to admit to himself that Hubert's most sinister manner in all his conversations and actions was deliberately intended to disturb the atmosphere. He could now very well understand the Baron's original alarm at his brother's coming.

One day when Voetheri was sitting alone in his office over his papers, Hubert entered, more serious and more composed than usual, and said in almost doleful tones, "I accept my brother's last proposals too. See that I get the two thousand guineas today, and I will leave tonight, on horseback and alone."

"With the money?" asked Voetheri.

"You're right," answered Hubert. "I know what you're going to say—the weight. Let me have it in bills of exchange on Isaac Lazarus of Königsberg. I shall ride there tonight. I am being driven away. The old man has set his evil spirits walking in this place."

"Do you mean your father, Baron?" asked Voetheri seriously.

Hubert's lips trembled, and he had to grip his chair to prevent himself from falling. Then, suddenly pulling himself together, he cried, "This very day, my dear sir!" and staggered with some effort out of the door.

"Now he realizes that no more deception is possible, that he can do nothing in the face of my resolution," said the Baron, making out the bill of exchange in favor of Isaac Lazarus of Königsberg. His hostile brother's departure lifted a weight from his mind, and that night at supper he was more cheerful than he had been for a long while. To everyone's considerable relief, Hubert had excused himself from the meal.

Voetheri slept in a rather out-of-the-way room whose windows gave onto the castle courtyard, and that night he was suddenly woken by what sounded to him like a distant and lugubrious whimpering. Yet though he strained his ears to listen, everything was still as death. He concluded therefore that what he had heard was merely the delusion of a dream. But a most strange feeling of fear and horror gained possession of him, and he could not stay in bed. Getting up, he crossed to the window, and before long he saw the castle gate opened and a figure with a burning torch in his hand come out and cross the yard. He recognized old Daniel, and watched him open up the stables, go in, and lead out a saddled horse. Then a second figure emerged from the darkness, well wrapped in furs, with a foxskin cap on his head. Voetheri recognized Hubert who, after a few moments' violent conversation with Daniel, went in again. Then the old servant led the horse back to its stall, shut the stable door, and, coming back again across the yard, bolted the castle gate behind him. Hubert had intended to ride away, but at just that moment he had remembered something—so much was obvious. It was also clear that Hubert was involved in some dangerous compact with the old steward, and Voetheri could hardly wait till morning to inform the Baron of the night's events. The question now was how to repel some wicked plot of Hubert's, which would explain his disturbed state on the day before.

Next morning, at the Baron's usual hour for rising, Voetheri heard a great deal of running about, of opening and shutting of doors, and the sound of confused voices and cries. Leaving his room, he met servants everywhere, who took no notice of him, but ran past him, up and down stairs and in and out of the rooms, with deathly pale faces. At last he learned that the Baron had disappeared; they had been searching for him for hours. Franz had been attending him when he went to bed, but he must have got up later and gone out in his dressing gown and slippers, with the candlestick in his hand; for these articles were missing. A prey to dark anticipations, Voetheri ran to the audience chamber, off which led the room that Wolfgang, like his father, had chosen for his bedroom. The tower postern stood wide open. "He's down there," cried Voetheri in terror. "Down in the abyss, shattered to pieces." He was right. Snow had fallen, and all that could clearly be made out from above was one stiff arm of the unfortunate man, protruding from the stones. It was many hours before workmen succeeded, at the peril of their lives, in climbing out on ladders tied together and bringing up the corpse on ropes. In his death agony the Baron had tightly gripped the silver candlestick, and the hand that held it was the only undamaged limb of his whole body, which had been hideously dashed to pieces by its fall onto the jagged stones.

With despair written in every line of his face, Hubert stumbled past, as the corpse was drawn up from the abyss and laid on a broad table in the hall, on the very spot where a few weeks before Baron Roderick had lain. Overwhelmed by the terrible sight, he cried, "Brother! Oh, my poor brother! Not for this did I pray the devils which possessed me." Voetheri trembled at these suspicious words. He felt he should strike Hubert down for his brother's murder. But Hubert lay senseless on the floor. They carried him to bed, where after the application of restoratives he fairly soon recovered. Then, very pale, with dark grief in his half-closed eyes, he visited Voetheri in his room. Almost too exhausted to stand, slowly he let himself down into an armchair, saying as he did so, "I desired my brother's death, because my father, by this stupid entail, left him the better half of the inheritance. Now he had met his end in a terrible fashion, and I succeed to the estates. But my heart's crushed within me. I shall never—can never be happy. I confirm you in your post, and you will receive the widest powers relative to the management of this property, on which I can never bear to live." He rushed out of the room, and a couple of hours later was on his way to Königsberg.

It appeared that the unfortunate Wolfgang had got up in the night, perhaps with the intention of going to another room off the hall, which contained a library. In a sleepy stupor he must have mistaken the door, opened the tower postern, stepped out and tumbled down. This explanation, however, did some violence to probabilities. If the Baron could not sleep and wished to fetch a book to read, a sleepy stupor was out of the question. Yet only in this condition could he have mistaken the door of the room, and opened the way to the tower instead. What is more, the tower postern was locked, and it would have taken him some trouble to get it open. "Oh, your worship," exclaimed the Baron's huntsman, Franz, after Voetheri had explained all these improbabilities to the assembled servants, "it certainly didn't happen like that."

"How else then?" Voetheri turned to Franz, a good honest fellow, who would have followed his master into the grave, but was unwilling to speak in front of the others. He had decided that what he had to say he would confide to the lawyer in private. Voetheri learned that the Baron had often spoken to Franz of the great treasures lying buried down there under the rubble, and that often at night, as if driven to it by an evil spirit, he would open the door, the key of which he had forced Daniel to give him; and there he would stand looking longingly down into the chasm for the alleged riches. So it seemed certain that, after the huntsman had left him on that fatal night, the Baron had paid another visit to the tower, had been seized by a sudden giddiness, and had tumbled down. Daniel, who seemed absolutely shattered by his master's terrible death, further suggested that it would be a good thing if the door were to be walled up; and this was done.

Baron Hubert von Ross, now inheritor of the entail, returned to Courland without ever again appearing at Rossitten. Voetheri received the full powers necessary for the administration of the estate. The building of the new castle was discontinued, while, in so far as was possible, the old building was put into good condition. Many years went by before Hubert appeared in Rossiten, one year in late autumn, and after some days spent with Voetheri in his room, returned to Courland. On passing through Königsberg he deposited and registered his will at the government office there.

During his stay in Rossitten the Baron, who seemed completely changed in his character, spoke a great deal about forebodings of his approaching death. These proved only too true, for in that very year he died; and his son, also called Hubert, came speedily over from Courland, followed by his mother and sister, to take possession of the rich entail. This young man appeared to have inherited all the bad qualities of his forebears; in the very first moments of his stay in Rossitten he showed himself to be conceited, overbearing, impetuous and avaricious. He then and there required a great number of changes in things that seemed to him inconvenient or unsuitable; he pitched the cook out of the house; he tried to beat the coachman but did not succeed, for the stubborn fellow had the insolence to prevent it. Indeed he was just beginning to assume the part of the severe master, when Voetheri resolutely opposed him, observing with decision that not a chair should be moved nor a cat leave the house against its wishes until the opening of the will. "You are here to serve the master of the estates," began the Baron, spluttering with rage, but Voetheri would not let him finish. For, measuring him with a penetrating glance, he observed, "Don't be in too much of a hurry, Baron. You can't expect to command here before the opening of the will. At present I alone am master, and I know how to meet force with force. Remember that by my authority as executor of your father's will, confirmed by the orders of the court, I am empowered to forbid your residence here at Rossitten. So, to avoid any unpleasantness, I advise you to return quietly to Königsberg."

His legal adviser's serious manner and decisive tone lent his words peculiar weight, and so it was that the young Baron found himself in danger of blunting his fine new horns on a brick wall. Realizing the weakness of his weapons, therefore, he decided to retreat, masking his shame behind a mocking laugh.

Three months went by, and the day fixed by the deceased for the opening of his will arrived; he had deposited it at Königsberg. Besides the law officers, the Baron and Voetheri, there was in the courtroom a young man of noble appearance who came in with the legal adviser; on his taking a bundle of documents from his inside pocket, he was assumed to be his secretary. The Baron looked contemptuously at him, as he did at almost everyone else, and angrily demanded that the wearisome and unnecessary ceremonial should be quickly concluded without many words or much writing. He did not understand what significance a will could have in matters of inheritance governed by an entail. It would depend entirely on his pleasure whether any provisions it contained should be observed or not. With one fleeting, disagreeable glance at the document the Baron recognized his late father's hand and seal, and while the clerk of the court prepared to read the will aloud, looked imperturbably out of the window, with his right arm dangling over the back of the chair and his left propped on the judgment table, playing a tattoo with his fingers on the green cloth. After a short preamble, the late Baron Hubert von Ross declared that he had never possessed the estate as inheritor of the entail, but had merely administered it for the only son of the late Baron Wolfgang von Ross, named Roderick after his grandfather; it was to him that the entail had fallen at his father's death, according to the family succession. Complete accounts of income and expenditure, of the present state of the property, etc., would be found among his papers. Wolfgang von Ross, according to Hubert's will, had met Mlle. Julie de St. Val in Geneva on his travels, and conceived such an affection for her that he had made up his mind never to be parted from her. She was very poor, and her family, although of good stock, were not among the noblest. For that reason he had not been able to reckon on the consent of old Roderick, whose whole endeavor was to raise the importance of his family and the estate in every possible way. He had ventured, however, to write to his father from Paris, informing him of his passion; and as might have been foreseen, the old man had declared peremptorily that he would choose a bride for the successor to the entail, and no other choice would be considered. Instead of crossing over to England, as it was said he had done, Wolfgang returned to Geneva under the name of Born and married Julie. She in the course of a year bore him a son, who at Wolfgang's death succeeded to the entail. For the fact that, although informed of the whole matter, the testator had kept a long silence and acted as if he were the true successor, he adduced a number of reasons arising from a previous agreement with Wolfgang. But these now appeared insufficient and fictitious.

The Baron stared thunderstruck at the clerk of the court, who was reading him this terrible news in a monotonous, strident voice; and when the reading was over, Voetheri stood up, took his young companion by the hand, and, with a deep bow to the court, announced: "Here, gentlemen, I have the honor to present to you Baron Roderick von Ross, successor to the Rossitten entail." Baron Hubert stared at the young man who had fallen out of a blue sky to rob him of the rich entail and a half of the Courland properties, with suppressed fury glowing in his eyes. Then, threatening him with his clenched fist, he ran out of the hall, powerless to utter a word. At the request of the members of the court, Baron Roderick produced the evidence proving him to be the person he claimed to be. He showed them an attested extract from the register of the church where his father had been married, stating that on a certain day Wolfgang Born, merchant, born in Königsberg, had been married with the blessings of the Church to Mlle. Julie de St. Val in the presence of the undersigned persons. He also showed them his certificate of baptism (he was baptized in Geneva as the legitimate son of the the merchant Born and his wife Julie, *née* de St. Val), and several letters from his father to his long-dead mother, all of which, however, were signed only with the letter W. Voetheri looked gloomily through all these papers and, apparently much disturbed, remarked, as he bundled them together again, "Well, God will help us!"

On the very next day Baron Hubert von Ross put in, through a lawyer whom he had chosen to represent him, a demand to the Königsberg courts for the immediate surrender of the entailed property of Rossitten. "It is clear as day," pleaded his advocate, "that the late Baron von Ross had no rights, testamentary or otherwise, to dispose of the said entail. This will is no more than a written statement laid before the courts, informing them that Baron Wolfgang von Ross left the entail to a surviving son. It is not, however, conclusive as evidence, and does not therefore prove the legitimacy of the alleged Baron Roderick von Ross. Furthermore, it is the business of that pretender to substantiate his alleged right of inheritance, which we herewith deny in due legal form, and to state his claim to the entailed estates, which now fall by right of succession to Baron Hubert von Ross. By the father's death the possession has passed directly to the son, and there is no need of a declaration of succession; for the order of succession to the entail cannot be revoked. The present owner, therefore, should not be disturbed in his possession by entirely unrecognized claims. What reasons the late Baron had for naming another successor are quite indifferent; it must be observed, however, that, as can be proved upon necessity from the papers of the deceased, he had a mistress in Switzerland, and it is therefore possible that the alleged nephew is in fact his own illegitimate son, on whom in a burst of contrition he wished to bestow this rich entail."

Probability seemed to speak strongly in favor of the circumstances stated in the will, and the judges were extremely indignant at the son's daring, in that last clause, to accuse his late father of a crime. Yet the case presented by Baron Hubert's lawyer seemed legally valid, and it was only Voetheri's indefatigable and insistent assurances that Baron Roderick's legitimacy could be most conclusively proved in a very short time, that succeeded in postponing the surrender of the entail and prolonging his own administration of the estate until final proof was established.

Voetheri realized only too well how hard it would be to fulfill his promise. He had rummaged through all the elder Roderick's papers without finding the trace of a letter or any other writing touching on Wolfgang's relationship with Mlle. de St. Val. He had thoroughly searched old Roderick's bedroom in Rossitten, and was sitting there, deep in thought, working at a statement for the Geneva lawyer, who had been recommended to him as an active and intelligent man, and to whom he looked for information that would establish the young Baron's case. It was midnight, and through the open bedroom door he saw the moon shining brightly into the adjoining hall. Suddenly there was a sound, as if someone were slowly and heavily climbing the stairs, and jangling and clattering with some keys. Voetheri got up and went into the hall, and there clearly heard someone approaching along the passage to the hall doors. They swung open almost instantly, and a man in night-clothes with death-pale, distorted features came slowly in, bearing a candlestick with burning candles in one hand and a great bunch of keys in the other. Voetheri immediately recognized the steward, and was just about to ask him what he wanted so late in the night when something strange and ghostly in the old man's whole appearance, and in the deathlike rigidity of his features, breathed on him with an icy breath. He realized that he was watching a sleep-walker. The old man crossed the room with even steps, making straight for the walled-up postern that had once led into the tower and, when he reached it, uttered a howling cry that issued from the depths of his being and echoed so eerily through the great hall that Voetheri trembled with fear. Then putting the candlestick on the floor and hanging the keys on his belt, Daniel began to scratch at the wall with both hands, till soon the blood was dripping from his nails; and all the while he cried and groaned, as if suffering under some nameless torture. Next he put his ear to the wall, with all the appearance of listening for something, and made a sign with his hand that seemed to be meant as a reassurance for someone. Leaning down to pick up the candlestick, he next paced evenly and quietly back to the door, while Voetheri followed him cautiously with a candle in his hand. Then the old man went downstairs, opened the great gate of the castle and slid quickly out. He crossed to the stable and, placing his candles, to Voetheri's astonishment, so carefully that the whole building was sufficiently well lit without the least danger of fire, he fetched saddle and bridle. Then, leading a horse out of its stall, he saddled it, accurately arranging the girths and stirrup buckles and even releasing a wisp of its mane from the headpiece of its bridle. Clicking his tongue, he took the beast by the rein, patting its neck with his free hand, and led it out. Once outside in the yard, he stood for a few moments as if to receive orders, which with a nod he apparently promised to obey. Then he led the horse back into its stall, unsaddled it and tied it up again. Taking up the candlestick, he afterwards locked the stable, returned to the castle and finally vanished into his room, carefully bolting the door behind him. Voetheri felt absolutely shattered by this experience. Suspicion of some terrible deed rose before him like a black ghost from hell, and refused to leave him. Obsessed by Baron Roderick's perilous situation, however, he felt that he must at least use what he had seen for the young man's advantage.

Next day, when just as dusk was falling Daniel came into his room for instructions on some household matter, Voetheri seized the old servant by both hands and, pressing him into a chair, began confidentially, "Listen, Daniel, my old friend, I have been meaning for a long time to ask you what you make of this muddle Hubert's strange will has landed us into. Do you think that this young man is really Wolfgang's son and the offspring of a legal marriage?"

Leaning away sideways over the back of the chair to avoid Voetheri's direct gaze, old Daniel exclaimed morosely, "Pah—he may be. On the other hand, he may not. It's nothing to me who may be master here."

"But surely," Voetheri persisted, drawing closer to the old man and laying a hand on his shoulder, "surely, since you had the old Baron's absolute confidence he didn't keep his son's affairs secret from you. Didn't he tell you of Wolfgang's marrying against his will?"

"I really can't remember a thing like that," answered the old man with a loud and ill-bred yawn.

"You're sleepy, fellow," said Voetheri. "Perhaps you had a disturbed night."

"As if I didn't know that," replied the old man coldly, "but I'll go now and order the dinner." At this he got up heavily from the chair, rubbing his stiff back and yawning once again even louder than before.

"Stop a moment, fellow," cried Voetheri, seizing his arm and trying to force him back into the chair.

The old man continued to stand, however, in front of the desk, supporting himself upon it with both hands. Then with his body bent over toward Voetheri he asked in a surly voice: "What is it then? What has the will got to do with me? What concern of mine is this quarrel about the property?"

"About that," Voetheri interrupted him, "we'll say no more. We have something else to talk about, my dear Daniel. You are surly and you're yawning, and that speaks of some unusual fatigue. It almost makes me think that it really was you who came last night."

"What about me last night?" asked the old man, remaining in his position.

"As I was sitting late last night," pursued Voetheri, "up there in the old Baron's bedroom beside the great hall, you came through the door, stiff and pale, you went over to the walled-up postern, and you scratched at it with both your hands, groaning as if you were in great pain. Are you a sleepwalker then, Daniel?"

The old man collapsed onto the chair that Voetheri quickly pushed forward under him. He uttered no sound, and his face was invisible in the darkness, but Voetheri observed that he was panting and that his teeth were chattering.

"Yes," the lawyer resumed after a short pause. "There's one odd thing about sleepwalkers. They have never the slightest memory next day of their very strange condition nor of any actions they performed, though these may seem to have been carried out in a waking state." Daniel remained quiet. "I have had experiences similar to that with you last night," Voetheri went on. "I had a friend who walked regularly at night, at the full moon. Sometimes he would even sit down and write letters. But the strangest thing about him was that if I whispered very softly in his ear, I could make him speak. He answered any question quite properly, and even things that he would have concealed in a waking state dropped involuntarily from his lips, as if he could not withstand the force that was working on him. Do you know, I believe even if a somnambulist had committed a crime and kept it secret for a very long time, he'd confess it if one questioned him under those strange conditions. It's a good thing to have a clear conscience, as we two have, my dear Daniel. Never mind how much we sleepwalk, no one will get us to admit to any crimes. But listen, Daniel, you wanted to go up into the observatory tower, didn't you when you were scratching so horribly on the walled-up postern? You want to perform experiments like old Baron Roderick, don't you? I'll ask you about that next time you walk in your sleep." The old man's trembling had increased all the time Voetheri was talking, and now, his whole body racked by terrible convulsions, he broke out in a shrill, unintelligible babble. Voetheri rang for the servants, who brought lights and carried the still-rigid Daniel like an unconscious automaton to his bed. After an hour of this terrible rigor, he fell into a deep state of unconsciousness resembling sleep. On waking he called for wine, which was given him, upon which he drove the servant, who wanted to watch beside his bed, out of the room and locked himself in as usual.

Voetheri had seriously intended to try the experiment when he had been describing it to Daniel. He had to admit to himself, however, that since the old man now knew, perhaps for the first time, of his sleepwalking, he would do everything possible to elude him; and that, furthermore, confessions made under such circumstances were no suitable foundation for a case at law. Nevertheless, he went into the hall just before midnight, in the hopes that Daniel, as is usual in such cases, might be powerless to resist his involuntary promptings. At midnight there was a great noise in the court, and he clearly heard the breaking of a window. Hurrying down, he was greeted in the corridor by a foul-smelling smoke which, he soon ascertained, was rising from the steward's window. Daniel was being carried out—stiff as a corpse, to be put to bed in another room. At midnight, the servants told him, a groom had been awakened by a strange, dull knocking. Something, he supposed, had happened to the old man, and he was hurriedly getting up to go to his aid when the porter in the court shouted "Fire! Fire! There's a blaze in the steward's room!" His shouts awoke several more servants, who ran up, but all endeavors to break in the steward's door were in vain. Everyone then rushed out into the court, but the porter had had the presence of mind to break the steward's window—his was a low room on the ground floor—to tear down the burning curtains, and put the fire out in a moment with a couple of buckets of water. They found Daniel lying in the middle of the floor in a deep faint, with the candlestick tightly grasped in his hand; it was the flaming candles that had caught the curtains and started the fire. Burning rags falling on the old man had scorched his eyebrows and a good deal of his hair, and if the watchman had not seen the fire he would have helplessly burned to death. Moreover, to their no small astonishment they found that the door was secured from the inside by two newly fixed bolts, which had not been there on the previous evening.

Voetheri realized that the old man had wanted to make it impossible for himself to get out of the room; there was no mistaking this blind compulsion. But he was now seriously ill. He did not utter a word, took very little nourishment, and stared straight in front of him, as if in the grip of some terrible thoughts, with death written on his features. He did not believe that the old man would ever rise from his bed again.

He had done everything possible for the young Roderick, and must calmly await the outcome. He wanted, therefore, to return to Königsberg, and had fixed his departure for the next day. But late in the evening, as he was putting his documents together, he stumbled across a small sealed packet addressed to him by the late Baron Hubert von Ross and marked: "To be read after the opening of my will." It was inexplicable that he had not noticed it before. He was just about to break the seal when suddenly the door opened, and Daniel entered with light ghostlike steps, carrying a black portfolio under his arm. This he laid down on the desk and, sinking on both knees, uttered a deep and deathlike sigh. Then convulsively grasping Voetheri's hands, he cried with the dull and hollow voice of the grave, "Do not let me die on the scaffold. God above shall be my judge!" After which, gasping with pain, he laboriously pulled himself up and left the room as he had come.

Voetheri spent the whole night reading the contents of the black portfolio and Hubert's packet. The two collections generally agreed and were sufficient to dictate his next moves. Immediately upon his arrival at Königsberg, he paid a call on the young Baron Hubert, who received him with highhanded rudeness. The remarkable outcome of this conversation, however, which began at midday and continued unbroken until late into the night, was that next day the Baron acknowledged before the court that he recognized the claimant to the entail according to his father's will, as the legitimate son of Baron Wolfgang von Ross, eldest son of Baron Roderick von Ross, born in wedlock with Mlle. Julie St. Val, and therefore rightful and legitimate successor to the entailed estate. When he left the court, his carriage, drawn by post-horses, was at the door; and he quickly drove out of the town, leaving his mother and sister behind. They would perhaps never see him again, he had written in a few cryptic lines.

Roderick's astonishment at this turn in affairs was considerable, and he pressed Voetheri to tell him how the miracle had happened and what secret forces had been at work. The lawyer put him off with promises of future enlightenment once he had taken over the estate. For the surrender of the entail could not take place immediately, since the courts would not be satisfied with Hubert's acknowledgment, but would require complete proof of Roderick's legitimacy. Voetheri recommended the young Baron to move to Rossitten, adding that Hubert's mother and sister were momentarily embarrassed by his precipitate departure and might prefer a quiet stay on the family estate to living in the expensive and noisy city. The delight with which Roderick accepted the idea of sharing a roof, at least temporarily, with the Baroness and her charming daughter, testified to the deep impression that charming child Seraphine had made on him. Indeed, the Baron put their residence at Rossitten to such good use that before many weeks had passed he had won the girl's love and the mother's consent to their marriage.

This was all too hasty for Voetheri, for so far Roderick's legitimation as Lord of Rossitten was still in doubt. But letters from Courland cut short this idyll at the castle. Hubert had not appeared on his estates, but had gone direct to Petersburg to join the army, and was now fighting against the Persians, with whom Russia was at war. This compelled the swift departure of the Baroness and her daughter for their properties, for everything there was in disorder. Roderick, looking upon himself as the accepted son-in-law, insisted on accompanying his beloved, and so when Voetheri returned to Königsberg the castle was as deserted as before. The steward's serious illness grew steadily so much worse that he was no longer expected to recover, and his post was given to the old huntsman Franz, Wolfgang's faithful servant.

At length, after long delays, the lawyer received satisfactory reports from Switzerland. The parson who had married Wolfgang had long been dead, but a note was found in the church register in his hand to the effect that the stranger, calling himself Wolfgang Born, whom he had married to Mlle. de St. Val, had proved his identity as Baron Wolfgang von Ross, eldest son of Baron Roderick von Ross of Rossitten. Furthermore, two other witnesses, a Geneva merchant and an old French captain who had moved to Lyons, were discovered, to whom Wolfgang had revealed his identity; and their statements on oath confirmed the parson's note in the register. With this evidence, drawn up in due form, in his hand, Voetheri now offered complete proof of his principal's rights, and there was nothing to prevent the transfer of the entail, which was to take place in the following autumn. Hubert did not survive his first battlefield, but met the same fate as his younger brother, who had fallen in the field a year before his father's death; the Courland estates, therefore, fell to Baroness Seraphine von Ross, and made a fine dowry for the fortunate Roderick.

It was early November when the Baroness, Roderick and his bride reached Rossitten, where the formal surrender of the entail was followed by the wedding of Roderick and Seraphine. Many weeks passed in wild rejoicings till finally the sated guests left one by one, to Voetheri's great satisfaction; for he did not want to quit Rossitten until he had initiated the young Baron into the financial details of his new properties. Roderick's uncle had kept the strictest accounts of income and disbursements, so that although the young Baron had received only a small annual sum for his expenses, the capital sum that had been found among the old Baron's effects had been considerably increased by the income unexpended during his minority. Except in the first three years, Hubert had not applied the revenues of the estate to his own needs, but had drawn up a statement of his liabilities to the young Baron secured upon his own share of the Courland estate.

Since the time of Daniel's sleepwalking Voetheri had chosen old Roderick's bedroom for his quarters, so as to be quite sure of overhearing any statement Daniel might thereafter volunteer. So it was there, and in the great castle hall adjoining, that the Baron visited Voetheri for business; and there one day the pair of them were sitting over a brightly burning fire at the great table, Voetheri with a pen in his hand noting down sums of money and adding up the Baron's capital, and the Baron with his elbows on the table peering into the open account books and weighty documents. Neither of them heard the dull roaring of the sea, nor the alarmed cries of the gulls that fluttered up and down, beating against the windowpanes, the certain sign of an approaching storm. Neither of them was perturbed by the wild howling of the wind, which blew up about midnight and roared through the castle, starting up uncanny noises in all the chimneys and narrow passages, whistlings and roarings that mingled in wild confusion. But when a final gust of wind had echoed through the whole edifice and the hall was suddenly flooded with the dull glow of the full moon, Voetheri casually exclaimed, "A bad storm," and the Baron, immersed in the prospect of the riches that had fallen to him, answered unconcernedly, turning over a page of the revenue accounts with a contented smile, "Yes, indeed, very stormy."

But, touched by the icy hand of fear, he started, when the door of the hall flew open and a pale, ghostly figure appeared, striding in with death written upon his face. Like everyone else, Voetheri had supposed Daniel to be lying helpless upon his bed, incapable of moving a limb. But here, under the spell of the full moon, he had begun his sleepwalking again. The Baron stared silently at the old man as he scratched at the wall, groaning as if his last hour had come. Then a dreadful fear seized the young man. With death-pale face and bristling hair, he sprang up, strode threateningly over to his aged servant, and cried in a loud voice that echoed through the hall, "Daniel, Daniel, what are you doing here at this hour?" Uttering that frightful whimpering howl he had given when Wolfgang had offered him the purse of gold, the old man collapsed. Voetheri called the servants, who lifted him up, but all efforts to revive him were in vain.

Then the Baron cried, as if beside himself, "O God! My God! Oh, wretch that I am, I have killed the poor old man! To call a sleepwalker means his certain death. Isn't that true? I shall never have another peaceful moment so long as I live!" The servants had borne away the body, and the Baron was still reproaching himself when Voetheri took him by the hand and led him in complete silence to the walled-up postern.

"The man who fell dead here at your feet, Baron Roderick," he said, "was your father's pitiless murderer." The Baron stared at him as if he were gazing on a ghost from hell, but Voetheri continued, "The time has now come to reveal to you the terrible secret that oppressed that monster, driving him to walk in his hours of sleep beneath a curse. The eternal powers have given the son vengeance over his father's murderer. The words that you thundered in that ghastly sleepwalker's ears were the last words that your unfortunate father spoke." Trembling and incapable of uttering a word, the Baron sat down beside Voetheri, who had taken a seat before the fire. Then the lawyer began to read to him the document that Hubert had left, with instructions that it should not be opened until after the reading of the will. Hubert cursed himself, in words that spoke the deepest sorrow, for the implacable hatred he had conceived toward his elder brother from the moment that old Roderick had drawn up the deed of entail. He had, however, been robbed of all weapons, for even if he were to succeed in slyly setting father and son at variance, it would be to no effect. For Roderick himself had not the power to rob his eldest son of the rights of primogeniture, and even if he were to lose all affection for him, his principles would have prevented his annulling the entail. Not until Wolfgang formed that connection in Geneva with Julie de St. Val did Hubert see any chance of ruining his brother. From then onwards he wickedly began, in secret understanding with Daniel, to force the old man to decisions that would lead to his son's undoing. He knew that, in old Roderick's mind, an alliance with one of the oldest families in the country was necessary in order to advance the estates to the first rank, for all eternity. The old Baron had read this alliance in the stars, and any wanton interference with the decree of the heavens would certainly bring destruction to the property. Wolfgang's marriage to Julie seemed to Roderick in this sense a criminal attempt against the will of that power which had supported him in his earthly endeavors, and any scheme to destroy Julie, the principal of evil that opposed him, appeared to him to be justified. Hubert knew that his brother loved this girl to distraction, and that to lose her would reduce him to misery and perhaps even cause his death. But he had an even stronger reason for actively collaborating in his father's plans; he had conceived a guilty passion for Julie, and hoped to win her for himself. By a special mercy of heaven, however, his most venomous attacks were shattered by Wolfgang's resolution; Wolfgang, in fact, succeeded in outwitting his brother. The solemnization of his marriage and the birth of a son remained completely unknown to Hubert. But with his premonitions of death, there came to old Roderick the conviction that Wolfgang had indeed married the abhorred Julie, and in the letter summoning his son to arrive at Rossitten on that certain day to take over the entail, he laid his curse upon him should he refuse to dissolve that alliance. Wolfgang burned the letter beside his father's corpse. The old Baron had written to Hubert that Wolfgang had married Julie, but would annul the marriage. Hubert considered this story the product of his father's imagination, and was much taken aback when Wolfgang at Rossitten not only confirmed the old man's suspicions with complete frankness, but added that Julie had borne him a son, and that he would shortly send his wife, who had hitherto known him as the merchant Born, the welcome news of his rich inheritance. He intended to go to Geneva and fetch her, but before he could put his plans into effect, he was overtaken by death.

Hubert kept the knowledge of his nephew's existence a complete secret, and took over the entail, which rightfully belonged to the child of Wolfgang and Julie. But before many years had passed, he deeply repented his act. For fate, with the spectacle of the growing enmity between his own two sons, reminded him in a most terrible way of his guilt. "You are a poor penniless creature," said the twelve-year-old elder brother to the younger. "I shall be master of Rossitten when Father dies, and you'll have to go down on your knees and kiss my hand for money to buy a new coat." The younger brother, stung to fury by his elder's contempt, threw at him a knife he happened to be holding, which wounded him most severely. Fearing an even worse tragedy, Hubert sent the younger boy to Petersburg, where he afterwards served as an officer under Suvarov, and was killed in battle during the French campaigns.

Shame prevented Hubert's acknowledging the secret of his dishonorable, treacherous conduct before the world. But he would not keep a penny more from the rightful owner of the property. He had inquiries made in Geneva and learned that Mme. Born had died from grief at the inexplicable disappearance of her husband, but that Roderick Born was being brought up by a good man who had taken charge of him. Hubert then introduced himself under an assumed name as a relative of Born's, explained that the merchant had been drowned at sea, and sent sums of money sufficient for the young heir's proper education. How scrupulously he set aside the income of the estate, and all the provisions of his will, we already know. Of his brother's death Hubert spoke in strangely veiled terms that left some mysterious occurrence to be presumed; one could not but suspect, indeed, that he had played at least an indirect part in some terrible crime. The contents of the black portfolio revealed the whole story. In addition to the treacherous correspondence between Hubert and Daniel, there was a further paper written and signed by the old steward. Voetheri read a confession that shook him to the marrow. At Daniel's instigation, Hubert had come to Rossitten. It was Daniel who had informed him of the discovery of the hundred and fifty thousand thalers. We know how Hubert was received by his brother, how when his hopes and plans were foiled he had wished to go, and how Voetheri held him back. But Daniel's mind was plotting a bloody revenge against the young man who had proposed to throw him out like a mangy dog. He stoked and stoked the fires consuming the desperate Hubert. On their wolf hunts in the pinewoods, in the winds and snowstorms, they came to an agreement for Wolfgang's destruction. "Get rid of him," muttered Hubert, taking his eyes off his aim as he leveled his gun. "Yes, get rid of him," grinned Daniel. "But not that way. Not that way." For he solemnly promised that he would murder the Baron and no one would be a penny the wiser. When Hubert finally got his money he regretted the plot, and tried to get away, to avoid all further temptation. Daniel it was that saddled the horse in the night and led it out of its stall, but just as Hubert was about to mount the old steward exclaimed in biting tones: "I thought, Baron Hubert, that you would stay on the estate, seeing that the entail has fallen to you. For the proud lord, your brother, is lying at this moment shattered in the pit below the tower."

Daniel had observed that Wolfgang would often get up in the night, tortured by his avarice, go to the postern that had once led into the tower, and look longingly down into the chasm where, the old servant had assured him, a great treasure still lay buried. On that fatal night, therefore, Daniel had posted himself at the door of the hall, and the moment he heard the Baron open the tower postern, he had crossed the room to where his master stood above the sheer abyss. Catching sight of his wicked servant behind him, with murder shining in his eyes, the Baron had turned and cried in terror, "Daniel, Daniel, what are you doing here at this hour?" "Down with you! Down with you, you mangy dog," Daniel insanely shrieked, and with a violent kick precipitated the unfortunate man into the chasm.

Appalled by this terrible crime, the young Baron could get no rest in the castle where his father had been murdered. So he moved to his estates in Courland, only coming to Rossitten once a year in autumn. Old Franz affirmed that Daniel, whose crime he suspected, often walked at the time of the full moon, and described the ghost in exactly the form in which Voetheri later met and laid it. The discovery of these events, so disgraceful to his father's memory, had also driven young Baron Hubert out into the world.

My great-uncle had told the whole story and, taking my hand, he added tenderly, the tears starting to his eyes, "Nephew, nephew, the evil fate, the powers of darkness that dwell in that castle, overtook her too, the lovely Seraphine. Two days after we left Rossitten the Baron arranged a final sleigh ride. He was driving his wife himself, when on the downhill slope the horses for some inexplicable reason suddenly took fright, and began wildly panting and snorting. 'The old man—the old man's behind us,' cried the Baroness shrilly. At that moment the sleigh was overturned and she was thrown out. They found her lifeless—she's dead. The Baron is inconsolable, he lives in the apathy of a dying man. We shall never go back to Rossitten, nephew." My great-uncle said no more, and it was with a heavy heart that I left his room; only time, the universal consoler, had strength to assuage the deep grief which I then thought would kill me.

Years passed. Voetheri was long in his grave and I had left my country. The storm of war, raging destructively right across Germany, had driven me north, to Petersburg. On my return, driving one dark summer night along the Baltic coast not far from Königsberg, I saw a great shining star in the sky before me. As I approached it I saw from its red flickering flame that what I had taken for a star was in fact a great fire. But I could not understand how it could stand so high into the air. "What sort of fire's that ahead of us, fellow?" I asked the postilion. "Oh," he replied. "That? That's no fire. That's the lighthouse at Rossitten." Rossitten! As the postilion spoke the name, the picture of those terrible autumn days I had spent there sprang vividly alive before my eyes.

I saw the Baron, Seraphine and the strange old aunts too, myself with my shining white face, all frizzed and powdered and dressed in soft sky-blue. Yes, myself, the lover sighing out his passionate, doleful ditties to his mistress's brow. Overwhelmed as I was by sadness, Voetheri's dry quips flickered before me like little lights, and amused me more than they had done then. So, sad and yet moved by some strange pleasure, I left the coach when it stopped at Rossitten in the early morning for the mail. I recognized the bailiff's house and asked for him. "Begging your pardon," said the clerk of the post-house, taking his pipe out of his mouth and removing his night cap. "Begging your pardon, there's no bailiff here. Here there's a public office, and the King's officer is still asleep, if you please." On questioning him further I learned that Baron Roderick von Ross, the last inheritor of the entail, had died sixteen years before without issue, and that the estate, according to the terms of the original deed, had fallen to the Crown. I climbed to the castle; it lay in ruins. An old peasant, who came out of the pinewoods and joined me in conversation, informed me that a great quantity of its masonry had been used for the lighthouse. He also knew something about the ghost, and told me how it still haunted the castle, and often appeared at the full moon, when terrible moans were to be heard from among the fallen stones. Poor old, shortsighted Roderick! What evil powers did you conjure up, which poisoned your stock in its earliest shoots, that stock which you thought to plant firm-rooted for all eternity?

Translated by J. M. Cohen

The Sandman

Nathanael to Lothar

Y ou certainly must be disturbed because I have not written for such a long, long time. Mother, I am sure, is angry, and Klara will imagine that I am spending my time in dissipation, having completely forgotten my pretty angel whose image is so deeply imprinted on my heart. But it's not so; I think of you all every day and every hour, and my lovely Klärchen appears to me in my sweet dreams, her bright eyes smiling at me as charmingly as when I was with you. Alas, how could I write to you in the tormented frame of mind that has disrupted all my thoughts! Something horrible has entered my life! Dark forebodings of some impending doom loom over me like black clouds that are impervious to every ray of friendly sunshine. I will now tell you what happened to me. I must tell you, but the mere thought of it makes me laugh like a madman. Oh, my dearest Lothar, how can I begin to make you realize, even vaguely, that what happened a few days ago really could have so fatal and disruptive an effect on my life? If you were here you could see for yourself; but now you will certainly think I am a crazy man who sees ghosts. In brief, this horrible thing I have experienced, the fatal effects of which I am vainly trying to shake off, is simply this: A few days ago, on October 30th, at twelve noon, a barometer dealer came into my room and offered me his wares. I bought nothing and threatened to kick him down the stairs, whereupon he left of his own accord.

You will surmise that only associations of the strangest kind that are profoundly entangled in my life could have made this incident significant, and that the character of this wretched dealer must have had an evil influence on me. In fact, this is the case. I will, with all my strength, pull myself together and calmly and patiently tell you enough about my early youth so that everything will appear clearly and distinctly to your keen mind. But just as I am about to begin, I can hear you laugh, and I can hear Klara say: "This is all childish nonsense!" Laugh! I beg you, have a good laugh! But, my God, my hair is standing on end, and it is in mad despair that I ask you to laugh at me—as Franz Moor asked Daniel. But back to my story.

Except at the noon meal, my brothers and sisters and I saw little of our father during the day. His work must have kept him very busy. After supper, which was served at seven in the old-fashioned way, we all went into father's workroom and sat at a round table. Father smoked and drank a large glass of beer. He often told us marvelous stories, and he would get so carried away that his pipe would keep going out and I would relight it for him with a piece of burning paper, which I thought was great fun. But there were occasions when he'd put picture books in our hands and sit silently in his armchair, blowing out billows of smoke till we all seemed to be swimming in clouds. Mother was very sad on such evenings, and hardly had the clock struck nine when she would say: "Now, children, off to bed with you! The Sandman is coming, I can already hear him. " And at these times I always really did hear something clumping up the stairs with a heavy, slow step; it must have been the Sandman. Once, this dull trampling step was especially frightening; and as my mother led us away, I asked her: "Oh, Mama, who is this nasty Sandman who always drives us away from Papa? What does he look like?"

"My dear child, there is no Sandman," my mother answered. "When I tell you that the Sandman is coming, it only means that you are sleepy and can't keep your eyes open any longer, as though someone had sprinkled sand into them."

Mother's answer did not satisfy me, for in my childish mind I was certain that she denied that there was a Sandman only to keep us from being afraid of him—I had surely always heard him coming up the stairs. Full of curiosity to learn more about this Sandman and what his connection was with us children, I finally asked the old woman who took care of my youngest sister what kind of man the Sandman was.

"Oh, dear Thanael," she replied, "don't you know that yet? He is a wicked man who comes to children when they refuse to go to bed and throws handfuls of sand in their eyes till they bleed and pop out of their heads. Then he throws the eyes into a sack and takes them to the half-moon as food for his children, who sit in a nest and have crooked beaks like owls with which they pick up the eyes of human children who have been naughty."

A horrible picture of the cruel Sandman formed in my mind, and in the evenings, when I heard stumbling steps on the stairs, I trembled with fear and dread. My mother could get nothing out of me but the stammered, tearful cry: "The Sandman! The Sandman!" Then I ran into the bedroom and was tortured all night by the horrible apparition of the Sandman. I was old enough to realize that the nurse's tale of the Sandman and his children's nest in the half-moon couldn't be altogether true; nevertheless, the Sandman remained a frightful specter; and I was seized with utmost horror when I heard him not only mount the stairs, but violently tear open the door to my father's room and enter. Frequently, he stayed away for a long time; then he came many times in succession. This continued for years, and I never got used to this terrible phantom. My image of the horrible Sandman grew no paler. His intimacy with my father occupied my imagination more and more. An insurmountable reluctance prevented me from asking my father about him; but if only I—if only I could solve the mystery and get to see this fantastic Sandman with my own eyes— that was the desire that increased in me year by year. The Sandman had directed my thoughts toward marvels and wonders which can so easily take hold of a childish mind. I liked nothing better than to hear or read horrible tales about goblins, witches, dwarfs, and such; but at the head of them all was the Sandman, of whom I was always drawing hideous pictures, in charcoal, in chalk, on tables, cupboards, and walls.

When I was ten my mother moved me from the nursery into a small room that opened off the corridor and was close to my father's room. As always, on the stroke of nine, when the mysterious step could be heard in the house, we had to scurry out. From my room I could hear him enter my father's, and soon thereafter

I seemed to detect a thin, strange-smelling vapor spreading through the house. As my curiosity to know the Sandman grew, so did my courage. When my mother had left, I would sneak out of my room into the corridor; but I could never discover anything, because the Sandman had already gone through the door by the time I got to a spot from which he would have been visible. Finally, driven by an uncontrollable impulse, I determined to hide in my father's room itself to await the Sandman.

I could tell one evening from my father's silence and my mother's sadness that the Sandman was coming. I pretended, therefore, to be very tired, left the room before nine o'clock, and hid in a dark corner close to the door. The front door groaned. Slow, heavy, resounding steps crossed the hall to the stairs. My mother hurried past me with the rest of the children. Softly, softly I opened the door of my father's room. He was sitting as usual, silent and rigid, his back to the door; he didn't notice me. I slipped quickly behind the curtain that covered an open cupboard in which my father's clothes were hanging. Closer, ever closer resounded the steps— there was a strange coughing, scraping, and mumbling outside. My heart quaked with fear and expectation. Close, close to the door, there was a sharp step; a powerful blow on the latch and the door sprang open with a bang! Summoning up every drop of my courage, I cautiously peeped out. The Sandman was standing in the middle of my father's room, the bright candlelight full on his face. The Sandman, the horrible Sandman, was the old lawyer Coppelius who frequently had dinner with us!

But the most hideous figure could not have filled me with deeper horror than this very Coppelius. Picture a large, broad-shouldered man with a fat, shapeless, head, an ochre-yellow face, bushy gray eyebrows from beneath which a pair of greenish cat's eyes sparkled piercingly, and with a large nose that curved over the upper lip. The crooked mouth was frequently twisted in a malignant laugh, at which time a pair of dark red spots would appear on his cheeks and a strange hissing sound would escape from between clenched teeth. Coppelius invariably appeared in an old-fashioned coat of ash gray, with trousers and vest to match, but with black stockings and shoes with small agate buckles. His little wig barely extended past the crown of his head, his pomaded curls stood high over his big red ears, and a broad hair bag stood stiffly out from his neck so that the silver clasp which held his folded cravat was visible. His whole appearance was loathsome and repulsive; but we children were most revolted by his huge, gnarled, hairy hands, and we would never eat anything they had touched. He noticed this and took pleasure in touching, under some pretext or other, some piece of cake or delicious fruit that mother had slipped on our plates, so that, tears welling up in our eyes, we were unable to enjoy the tidbit intended for us because of the disgust and abhorrence we felt. He did the same thing on holidays when each of us received a glass of sweet wine from our father. He would pass his hand over it or would even raise the glass to his blue lips and laugh demoniacally, and we could only express our indignation by sobbing softly. He always called us "the little beasts"; and when he was present, we were not to make a sound. How we cursed this horrible man who deliberately and malevolently ruined our slightest pleasure! Mother seemed to loath the repulsive Coppelius as much as we did; the moment he appeared, her gaiety, her lightheartedness, and her natural manner were transformed into dejected brooding. Father behaved toward him as if he were a superior being whose bad manners must be endured and who must be humored at any cost. Coppelius needed only to hint, and his favorite dishes were cooked and rare wines were served.

When I now saw this Coppelius, then, the terrible conviction that he alone was the Sandman possessed me; but the Sandman was no longer the hobgoblin of the nurse's tale, the one who brought the eyes of children for his brood to feed upon in the owl's nest in the half-moon. No! He was a horrible and unearthly monster who wreaked grief, misery, and destruction—temporal and eternal—wherever he appeared.

I was riveted to the spot, spellbound. At the risk of being discovered and, as I could clearly anticipate, severely punished, I remained watching, my head stretched out through the curtain. My father greeted Coppelius ceremoniously. "To work!" Coppelius cried in a hoarse, jarring voice, throwing off his coat. Silently and gloomily my father took off his dressing gown, and both of them dressed in long black smocks. I did not see where these came from. My father opened the folding door of a wall cupboard, but what I had always believed was a cupboard was not. It was rather a black recess that housed a little hearth. Coppelius went to the hearth, and a blue flame crackled up from it. All kinds of strange utensils were about. God! As my old father now bent over the fire, he looked completely different. His mild and honest features seemed to have been distorted into a repulsive and diabolical mask by some horrible, convulsive pain. He looked like Coppelius, who was drawing sparkling lumps out of the heavy smoke with the red-hot tongs he wielded and then hammering the coals furiously. It seemed as if I saw human faces on all sides—but eyeless faces, with horrible deep black cavities instead.

"Give me eyes! Give me eyes!" Coppelius ordered in a hollow booming voice. Overcome by the starkest terror, I shrieked and tumbled from my hiding place to the floor. Coppelius seized me. "Little beast! Little beast!" he bleated, baring his teeth. He dragged me to my feet and flung me on the hearth, where the flames began singeing my hair. "Now we have eyes, eyes, a beautiful pair of children's eyes!" he whispered. Pulling glowing grains from the fire with his naked hands, he was about to sprinkle them in my eyes when my father raised his hands entreatingly: "Master! Master!" he cried, "leave my Nathanael his eyes!" "Let the child keep his eyes and do his share of the world's weeping," Coppelius shrieked with a shrill laugh, "but now we must carefully observe the mechanism of the hands and feet." He thereupon seized me so violently that my joints cracked, unscrewed my hands and feet, then put them back, now this way, then another way. "There's something wrong here! It's better the way they were! The Old Man knew his business!" Coppelius hissed and muttered. But everything around me went pitch black; a sudden convulsive pain flashed through my nerves and bones—I felt nothing more.

A gentle, warm breath passed across my face, and I awoke as from the sleep of death, my mother bending over me.

"Is the Sandman still here?" I stammered.

"No, my dearest child, he left long ago and will do you no harm," my mother said, kissing and cuddling her reclaimed darling.

Why should I bore you, my dear Lothar? Why should I go into such copious detail when so much remains to be said? Suffice it to say that I had been caught spying and had been manhandled by Coppelius. My fear and terror had brought on a violent fever, which kept me ill for many weeks. "Is the Sandman still here?"

were my first words after regaining consciousness, the first sign of my recovery, my deliverance. I have only to tell you now about the most horrible moment in all the years of my youth; then you will be convinced that it is not because of faulty vision that everything seems devoid of color to me, but that a somber destiny has really hung a murky veil over my life, which I will perhaps tear through only when I die.

Coppelius was not seen again; it was said that he had left the town.

It was about a year later, when we were once more sitting at the round table as was our custom. Father was very cheerful and was telling us entertaining stories about his youthful travels. As the clock struck nine, we suddenly heard the front door groan on its hinges and, leaden steps resounded across the hall and up the stairs.

"It's Coppelius," my mother said, growing pale.

"Yes, it is Coppelius," father repeated in a faint, broken voice. Tears welled in mother's eyes.

"But Father, Father!" she cried, "must it be like this?"

"It is the last time!" he answered, "I promise you this is the last time he will come here. Now go, take the children with you. Go, go to bed! Good night!"

I felt as if I had been turned into cold heavy stone—I couldn't catch my breath! But as I stood there, motionless, my mother seized me by the arm. "Come, Nathanael, do come!" I let myself be led to my room. "Calm yourself, calm yourself and go to bed!" my mother cried to me. "Go to bed and go to sleep. Sleep!" But tormented by an indescribable fear, I couldn't close my eyes. The detestable and loathsome Coppelius stood before me with fiery eyes, laughing at me malevolently. I tried in vain to obliterate his image from my mind. It must have been about midnight when there was a terrifying explosion—like the firing of a cannon. The entire house resounded with the detonation; there was a rattling and clattering past my door. The front door slammed shut violently.

"That is Coppelius!" I cried in terror, springing out of bed. Then there was a shriek, a wail of heartrending grief. I rushed to my father's room. The door was open, and suffocating smoke rolled toward me. The maid shrieked, "Oh, the master! Oh, the master!"

My father lay dead in front of the smoking hearth, his face charred black and his features hideously contorted; my brothers and sisters were sobbing and moaning around him—my mother unconscious beside him! "Coppelius, you vile Satan, you've murdered my father!" I cried, and lost consciousness.

When my father was placed in his coffin two days later, his features were once more serene and gentle, as they had been in life. My soul drew consolation from the thought that his alliance with the satanic Coppelius could not have thrust him into everlasting perdition.

The explosion had awakened the neighbors; the tragedy was talked about and reached the ears of the authorities, who wanted to proceed against Coppelius and hold him accountable. But Coppelius had vanished from town without leaving a trace.

So, my dear friend, when I now tell you that this barometer dealer was the infamous Coppelius himself, you will not blame me for regarding this apparition as foreboding some frightful disaster. He was dressed differently, but Coppelius's figure and face are too deeply etched on my mind for me possibly to make a mistake. In addition, Coppelius has hardly changed his name. I have been told that he claims to be a Piedmontese skilled craftsman, Giuseppe Coppola.

I am determined, regardless of the consequences, to deal with him and to avenge my father's death.

Do not tell my mother anything of this loathsome monster's presence here. Give my love to dear, sweet Klara. I will write to her when I am in a calmer frame of mind. Farewell, etc., etc.

Klara to Nathanael

Despite it's being true that you have not written for a long time, I believe that I am still in your thoughts. You surely had me most vividly in mind when you intended sending your last letter to Lothar, because you addressed it to me instead. I opened the letter with delight and did not realize my error until I read: "Oh, my dearest Lothar." I should have stopped reading and given the letter to your brother. Even though you have often reproached me, in your innocent, teasing manner, for being so serene and womanly in disposition that if the house were about to collapse I would quickly smooth a misplaced crease out of a curtain—like the woman in the story—before escaping; nevertheless, I can hardly tell you how deeply the beginning of your letter shocked me. I could barely breathe; everything swam before my eyes. Oh, my dearest Nathanael, what horrible thing has entered your life? To be parted from you, never again to see you—the thought pierced my breast like a red-hot dagger. I read on and on. Your description of the repulsive Coppelius horrifies me. For the first time I learned about the terrible, violent way your dear old father died. My brother Lothar, to whom I gave this letter, tried with little success to calm me. The horrid barometer dealer Giuseppe Coppola followed my every step, and I am almost ashamed to admit that he even disturbed my normally sound and restful sleep with all kinds of horrible dream images. Soon, however—by the very next day, in fact—I saw everything differently. Do not be angry with me, my dearest one, if Lothar tells you that despite your strange presentiment that Coppelius will harm you, I am still cheerful and calm.

I will frankly confess that in my opinion all the fears and terrors of which you speak took place only in your mind and had very little to do with the true, external world. A loathsome character old Coppelius may have been, but what really lead to the abhorrence you children felt stemmed from his hatred of children.

Naturally, your childish mind associated the dreadful Sandman of the nurse's tale with old Coppelius—who would have been a monster particularly threatening to children even if you had not believed in the Sandman. The sinister business conducted at night with your father was probably nothing other than secret alchemical experiments, which would have displeased your mother because not only was a great deal of money being squandered, but, as is always the case with such experimenters, your father's mind was so imbued with an illusory desire for higher knowledge that he may have become alienated from his family. Your father, no doubt, was responsible for his own death through some carelessness or other, and Coppelius is not guilty of it. Let me tell you that yesterday I asked our neighbor, an experienced chemist, whether experiments of this kind could possibly lead to such a sudden lethal explosion. "Absolutely," he replied, and continued, at length and in detail, to tell me how such an accident could occur, mentioning so many strange-sounding names that I can't recall any of them. Now, you will be annoyed with your Klara and will say, "Such a cold nature is impervious to any ray of the mysterious which often embraces man with invisible arms. Like the simple child who rejoices over some glittering golden fruit that conceals a fatal poison, she sees only the bright surface of the world."

Oh, my dearest Nathanael, do you not believe that even in gay, easygoing, and carefree minds there may exist a presentiment of dark powers within ourselves that are bent upon our own destruction? But forgive me, simple girl that I am, if I presume to tell you what my thoughts really are about such inner conflicts. I will not, to be sure, find the right words; and you will laugh at me—not because what I say is foolish, but because I express my ideas so clumsily.

If there is a dark power that treacherously attaches a thread to our heart to drag us along a perilous and ruinous path that we would not otherwise have trod; if there is such a power, it must form inside us, from part of us, must be identical with ourselves; only in this way can we believe in it and give it the opportunity it needs if it is to accomplish its secret work. If our mind is firm enough and adequately fortified by the joys of life to be able to recognize alien and hostile influences as such, and to proceed tranquilly along the path of our own choosing and propensities, then this mysterious power will perish in its futile attempt to assume a shape that is supposed to be a reflection of ourselves. "It is also a fact," Lothar adds, "that if we have once voluntarily surrendered to this dark physical power, it frequently introduces in us the strange shapes which the external world throws in our way, so that we ourselves engender the spirit which in our strange delusion we believe speaks to us from that shape. It is the phantom of our own ego, whose intimate relationship, combined with its profound effect on our spirits, either flings us into hell or transports us to heaven." You see, dear Nathanael, that my brother Lothar and I have fully discussed the matter of dark powers and forces—a subject which I have outlined for you not without difficulty and which seems very profound to me. I do not completely understand Lothar's last words; I have only an inkling of his meaning, and yet it seems to be very true. I beg you to cast the hateful lawyer Coppelius and the barometer man Giuseppe Coppola from your thoughts. Be convinced that these strange figures are powerless; only your belief in their hostile influence can make them hostile in reality. If profound mental agitation did not speak out from every line in your letter, if your frame of mind did not distress me so deeply, I could joke about Sandman the lawyer and barometer dealer Coppelius. Cheer up, please! I have decided to be your guardian angel, and if ugly Coppola takes it into his head to plague you in your dreams, I will exorcise him with loud laughter. Neither he nor his revolting fists frighten me at all; as a lawyer he is not going to spoil my tidbits, nor, as a Sandman, harm my eyes.

Ever yours, my dearest beloved Nathanael, etc., etc., etc.

Nathanael to Lothar

I am very sorry that Klara recently opened and read my letter to you through a mistake occasioned by my distraction. She has written me a very thoughtful and philosophical letter in which she proves, in great detail, that Coppelius and Coppola exist only in my mind and are phantoms of my ego that will vanish in a moment if I accept them as such. As a matter of fact, one would not think that Klara, with her bright, dreamy, childlike eyes, could analyze with such intelligence and pedantry. She refers to your views. The two of you have discussed me. No doubt you are giving her lessons in logic so that she is learning to sift and analyze everything very neatly. Do stop that! By the way, it is probably quite certain that the barometer dealer Giuseppe Coppola cannot possibly be the old lawyer Coppelius. I am attending lectures by the physics professor who just came here recently and who, like the famous naturalist, is called Spalanzani and is of Italian origin. He has known Coppola for many years; besides which, one can tell from his accent that he is really a Piedmontese. Coppelius was a German, but, it seems to me, not an honest one. I am still a little uneasy. You and Klara may still consider me a morbid dreamer; however, I cannot get rid of the impression that Coppelius's damned face makes on me. I am very happy that he has left the city, as Spalanzani told me. This professor is an eccentric fellow. A small, chubby man with big cheekbones, a thin nose, protruding lips, and small piercing eyes. But better than from any description, you can get a picture of him if you look at a picture of Cagliostro as painted by Chodowiecki in any Berlin pocket almanac. Spalanzani looks just like that.

Recently, when I went up the steps, I noticed that the curtain that usually covers the glass door was not completely drawn across. I do not even know why I was curious enough to peek, but I did. A tall, very slender, beautifully dressed, beautifully proportioned young lady was sitting in the room in front of a small table, on which she had placed her outstretched arms, with hands clasped. She was sitting opposite the door, so I could see her divinely beautiful face. She did not seem to notice me; indeed, her eyes seemed fixed, I might almost say without vision. It seemed to me as if she were sleeping with her eyes open. I became very uneasy and therefore stole quietly away to the neighboring lecture room. Later, I discovered that the figure I had seen is Spalanzani's daughter, Olympia, whom he, for some strange reason, always keeps locked up so that no one can come near her. Perhaps, after all, there is something wrong with her; maybe she is an idiot, or something like that. But why do I write you about all this? I can tell you better and in greater detail when I see you. By the way, I am planning to visit you in two weeks. I must see my dear, sweet, lovely Klara again. The irritation which, I must confess, possessed me after the arrival of that disagreeable analytical letter will have vanished by then. For this reason I am not writing to her today. A thousand greetings, etc., etc., etc.

Gentle reader, nothing can be imagined that is stranger and more extraordinary than the fate that befell my poor friend, the young student Nathanael, which I have undertaken to relate to you. Have you, gentle reader, ever experienced anything that totally possessed your heart, your thoughts, and your senses to the exclusion of all else? Everything seethed and roiled within you; heated blood surged through your veins and inflamed your cheeks. Your gaze was peculiar, as if seeking forms in empty space invisible to other eyes, and speech dissolved into gloomy sighs. Then your friends asked you: "What is it, dear friend? What is the matter?" And wishing to describe the picture in your mind with all its vivid colors, the light and the shade, you struggled vainly to find words. But it seemed to you that you had to gather together all that had occurred—the wonderful, the magnificent, the heinous, the joyous, the ghastly—and express it in the very first word so that it would strike like lightning. Yet, every word, everything within the realm of speech, seemed colorless, frigid, dead. You tried, tried again, stuttered and stammered, while the insipid questions asked by friends struck your glowing passion like icy blasts until it was almost extinguished. If, like an audacious painter, you had initially sketched the outline of the picture within you in a few bold strokes, you would have easily been able to make the colors deeper and more intense until the multifarious crowd of living shapes swept your friends away and they saw themselves, as you see yourself, in the midst of the scene that had issued from your soul.

Sympathetic reader, no one, I must confess, asked me about the history of young Nathanael; you are, however, surely aware that I belong to that remarkable species of authors who, when they carry something within themselves as I have just described it, feels as if everyone who approaches—indeed, everyone in the whole world—is asking "What is it? Do tell us, dear sir!"

I was most strongly compelled to tell you about Nathanael's disastrous life. The marvelous and the extraordinary aspects of his life entirely captivated my soul; but precisely for this reason and because, my dear reader, it was essential at the beginning to dispose you favorably toward the fantastic—which is no mean matter—I tormented myself to devise a way to begin Nathanael's story in a manner at once creative and stirring: "Once upon a time," the nicest way to begin a story, seemed too prosaic. "In the small provincial town of S——, there lived"—was somewhat better, at least providing an opportunity for development toward the climax. Or, immediately, *in medias res:* " 'Go to hell!' the student Nathanael cried, his eyes wild with rage and terror, when the barometer dealer Giuseppe Coppola—" In fact, that is what I had written when I thought I noticed something humorous in Nathanael's wild look—but the story is not at all comic. There were no words I could find that were appropriate to describe, even in the most feeble way, the brilliant colors of my inner vision. I resolved not to begin at all. So, gentle reader, do accept the three letters, which my friend Lothar has been kind enough to communicate, as the outline of the picture to which I will endeavor to add ever more color as I continue with the story. As a good portrait painter, I may possibly succeed in making Nathanael recognizable even if the original is unknown to you; and you may feel as if you had seen him with your own eyes on very many occasions. Possibly, also, you will come to believe that real life is more singular and more fantastic than anything else and that all a writer can really do is present it as "in a glass, darkly."

To supply information necessary for the beginning, these letters must be supplemented by noting that soon after the death of Nathanael's father, Klara and Lothar, children of a distant relative who had likewise died and left them orphans, were taken in by Nathanael's mother. Klara and Nathanael soon grew strongly attached to each other, to which no one in the world could object; hence, when Nathanael left home to continue his studies at G——, they were engaged. His last letter is written from G——, where he is attending the lectures of the famous professor of physics Spalanzini.

I could now confidently continue with my story, but even at this moment Klara's face is so vividly before me that I cannot avert my eyes, just as I never could when she gazed at me with one of her lovely smiles. Klara could not be considered beautiful; all who profess to be judges of beauty agreed on that. Nevertheless, architects praised the perfect proportions of her figure, and painters considered her neck, shoulders, breasts almost too chastely formed. Yet on the other hand, they adored her glorious hair and raved about her coloring, which reminded them of Battoni's Magdalen. One of them, a veritable romantic, elaborated an old comparison between her eyes and a lake by Ruïsdael, in which the pure azure of a cloudless sky, the woodlands and flower-bedecked fields, and the whole bright and varied life of a lush landscape are reflected. Poets and musicians went even further and said, "That is nonsense about a lake and a mirror! Can we look at the girl without sensing heavenly music which flows into us from her glance and penetrates to the very soul until everything within us stirs awake and pulsates with emotion? And if we cannot then sing splendid tunes, we are not worth much; the smile flitting about her lips will tell us this clearly enough when we have the courage to speak out in her presence something that we profess to be a song when, in fact, it is only a disconnected jumble of notes strung together."

And this really was the case. Klara had the spirited imagination of a gay, innocent, unaffected child, the deep sympathetic feelings of a woman, and an understanding that was clear and discriminating. Dreamers and visionaries had bad luck with her; for despite the fact that she said little—she was not disposed to be talkative—her clear glance and her rare ironical smile asked, "Dear friends, how can you suppose that I will accept these fleeting and shadowy images for true shapes which are alive and breathe?" For this reason, many chided Klara for being cold, without feeling, and unimaginative; but others, those whose conception of life was clearer and deeper, were singularly enamored of this tenderhearted, intelligent, and childlike girl, though no one cared for her so much as Nathanael, who had a strong proclivity for learning and art. Klara clung to her lover with all of her soul, and when he parted from her, the first clouds passed over her life. With what delight she flew into his arms when he returned to his native town (as he had promised he would in his last letter to Lothar) and entered his mother's room. It turned out as Nathanael had believed it would: the instant he saw Klara again thoughts about the lawyer Coppelius or Klara's pedantic letter—all his depressions vanished.

Nevertheless, Nathanael was right when he wrote to his friend Lothar that the abhorrent barometer dealer Coppola had exercised a disastrous influence on his life. This was evident to everyone for even in the first few days of his visit Nathanael seemed completely changed; he surrendered to gloomy brooding and behaved in a manner more strange than they had known before. All of life, everything, had become only a dream and a presentiment; he was always saying that any man, although imagining himself to be free, was in fact only the horrible plaything of dark powers, which it was vain to resist. Man must humbly submit to whatever fate has in store for him. He went so far as to insist that it was foolish to believe that man's creative achievements in art or science resulted from the expression of free will; rather, he claimed that the inspiration requisite for creation comes not from within us but results from the influence of a higher external principle.

To the clear-thinking Klara all this mystical nonsense was re-

292 · E. T. A. Hoffmann

pugnant in the extreme, but it seemed pointless to attempt any refutation. It was only when Nathanael argued that Coppelius was the evil principle that had entered him and possessed him at the moment he was listening behind the curtain, and that this loathsome demon would in some terrible way destroy their happiness, that Klara grew very serious and said, "Yes, Nathanael, you are right; Coppelius is an evil and malignant principle. His effect can be no less diabolical than the very powers of hell if they assume living form, but only if you fail to banish him from your mind and thoughts. He will exist and work on you only so long as you believe in him; it is only your belief that gives him power."

Nathanael was greatly angered because Klara said that the demon existed only in his own mind, and he wanted to begin a disquisition on the whole mystic doctrine of devils and sinister powers, but Klara terminated the conversation abruptly by making a trivial remark, much to Nathanael's great annoyance. He thought that profound secrets were inaccessible to those with cold, unreceptive hearts, without being clearly aware that he included Klara among these inferior natures; and therefore he did not cease trying to initiate her into these secrets. Early in the morning, when Klara was helping to prepare breakfast, he would stand beside her and read to her from various occult books until she begged, "But my dear Nathanael, what if I have to accuse you of being the evil principle that is fatally influencing my coffee? For if I please you and drop everything to look into your eyes as you read, my coffee will boil over and no one will have breakfast." Nathanael slammed his book shut and rushed to his room indignantly.

Nathanael had formerly possessed a notable talent for writing delightful and amusing stories, to which Klara would listen with enormous pleasure; now, however, his tales were gloomy, unintelligible, and shapeless so that although Klara spared his feelings and did not say so, he probably felt how little they interested her. Above all, Klara disliked the tedious; and her uncontrollable drowsiness of spirit was betrayed by her glance and by her word. In truth, Nathanael's stories were really very boring. His resentment of Klara's cold, prosaic disposition increased; she could not conquer her dislike of his dark, gloomy, and dreary occultism; and so they drifted further and further apart without being conscious of it. Nathanael was forced to confess to himself that the ugly image of Coppelius had faded in his imagination, and it often cost him great effort to present Coppelius in adequate vividness in his writing where he played the part of the sinister bogeyman. Finally it occurred to him to make his gloomy presentiment that Coppelius would destroy his happiness the subject of a poem. He portrayed himself and Klara as united in true love but plagued by some dark hand that occasionally intruded into their lives, snatching away incipient joy. Finally, as they stood at the altar, the sinister Coppelius appeared and touched Klara's lovely eyes, which sprang into Nathanael's own breast, burning and scorching like bleeding sparks. Then Coppelius grabbed him and flung him into a blazing circle of fire that spun round with the speed of a whirlwind and, with a rush, carried him away. The awesome noise was like a hurricane furiously whipping up the waves so that they rose up like white-headed black giants in a raging inferno. But through this savage tumult he could hear Klara's voice: "Can't you see me, dear one? Coppelius has deceived you. That which burned in your breast was not my eyes. Those were fiery drops of the blood from your own heart. Look at me. I have still got my own eyes." Nathanael thought: "It is Klara: I am hers forever." Then it was as though this thought had grasped the fiery circle and forced it to stop turning, while the raging noise died away in the black abyss. Nathanael looked into Klara's eyes; but it was death that, with Klara's eyes, looked upon him kindly. While Nathanael was composing his poem he was very calm and serene; he reworked and polished every line, and since he fettered himself with meter, he did not pause until everything in the poem was perfect and euphonious. But when it was finally completed and he read the poem aloud to himself, he was stricken with fear and a wild horror and he cried out, "Whose horrible voice is that?" Soon, however, he once more came to understand that it was really nothing more than a very successful poem, and he felt certain that it would arouse Klara's cold nature, although he did not clearly understand why Klara should be aroused by it or what would be accomplished by frightening her with these hideous visions that augured a terrible fate and the destruction of their love.

They were sitting in his mother's little garden. Klara was extremely cheerful because Nathanael had not plagued her with his dreams and foreboding for the three days he had devoted to writing the poem. Nathanael also chatted gaily about things that amused her, as he had in the past, so that Klara remarked, "Now I really do have you back again. Do you see how we have driven out the hateful Coppelius?"

Nathanael suddenly remembered that the poem he had intended to read to Klara was in his pocket. He took the sheets from his pocket and started reading while Klara, anticipating something boring as usual and resigning herself to the situation, calmly began knitting. But as the dark cloud of the poem grew ever blacker, the knitting in her hand sank and she stared fixedly into Nathanael's eyes. But Nathanael was carried inexorably away by his poem; passion flushed his cheeks a fiery red, and tears flowed from his eyes. When he finally finished, he uttered a groan of absolute exhaustion; he grasped Klara's hand and sighed, as though dissolving in inconsolable grief, "Alas! Klara, Klara!"

Klara pressed him tenderly to her bosom and said in a voice at once soft but very slow and somber, "Nathanael, my darling Nathanael, throw that mad, insane, stupid tale into the fire." Nathanael then sprang indignantly to his feet, thrust Klara away, cried, "You damned, lifeless automaton," and ran off. Klara, deeply hurt, wept bitter tears, sobbing, "He has never loved me because he does not understand me."

Lothar came into the arbor; Klara had to tell him everything that had happened. He loved his sister with all his soul, and every word of her complaint fell like a fiery spark upon his heart so that the indignation that he had long felt toward the visionary Nathanael flared into furious rage. He ran to find Nathanael and in harsh words reproached him for his insane behavior toward his beloved sister. Nathanael, incensed, answered in kind, "Crazy, conceited fool!" and was answered by "Miserable commonplace idiot!" A duel was inevitable, and they agreed to meet on the following morning behind the garden and to fight, in accordance with the local student custom, with sharpened foils. They stalked about in silence and gloom. Klara, who had overheard and seen the violent argument, and who had seen the fencing masters bring the foils at dusk, suspected what was to happen. They both reached the dueling ground and cast off their coats in foreboding silence, and with their eyes aglow with the lust of combat, they were about to attack when Klara burst through the garden door. Through her sobs she cried: "You ferocious, cruel beasts! Strike me down before you attack each other. How am I to live when my lover has slain my brother, or my brother has slain my lover?"

Lothar lowered his weapon and gazed in silence at the ground, but in Nathanael's heart the affection he had once felt for lovely Klara in the happiest days of youth reawoke with a lacerating sorrow. The murderous weapon fell from his hand, and he threw himself at Klara's feet: "Can you ever forgive me, my one and only, beloved Klara? Can you ever forgive me, my dear brother Lothar?" Lothar was touched by his friend's profound grief, and all three embraced in reconciliation, with countless tears, vowing eternal love and fidelity.

Nathanael felt as if a heavy burden that had weighed him to the ground had been lifted, as if by resisting the dark powers that had gripped him he had saved his whole being from the threat of utter ruin. He spent three blissful days with his dear friends and then returned to G——, where he intended to remain for another year before returning to his native town forever.

Everything that referred to Coppelius was kept from Nathanael's mother, for they knew that it was impossible for her to think of him without horror, since like Nathanael, she believed him to be guilty of her husband's death.

Upon returning to his lodgings, Nathanael was completely astonished to find that the whole house had been burned down; nothing remained amid the ruins but the bare outer walls. Although the fire had started in the laboratory of the chemist living on the ground floor and had then spread upwards, some of Nathanael's courageous and energetic friends had managed, by breaking into his room on the upper floor, to save his books and manuscripts and instruments. They had carried them undamaged to another house and had rented a room there, into which Nathanael immediately moved. It did not strike him as singular that he now lived opposite Professor Spalanzini, nor did it seem particularly strange to him when he discovered that by looking out of his window he could see where Olympia often sat alone, so that he could clearly recognize her figure, although her features were blurred and indistinct. It did finally occur to him that Olympia often sat for hours at a small table in the same position in which he had seen her when he had first discovered her through the glass door, doing nothing and incessantly gazing across in his direction. He was forced to confess to himself that he had never seen a lovelier figure, although, with Klara in his heart, he remained perfectly indifferent to the stiff and rigid Olympia; only occasionally did he glance up from his book at the beautiful statue—that was all.

He was writing to Klara when there was a soft tap at the door. At his call, the door opened and Coppola's repulsive face peered in. Nathanael was shaken to the roots. Remembering, however, what Spalanzini had said to him about his compatriot Coppola and what he had solemnly promised his sweetheart regarding the Sandman Coppelius, he felt ashamed of his childish fear of ghosts and forcibly pulled himself together and said as calmly as possible, "I don't want a barometer, my good friend, do go away."

Coppola, however, came right into the room and said in a hoarse voice, his mouth twisted in a hideous laugh, his little eyes flashing piercingly from beneath his long, gray eyelashes, "Oh, no barometer? No barometer! I gotta da eyes too. I gotta da nice eyes!" Horrified, Nathanael cried, "Madman, how can you have eyes? Eyes?" But Coppola instantly put away his barometers and, thrusting his hands in his wide coat pockets, pulled out lorgnettes and eyeglasses and put them on the table. "So, glasses—put on nose, see! These are my eyes, nice-a eyes!" Saying this, he brought forth more and more eyeglasses from his pockets until the whole table began to gleam and sparkle. Myriad eyes peered and blinked and stared up at Nathanael, who could not look away from the table, while Coppola continued putting down more and more eyeglasses; and flaming glances crisscrossed each other ever more wildly and shot their blood-red rays into Nathanael's breast.

Overcome by an insane horror, Nathanael cried, "Stop, stop, you fiend!" He seized Coppola by the arm even as Coppola was once more searching in his pocket for more eyeglasses, although the table was already covered with them. Coppola gently shook him off with a hoarse revolting laugh and with the words "Oh! None for you? But here are nice spyglasses." He swept the eyeglasses together and returned them to the pocket from which they had come and then produced from a side pocket a number of telescopes of all sizes. As soon as the eyeglasses were gone Nathanael grew calm again, and focusing his thoughts on Klara, he

clearly saw that this gruesome illusion had been solely the product
of his own mind and that Coppola was an honest optician and
maker of instruments and far removed from being the ghostly
double and revenant of the accursed Coppelius. Besides, there was
nothing at all remarkable about the spyglasses that Coppola was
placing on the table now, or at least nothing so weird about them
as about the eyeglasses. To make amends for his behavior, Nathanael decided actually to buy something, picked up a small, very
beautifully finished pocket spyglass, and in order to test it, looked
through the window. Never in his life had he come across a glass
that brought objects before his eyes with such clarity and distinct-
ness. He involuntarily looked into Spalanzini's room. Olympia, as
usual, sat before the little table, her arms upon it, her hands folded.
For the first time now he saw her exquisitely formed face. Only
her eyes seemed peculiarly fixed and lifeless. But as he continued
to look more and more intently through the glass, it seemed as
though moist moonbeams were beginning to shine in Olympia's
eyes. It seemed as if the power of vision were only now starting
to be kindled; her glances were inflamed with ever-increasing life.
  Nathanael leaned on the window as if enchanted, staring steadily upon Olympia's divine beauty. The sound of a throat being
cleared and a shuffling of feet awakened him from his enchantment. Coppola was standing behind him. "*Tre zechini*—three ducats," Coppola said. Nathanael had completely forgotten the
optician. He quickly paid the sum requested. "Nice-a glass, no?
Nice-a glass?" Coppola asked in his hoarse and revolting voice, smiling maliciously. "Yes, yes, yes," Nathanael answered irritably.
"Goodbye, my friend." But only after casting many peculiar side-
long glances at Nathanael did Coppola leave the room. Nathanael
heard him laughing loudly on the stairs. "Ah," thought Nathanael, "he's laughing at me because I overpaid him for this little
spyglass." But as he quietly voiced these words he seemed to hear
a deep sigh, like a dying man's, echoing through the room. Terror
stopped his breath. To be sure, it was he who had deeply sighed;
that was obvious. "Klara is absolutely right," he said to himself,
"in calling me an absurd visionary, yet it is ridiculous—more than
ridiculous—that I am so strangely distressed by the thought of
having overpaid Coppola for the spyglass. I see no reason for it."
Then Nathanael sat down to finish his letter to Klara, but a glance

through the window showed him that Olympia still sat as before, and as though impelled by an irresistible power, he jumped up, seized Coppola's spyglass, and could not tear himself away from the alluring vision of Olympia until his friend Siegmund called for him to go to Professor Spalanzini's lecture. The curtain was tightly drawn across the fateful door so that he could not see Olympia; nor could he see her for the next two days from his own room, despite the fact that he scarcely ever left his window and, almost without interruption, gazed into her room through Coppola's glass. Moreover, on the third day curtains were drawn across the window, and Nathanael, in despair, driven by longing and ardent passion, rushed out beyond the city gates. Olympia's image hovered before him in the air, emerged from the bushes, and peered up at him with great and lustrous eyes from the shining brook. Klara's image had completely faded from his soul. He thought of nothing but Olympia, and he lamented aloud, in a tearful voice, "Oh! My lofty and lovely star of love, have you arisen only to disappear again and leave me in the gloomy night of dark despair?"

As he was about to return home, he became aware of great noise and activity in Spalanzini's house. The doors were open and various kinds of gear were being carried in. The first-floor windows had been removed from their hinges, maids with large dust-mops were busily rushing about, sweeping and dusting, while inside the house carpenters and upholsterers were banging and hammering. Nathanael stood absolutely still in the street, struck with amazement. Siegmund then joined him and asked with a laugh: "Well, what do you think of our old Spalanzini now?" Nathanael assured him that he could say nothing, since he knew absolutely nothing about the professor, but that, much to his astonishment, he had noticed the feverish activity that was taking place in the silent and gloomy house. Siegmund told him that Spalanzini was going to give a great party, a concert and a ball, the next day and that half the university had been invited. Rumor had it that Spalanzini was going to present his daughter Olympia to the public for the first time, after so long having carefully guarded her from every human eye.

Nathanael received an invitation, and at the appointed hour, when carriages were driving up and lights gleamed in the decorated rooms, he went to the professor's house with palpitating heart. The gathering was large and dazzling. Olympia appeared, elegantly and tastefully dressed. No one could help but admire her beautifully shaped face and her figure. On the other hand, there was something peculiarly curved about her back, and the wasplike thinness of her waist also appeared to result from excessively tight lacing. There was, further, something stiff and measured about her walk and bearing that struck many unfavorably, but it was attributed to the constraint she felt in society. The concert began. Olympia played the piano with great talent and also skillfully sang a *bravura* aria in a voice that was high-pitched, bell-like, almost shrill. Nathanael was completely enchanted; he was standing in the back row and could not precisely distinguish Olympia's features in the dazzling candlelight. Surreptitiously, he took Coppola's glass from his pocket and looked at her. Oh! Then he perceived the yearning glance with which she looked at him, and he saw how every note achieved absolute purity in the loving glance that scorched him to his very soul. Her skillful roulades appeared to him to be the heavenly exaltations of a soul transfigured by love; and, finally, when the cadenza was concluded, the long trill echoed shrilly through the hall and he felt as if he were suddenly embraced by burning arms. No longer able to contain himself, rapture and pain mingling within him, he cried: "Olympia!" Everyone looked at him; many laughed. The cathedral organist pulled a gloomier face than before and simply said, "Now, now!"

The concert was over. The ball began. Oh, to dance with her! That was his one desire. But how could he summon up the courage to ask her, the queen of the ball, to dance with him? And yet, without really knowing how it happened, just as the dance began he found himself standing close to her and she had not yet been asked to dance. Barely able to stammer a few words, he grasped her hand. It was cold as ice. A deathly chill passed through him. Gazing into Olympia's eyes he saw that they shone at him with love and longing; and at that moment the pulse seemed to beat again in her cold hand, and warm life-blood to surge through her veins. In Nathanael's heart, too, passion burned with greater intensity. He threw his arms around the lovely Olympia and whirled her through the dance. He had thought that he usually followed the beat of the music well, but from the peculiar rhythmical evenness with which she danced and which often confused him, he was aware of how faulty his own sense of time really was. Yet he would dance with no other partner, and he felt that he would murder anyone else who approached Olympia to ask her to dance. But this occurred only twice; to his amazement Olympia remained seated on each occasion until the next dance, when he did not fail to lead her out to the dance floor. If Nathanael had had eyes for anything but the lovely Olympia, there would inevitably have been a number of disagreeable quarrels; for it was obvious that the carefully smothered laughter which broke out among the young people in this corner and that, was directed toward the lovely Olympia, whom they were watching curiously for an unknown reason. Heated by the quantity of wine he had drunk and by the dancing, Nathanael had cast off his characteristic shyness. He sat beside Olympia, her hand in his, and with fervor and passion he spoke of his love in words that no one could understand, neither he nor Olympia. But perhaps she did, for she sat with her eyes fixed upon his, sighing again and again, "Ah, ah, ah!" Whereupon Nathanael answered: "Oh, you magnificent and heavenly woman! You ray shining from the promised land of love! You deep soul, in which my whole being is reflected," and more of the same. But Olympia did nothing but continue to sigh, "Ah, ah!"

Professor Spalanzini passed the happy couple several times and smiled at them with a look of strange satisfaction. It seemed to Nathanael, although he was in a very different, higher world, that it was suddenly getting noticeably darker down here at Professor Spalanzini's. When he looked around him, it was with great consternation that he saw that only two lights were burning in the empty room and that they were about to go out. The music and the dancing had ceased long ago. "We must part, we must part!" he cried in wild despair, then kissed Olympia's hand. He bent down to her mouth; icy lips met his burning ones. Just as when, touching her cold hand, he had felt a shudder seize him, the legend of the dead bride flashed suddenly through his mind. But Olympia drew him close to her, and the kiss seemed to warm her lips into life. Professor Spalanzini walked slowly through the empty room, his steps echoing hollowly, and in the flickering light cast by the candles, his figure assumed a sinister and ghostly appearance.

"Do you love me? Do you love me, Olympia? Just one word! Do you love me?" Nathanael whispered.

But as she rose, Olympia only sighed, "Ah, ah!"

"Yes, you, my lovely, wonderful evening star," said Nathanael, "you have risen for me and will illuminate and transfigure my soul forever."

"Ah, ah!" Olympia replied as she walked away. Nathanael followed her; they stood before the professor.

"You had a most lively conversation with my daughter," the professor said with a smile. "If you enjoy talking with this silly girl you are welcome to come and do so."

Nathanael left, his heart ablaze with all of heaven.

Spalanzini's ball was the talk of the town for the next few days. Despite the fact that the professor had done everything to put on a splendid show, the wags found plenty of fantastic and peculiar things to talk about. Their favorite target was the rigid and silent Olympia, who, her beautiful appearance notwithstanding, was assumed to be hopelessly stupid, which was thought to be the reason Spalanzini had so long kept her concealed. Nathanael heard all this, not without inner fury, but he said nothing. "What would be the use," he thought, "of proving to these fellows that it was their own stupidity which precluded them from appreciating Olympia's profound and beautiful mind."

"Do me a favor, brother," Siegmund said to him one day, "and tell me how it is possible for an intelligent fellow like you to have fallen for that wax-faced, wooden puppet across the way?"

Nathanael was about to lose his temper, but he quickly gained control of himself and replied, "Tell me, Siegmund, how do you account for the fact that a man who is able to so readily to discern beauty has not seen the heavenly charms of Olympia? Yet, thank heaven you are not my rival, for if you were a rival, the blood of one of us would be spilled."

Siegmund, seeing how things were with his friend, adroitly switched tactics, and after commenting that there was no point in arguing about the object of a person's love, he added, "It's very strange, however, that many of us have come to the same conclusion about Olympia. She seems to us—don't take this badly, my brother—strangely stiff and soulless. Her figure is symmetrical, so is her face, that's true enough, and if her eyes were not so completely devoid of life—the power of vision, I mean—she might be considered beautiful. Her step is peculiarly measured; all of her movements seem to stem from some kind of clockwork. Her playing and her singing are unpleasantly perfect, being as lifeless as a music box; it is the same with her dancing. We found Olympia to be rather weird, and we wanted to have nothing to do with her. She seems to us to be playing the part of a human being, and it's as if there really were something hidden behind all of this."

Nathanael did not surrender to the bitterness aroused in him by Siegmund's words; rather, mastering his resentment, he merely said, very gravely, "Olympia may indeed appear weird to you cold and unimaginative mortals. The poetical soul is accessible only to the poetical nature. Her adoring glances fell only upon *me* and irradiated my feelings and thoughts. I discover myself again only in Olympia's love. That she does not indulge in jabbering banalities like other shallow people may not seem right to you. It's true that she says little; but the few words she does utter are in a sacred language that expresses an inner world imbued with love, with the higher, spiritual knowledge gathered from a vision of the world beyond. But you have no feeling for these things; I am wasting my breath."

"God protect you, brother," said Siegmund very gently, almost sadly. "It does seem to me that you are moving in an evil direction. You may depend upon me if—no, I'll say nothing more." It suddenly dawned upon Nathanael that his cold, unimaginative friend Siegmund sincerely wished him very well, and so he warmly shook his outstretched hand.

Nathanael had completely forgotten that there was in the world a Klara whom he had once loved; his mother, Lothar—all had disappeared from his mind. He lived only for Olympia, beside whom he sat every day, hour after hour, carrying on about his love, about mutual sympathy kindled into life, and about their psychic affinity—and Olympia listened to all of this with great reverence. From deep within his desk, Nathanael dug up everything he had ever written—poems, fantasies, visions, romances, tales—and the number was increased daily by a plethora of hyperbolic sonnets, verses, and canzonets; and all of this he read to Olympia tirelessly for hours at a time. Never before had he had such a splendid listener. She neither embroidered nor knitted; she did not look out of the window nor feed a bird nor play with a lapdog or kitten; she did not twist slips of paper or anything else around her fingers; she had no need to disguise a yawn by forcing a cough. In brief, she sat for hours on end without moving, staring directly into his eyes, and her gaze grew ever more ardent and animated. Only when Nathanael at last stood up and kissed her hand and then her lips did she say, "Ah, ah!" and then add, "Goodnight, my dearest."

When Nathanael returned to his own room, he cried, "How beautiful, how profound is her mind! Only you, only you truly understand me." He trembled with rapture when he thought of the marvelous harmony which daily grew between him and Olympia; it seemed to him as if she expressed thoughts about his work and about all of his poetic gifts from the very depth of his own soul, as though she spoke from within him. This must, to be sure, have been the case, for Olympia never spoke any word other than those already recorded. But even in clear and sober moments, those, for example, which followed his awaking in the morning, when Nathanael was conscious of Olympia's utter passivity and taciturnity, he merely said, "What are words? Mere words! The glance of her heavenly eyes expresses more than any commonplace speech. Besides, how is it possible for a child of heaven to confine herself to the narrow circle demanded by wretched, mundane life?"

Professor Spalanzini appeared to be most pleased by the intimacy that had developed between his daughter and Nathanael, and he gave Nathanael many ummistakable signs of his delight. When, at great length, Nathanael ventured to hint delicately at a possible marriage with Olympia, the professor's face broke into a smile and he said that he would allow his daughter to make a perfectly free choice. Emboldened by these words, and with passion inflaming his heart, Nathanael determined to implore Olympia the very next day to put into plain words what her sweet and loving glances had told him—that she would be his forever. He searched for the ring his mother had given him when he had left. He intended to present it to Olympia as a symbol of his devotion and the joyous life with her that had flowered. While looking for the ring he came upon his letters from Klara and Lothar; he cast them aside indifferently, found the ring, put it in his pocket, and hurried with it across to Olympia.

While still on the stairs, he heard a singular hubub that seemed to come from Spalanzini's study. There was a stamping, a rattling, pushing, a banging against the door, and, intermingled, curses and oaths, "Let go! Let go! Monster! Villain! Risking body and soul for it? Ha! Ha! Ha! Ha! That wasn't our arrangement! I, I made the eyes! I made the clockwork! Damned idiot, you and your damned clockwork! Dog of a clockmaker! Out! Let me go!" The voices causing this uproar belonged to Spalanzini and the abominable Coppelius. Nathanael rushed in, seized by a nameless dread. The professor was grasping a female figure by the shoulders, the Italian Coppola had her by the feet, and they were twisting and tugging her this way and that, contending furiously for possession of her. Nathanael recoiled in horror upon recognizing the figure as Olympia's. Flaring up in a wild rage, he was about to tear his beloved from the grasp of these madmen when Coppola, wrenching the figure from the professor's hand with the strength of a giant, struck the professor such a fearful blow with it that he toppled backwards over the table on which vials, retorts, flasks, and glass test tubes were standing—everything shattered into a thousand fragments. Then Coppola threw the figure over his shoulder and with a horrible, shrill laugh, ran quickly down the stairs, the figure's grotesquely dangling feet bumping and rattling woodenly on every step. Nathanael stood transfixed; he had only too clearly seen that in the deathly pale waxen face of Olympia there were no eyes, but merely black holes. She was a lifeless doll. Spalanzini was writhing on the floor; his head and chest and arm had been cut by the glass fragments and blood gushed from him as if from a fountain. But he summoned up all his strength: "After him, after him! What are you waiting for! Coppelius—Coppelius has stolen my best automaton. Worked at it for twenty years—put everything I had into it—mechanism—speech—movement—all mine. The eyes—the eyes stolen from you! Damn him! Curse him! After him! Get me Olympia! Bring back Olympia! There are the eyes!"

And now Nathanael saw something like a pair of bloody eyes staring up at him from the floor. Spalanzini seized them with his uninjured hand and flung them at Nathanael so that they hit his breast. Then madness racked Nathanael with scorching claws, ripping to shreds his mind and senses.

"Whirl, whirl, whirl! Circle of fire! Circle of fire! Whirl round, circle of fire! Merrily, merrily! Aha, lovely wooden doll, whirl round!"

With these words Nathanael hurled himself upon the professor and clutched at his throat. He would have strangled him if several people who had been attracted by the noise had not rushed in and torn the raging Nathanael away, thus saving the professor, whose wounds were then bandaged. As strong as he was, Siegmund was unable to subdue the madman, who continued to scream in a horrible voice, "Wooden doll, whirl round!" and to flail about with clenched fists. Finally, several men combined their strength and flung Nathanael to the ground and tied him up. Nathanael's words turned into a heinous bellow, and in a raging frenzy, he was taken away to the madhouse.

Before continuing my narration, gentle reader, of what further happened to the unhappy Nathanael, I can assure you, in case you are interested in Spalanzini, that skillful craftsman and maker of automatons, that his recovery from his wounds was complete. He was, however, forced to leave the university because Nathanael's story had caused a considerable scandal and because opinion generally held that it was an inexcusable deceit to have smuggled a wooden doll into proper tea circles, where Olympia had been such a success, and to have palmed it off as a human. If fact, lawyers held that it was a subtle imposture and considered it felonious because it had been so craftily devised and was directed against the public so that, except for some astute students, it had gone undetected, notwithstanding the fact that everyone now claimed wisdom and pointed to various details which they said had struck them as suspicious. They did not, however, bring any clues to light. Why, for example, would anyone have had his suspicions aroused by the fact that Olympia, according to an elegant tea party-goer, had sneezed more often than she had yawned? This elegant gentleman was of the opinion that the sneezing had really been the sound of the concealed clockwork winding itself up—concomitantly, there had always been an audible creaking—and so on. The professor of poetry and rhetoric took a pinch of snuff, snapped the lid shut, cleared his throat, and solemnly declared, "Most honorable ladies and gentlemen, do you not see the point of it all? It is all an allegory, an extended metaphor. Do you understand? *Sapienti sat.*"

But many honorable gentlemen were not reassured by this. The story of the automaton had very deeply impressed them, and a horrible distrust of human figures in general arose. Indeed, many lovers insisted that their mistresses sing and dance unrythmically and embroider, knit, or play with a lapdog or something while being read to, so that they could assure themselves that they were not in love with a wooden doll; above all else, they required the mistresses not only to listen, but to speak frequently in such a way that it would prove that they really were capable of thinking and feeling. Many lovers, as a result, grew closer than ever before; but others gradually drifted apart. "One really can't be sure about this," said one or another. At tea parties, people yawned with incredible frequency and never sneezed, in order to ward off all suspicion. Spalanzini, as has been noted, had to leave the place in order to escape criminal charges of having fraudulently introduced an automaton into human society. Coppola had also disappeared.

Nathanael awoke as from a deep and frightful dream, opened his eyes, and experienced an indescribable sensation of bliss warmly permeating his body. He lay on his own bed in his own room at home, Klara bending over him, his mother and Lothar standing nearby.

"At last, at last, my darling Nathanael, you have recovered from your terrible illness and are once more mine!" cried Klara with deep emotion, clasping him in her arms. Bright scalding tears streamed from his eyes, so overcome with mingled feelings of sorrow and delight was he, and he gasped, "Klara, my Klara!"

Then Siegmund, who had faithfully stood by his friend in his hour of need, entered the room; and Nathanael shook his hand. "My faithful brother, you have not deserted me."

Every vestige of insanity had disappeared and Nathanael soon recovered his strength again under the tender care of his mother, sweetheart, and friends. Good luck had, in the meantime, visited the house—an old miserly uncle, from whom they had expected nothing, had died and left not only a considerable fortune but a small estate that was pleasantly situated not far from the town. And there they resolved to go and live, Nathanael and Klara, whom he was to marry, and his mother and Lothar. Nathanael had grown more gentle and childlike than ever before, and for the first time could fully appreciate the heavenly purity of Klara's noble spirit. No one ever reminded him, even most remotely, of what had taken place. But when Siegmund said goodbye to him, he remarked, "By heaven, brother, I was on the wrong road. But an angel guided me to the path of light just in time. It was Klara." Siegmund would let him say nothing else for fear that the wounding memories of the past might flare up in him too vividly.

The time came when these four lucky people were to move into their property, and as they were walking through the streets at noon, after having made many purchases, the high tower of the town hall cast its huge shadow over the marketplace. "Oh!" said Klara, "Let us climb to the top once more and look at the distant mountains!" No sooner said than done. Nathanael and Klara climbed the tower; his mother and the servant went home. Lothar, not wishing to climb so many steps, remained below. There the two lovers stood arm in arm on the topmost gallery of the tower looking down into the fragrant woods beyond which the blue mountains rose up like a giant city.

"Just look at that strange little gray bush," Klara cried. "It really seems to be coming toward us." Nathanael automatically felt his side pocket, where he found Coppola's spyglass, and looked to one side. Klara was standing in front of the glass. Then there was a convulsive throbbing in his pulse. Deathly pale, he stared at Klara; but soon streams of fire flashed and spurted from his rolling eyes. He roared horrendously, like a hunted beast, leaped high into the air, and bursting with horrible laughter, he shrieked in a piercing voice, "Whirl wooden doll! Whirl wooden doll!" And seizing Klara with superhuman strength he tried to hurl her from the tower, but Klara, with a strength born of the agony of desperation, clung tightly to the railing. Lothar heard the madman raving, and he heard Klara's cry of terror. He was seized with a terrible foreboding and raced up the stairs. The door leading to the second flight was shut. Klara's cries were growing fainter and fainter. Mad with rage and fear, he pushed against the door, which finally burst open. "Help! Save me, save me!" Her voice faded in the air. "She is dead, murdered by that madman," Lothar cried. The door leading to the gallery was also locked, but his desperation endowed him with the strength of a giant and he tore it from its hinges. Good God! Klara was in the grasp of Nathanael the madman, hanging in the air over the gallery railing, to which she barely clung with one hand. Quick as lightning, Lothar seized his sister and pulled her back, at the same instant smashing the madman in the face with his fist so hard that he reeled back and let go of his victim.

Lothar raced down the stairs with his unconscious sister in his arms. She was saved. Nathanael dashed around the gallery, leaping up in the air and shouting, "Circle of fire! Whirl round, circle of fire! Whirl round!" A crowd gathered quickly, attracted by the wild screaming; and in the midst of them there towered the gigantic figure of the lawyer Coppelius, who had just arrived in town and had come directly to the marketplace. Some wanted to go up and overpower the madman, but Coppelius laughed and said, "Ha, ha! Just wait; he'll come down on his own." And he looked up with the rest. Nathanael suddenly froze, leaned forward, caught sight of Coppelius, and with a shattering scream of "Ah, nice-a eyes, nice-a eyes!" jumped over the railing.

Nathanael lay on the pavement with his head shattered, but Coppelius had vanished in the crowd.

Many years later it was reported that Klara had been seen in a remote district sitting hand in hand with a pleasant-looking man in front of the door of a splendid country house, two merry boys playing around her. Thus it may be concluded that Klara eventually found that quiet, domestic happiness that her cheerful nature required and that Nathanael, with his lacerated soul, could never have provided her.

Translated by L. J. Kent
and E. C. Knight

ACKNOWLEDGMENTS

Every reasonable effort has been made to locate the owners of rights to previously published translations reprinted here. We gratefully acknowledge permission to reprint the following material:

"The Golden Pot," "Councillor Krespel," "Mademoiselle de Scuderi," "The Mines of Falun," and "The Sandman," reprinted from *Selected Writings of E. T. A. Hoffmann,* edited and translated by Leonard J. Kent and Elizabeth C. Knight: *The Tales,* Vol. 1, by permission of the University of Chicago Press. Translation © 1969 by The University of Chicago.